DATE DUE

AP 5-01			

DEMCO 38-296

Mesopotamian Civilization

Mesopotamian Civilization

The Material Foundations

D. T. Potts

Cornell University Press

ITHACA, NEW YORK

First published 1997 by Cornell University Press.

Library of Congress Cataloguing-in-Publication Data
Potts, Daniel T.
Mesopotamian civilization: the material foundations / D.T. Potts.
p. cm.
Includes bibliographical references and index.
ISBN 0–8014–3339–8
1. Middle East—Civilization—To 622. 2. Ethnology—Middle East.
3. Physical geography—Middle East. I. Title.
DS57.P67 1996
939.4—dc20 96–34832

Printed in Great Britain

Contents

Preface and Acknowledgements

I made the decision to write this book one day in 1993 after attending an informal seminar at the University of Sydney organized by a group of postgraduates from various branches of archaeology (Classical, Western Asiatic, Pacific and Australian). The subject of the seminar that week was a recent article which examined the archaeological evidence of standardization and specialization in ceramic manufacture in northern Mesopotamia. I listened to a somewhat tortuous discussion of how standardization and specialization could be detected in the archaeological record until I could no longer restrain myself from pointing out that the authors of the article under discussion certainly ought to have used the available cuneiform evidence for ceramic production in Mesopotamia as it would have answered a number of their questions. This was something of a conversation-stopper, but walking back to my office from the seminar I realized that it was completely unrealistic to think that the most relevant article on the subject, which happened to be in German and was published in a journal to which my university library did not subscribe, should have been known to any of the students present at the seminar. I also realized that a discussion of ceramic production from both an archaeological and a philological perspective was nowhere available in any of the books which I routinely put on my undergraduate reading lists when teaching Mesopotamia. Indeed, the same applied to subjects like metallurgy and agriculture, and it was then that I decided to try to write the sort of book which contained the kinds of information of which I most wanted my students to be aware.

That book should literally present Mesopotamian civilization from the ground up. The general books available for teaching Mesopotamia are for the most part concerned with the superstructure of a 'great civilization' – its art, architecture, monuments, history and literature. Before exposing students to these topics I wanted them to have a grasp of Mesopotamia's material infrastructure. What were the basic ingredients – the soils, the water regime, the climate, the landforms? How did the area come to be populated in the first place? Once there, how did the earliest Mesopotamians survive? What were the foundations of their subsistence base? What inedible natural resources did they have at their disposal? What was produced, how and by whom? How did the region's religious ideals reflect the basic conditions of life in the alluvial plain of southern Mesopotamia? What do we know of the kinship system of southern Mesopotamian society? What kinds of attitudes towards death and the afterlife prevailed? What significant input into Mesopotamian civilization came from the East, and what from the West?

The actor Peter Ustinov once published a book called *My Russia*. This book is *my* Mesopotamia. Although I have resisted the temptation to give this work such a title, the fact remains that a comparison of the

bibliography cited here with that of any of the other general works on Mesopotamia currently on the market will reveal just how different the approach
taken here is to that of orthodox Mesopotamianists. I am well aware that
there are dozens of scholars with an expertise in one or another aspect of
Mesopotamian studies who could have told a much more detailed story of
any of the subjects dealt with here. The fact is, however, that few of these
scholars attempt to write books like this one. Nicholas Postgate's *Early
Mesopotamia* (Postgate 1994) and Roger Moorey's *Ancient Mesopotamian
materials and industries* (Moorey 1994) are happy exceptions, for which I
have enormous respect, but none of the other general books of which I am
aware treats the material foundations of Mesopotamian civilization from
the perspective of the present work. Archaeological books tend to stick to
material culture, particularly focusing on architecture, ceramics and statuary, all presented in a straightforward, chronological fashion. Art historical
works tend to ignore all aspects of material culture which do not qualify as
'art', objectifying Mesopotamia as a series of cylinder seals, statues and
reliefs, as though these speak for themselves, imparting the 'essence' of the
ancient Mesopotamian spirit to the modern viewer. Historical and Assyriological studies tend, not unnaturally, to concentrate on the history, literature, religion, law and economic institutions of Mesopotamia, without
ever linking these to the material foundations of the civilization.

What is offered here is an admittedly imperfect attempt to bridge the gap
between Assyriology and Mesopotamian archaeology on topics of an often
materialist nature which I consider important for an understanding of
what *made* Mesopotamia. It may sound like old-fashioned Marxism to say
that I would rather my students knew about Mesopotamian soils than
banquet scenes on cylinder seals, or about wool classes rather than Etana,
but the fact remains that whereas the subjects omitted here are adequately
covered in a dozen general works on Mesopotamia by eminent scholars,
those covered are often treated only in specialist literature, much of it
inaccessible to English-speaking students because it is written in Italian,
German and French. Had the scholars best qualified to write a book of the
present sort done so, I should never have attempted one myself.

In conceiving this book I had hoped it would read something like an
ethnography of ancient Mesopotamia, combining an understanding of its
material and its mental culture. I have not been able to realize that hope in
the time allocated for the writing of this book, nor do I any longer feel
equipped to carry out such a task. This book therefore falls well short of
the mark I had originally set for myself, but it may still prove of some
utility if it encourages students to think about Mesopotamia in a way to
which they have not been accustomed, and particularly if it encourages
qualified scholars to adopt a more wide-ranging, synthetic approach to a
body of evidence which is uniquely suited to a holistic, anthropological
approach. Geographically I have limited the work to southern Mesopotamia (cf. Chapter I) because this is the area from which the best documentation comes. Assyria is but rarely mentioned. Nor is there any attempt to be
comprehensive in chronological terms. While most of the cases discussed
date to the third millennium BC, a smattering come from the second and

first millennia, but the evidence is not presented in a rigorous way from earliest to latest. Such a comprehensive approach would have exceeded the length limits of the present work, and would have turned this from a series of essay-like chapters into something approaching a selective encyclopaedia. Indeed, the end result has been a baker's dozen – thirteen essays on different aspects of ancient Mesopotamia, with a short conclusion containing some reflections on Mesopotamian studies in general.

My intellectual debt to German scholarship is profound, and is amply illustrated by the many works in German cited in the bibliography and references. My first, serious introduction to Mesopotamia came during a five-year period (1981–86) as a junior faculty member in the Institut für Vorderasiatische Altertumskunde of the Free University of Berlin. Far more important for me than the superb library there was the daily contact with Kilian Butz, Bob Englund, Karlheinz Kessler, Hartmut Kühne, Hans Nissen and Johannes Renger, not to mention a steady stream of visitors, the most influential of whom on my intellectual development were without doubt Jean-Pierre Grégoire (Paris), Blahoslav Hruška (Prague), Giovanni Pettinato (Rome) and Marcel Sigrist (Jerusalem). In addition, the many fine students we had in those years enriched the subject which, to a great extent, I learned as I taught. I am only too aware of how deficient much of my own understanding of ancient Mesopotamia is in comparison to the above mentioned friends and colleagues, but I hope they derive some satisfaction from knowing that, were it not for their influence, I should never have been able to write this book. It is, I think, unnecessary to mention in any greater detail just what I learned from each of these individuals, but I must single out the inspiration of the late Kilian Butz whose perspective was always fresh, controversial, provocative and unceasingly inquisitive.

At such a distance from my Mesopotamian colleagues I have often been forced to fax or e–mail queries and pray for a speedy reply. I should like to thank Dr Robert K. Englund (Berlin), Professor Wolfgang Heimpel (Berkeley), Professor Jean-Louis Huot (Paris), Dr Ingolf Thuesen (Copenhagen), Professor Hans-Peter Uerpmann (Tübingen) and Professor Norman Yoffee (Ann Arbor) for promptly responding to such cries from the wilderness. I am sure to have forgotten other friends who helped me in a similar manner, and beg their indulgence for so doing. Peter Magee prepared the index for which I am extremely grateful. I also owe a great deal to my Sydney students who sat through the first, very rough version of these chapters as a series of lectures on Mesopotamia. The often bewildered looks on their faces pointed out to me more often than not where I had to clarify and elaborate on a particular point. In order to help readers of the present work navigate their way through the welter of names present, a general chronological chart (p. xi) is included which lists the names of the principal sites and persons mentioned in the text. Further clarification is offered in the index as well.

It is a pleasure to acknowledge the encouragement I have received from Professor John Baines (Oxford) and Professor Norman Yoffee (Ann Arbor) since the idea of writing this book first occurred to me. Dr Jeremy Black (Oxford) also took the time to read the first draft and provide valuable comments and corrections.

Finally, my family would no doubt have preferred to see me more during the writing of this book, but I appreciate the time which I have been able to spend working on it even when it meant that their patience was worn thinner than usual. My wife Hildy gave birth to our third child, Hallam, just before I began to write in earnest, and she suffered through the gestation of this book in often trying times. I dedicate this book to our first son Morgan, who wants to be a Viking archaeologist.

D. T. Potts
Edwin Cuthbert Hall Professor of Middle Eastern Archaeology
University of Sydney

Chronological table

showing the main places and persons mentioned in the text

Years	Period	Important Places mentioned in the Text	Important Persons mentioned in the Text
6000	pre-Ubaid	Choga Mami, Tell Oueili, Tell Rihan III, Umm Dabaghiyah, Yarim Tepe I & II, Maghzaliyah	
5500	Samarran	Tell es-Sawwan	
5000–3800	Ubaid	Eridu, Hajji Muhammad, Tell al-ʻUbaid, Ur, Tello, Tell Chragh, Tell Madhhur, Tell el-Saadiya, Tell Abada, Tepe Gawra	
3800	Early Uruk	Uruk/Warka, Tepe Gawra, Kullaba	
3400	Late Uruk	Uruk, Jamdat Nasr, Adab, Ur, Larsa, Umma, Tell Chragh, Tell Uqair	
3100	Jamdat Nasr	Uruk, Jamdat Nasr, Shuruppak, Zabala, Ur, Adab, Kish, Umma, Larsa, Eshnunna, Fara, Tell Gubba	
2900	ED I	Ur, Uruk, Kish, Kheit Qasim	
2700	ED II	Fara, Tell Asmar, Abu Salabikh	
2600	ED III	Lagash, Tello, Girsu, Tell al-Hiba, Ur Ebla, Tell al-ʻUbaid, Abu Salabikh, Kish	Ur-Nanshe, Eanatum, Enmetana, Lugalanda, Baragnamtara, Shagshag, Urukagina

Date	Period	Sites	Rulers
2350	Old Akkadian	Tell Taya, Umma, Agade, Urú, Uch Tepe, Tell Asmar	Sargon of Akkad, Rimush, Manishtushu, Naram-Sin
2100	Ur III	Ur, Girsu, Guabba, Umma, Adab, Bad-Tibira, Larsa, Nigin, Karhar, Drehem, Puzrish-Dagan, Uruk, Nippur	Gudea, Ur-Ningirsu, Pirigme, Ur-Nammu, Shulgi, Amar-Sin, Shu-Sin, Ibbi-Sin, Ur-Meme, Ur-Lisi, Ajakalla, Aradani
2000	Isin-Larsa	Isin, Larsa, Tell Bazmosian, Qurtass, Tell Yelkhi, Tell edh-Dhiba'i	Ishbi-Erra, Ishme-Dagan, Lipit-Ishtar, Nur-Adad, Sinkashid, Siniddinam, Rim-Sin
1800	Old Babylonian	Sippar, Dilbat, Nipur, Babylon, ed-Der, Diqdiqqah, Khafajah, Tell Ischali, Tell Harmal, Tell Shemshara, Mari, Mashkan-Shapir, Eshnunna	Hammurapi, Samsu-iluna, Abi-eshuh
1600	Kassite (Middle Babylonian/Assyrian)	Nippur, Tell Kirbasi, Tell Bazmosian, Nuzi, Tell Keseran	Agum, Nazi-Maruttash, Tukulti-Ninurta, Enlil-nadin-ahi
1100	Isin II	Sealand	Nebuchadrezzar I
900	Neo-Assyrian/Neo-Babylonian	Dur-Sharruken, Nimrud, Tell al-Lahm, Suhi, Dur-Yakin	Nabuapplaidina, Shamash-resh-usur, Sargon II, Sennacherib, Esarhaddon, Assurbanipal, Merodach-Baladan
600	Chaldean	Babylonian, Borsipa, Tell al-Lahm	Nebuchadrezzar II, Neriglissar, Nabonidus, Nitokris
539	Achaemenid	Sippar	Cyrus, Cambyses, Darius I, Xerxes I, Artaxerxes I & II
333	Seleucid	Uruk, Pallacopas canal, Alexandria, Larsa, Seleucia, Babylon, Borsippa, Teredon, Nippur	Alexander, Seleucus I–III, Antiochus I–IV, Anu-uballit Nikarchos, Anu-uballit Kephalon
139	Parthian	Uruk, Ctesiphon, Nippur	
0 BC/AD			
226	Sasanian	Hira, Ctesiphon, Kish	Kavadh I, Khusrau II
637	Islamic Conquest		

List of Figures

List of Tables

I The Country and its Climate

INTRODUCTION

Before we can begin to appreciate the cultures which inhabited southern Mesopotamia, it is essential that we have some understanding of the climate and environment of this region. The contributions of the two major rivers which drain southern Mesopotamia, the Euphrates and Tigris, are indisputable. The salt and silt brought south by these rivers created the landscape upon which the area's inhabitants lived. The water they brought, diverted into artificial canals, was the basis of their subsistence. How greatly the ancient landscape may have differed from the modern must also be investigated. If we ignore any of these factors then we ignore the foundations on which Mesopotamian civilization was built.

TODAY'S CLIMATE

Most of the developments discussed in this book took place in what is today lower Iraq, primarily within that parallelogram of land which is bounded on the north by the Tigris; on the south and west by the Hillah branch of the Euphrates and on the east by the Shatt al-Gharraf, a tributary of the Tigris which runs from Kut al-Amara south to Nasiriyyah on the Euphrates (Fig. I.1). Like the rest of southern Iraq this area today enjoys a 'dry "continental" variant of the Mediterranean type' (Brice 1966:36) climate (Table I.1), experiencing relatively wet winters (November–March) as a by-product of eastward-moving cyclones and hot, dry summers (May–October). Mean annual precipitation can vary by as much as 50 per cent from year to year (Larsen 1975:48), but with average annual rainfall at 115–135 mm (figures are for 1929–59) the area never attains the recommended annual minimum of 240 mm needed for dry-farming (Charles 1988:1). Indeed, according to precipitation data recorded at Diwaniyah, near the middle of the Hillah branch of the Euphrates (1929–58), Hai, on the upper Shatt al-Gharraf (1941–58) and Nasiriyyah, at the junction of the Shatt al-Gharraf and Euphrates (1941–58), 200 mm of rainfall were recorded on only three occasions in the years for which records are available (Adams 1981:12; cf. Oates and Oates 1977:113). Thus agriculture is for all intents and purposes unthinkable without the aid of irrigation.

Aggregate rainfall figures are, however, very misleading for the simple fact that they mask the all-important aspect of timing. Less than the theoretically required annual minimum needed for dry-farming, if it falls at the appropriate points in the growing season, will produce an excellent yield, while more than adequate rainfall, if it comes too early or too late in the growing season, will result in crop failure. Indeed, if the major rainfalls occur after March they can have little influence on harvest yields and the

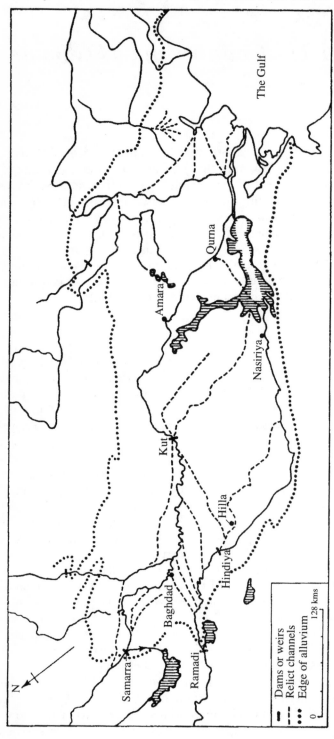

Figure I.1 Map of lower Iraq showing the area of principal concern in this book (after Brice 1966: Fig. 43)

	January	April	July	October	
Diwaniyah	10	22.2	32.9	25.7	Mean Monthly Temperature (°C)
	70	46	28	39	Mean Relative Humidity (%)
	18.8	14.5	0.2	0.8	Mean Monthly Rainfall (mm)
Baghdad	9.3	21.7	34.4	25.2	Mean Monthly Temperature (°C)
	71	47	23	36	Mean Relative Humidity (%)
	22	43	0	6.3	Mean Monthly Rainfall (mm)

Table I.1 *Temperature, Humidity and Rainfall Figures for Diwaniyah and Baghdad* (from Charles 1984: Tables 1, 6, 7)

rainfall will, in a sense, have been wasted (Adams 1981:12). Moreover, if rain in January is not accompanied by sufficiently warm temperatures (+10° C) plant growth will be interrupted (Oates and Oates 1977:113). Yearly averages are also misleading in that they often obscure great swings in precipitation which characterize the region, and while winter rainfall is essential for crop growth, it can also wreak havoc as violent winter storms often cause terrible flooding and soil erosion (Charles 1988:2). Such would undoubtedly have been the case in 1894 when 152.4 mm of rain were recorded on a single February day in Baghdad, whereas annual figures measured at the capital in other years have been as little as 50.8 mm (Cressey 1958:449).

Dew must also be taken into account as a supplement to rainfall and irrigation in an arid environment. The Greek natural philosopher Theophrastus noted that, 'In Egypt, Babylon and Bactra, where the country receives no rain, or but little, the dews are sufficient nourishment' (*Hist. Plant.* VIII vi 6). Studies in the Negev have shown that annual dewfall there may reach 37 mm, contributing significantly to plant growth (Evenari, Shanan and Tadmor 1971:35), and in southern Mesopotamia dew, particularly during the winter, 'undoubtedly provides useful additional moisture' (Oates and Oates 1977:113).

PALAEOCLIMATE

It is, of course, important to question just how relevant the current climatic regime in southern Iraq is for a study of the region in more remote antiquity. Views on this point are, as the saying goes, as changeable as the weather. In an influential paper published in 1957, P. Buringh stated categorically, 'Since man entered the Lower [Mesopotamian] Plain some 5 or 4000 years BC no important changes in climate occurred' (Buringh 1957:32), and it is probably fair to say that most scholars subscribe to the view that climatic change in the region since the beginning of the Holocene (c. 8000 BC) has been minimal and generally insignificant. As an example we may cite R.McC. Adams who has concluded that no evidence exists which would suggest 'that the climate of the region since the Pleistocene was for a time sufficiently wetter to permit sustained, significant dry agriculture on the alluvial plains' (Adams 1981:12). It is, however, one thing to say that climatic conditions in the past were not so different from those of today to permit 'sustained, significant' dry-farming, and quite another to acknowledge that, within what has always been a generally arid climate, minor climatic changes – towards either wetter or drier conditions – may have had significant implications for the flora, fauna and human populations of the area. Carefully weighing the palaeoclimatic evidence from pollen cores in the nearby Zagros mountains, for example, David and Joan Oates have concluded that, while the ancient climate was certainly arid in general, minor climatic variations *can* be detected through space and time. Thus they cite evidence for marsh formation near Umm Dabaghiyah in the north Mesopotamian *Jazirah* which suggests 'that the area was undoubtedly wetter *c*. 6,000–5,000 BC', while data from northeastern Arabia demonstrate that the climate to the south of Basra experienced 'a relatively wet phase sometime betwen 5,500-3,500 BC'[1] (Oates and Oates 1977:116–17).

Much of the relevant data for the existence of these wet phases comes from recent advances in worldwide climatology, but the results of those wet phases have long been observable on the ground. Since the 1960s the existence of fossil playa lake beds in the Rub al-Khali desert of southern Saudi Arabia has been known (McClure 1971:29), the formation of which can be attributed to periods of higher precipitation, while two major wadi systems in eastern Arabia, the Wadis Batn and Sahba, owe their existence to periods of intense run-off as a result of greater precipitation during the Pleistocene. A major breakthrough in understanding the causes of the Holocene wet phases came in 1981 when John Kutzbach showed that 'the earth's orbital parameters during the early Holocene may have influenced climate through their effect on the seasonal cycle of solar radiation' (Kutzbach 1981:59). In effect, a slight shift in the earth's orbit was responsible for solar radiation values *c*. 7000 BC which were 6–7 per cent higher than those of the present day. Solar radiation in the period between June and August is important because it warms the landmasses, accounting for intensified summer monsoon circulation over the African-Eurasian zone. This translates into a precipitation rate *c*. 8 per cent higher than present in the summer months 9000 years ago, generally corroborating the earlier C14 dates (8000 and 3000 BC) available from mid-Holocene palaeo-lakes in the area (Kutzbach 1981:60–1).

Kutzbach's findings were fully confirmed by H.A. McClure in his study of playa lake formation and palaeoclimate in the Rub al-Khali (McClure 1984, 1988:9-13). McClure found that the mid-Holocene wet phase seems to have ended *c*. 4000 BC (Fig. I.2) with the onset of hyper-aridity and the retreat of the summer monsoon to its present position (McClure 1984:213). According to several authorities, this warming trend continued to gain momentum over the next two millennia, reaching approximately modern levels of aridity around 1000 BC (Kay and Johnson 1981:259; Sanlaville 1992:23). The northward displacement of the summer monsoon is certain to have been responsible for the markedly moister conditions during the sixth millennium BC suggested by the pollen cores from the *Jazirah* as mentioned above, and even if the mid-Holocene wet phase was not characterized by enough precipitation to permit dry-farming in the southern alluvium, it must have had a positive impact on the region, encouraging a proliferation of wildlife and in part prompting the earliest settlement of the region (see Chapter II).

That micro-variations in climate have continued to occur even since the onset of hyper-aridity is borne out by several episodes for which we have written documentation. Thus, for example, in the tenth century AD the date palm is known to have flourished in northern Iraq around Jabal Sinjar

Epoch	Yrs BP	Palaeoclimate	Palaeogeography
H O L O C E N E	6,000 - PRESENT	HYPER-ARID HOT INTENSE WINDS	PRESENT ASPECT
	10,000 - 6,000	WET (SUB-PLUVIAL) LIGHT/MODERATE MONSOON PRECIPITATION; LOCALLY COOLER THAN PRESENT (?)	LOCAL LAKES IN INTERDUNES AND DUNE PROFILES; PARTLY STABILIZED DUNES WITH SUBDUED CRESTS; MODERATE GRASSLAND; WEAK PALAEOSOL DEVELOPMENT LOCALLY.
LATE PLEISTOCENE	20,000 - 10,000	HYPER-ARID HOT INTENSE WINDS	SALT DUNES WITH HIGH, ACTIVE AND COMPLEX CRESTS; REG PLAINS AS INTERDUNES; SPARSE GRASSLAND.
	32,000 - 20,000	WET (PLUVIAL) HEAVY (?) MONSOON PRECIPITATION; COOLER REGIONALLY THAN PRESENT.	LOCAL LAKES IN INTERDUNE LOWS; WIND-RIFT DUNES AND FURROWS ON A RE-WORKED PLAIN OF OLD ALLUVIUM; LOCALLY LUSH GRASS AND SHRUBLAND; PALAEOSOL DEVELOPMENT?
EARLIER PLEISTOCENE	? - 32,000	ARID WARM	INFERRED: LOCAL LAKES DURING WET PHASES; PLAIN OF OLD ALLUVIUM IN PROCESS OF RE-WORKING INTO WINDRIFT DUNES AND FURROWS; LUSH GRASS AND SHRUBLAND.
	?	WET (PLUVIAL) MONSOON PRECIPITATION (?); COOLER THAN PRESENT.	

Figure I.2 Phases of climatic change in the Rub al-Khali (after McClure 1988: Fig. 1)

and Tell Afar, whereas today, although it grows in the north, it does not bear fruit north of Hit (Oates and Oates 1977:117). This is a clear sign that conditions in northern Iraq *c.* 1000–1100 AD were warmer than those of the present day.

Similarly, climatic micro-variations have been detected in the second and first millennia BC on the basis of cuneiform evidence. Neumann and Sigrist have found that barley harvest dates in late Old Babylonian (*c.* 1800–1650 BC) texts from Sippar and Dilbat fall in late March/early April, while the barley harvest in Neo-Babylonian (*c.* 600–400 BC) texts from Babylon, Sippar and Nippur occurred in late April/early May. Thus, the maximum range of variation between the the two periods is in the order of three to eight weeks (Neumann and Sigrist 1978:249). This represents a harvest commencing *c.* 10–20 days earlier in the Old Babylonian period and 10–20 days later in the Neo-Babylonian period than is currently the case. While it is always possible that the observable time difference is due to the adoption of an early-maturing type of barley (neither the archaeobotanical nor the cuneiform evidence is sensitive enough to reflect such a difference in strains of barley; cf. Chapter II), Neumann and Sigrist suggest that the shift in harvest dates reflects climatic conditions in the Old Babylonian period which were *warmer* than those at present, and conditions in the Neo-Babylonian period which were *cooler* than today's climate. In other words, the growing season was longer in the latter period when the climate was slightly cooler than today.

The relationship between cooler weather and higher rainfall has been established empirically through studies elsewhere in Western Asia[2] and is basically intuitive, since 'rainfall in the Near East is usually associated with the passage of depressions, and especially with the passage of *cold fronts*; rain frequently falls in the unstable cold air just "behind" the front' (Neumann and Sigrist 1978:241). From all of this one can conclude that microvariations *did* occur in ancient Mesopotamia and while they were not of a magnitude as to permit dry-farming in the south, they were certainly not without consequences for the settled agricultural and herding population of the alluvium.

Finally, it is not without interest to note that, at the turn of the century, at both Jahrah in Kuwait and Hofuf in eastern Saudi Arabia, where the climate was as arid if not more arid than that of southern Mesopotamia, small stands of wheat and barley were grown in the winter months by bedouin *without the aid of irrigation* (Lorimer 1908:656, 898). Thus, while irrigation was the *sine qua non* of large-scale agriculture in Mesopotamia, slightly different conditions may have permitted small-scale experimentation with agriculture in the alluvium even before the development of the earliest irrigation technology.

Irrigation, of course, was required for sustained, efficient cultivation and it is to the sources of water for irrigation that we now turn. Although, as we have seen, precipitation in southern Mesopotamia is of less consequence than water obtained by irrigation, it is precipitation, in this case snowfall over the mountains of Turkey, which accounts for the very existence of Mesopotamia's great rivers.

THE RIVERS EUPHRATES AND TIGRIS

In theory, the water for irrigation in southern Mesopotamia could have come from either the Euphrates or the Tigris, but in order to understand why and how water was used from one or the other river through time and why most ancient settlements in this area are located so far from the rivers today, it is important to understand something of the river regimes them-selves during the past five or six millennia. We shall consider the Tigris first, before turning to the Euphrates.

The Tigris

The headwaters of the Tigris lie in the Taurus mountains of eastern Turkey. With a total length of *c.* 2032 km, the Tigris drains an area of 68,975 sq. km above the head of its delta at Samarra. As more than half of the Tigris' drainage area is comprised of mountainous and piedmont terri-tory, it loses far less water to evaporation than does the Euphrates, which crosses a vast expanse of desert-steppe on its way to the Gulf. Unlike the Euphrates, which has no tributaries in Iraq, the volume of water carried by the Tigris is augmented by additions from the Greater and Lesser Zab, the Adhaim and the Diyala. As we have seen, annual rainfall in Iraq, even in the north, is relatively inconsequential and, as with the Euphrates, it is the quantity of melting snow in the mountains during the spring which deter-mines the water budget of the Tigris, not the amount of water added by winter rainfall. That quantity can vary greatly, for while the snowline in the Turkish mountains normally remains at around 1000 m above sea-level (m.a.s.l.), it has been known to rise to over 3000 m.a.s.l. (Cressey 1958:449), and such a vast increase in melted snow consequently means greatly increased run-off and therefore stream flow. Thus, when the Tigris is in spate in March/April, high water levels of more than 6 m above its minimum level have been recorded. Gauge readings of 218.9 (highest, 1935) and 212.6 m.a.s.l. (lowest, 1925) were recorded at Mosul during the first half of this century, which translates into a maximum discharge of 6200 as opposed to a minimum discharge of 88 cubic metres of water per second (cumecs) (Cressey 1958:450). At Baghdad the difference between high and low water levels is even more dramatic. There the Tigris in spate has been known to carry eighty times the water carried at low water, and, in full flood, to reach a velocity of 10 knots. The discharge of the Tigris at Bagh-dad in spate approaches 13,000 cumecs, while at low water it carries only 158 cumecs. Moreover, as the discharge level of the Tigris increases the river has been known to double its volume in only two days.

Because its gradient is much steeper than that of the Euphrates (Fig. I.3), and because it loses much less water to evaporation (see below), the dis-charge of the Tigris is consequently greater than that of the Euphrates and for this reason the Tigris has incised a much deeper bed than the Euphra-tes. In the opinion of most scholars, this made the Tigris generally unsuit-able for gravity-flow irrigation, since its water had to be lifted up and out of the river in order for it to be brought to the fields. As Adams wrote three decades ago, 'With only the hand-operated *shādūf* [3] (Fig. I.4) having been common in much of earlier antiquity, water could not have been drawn profitably from the deep bed of the Tigris. But with the introduction of pulleys and animal traction in Assyrian or later times this became com-paratively easy' (Adams 1965:65). This circumstance surely accounts for the greater exploitation of Tigris water for purposes of irrigation in the

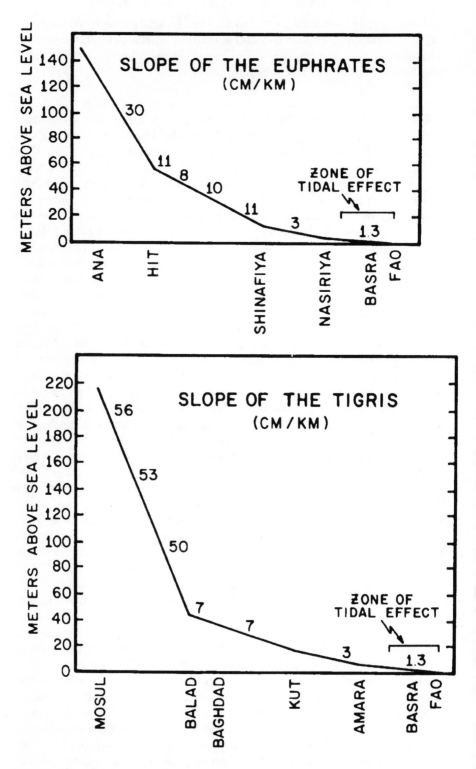

Figure I.3 Slopes of the Euphrates and Tigris (after Gibson 1972: 21, Table 2)

Figure I.4 Depiction of a *shaduf* on a Mesopotamian cylinder seal (after Butz 1984: Abb. 9)

later periods of Mesopotamian history once mechanical devices had been developed. For this reason, far from being a 'land of the twin rivers', southern Mesopotamia has generally been looked upon as a 'land of one river', namely the Euphrates, by most scholars.

Recently, the notion that life in lower Mesopotamia depended almost entirely on the Euphrates has been challenged by W. Heimpel. Heimpel points out that in the late third millennium BC the inhabitants of Lagash considered the Tigris their main source of water, while records from Nippur attest to the diversion of Tigris water to alleviate a water shortage during the Kassite period (Heimpel 1987:316–17, 1990:205–06). The role of the Tigris will be considered in more detail below when we examine the ancient system of watercourses in southern Mesopotamia.

The Euphrates
The Euphrates rises in central Turkey at the confluence of the Kara Su and the Murad Su and runs for approximately 2720 km, draining an area of 163,120 sq. km above the head of its delta at Ramadi. This represents an area nearly three times as great as the drainage of the Tigris. Like the Tigris, the Euphrates owes its existence to melting mountain snows, in this case the snows of the Kurdish mountains, but the Tigris is affected by the spring thaw sooner than the Euphrates, which only reaches full spate in April/May.

The upper Euphrates cuts through the Kurdish plateau, spreading out below Bireçik, from which point onward it is flanked by cliffs and terraces up to 100 m high until it reaches the head of the combined Tigris-Euphrates delta at Ramadi (Brice 1966:229). The volume of water in the middle Euphrates is supplemented modestly by what it receives from two tributaries in northern Syria, the Balikh and Khabur rivers. Unlike that of the Tigris, the gradient of the Euphrates is gentle, producing a slower river. The slowness of the Euphrates, combined with the fact that it crosses a vast stretch of desert-steppe, means that much of its water is lost to evaporation. Thus, the mean annual discharge of the Euphrates at Hit is only *c.*

710 cumecs, compared to a mean annual discharge of 1240 cumecs for the Tigris at Baghdad. The difference between the rivers can also be expressed in terms of minimum/maximum discharge figures. Thus, whereas the minimum/maximum ratio of the Tigris at Baghdad is 1:80, that of the Euphrates is only 1:28.

Between Ramadi and Musaiyib no fewer than six major canals siphon water off the Euphrates from its east bank before the river reaches the Hindiyah Barrage where it divides, one branch running south past Kufa, another heading southeast to Hillah and Diwaniyah. These two branches converge south of Samawa, flowing jointly past Nasiriyyah, where they are joined by the Shatt al-Gharraf, and on through the Hor al-Hammar to Qurna where the Tigris meets them. The combined waters of the Tigris and Euphrates, known as the Shatt al-Arab, then flow on past Basra to Fao and the head of the Arabian Gulf. Much of the water in the Euphrates and Tigris, however, never reaches the Arabian Gulf, but is siphoned off for irrigation, lost to evaporation or dissipated in a series of swamps and marshes. The 'progressive downstream shrinkage' resulting from evaporation, irrigation and flood diversion is also reflected in diminished discharge rates of the Euphrates as one moves south. Thus, maximum flow rates at Hit, Hindiyyah and Nasiriyyah amount to 5200, 2880 and 1740 cumecs respectively, a clear indication of the ever-diminishing amount of water in the Euphrates as the river flows towards the Gulf. Indeed, of the 27 cu. km of water in the Shatt al-Arab, fully 22 cu. km originate in the Karun, a tributary which drains the Khuzistan province of southwestern Iran (Cressey 1958:455).[4] In fact, total water loss due to evaporation on irrigated land in Iraq from the combined Tigris and Euphrates amounts to no less than 30,000,000,000 cu. m or 30 cu. km of water per year. As G.B. Cressey noted many years ago, the 'average drop of rain' falling into the Euphrates, Tigris and Karun has only one chance in twelve of ever reaching the Gulf (Cressey 1958:443).

R.McC. Adams has described the regime of the Euphrates as an 'anastomising' one, defined as 'a natural pattern of multiple channels, separating and rejoining' in a series of meanders, in contrast to the Tigris which follows a single, incised bed throughout its course (Adams 1981:7–8). This tendency, when combined with the frequent efforts of farmers and governments to alter the Euphrates' flow by means of artificial diversions such as barrages, weirs, cataracts and canals, has resulted in a river which, throughout its history, has consistently shifted its bed. For the student of ancient Mesopotamia these shifts become immediately apparent when consulting a map showing the locations of the famous cities of Sumer and Akkad (Fig. I.5).

If it seems that undue attention is being paid here to the Tigris and Euphrates themselves, and not enough to the countryside on which the ancient Mesopotamians in fact existed, it is for the simple reason that the rivers literally *created* the landscape on which those human actors lived and died. Unlike rivers in many other parts of the world, the Tigris and Euphrates, once they reach their delta, do not wind their way through an ancient landscape which they have known, as it were, for millennia. On the

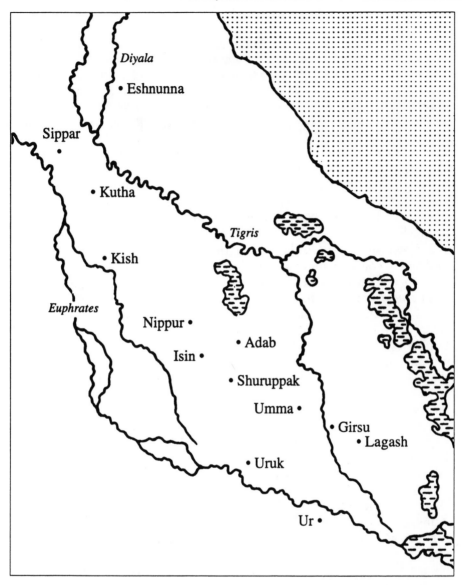

Figure I.5. Distribution of some of the main sites in southern Mesopotamia during the Ur III period (after Steinkeller 1987b: Fig. 1)

contrary, the lower Mesopotamian plain is like a canvas on which, each year, the twin rivers paint a new picture by depositing millions of tons of silt and salt, blanketing the land surface of the previous year. The same process, moreover, has wider ramifications which affect all aspects of the rivers' behaviour, irrigation patterns and agriculture in the region. Thus, the importance of the Tigris and Euphrates in helping to shape Mesopotamian civilization can hardly be overestimated.

Of Silt and Salt

The silt and salt content of the Euphrates and Tigris are, to a large extent, responsible for the landscape of southern Mesopotamia. In spate the Euphrates carries 1000–4000 parts per million (ppm) of sediment, while the Tigris has had up to 25,000 ppm at peak, levels which are four to five times greater than those found in the Nile (Charles 1988:8). Expressed in another way, it was estimated before World War II that the Euphrates carried an average 553 dry g of silt per cu. m of water, while the Tigris bore with it 787 dry g per cu. m of water (Gibson 1972:20), although this figure can triple when the river is in spate. In the 1950s the geographer G.B. Cressey estimated that the Tigris deposited *c.* 40,000,000 cu. m of sediment annually, 90 per cent of it in the lower alluvial plains between Baghdad and Basra (Cressey 1958:448–9). The figure for the Euphrates is lower, but not by much.

Silt deposition *within* the bed of the Euphrates is also an important problem to consider, for to a great extent it determines the behaviour of the river once it enters the delta. The steepness of the Euphrates' banks north of Hit means that flooding is not a problem, although it also means that it is difficult, if not impossible, without the aid of diesel pumps, to raise the water up and over its banks to be put to use in irrigation. From the time the Euphrates finally reaches the head of the combined Tigris-Euphrates delta at Ramadi, however, silt deposition in the river's bed changes the regime of the river markedly. The fact that the Euphrates is slower than the Tigris (see above) means that silt deposition along its bed is greater. Thus, while high water on the Euphrates is only 3.3 m above minimum flow levels, the constant deposition of silt and dissolved chemicals raises the river's bed, such that it frequently flows *above* the level of the surrounding plain (Fig. I.6). Indeed, from Ramadi southward, flooding will result unless steps are taken to prevent it. When the Euphrates overflows its banks, floodwater can destroy houses, fields, crops and elements of the irrigation system itself (Kay and Johnson 1981:253), as well as creating pools which, if not drained, make once-arable land into a marsh suited only for wild fowl and summer grazing following evaporation in the torrid months of the year (Adams and Nissen 1972:86). Thus, at Ramadi the Euphrates is only inhibited from spilling out of its bed by means of artificial embankments (Gibson 1972:25; cf. Brice 1966:241).

In addition to silt, the Euphrates carries on average 445 ppm chemical content, while the Tigris carries 250 ppm chemical content. The

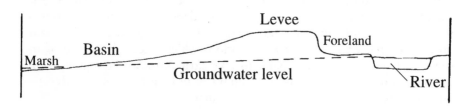

Figure I.6 Cross-section of a river levee and basin (after Oates and Oates 1977: Fig. 3)

significance of the chemical content of both rivers becomes clear when we recall that evaporation loss from the combined waters of both rivers, amounting to no less than 30,000,000,000 cu. m of water annually, leaves an estimated 22,000,000 metric tons of dissolved chemicals on the arable land of the country each year (Cressey 1958:448). Not all of this, however, is salt (sodium chloride), for lime and gypsum are also prominent components of the chemical content of the two rivers. Considering for the moment salt alone, the rivers carry on average between 10 and 50 ppm salt, but the figure rises to between 400 and 500 ppm at certain times of the year (NB 400 ppm = 400 mg/l). Thus, 475 ppm have been recorded in the Tigris at Baghdad in the month of December, while 462 ppm have been recorded in the Euphrates near Nasiriyyah in the month of September. These figures fall into the 'medium salinity range'. This, however, is nothing compared to the concentration of 900 ppm in the Diwaniyah canal during autumn and winter (Charles 1988:8–9).

When the Tigris and Euphrates are in spate salt concentration will naturally be diluted by the extra amounts of water being carried, but the further south one is, the less water there is in the rivers, and the greater the salinity level in ppm. Indeed, even a relatively low salinity rate of 100 ppm is still substantial for when water with 100 ppm salt content is used in an intensive irrigation situation, '1 m of water (depth of irrigation) applied to the land is equivalent to 1000 kg of salt per ha' (Charles 1988:9). To put it another way, 'If we assume a good irrigation water of 400 ppm of soluble salts and a total depth of irrigation requirement per year of about 1,500 mm, the amount of salt added to the soil annually amounts to about 6 tons/ha. If it is also assumed that due to lack of leaching, improper irrigation practices and bad infiltration the salts brought with the irrigation water are allowed to accumulate in the upper 50 cm of the soil profile, it can be found by simple arithmetic that the salt content of this soil depth will increase by about 0.50 per cent in a period of less than 7 years. This level of salinity is too high for the economical production of most agricultural crops' (A. Arar cited in Butz 1979:277).

Obviously, therefore, the salt and silt content of the Euphrates and Tigris has the greatest implications for determining the nature of the soils found in southern Mesopotamia and more particularly their utility for the human inhabitants of the area. It is to this subject that we now turn.

CLASSIFICATION OF LAND AND GENERAL SOIL CHARACTERISTICS

In the 1950s W.L. Powers classified the cultivable land of Iraq as follows: 6 per cent excellent, 68 per cent good and 23 per cent mediocre (Butz 1979:260). He was hardly the first to carry out such an exercise, however. Already in the late Early Dynastic period we find a wide range of Sumerian terms (Hruška 1985a; cf. G. Pettinato cited in Butz 1979:262) which were used to describe the arable and non-arable land of southern Mesopotamia, including 'best' (*sig₅*), 'good' (*muru$_x$*), 'mediocre' (*hul* or *hul-sum*), 'bad' (*murgu$_x$*) and 'non-draining/infertile' (*ù*). To these may be added a variety of other designations distinguishing, for example, 'steppe' (*eden*), 'economic hinterland of the city' (*uru-bar, é-duru₅*), 'settled land' (*LAGAB × SIG₅*), 'dry land' (*kislah*), 'fallow land/pasture' (*ki-ú-du₁₁-ka*), 'area with salt appearing' (*du₆-mun*), 'heavily salinated land' (*ki-mun*) and 'damp land' (*ki-duru₅*).

The traditional view of Mesopotamia is that it has always been poor in natural resources (but see Chapter IV), yet rich in agricultural fertility. The latter part of this equation, however, is a myth which is contradicted by every soil scientist who has ever worked in Iraq. The notion of Mesopotamia's legendary fertility can be traced back to Herodotus, who in Book I 93 of his *History* wrote:

> Of all the countries that we know there is none which is so fruitful in grain. It makes no pretension indeed of growing the fig, the olive, the vine, or any other tree of the kind; but in grain it is so fruitful as to yield commonly two-hundred-fold, and when the production is the greatest, even three-hundred-fold. The blade of the wheat-plant and the barley-plant is often four fingers in breadth. As for the millet and the sesame, I shall not say to what height they grow, though within my own knowledge; for I am not ignorant that what I have already written concerning the fruitfulness of Babylonia must seem incredible to those who have never visited the country.

Quite apart from the fact that these are unachievable yields (cf. Chapter III), it is simply not true that the soils of Mesopotamia are as fertile as Herodotus would have us believe. Agricultural yields are influenced by a multiplicity of factors including climate (adequate temperature regime), topography (resistance to erosion; accessibility for farmers), water budget (and ability to irrigate and for drainage), soil quality (texture, structure, soil depth, mineral content, nitrogen), fertility (organic content (humus), ph-value) and salt and alkali content (Butz and Schröder 1985:166). Soil texture and structure are dependent on the size and arrangement of the soil particles. Texture is determined by the relative proportions of sand, silt and clay, structure by the arrangement of individual soil particles and their aggregates. Soil particles are bound together by a variety of chemicals which are formed by soil micro-organisms, fungal activity, plant roots and decaying organic matter. Good soil aggregation is vital for the maintainance of good aeration and permeability. Aggregation also hinders the collapse of soil structure. Good soils, which retain water well, making it available to plants, are characterized by a balance between large, air-filled pores and small, water-filled pores (Charles 1988:21).

During the 1950s, when a great deal of land reclamation and agricultural study was conducted in Iraq, the soil scientists who worked there were uniformly of the opinion that the soil structure of southern Mesopotamia was poor, showing little particle aggregation. In a famous experiment J.C. Russel showed that '97 per cent of a dry cloddy soil taken from a field would pass through a 0.25 mm sieve after 30 minutes of soaking i.e. only 3 per cent remained aggregated' (Charles 1988:21). It should be obvious then that saturation, as experienced during irrigation, will do severe damage to soils with the poor structure of those found in southern Mesopotamia.

Poor soil structure is also responsible for the fact that the upper soil horizon in southern Mesopotamia is characterized by 'low hydraulic conductivity' which contributes to a 'high groundwater table due to the restricted drainage outflow' (Butz 1979:263).

Let us move now from soil structure to fertility. Soil fertility can be defined as 'total amount of plant nutrients contained in the soil, or as the overall potential of the soil for producing crops on a sustained basis, in which case the general condition of the soil, its organic matter content and the cycling of nutrients must also be considered' (Charles 1988:22). Contrary to Herodotus and the prevailing image which most laymen and not a few scholars have of Mesopotamia, the soils of Iraq have been described as 'low in . . . natural fertility level' (Butz 1979:263). Why should this be the case? As Charles has noted, 'In alluvial soils plant nutrients are released by the breakdown of sediment particles, the rate of release being greatest in hot, wet conditions, while nitrogen is fixed from the atmosphere by certain plants and organisms. To be utilised by the plant the nutrients must be dissolved in the soil water' (Charles 1988:22). Since ground cover is thin in an arid environment like southern Iraq, the organic content of the soil will be lower than in a temperate climate with more plant life. Soil scientists classify as 'desert soils' those soils having less than 1 per cent organic matter; 'semi-desert soils' as those with less than 2 per cent organic matter; and 'fertile temperate soils' as those with 3–5 per cent organic matter. Generally speaking, the soils of lower Mesopotamia have 0.05 per cent or less organic matter, making them very low in fertility.

Furthermore, although they are characterized by 'relatively high amounts of gypsum and lime' (Butz 1979:263), the Mesopotamian soils contain little nitrogen and phosphorus as there is little chance for the chemical breakdown of rock fragments. Additionally, the silt which comes with the floods may be mineral-rich, but as the structure of the soils is not very good, particularly in terms of porosity, the soil often becomes clogged and in effect smothered by the overlay of silt which in fact damages its productivity (Butz and Schröder 1985:176) as flood deposits consist generally of fine silt and clay particles with low porosity making for a poor 'infiltration rate'. On the other hand, the water-retention capacity of silt is high once water is in, making leaching difficult and salt retention a problem. Hence, salt crusts will form on the surface of regularly cultivated soils because of their poor structure (Charles 1988:23). For this reason hoeing and ploughing are so important to turn over the soils (see Chapter III).

Intuitively it might seem that artificial fertilization would compensate for low natural fertility, but this is a problem because of the arid climate, for if organic material (human or animal dung) is added to soil in a climatic regime like that of Iraq, it quickly disappears due to the combination of low humidity and high temperatures (Charles 1988:23). To conclude, in 1960 the soil scientist P. Buringh summed up the situation in southern Iraq in the following words: 'The natural fertility of the soils of the Lowland Mesopotamian Plain is . . . low. This conclusion is in contradiction to the general opinion, written in many articles and books, in which the plain is prized for its high fertility' (quoted in Charles 1988:23).

RIVER LEVEE AND RIVER BASIN SOILS

As noted above, the entire landscape of the Mesopotamian delta is a product of the silt and salt deposited by the Tigris and Euphrates. The flood levees on either side of the Euphrates, built up through successive floods and the deposition of silt, can reach over 1 km in width. The backslopes of the levees occupy virtually another 2 kms on either side of the river, while the depressions between the watercourses (the Hillah and Hindiyyah branches of the Euphrates, the Tigris, the Shatt al-Gharraf and the thousands of canals which emanate from them) where floodwater collects (Hunt 1988:189–206), form a mosaic of semi-permanent marshes and lakes (Fig. I.7) (Cressey 1958:457).

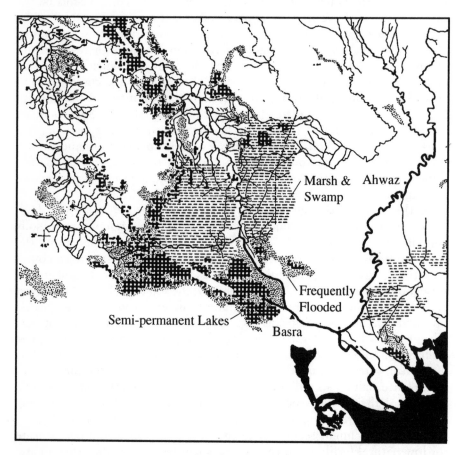

Figure I.7 Distribution of marshes, swamps and lakes in southern Mesopotamia *c. 1958* (after Cressey 1958: 457)

Because of the fact that the coarser, heavier river sediments are deposited before the lighter ones, two types of alluvial soils are formed in southern Mesopotamia, those along the raised levees of the rivers, and those in the basins some distance away. These have been described many times in the literature by scholars such as Buringh (1957:33–4), Adams (1965:7-9) and the Oates (Oates and Oates 1977:121–2), and the account which follows is an amalgam of prevailing views.

River Levee Soils
River levee soils are formed of the heaviest sediments carried by the river, since these are the first to be deposited when the river floods its banks. As the floodwaters overflow the river's bank they lose velocity, depositing the heaviest sediments first. This occurs along the river's banks, creating raised levees of 'relatively coarse textured soils' while the lighter sediments, suspended in water, are deposited further away in the river basins (Charles 1988:8) (see below). A similar process occurs whenever river water is siphoned off into a canal, for the water again loses velocity once it leaves the river and the coarser particles sink to the bottom of the canal, while the lighter ones remain suspended. Borne along with the irrigation water when it is let out onto the fields, fine 'irrigation sediment' is thus spread over extensive areas of cultivation (Charles 1988:8).

Because the river levees are elevated, drainage is usually better than average, and the ground surface is therefore further away from the watertable than in more low-lying areas. In addition, groundwater salt content in the levees is diluted by seepage of water from the river itself. On the other hand, irrigation is made difficult by the height of the levee which can only be irrigated using a mechanical device, such as a hand-operated *shaduf*, attested by the Early Dynastic period (Fig. I.4), or diesel pump to raise the water. Thus, the levees are optimal areas for the cultivation of a wide variety of crops, including date palms, in the shadow of which smaller fruit trees, cereals, legumes and vegetables can be grown. Date-palm shade creates a micro-climate of cooler than average temperature and higher than average humidity, and the rooting system of the date-palm stabilizes the soil, improving permeability and structure. In more recent times the river banks have also been used for the cultivation of summer vegetables after flooding.

River Basin Soils
When the Tigris or Euphrates floods, the floodwaters spread out for several kilometres after surmounting the levees. This results in standing water for a period of time until it is absorbed by the soil, evaporates or drains back into a canal. In such a situation no less than 5–10 cm of sediment can be deposited by a single flood (Charles 1988:25), concentrating the finest clays where standing water was present longest, i.e. in the lower lying basins which are below the elevation of the river and levees and thus closer to the watertable. The finer sediments have lower permeability, making them more liable to drain poorly. There is, however, a range of basin soils extending from silty clay loams to clay (Fig. I.8). Their suitability for cultivation depends largely on their distance from the river. The closer one moves to the river, the deeper the watertable (e.g. 1.5–2.5 m) and the coarser the soils. These are more easily cultivated than the more distant, clayey soils which are less permeable and closer to the water-table.

Studies conducted around Hillah have shown that groundwater must be

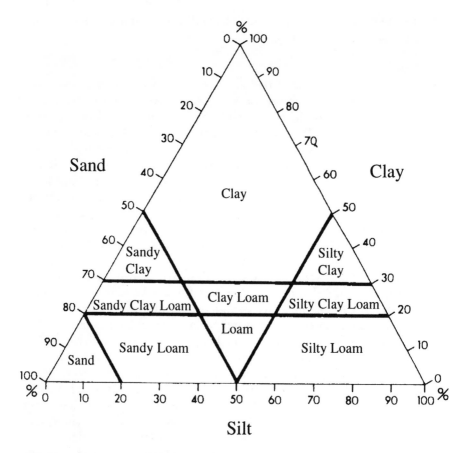

Figure I.8 Textural classification of soil (after Vita-Finzi 1978: 74)

at least 2 m from the surface at the beginning of summer or else salinization will occur (cf. the discussion of optimal groundwater level for barley in
Chapter III). Salinization occurs in several circumstances. It can happen as
a result of capillary movement of water to the surface due to evaporation,
which transports salts into the root zone. Similarly, where there is standing
water, capillary action will bring water and salts to the surface. When the
standing water has evaporated a layer of salt will be left in the top layers of
the soil (Charles 1988:25).

Basin soils are generally used for growing winter cereals, legumes, flax
and a wide range of vegetables in crop-fallow alternation. These soils are
poorer than those of the levee zone, since they are less permeable and tend
to become more easily salinized, waterlogged and covered with a saline
surface crust. Nevertheless, basin soils make up the bulk of the area under
cultivation today as they are more easily fed by gravity-flow irrigation from
feeder canals than the higher levees.

THE COURSE OF THE RIVERS TIGRIS AND EUPHRATES

It is an understatement to say that the delta of the Tigris and Euphrates rivers today looks nothing like it did in antiquity. Settlement patterns have changed dramatically during the past 7000–8000 years (Adams 1981). Two characteristics of the Tigris and Euphrates rivers' regimes have attracted particular attention in the Western literature: the tendency of the Euphrates to flood, thereby causing massive damage and frequent changes of course, and the degree to which silt deposited by the Euphrates has, as it were, 'projected' the base of the delta progressively south such that the head of the Arabian Gulf is now far from where it would have been in antiquity. A brief look at how the Euphrates assumed its present configuration will help explain the great discrepancy between the positions of the great sites of antiquity and those of the rivers today. Recent studies of the terminology of water management facilities in Mesopotamia demonstrate that a wide range of technical terms exist to describe the sorts of dams, dykes, weirs, barrages, sluices, regulators and reservoirs used to control the flow of water in ancient Mesopotamia (Hruška 1988a:61–4; Steinkeller 1988:74–9; van Soldt 1988:113–117; van Driel 1988: 136–41; Powell 1988:162–70), and it is clear that the capacity existed already in antiquity to substantially modify natural watercourses, to create artificial ones for specific purposes, and to intentionally or inadvertently set in motion physical processes whereby canals were so modified by the forces of nature that they were, in effect, turned into rivers, no longer under human control.

Ancient Mesopotamian canal names bear witness to the water management activities of numerous monarchs. Canal (Sum. *e*, Akk. *ikum*) names such as the *e-^{d}šul-gi* and *e-šarrum-kin*, i.e. canals built by Shulgi and Sargon, as well as many others mentioned in royal inscriptions and year formulae, confirm that the construction of irrigation canals was an achievement worth commemorating by the use of the ruler's name in identifying the new watercourse (Stol 1980:357, 364). Since the late nineteenth century work of such scholars as F. Delitzsch (Delitzsch 1881) and A. Delattre (Delattre 1888:480–507), many discussions of the numerous inscriptions commemorating irrigation works by Mesopotamian kings have appeared over the years. Without making an exhaustive survey of this subject, a number of examples may be cited which illustrate direct royal involvement in hydraulic management.

In the late Early Dynastic III period, Urukagina of Lagash included in a royal inscription the following: 'For Nanshe, he dug the Ninadua-canal, her beloved canal, and extended its far end to the sea' (Cooper 1986:70). Ur-Nammu, founder of the Ur III empire, reported a similar act as follows: 'For Nanna, first born son of Enlil, his master, did Ur-Nammu, the mighty male, king of Ur, king of Sumer and Akkad, when he built the temple of Enlil, here dig the canal the name of which is *^{d}Nanna-gú-gal* as boundary-canal, and connected its tail end with the sea' (Jacobsen 1960:178).

Pre-Sargonic and later kings were also active in the construction of weirs (Sum. *^{giš}KES-rá*, Akk. *erretu ša nāri*) to temporarily dam up water in reservoirs for future use. After describing his construction of a new canal for Ningirsu which he called Lumagimdu ('Sweet as Luma'), Eanatum of

Lagash says he built the reservoir of Lumagimdu (Cooper 1986:42) which, some years later, his nephew Entemena restored using '648,000 fired bricks and 1840 *gur* [*c.* 264,960 l, calculation after Powell 1990:497]' of bitumen (Cooper 1986:66). Because of the number of references to it on clay cones picked up there during the Ur excavations by Sir Leonard Woolley's workmen, the unexcavated site of Diqdiqah, near Ur, is thought by Jacobsen to cover a weir built by Ur-Nammu (Jacobsen 1960:182). A similar structure, excavated by the French at Tello (Fig. I.9), is thought by some scholars to be the weir built by Pirigme (2117–2115 BC), son of Ur-Ningirsu and a prince

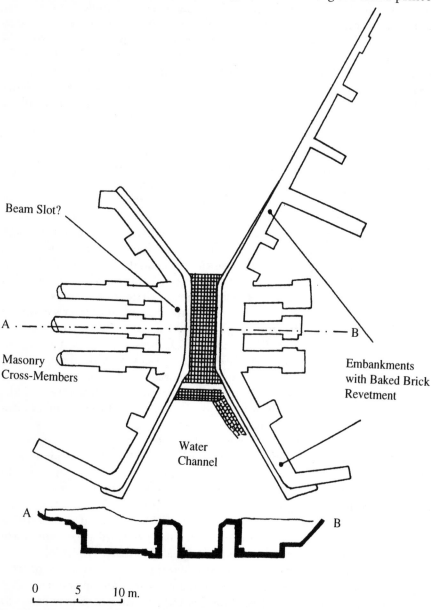

Figure I.9 The 'weir' of Pirigme at Tello (after Pemberton, Postgate and Smyth 1988: Fig. 9)

of Lagash, which is commemorated in a brick inscription (Barrelet 1965:100–18; cf. Sollberger and Kupper 1971:118–19, Nissen; 1975:26).

A long list of Old Babylonian kings considered their work on the canals of southern Mesopotamia significant enough to mention in their year formulae, following the format, 'Year (in which): the NN canal was dug' or 'Year (in which): PN dug the NN canal'. Such year formulae are attested in the reigns of many Old Babylonian rulers.[5] Nor were their Assyrian counterparts, such as Ashur-uballit I, Tukulti-Ninurta I, Assurnasirpal II and Sennacherib, any less attentive to the construction of canals, particularly along the tributaries of the Tigris (Stol 1980:364–5; Simonet 1977: 157–68). The year formulae make it clear that the provisioning of their people with sweet water, and the opening up of new tracts of land for agricultural exploitation, were of paramount concern to these kings.

In cases where the river had shifted beds and/or canals had gone dry, as has so often been documented in more recent times, the agricultural population could be left destitute and was forced to disperse, fending for itself as best it could. It is perhaps for this reason that several kings, including Ishme-Dagan of Isin (1953–1935 BC), Nur-Adad of Larsa (1865–1850 BC) and Hammurapi of Babylon (1792–1750 BC), speak of collecting and resettling the scattered people of a particular city or area (Edzard 1957:116–117). In discussing this phenomenon, Edzard has noted that a shift in the bed of the Euphrates near Musaiyib in 1820 caused 40,000 people to abandon the town of Hillah, and he suggests that similar catastrophes could have dispersed those ancient populations whom the Old Babylonian kings say they returned to their settlements (Edzard 1957:117).[6]

On a more individual level, the famous Old Babylonian law code known as the *Code of Hammurapi* contains several paragraphs (§§53–56) relating to damages to be paid (Renger 1990a:38) should a farmer not maintain properly the banks of his irrigation ditches or let water overflow onto another man's fields, thereby causing crop damage (Driver and Miles 1952–55:150–154[I], 31[II]).

Thus, we see a clear recognition by early Mesopotamian monarchs of their responsibilities vis-à-vis the population in respect to maintaining the canal system. Indeed the *topos* of a king providing his people and land with abundance through the provision of a new canal is amply attested in the cuneiform sources (Renger 1990a:34). As J. Renger has observed, 'Letters and administrative documents clearly show the emphatic and permanent concern of the central royal administration in all matters pertaining to irrigation' (Renger 1990a:36). Similar attitudes, combined with a clear sense of geomorphological reality, can be found in much later 'Western' accounts of Babylonia beginning with Herodotus. 'The whole of Babylonia is, like Egypt, intersected with canals' (*Hist.* I 193), Herodotus wrote, but when he suggested that the Euphrates, unlike the Nile, 'does not . . . overflow the corn-lands of its own accord, but is spread over them by hand, or by the help of engines', he was sorely mistaken, and it has consequently been suggested that Herodotus must have crossed Babylonia in a season when the water level was low, and never witnessed the river in spate (Delattre 1888:456).

Nevertheless, Herodotus and later historians preserve a good deal of information on the diversion of Mesopotamian rivers and canals for military and strategic purposes, extending back in time into the Neo-Babylonian period (Fig. I.10) when, Herodotus tells us, a queen called

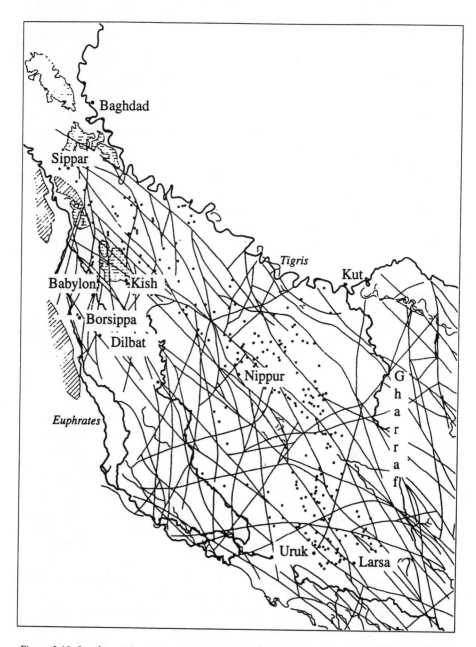

Figure I.10 Southern Mesopotamia in the Neo-Babylonian period showing the distribution of levees visible from satellite imagery and the locations of some principal ancient sites (after van Driel 1988: 148, Map 1)

Nitokris[7] altered the course of the Euphrates as it ran past Babylon. Herodotus describes how Nitokris made Babylon less vulnerable to Median attack by temporarily diverting the Euphrates into a great basin which she excavated 'a great way above Babylon, close alongside the stream'. Nitokris is said to have used the earth from the excavation to construct embankments which she reinforced with stone; and to have turned the Euphrates, which formerly ran straight through Babylon, into a meandering river 'by certain excavations which she made at some distance up the stream . . . that the stream might be slacker by reason of the number of curves, and the voyage be rendered circuitous . . . to prevent the Medes from holding intercourse with the Babylonians, and so to keep them in ignorance of her affairs' (*Hist.* I 185–7).

Elsewhere Herodotus describes how Cyrus the Great took vengeance on the Diyala, or 'Gyndes' river (Forbiger 1844:608), because of the fact that one of the sacred white horses accompanying his party had been drowned in its swift current (*Hist.* I 189). Cyrus is said to have temporarily called off his attack on Babylon in order that his troops might be put to work digging 360 canals, 180 on either side, running off the river in all directions and lowering its level 'so to break its strength that in future even women should cross it easily without wetting their knees'. However we are to interpret this story, Herodotus gives us a more pragmatic example of Cyrus' modification of waterways in the capture of Babylon. Having deployed part of his army 'at the point where the river enters the city, and another body at the back of the place where it issues forth, with orders to march into the town by the bed of the stream, as soon as the water became shallow enough', Cyrus is said to have 'turned the Euphrates by a canal into the basin [dug by the Neo-Babylonian queen Nitokris mentioned above], which was then a marsh, on which the river sank to such an extent that the natural bed of the stream became fordable. Hereupon the Persians who had been left for the purpose at Babylon by the river side, entered the stream, which had now sunk so as to reach about midway up a man's thigh, and thus got into the town' (*Hist.* I 189).

In 400/401 BC, during the fabled retreat of the 10,000 Greek mercenaries who fought for the younger Cyrus in his bid to overthrow his brother Artaxerxes II, Xenophon described topographic conditions near Babylon. He described 'a two days' march of 24 miles in the course of which they [the 10,000] crossed two canals, one of them by a permanent bridge and the other by a pontoon bridge of seven boats. The canal water was supplied from the river Tigris, and from the canals ditches were cut to extend over the country, big ones at first and then smaller ones, until in the end they were just little channels like we have in Greece for the millet fields' (*An.* II iv 13). Commentators are divided on the question of whether Xenophon was mistaken in assuming the water in the canals which he crossed came from the Tigris.[8]

Speaking of the Pallacopas canal, Arrian says that, prior to the arrival of Alexander the Great, 10,000 Babylonians were engaged annually for three months in the labour of closing the Pallacopas, a major canal running off the right bank of the Euphrates some 800 stadia north of Babylon near modern Anbar (Meissner 1896:8). This canal was dug late in the Neo-Babylonian period, perhaps by Nebuchadrezzar (604–562 BC), and is attested in cuneiform sources beginning with the reign of Neriglissar (559–556 BC) as the *nār Pal-lu-kat*, a name which conforms perfectly with the variant spelling *Pallacottas* preserved by Appian[9] (fl. pre-AD 100). Indeed, the sluice of the canal (*bāb nāri*), to which Arrian may have been alluding when he talked of the work of 'closing' the Pallacopas, is mentioned in sources from the reign of Nabonidus (555–539 BC) (Meissner 1896:9; cf. Jacobsen 1960:177, n. 6).

Both Arrian and Strabo preserve information concerning Alexander the Great's intervention in the realm of Babylonian canal and river management. One of Alexander's own admirals, Aristobulus, quoted by Strabo, says that Alexander 'inspected the canals and with his multitude of followers cleared them; and that he likewise stopped up some of the mouths and opened others' (*Geog.* 16 i 11). Further, Strabo records that the Euphrates was once again made navigable as far north as Babylon thanks to Alexander, who removed the artificially constructed cataracts which 'the Persians [Achaemenids], wishing on purpose to prevent voyaging up these rivers [speaking of both the Tigris and Euphrates], for fear of attacks from without, had constructed' (*Geog.* 16 i 9). Indeed, Alexander the Great's brief stay in Babylonia resulted in the accumulation and transmission of a good deal of knowledge about the regime of the Euphrates, the modalities of artificial canal construction and maintenance, and the dangers of lake, marsh and swamp formation through the flooding of both natural and artificial watercourses. Later testimony on the Babylonian canal system can be found in the works of, e.g. Polybius (IX 43) and Ammianus Marcellinus (XXIV 2).

Responsibility for managing the river regime as the sign of a good sovereign, and the failure to do so as the sign of a despotic and corrupt regime, is a *topos* which is found in various ancient and modern sources. Thus Strabo (*Geog.* 16 i 10) writes:

> Now it is impossible, perhaps, altogether to prevent overflows of this kind, but it is the part of good rulers to afford all possible aid. The aid required is this: to prevent most of the overflowing by means of dams, and to prevent the filling up effected by the silt, on the contrary, by keeping the canals cleared and the mouths opened up. Now the clearing of the canals is easy, but the building of dams requires the work of many hands; for, since the earth readily gives in and is soft, it does not support the silt that is brought upon it, but yields to the silt, and draws it on, along with itself, and makes the mouth hard to dam. And indeed there is also need of quick work in order to close the canals quickly and to prevent all the water from emptying out of them. For when they dry up in the summer, they dry up the river too; and when the river is lowered it cannot supply the sluices with water at the time needed, since the water is needed most in summer, when the country is fiery hot and scorched; and it makes no difference whether the crops are submerged by the abundance of water, or are destroyed by thirst for water. At the same

time, also, the voyages inland, with their many advantages, were always being thwarted by the two above-mentioned causes, and it was impossible to correct the trouble unless the mouths of the canals were quickly opened up and quickly closed, and unless the canals were regulated so that the water in them neither was excessive nor failed.

But modifications to the river and canal regime could result, not just from bad government, as Strabo implies, but from military intervention and neglect. Thus McG. Gibson has suggested that the Mongol invasion of Iraq under Hulaku, grandson of Genghis Khan, in 1258 was primarily destructive, not so much in physically destroying canals, but rather in causing the deaths of most of the senior officials engaged in managing the irrigation system of the country (Gibson 1972:25), although the historian S.H. Longrigg has suggested that, 'most ruinous of Hulaku's acts had been the studied destruction of dykes and headworks whose ancient and perfected system had been the sole source of wealth. Disordered times, and the very fewness of the spiritless survivors, forbade repair; and the silting and scouring of the rivers once let loose, soon made the restoration of control the remote, perhaps hopeless, problem to-day [1925] still unsolved' (Longrigg 1925:13). So altered was the state of the rivers during the medieval era that, at the turn of the present century, G. LeStrange wrote, 'During the middle-ages the physical conditions in 'Irâk were entirely different from what they are now, by reason of the great changes which have come to pass in the courses of the Euphrates and Tigris' (LeStrange 1905:25–6).

In the late eighteenth century an ambitious programme of construction was undertaken with a view to diverting water from the Euphrates north of Babylon to Najf. The resulting dam, known as the 'Hindiyyah Barrage' after its Indian builder, 'Asif ul Daulah, created what was known as the Hindiyyah canal and is today a second major arm of the Euphrates. By 1830 the Hillah branch of the Euphrates was nearly dry as a result of this diversion. Haji Muhammad 'Ali Ridha Pasha, governor of Baghdad from 1831 to 1842, as well as Najib Pasha, his successor from 1842 to 1852, both attempted to dam the Hindiyyah and divert some of its waters to the Hillah branch, but without success. 'Umr Pasha constructed a mud and brushwood weir in 1854, but even the constant repairs undertaken over the subsequent three decades proved inadequate to the force of the Hindiyyah. With the Hillah branch nearly dry by 1885, M. Schoenderfer, a French engineer, was commissioned to build a new barrage. This solid brick structure, some 200 m wide, finally burst in July 1903, 'the immediate result of which was to leave the lower Euphrates river-bed dry for a distance of nearly 150 miles, the whole volume of water passing down the Hindiye canal' (Cadoux 1906:271). Schoenderfer's barrage was not replaced until a decade later by Sir William Willcocks' barrage which finally restored water to the Hillah (Longrigg 1925:311, n. 1).

To this same propensity for bursting over its levee and changing course or simply pouring out to form a swamp or marsh can be ascribed the difficulty of determining the former course of the Euphrates. A glance at a map of modern Iraq suffices to show that, with the exception of Babylon, the important ancient sites of the south lie along neither the Hillah nor the Hindiyyah branch of the Euphrates, let alone the lower Tigris, but along a series of relict effluents which branched off from the main course of the Euphrates in the vicinity of ancient Sippar, near the point where it runs closest to the Tigris. Visiting Mesopotamia in 1765, Carsten Niebuhr had already noted the course of a dry watercourse called the Hafar or Jarri Zaade (Fig. I.11) heading south from Hit on the Euphrates towards Kufa, which later scholars identified with the ancient Pallacopas/Pallacottas canal, described above (Delattre 1888:473; cf. Meissner 1896:4–5). In 1857 the great Orientalist Sir Henry C. Rawlinson wrote, 'There is, of course, very great difficulty, owing to the shifting nomenclature and the fluctuating topography of the country, in ascertaining the sites of the different cities, which, as we descend from the early Chaldaean to the Assyrian period, appear to have risen into temporary importance on the lower Euphrates' (Rawlinson 1857:185). One of the British Museum's contracted excavators during the second half of the nineteenth century, Hormuzd Rassam, made numerous observations on the course of the canals in the neighbourhood of Sippar in northern Babylonia (Rassam 1885:176–7), while Robert Koldewey, the excavator of Babylon, devoted a chapter of his popular work on the excavations there to the regime of the Euphrates and the changes which its course had undergone in recent times (Koldewey 1913:16–23). Notwithstanding the difficulties of untangling the many thousands of canals which cross-cut southern Mesopotamia numerous scholars (e.g. T. Jacobsen, A. Sousa, P. Buringh, J.J.L. van der Kloes, E. de Vaumas, D. Coquerillat, R.McC. Adams, H. Gasche, R. Paepe, McG. Gibson and H.J. Nissen) have studied these watercourses and the thousands of relict canal levees associated with them on the ground, while others (e.g. A. Goetze, H. Sauren, G. van Driel, P. Steinkeller, K. Nashef, F. Carroué and R. Zadok) have isolated the names of the principal canals and natural waterways in southern Mesopotamia in the cuneiform sources of different periods and tried to reconstruct the riverine and canal system by combining this information with the topographic and geomorphological evidence. As the available aerial photographs and satellite images of southern Iraq show, however, there is an absolutely overwhelming number of channels of varying age which criss-cross the countryside, making it very difficult to link written references to named canals with specific scars on the landscape. It is, moreover, obvious that the precise pattern of waterways has changed constantly through time.

In a landmark study the late Thorkild Jacobsen sketched in the main lines of these watercourses, based both on literary evidence and limited surface survey. He isolated six main streams (Fig. I.12) departing from the present day Euphrates in the area of Sippar: the Zubi canal, the Irnina, the Arahtum and Apkallatum, the Me-Enlilak, the Iturungal[10] and Id-ninaki-gena and Nanna-gu-gal, and the Isinnitum (Jacobsen 1960:176–8). For the most part Jacobsen's reconstruction has stood the test of time, although, as noted above, W. Heimpel now suggests that the watercourse which flowed past Girsu, Umma and Adab, was in fact the Tigris (Heimpel 1990:213), and not a branch of the Euphrates.

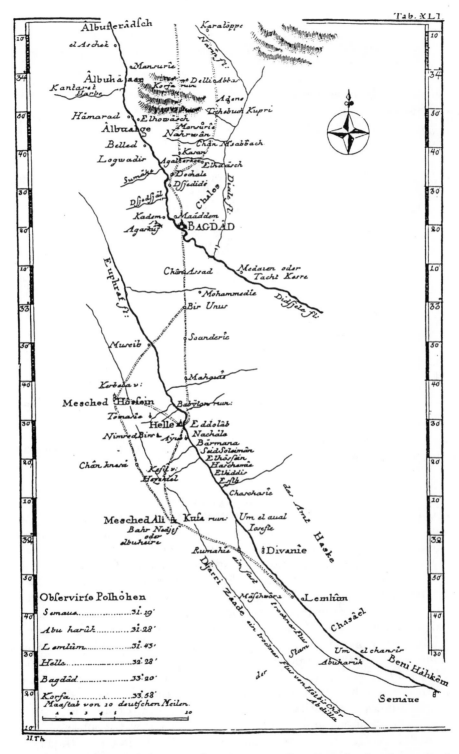

Figure I.11 Carsten Niebuhr's route from Samawa to Kara Tepe showing the course of the Jarri Zaade (after Rasmussen 1990: 283)

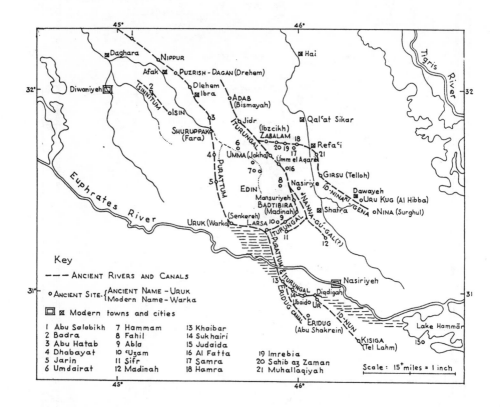

Figure I.12 Jacobsen's reconstruction of the main watercourses of southern Mesopotamia (after Jacobsen 1960: Pl. XXVIII)

These major waterways, along with many more minor canals, formed a network of links which were generally of far greater importance than the land routes between cities, which in any case 'usually follow the raised banks of canals' (Oates 1977:101–7). Thus, in southern Mesopotamia distances must not be calculated simplistically in terms of distance as the crow flies, but in terms of accessibility via navigable watercourses. Two towns separated by cultivated fields and pasture may be 'farther apart', even if the absolute distance between them is not great, than two towns linked by a waterway. To cite but one example, the waterway connecting Adab, Umma, Bad-Tibira, Larsa and Ur has been described as the main commercial artery in southern Mesopotamia during the Ur III period (Nissen 1975:27) (Fig. I.5), and it is clear that the canals and rivers of the south were the highways of antiquity. Only in the case of detailed, site-specific studies is it possible to come to even an approximate understanding of the locations and identifications of specific watercourses in and around individual sites, as Sauren has done for Umma in the Ur III period (Sauren 1966).

Years of survey by Adams and the publications which have grown out of his work have shown that the linear patterning of sites is a clear indication of the close correlation between ancient settlement locations and both canals and natural watercourses. This is borne out, moreover, by an examination of the geographical place-names mentioned in the earliest extant written records, the late fourth millennium BC Archaic texts from Uruk, one of southern Mesopotamia's premier population centres. No fewer than twenty-four economic texts of Uruk IV date (*c.* 3400–3100 BC) contain recognizable toponyms (Nissen 1985:230). Their frequency of occurrence is as follows: Uruk (×10), Adab (×8), Ur (×3), Larsa (×1) and Umma (×1). Fig. I.13 shows the placement of these cities. It is a truncated list of less than half a dozen sites, located along three of the watercourses discussed above, viz. the Purattum (Uruk), the Iturungal (or Tigris?) (Adab, Umma and Larsa), and the Id-Nun (Ur).[11]

In the Uruk III period (*c.* 3100–2900 BC) no fewer than 152 economic texts can be counted with toponyms (Nissen 1985:231). In order of frequency, they are as follows: Uruk (×57), Shuruppak (×31), Zabala (×31), Ur (×14), Dilmun (×11), Adab (×8), Kish (×7), Umma (×7), Larsa (×2) and Eshnunna (x1). Like the Uruk IV texts, most of these names (Fig. I.14) can be located in the lower reaches of the Purattum and Iturungal, with the exception of Kish (northern Babylonia), Eshnunna (Diyala region), Dilmun (Gulf region), and Aratta (semi-mythical land in eastern Iran).

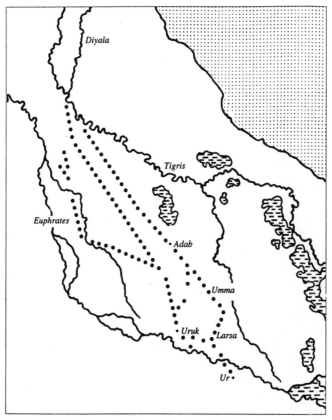

Figure I.13 Distribution of towns mentioned in economic texts of Uruk IV date

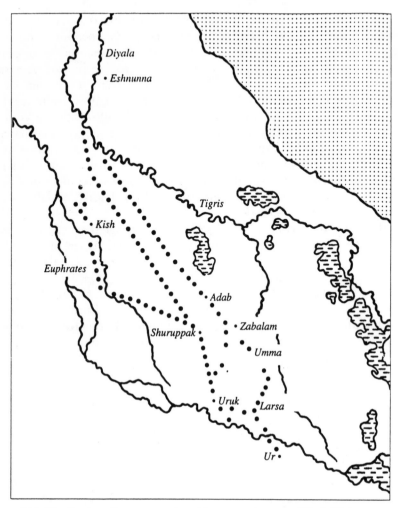

Figure I.14 Distribution of towns mentioned in economic texts of Uruk III date

THE PROGRADATION OF THE TIGRIS-EUPHRATES DELTA

Alongside the ongoing discussion of human- and nature-induced changes to the river and canal regime of southern Mesopotamia, we should also consider another key problem in the creation of the alluvial landscape, namely the degree to which the area from Ur to the south has been modified by millennia of silt deposition. As in the case of ancient Mesopotamia's watercourses, this too is a topic which has attracted interest since late antiquity. As indicated above by Strabo's disquisition on the responsibilities of all good rulers in southern Mesopotamia, the enormous amount of silt carried by the Euphrates was well known to ancient writers, and Strabo (*Geog.* 16 i 10) describes Alexander's own efforts to inspect and clean canals, and to divert streams in order to ensure navigability (cf. the discussion of this episode in Chesney 1850:367). Moreover, the deposition of silt at the mouth of the Euphrates was discussed in some detail by Pliny, who says that progradation occurred more rapidly in the Tigris-Euphrates delta than anywhere else in the world. To illustrate this he tells us (*Nat. Hist.* VI xxxi) that at the time of the foundation of the settlement of Alexandria (cf. Chapter XIII) in southernmost Mesopotamia by Alexander the Great in 324 BC, the city was 10 stadia (c. 1.8 km; for the length of the stadium see Reinmuth 1979:337) from the sea; by the time of Augustus, Juba reports (1 BC – AD 4) that it was 50 miles from the sea; and by Pliny's own lifetime (d. AD 79), according to contemporary Arab merchants ('*legati Arabum nostrique negotiatores*') it was no less than 120 miles from the mouth of the Euphrates to the town (*Nat. Hist.* VI xxvi–xxvii).

When European travellers began to visit lower Mesopotamia observations on the courses of canals and waterways began to supplement the knowledge gleaned from a careful reading of the classical authors. In 1835 C.T. Beke published a paper in which he argued that the head of the Arabian Gulf had originally stood near Samarra and had been progressively translated southward through the build-up of alluvium over the millennia (Beke 1835:40–6). W.G. Carter's paper of the same year calculated that progradation had occurred at the rate of 300 km in no less than 340 years, equalling a rate of 882.35 m per year.[12]

A year later (16 March – 28 October 1836) the British Euphrates Expedition under the command of Lt.Col. F.R. Chesney explored the possibilities of using the overland route through Syria via the Euphrates or Tigris and the Arabian Gulf as a highway to India (Pallis 1954:17). This brought about yet another reconsideration of the hydrology of the rivers and the geomorphology of their delta by the expedition surgeon and geologist, W.F. Ainsworth, who in 1838 published a detailed consideration of his geomorphological and hydrological observations in concert with the testimony of the Greek and Latin sources (Ainsworth 1838). The question continued to fascinate fieldworkers in the area over the next couple of decades, and in 1857, following the mid-century hiatus in Mesopotamian exploration occasioned by the Crimean War, W.K. Loftus proposed a progradation rate of 23 m per year (Loftus 1857:282; cf. Genthe 1896:57; Weissbach 1931:1085). In the same year, however, Sir Henry C. Rawlinson suggested a rate of c. 58.6 m per year. Critical of Pliny, yet committed to the belief that the ruins of Ur, which he described as 'now 150 miles from the sea', were those of a 'maritime people', Rawlinson wrote, 'Pliny, however, carries this theory of an accretion of land at the mouth of the Euphrates to an absurd extent . . . . The average increase of territory I believe to be about a mile in 30 years, which would give an aggregate of 133 miles for the whole period of history, our earliest Chaldæan antiquities dating from about 2200 BC' (Rawlinson 1857:186). Thus, whereas Pliny's figures represent progradation on the order of 120 km over 400 years (Genthe 1896:56), Rawlinson distributed his 133 miles of deltaic advance over nearly 4000 years. The climax to what one could call the era of progradation studies came in 1900 when the distinguished French engineer, archaeologist and numismatist J. de Morgan published an influential study basing himself on Neo-Assyrian and Greek sources and using Rawlinson's estimate of progradation as a bench-mark for his calculations. De Morgan proposed that when Sennacherib campaigned against the Elamites c. 696 BC and

Alexander's admiral Nearchus sailed in 325 BC along the coast of Susiana and up the Pasitigris (Karun) to Susa, the head of the Gulf was situated almost as far north as modern Kut al-Amara (de Morgan 1900:10–23; cf. Hansman 1978:49–61; Tomaschek 1890:80ff) (Fig. I.15). Twenty years later the German Assyriologist Bruno Meissner, while suggesting that the head of the Gulf in antiquity may have lain somewhere in the region of the modern Hor al-Hammar, nevertheless expressed a more sober attitude when he admitted that it would probably never be possible to confirm the exact position of the ancient shoreline using dubious calculations of annual silt deposition (Meissner 1920:5).

The theory of progradation remained dominant throughout the first half of the twentieth century and we find it, for example, in most works devoted to ancient Mesopotamia at this time. In 1952, however, just as one of the most influential archaeologists of all time, V. Gordon Childe, was paraphrasing de Morgan's argument yet again (Childe 1952:103), the British geologists G.M. Lees and N.L. Falcon published a revolutionary article in which they argued that tectonic subsidence through time had more than cancelled out the effects of siltation, and dismissing the arguments of their

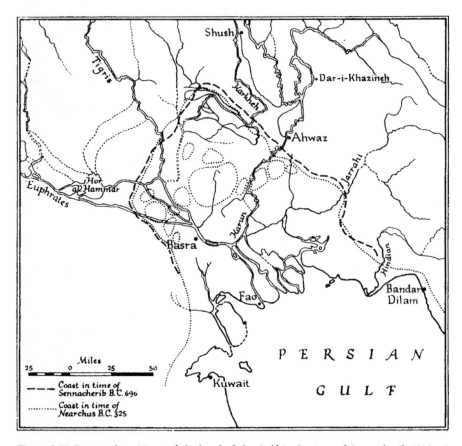

Figure I.15 Proposed positions of the head of the Gulf in the time of Sennacherib (696 BC) and Nearchus (325 BC) according to J. de Morgan (after Lees and Falcon 1952: Fig. 2)

predecessors, they found 'no acceptable historical evidence that the head of the Gulf was ever very far up-country from its present position' (Lees and Falcon 1952:39). Lees' and Falcon's position was quickly adopted by most scholars in the field but in 1975 de Morgan's suggestion was revived by C.E. Larsen, who suggested that the geomorphological situation in lower Mesopotamia was far more complex than had been assumed by any of his predecessors (Larsen 1975). Larsen looked at a wide range of variables, particularly the Flandrian Transgression, an episode of worldwide rise in sea-level which began *c.* 17,000 BP. In the late Pleistocene the Arabian Gulf was merely a trough which carried the combined effluence of the Tigris-Euphrates system in the form of a river to the Arabian Sea. Sea-levels rose by fits and starts, most rapidly between *c.* 12,000 and 8,000 BP (Potts 1990, I:13). Larsen argued that, 'as sea level rose to near present levels or above, it clearly displaced the shoreline inland to the Hor al-Hammar . . . Alluvial deposits on the surface of the Hammar Formation and seaward of the Hor al-Hammar can most reasonably be interpreted by delta advance, following the attainment of a near present sea level (*c.* 4000–3000 BC). This suggests at least 150 to 180 km of progradation during the last 5000 years' (Larsen 1975:53). Thus, by Larsen's reckoning progradation took place at the rate of 30–36 m per year. In his opinion, 'Cuneiform sources . . . that relate the third millennium cities of Ur and Eridu to the sea appear to have more validity than was previously thought' (Larsen 1975:57).

Just as the earlier views of de Morgan or Lees and Falcon were enthusiastically taken up by many of their contemporaries, we find Larsen's neoprogradation hypothesis cautiously embraced by authorities including Adams (Adams 1981:54) and J.-L. Huot (Huot 1989:66). P. Sanlaville has recently reviewed the geomorphological evidence yet again, combining it more judiciously with the available data on sea-level changes in the Arabian Gulf and coming to the conclusion that, while the situation is far more complex than most of his predecessors have allowed, the ancient coastline of the Gulf has indeed changed as a result of sea-level change, progradation and subsidence. To understand Sanlaville's arguments, however, it is necessary to first review his data on sea-level changes which shows

- sea-levels some 15–20 m lower than those of today at the start of the Ubaid period (*c.* 5500 BC) attaining approximately modern levels by the end of the Ubaid period (*c.* 3800 BC), after which
- sea-level continued to rise reaching maximum levels of *c.* 1–2 m above modern sea-level *c.* 3500 BC, followed by
- retreat to approximately modern sea-level by *c.* 2800 BC, after which
- sea-levels oscillated within a narrow band of ± 0-1 m until roughly the time of Christ when they may have been in the order of 2 m below modern levels, after which
- sea-level rose to approximately modern levels by *c.* AD 1000 (Sanlaville 1989: Fig. 7).

It is clear that, in an area of such low elevation as southern Mesopotamia, changes in sea-level can have serious ramifications. While it is often difficult to find precise elevations in archaeological reports from this area, the elevation of the plain of the Euphrates today near Tell Oueili is said to lie at 6 m above mean sea-level (Calvet 1983:15), while at Uruk the surface of the Eanna sounding stands at approximately 7 m above mean sea-level. A better appreciation of just how 'flat' southern Mesopotamia is and was, however, can be gained when we take into account that sterile soil at Eanna was reached at 0.99 m above mean sea-level. Thus, when the area was first occupied, it had an elevation of scarcely 1 m. This flatness is to a certain extent masked at a site like Uruk by the fact that another 6 m of cultural deposits overlie sterile soil (Adams and Nissen 1972:6). At Musaiyib on the middle Tigris roughly 6 m of alluvial deposits have accumulated in the area since the second half of the third millennium BC, while Adams estimates that in the Diyala region the build-up is in the order of 8 m of sediment since the fourth millennium, an accumulation of roughly 20 cm per century (Adams 1965:9–10).

H.J. Nissen has argued that sea-levels upwards of 2.75 m higher than today made much of lower Mesopotamia uninhabitable during the Ubaid period, until a recession of sea-level occurred *c.* 3500 BC which removed surface water from lower Babylonia (Nissen 1988a:41–2, 1988b:145; Adams and Nissen 1972:9–11). This view, however, has been challenged by Oates (Oates 1993:147, cf. 1991:23) and is indeed contradicted by Sanlaville's latest research, for it is clear that, if anything, sea-level during the entire Ubaid period was substantially lower than it is today (Fig. I.16), and cannot be adduced as an explanation for an absence of settlement. In other words, the area did not lie under water prior to the regression posited by Nissen at *c.* 3500 BC Sanlaville has pointed to highs of *c.* 1 m above modern sea-level *c.* 2600–2200 BC, and of *c.* 0.5–0.8 m above modern sea-level around 1600–1200 BC. Obviously, if one discounts the deposition of alluvial deposit noted above, and recalls that the elevation of virgin soil at Uruk is only *c.* 1 m, then a change in sea-level of up to 1 m in the mid-third millennium BC could theoretically, and in the absence of other, mitigating factors, have brought much of southern Mesopotamia under water. This, in fact, is what Sanlaville has argued, echoing Larsen in suggesting that cuneiform sources linking Ur and Eridu with water are correct (Sanlaville 1992:19). In making this suggestion, however, no attention has been paid to the very forceful arguments made some years ago by H. Waetzoldt, to which we now turn.

Waetzoldt has emphasized that, had Ur, Eridu or Tello been situated on an inland arm of the Gulf, one would have expected to find significant amounts of saltwater fish remains at all of them (Waetzoldt 1981:163).[13] In fact, as a recent study of fish remains from sites in southern Mesopotamia (Abu Salabikh, Nippur, Umm al-Hafriyat, Uruk, Isin and Tell al-Hiba) has shown, all of the excavated sites for which faunal data exist are characterized by higher proportions of sweetwater than salt or brackish water species in the faunal inventory (von den Driesch 1986: 37, Table 2). While this might seem, *per se*, a strong argument against the location of these sites on salt-water, the situation with regard to fishing in ancient Mesopotamia was never so clear cut. The state-controlled fishermen of the Ur III period at Girsu (Tello), for example, fished in inland canals, marshes and ponds, as

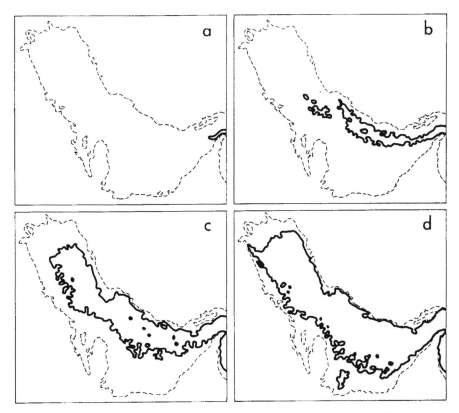

Figure I.16 Approximate positions of the head of the Gulf at *c.* (a) 18,000 BC, (b) 12,000 BC, (c) 8000 BC and (d) 6000 BC (after Vita-Finzi 1978: 129, Fig. 83)

well as in the Gulf (Englund 1990:6–7), and must have delivered a mixture of both salt and freshwater fish for temple offerings.[14]

More significant is the fact, pointed out by Waetzoldt, that in the so-called 'messenger texts' from Girsu, which concern the official couriers of the Ur III empire,[15] the Sumerian term *a-ab-ba* is used to designate both freshwater expanses and the open sea. Thus, some texts (e.g. RTC 338:5; ITT 3:5174:7ff.) stipulate the distance travelled between Girsu and the *a-ab-ba* as no more than two days, which, depending on whether the distance was covered on foot or by boat via the canals, could mean anywhere from 30–80 km. On the other hand, a text (ITT 5:6946:1) concerning Guabba (see Edzard and Farber 1974:63–5 for this toponym), a town which must have been some 50–60 km southeast of Girsu, states that it took twenty-six people eighteen days to reach the *a-ab-ba*. Again, we are not informed as to whether the travel was undertaken by boat or on foot, but this must represent a fairly healthy distance, perhaps anywhere from 150 to 500 km. Whereas the texts concerning Girsu would seem to be referring to a relatively nearby body of water, possibly a lake, marsh or swamp, the text concerning Guabba obviously implies that the *a-ab-ba* was situated at a considerable distance from the city and is likely to denote the Arabian Gulf (Waetzoldt 1981:165, Edzard 1993:2).

The same caveats noted by Waetzoldt must also be applied to the accounts of Sennacherib's campaign against Elam in 696 BC, according to which 'the ships of my warriors reached the swamps at the mouth of the river where the Euphrates carries its waters into the fearful sea', a point close to the intersection of the Ulai, or Eulaeus, river, the modern Karkheh, and the Tigris (Hansman 1978:53). In all these cases, however, whether Ur and Eridu in the third millennium, or the expedition of Sennacherib against Elam, references to 'the sea' must be treated cautiously. Not only has Waetzoldt shown that, in early sources, the same terms are used for marsh/swamp and open water, but more recently S.W. Cole has demonstrated clearly that a large marsh around the site of Borsippa, southwest of Babylon and far from even the northernmost line of the Gulf projected by de Morgan or Larsen, was routinely called the 'sea' (Akk. *tamirtu*) in texts dating to the Neo-Assyrian, Neo-Babylonian and Achaemenid periods (Cole 1994:81–109). Clearly, therefore, references to 'the sea' are ambiguous and must be examined more closely in conjunction with other types of evidence before they are taken to refer to the open waters of the Gulf itself. Indeed, this point is brought home forcibly by the very designation of southernmost Mesopotamia from the eary second millennium BC onwards.

In cuneiform sources southernmost Mesopotamia was known as *māt tāmti(m)* (Sum. *KUR A.AB.BA*), the 'Sealand' (Brinkman 1993:6). The texts which record the activities of the kings of the First Sealand Dynasty show conclusively that Ili-ma-AN*, its founder, was a contemporary of the Old Babylonian kings Samsu-iluna (1749–1712 BC) and Abi-eshuh (1711–1684 BC). By the reign of Nazi-Maruttash (1307–1282 BC) the Kassites had annexed the Sealand. A recently published text from Tell Kirbasi, on the south side of the central Hor al-Hammar some 30 km west of Basra (between Tells Aqram and Abu Salabikh), is a record from the sixteenth year of Nazi-Maruttash which enumerates forty-seven head of cattle (Kessler 1992). On analogy with a small group of texts from Nippur which mention cattle from the Sealand, K. Kessler has suggested that this region was one of the principal stockbreeding regions of the Kassite state, providing cattle for the capital Dur-Kurigalzu which were then distributed, *inter alia*, to the temple at Nippur. Grain and dates from the Sealand are also mentioned in Kassite texts from Nippur, suggesting that the area was agriculturally important as well at this time. In the Neo-Assyrian period the Sealand was the home of the important Chaldaean tribe, Bit-Jakin, against whom numerous Assyrian monarchs campaigned. In the Neo-Babylonian period the Sealand remained a province of the empire, at least through the reign of Nebuchadrezzar II (604–562 BC), and it again became one under the Achaemenid king Cambyses (529–522 BC) (Joannès 1990:177).

While B. Meissner could claim in 1920 that the lack of mounds in this region made it certain that it had been under water (Meissner 1920:4), G. Roux's survey of the Hor al-Hammar (Fig. I.17) showed that this was purely a result of insufficient exploration (Roux 1960:30), for there is in fact a string of mounds 'extending in an almost straight line from Tell Lahm to a point 23 miles north of Basrah' which, Roux suggests 'provides a strong argument against the classical theory according to which the whole

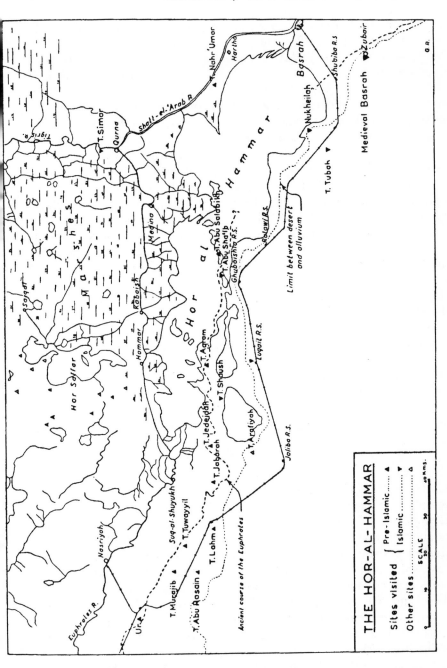

Figure I.17 Archaeological sites in the Hor al-Hammar (after Roux 1960: Map 1)

of this region was under sea-water from prehistoric times to the dawn of the Christian era' (Roux 1960: 30). The existence of sites such as Tells Kirbasi, al-Lahm, Aqram and Abu Salabikh in the area of the modern Hor al-Hammar underscores the fact that, from at least the early second millennium BC[16] onwards, this was a populated area which, while it may have been marshy, was certainly not submerged beneath the Gulf. Rising no more than 2 m above the water line, Tell Kirbasi is today periodically surrounded by water, yet it is difficult to imagine that a site like this was located on an island in the Kassite period, for there is little reason to suppose that if this were the case, Tell Kirbasi or indeed the Sealand generally would have been cited as a source of cattle and cereals. Thus, de Morgan's suggested shoreline in the time of Sennacherib would place under water sites such as Tell al-Lahm which we now know were occupied during the Neo-Assyrian period! The discovery of a cylinder of Nabonidus (555–539 BC) at Tell al-Lahm (Saggs 1957:190; cf. Jacobsen 1960:183; Röllig 1976–80:621; Vértesalji 1980–83:431–3; Nashef 1982:168–9; Zadok 1985:200–1), moreover, confirms that 150 years after Sennacherib's time, the region was most definitely not submerged, and indeed Sanlaville's sea-level curve shows that sea-levels throughout the second millennium BC were only marginally higher (less than 1 m) than they are today, while from the Neo-Assyrian through the latter part of the Parthian era, they were, contrary to de Morgan's belief, significantly *lower* than modern levels.

This is not to say, however, that the entire area of southernmost Mesopotamia was dry land, or that references to 'the sea' in Sennacherib's account or in texts relating to Ur and Eridu do not refer to some inland body or bodies of water which actually existed. As Waetzoldt showed, the term *a-ab-ba* was used extensively in the messenger texts, and the ziggurat of Nigi (modern Zurghul), a town situated on a canal leading from Girsu to Guabba, was described by Gudea as a 'mountain rising from the water' (Black 1989–1990:71). Judging by references in the Early Dynastic 'List of Geographical Names' to an *ambar-gal*, or 'Great Swamp' (Sum. *ambar* = Akk. *appāru*), which D. Frayne believes may represent the Hor as-Suwaiqiah (Frayne 1991:391; Waetzoldt 1981:167ff. Gibson 1972:24),[17] the creation of marshland and swamps, such as today's Hor al-Hammar, was a process which went on throughout antiquity. Adams and Nissen have described southern Mesopotamia as a mosaic 'in which swamps, arid steppes, gardens, and field were continuously interspersed' (Adams and Nissen 1972:86), and more recently Adams has suggested, 'We may have to deal in the past, as to a lesser extent we still do today, not with a well-defined shoreline but with a progression of swamps and more and more open, more brackish or saline lagoons' (Adams 1981:16). Nevertheless, this does not necessarily mean that the Hor al-Hammar itself existed when the sites found by Roux were inhabited. As Roux himself remarked, the existence of relict canals near Tell Abu Salabikh and a well at Tell Aqram suggest that the region was once cultivated, as indeed the Kassite cuneiform sources cited above confirm, and drier than it is today. Indeed Roux was told by local informants in the 1950s 'that in their fathers' time the area now occupied by the lake [Hor al-Hammar] was made of cultivated fields and that it was possible to walk or ride on dry land from Kubaish to Basrah' (Roux 1960:30–1 and n. 54). Even if this is a bit of apocryphal folklore, the fact remains that no clear consensus exists as to when the Hor al-Hammar as we now know it was formed.

Roux, for example, was struck by the absence of references to it in the Arab geographers and by the fact that Chesney did not mention it in his Survey report. In fact it may be a very young swamp indeed. The British *Naval Intelligence Handbook* of 1944 ascribed its formation to the flood which ensued sometime after 1870, when the right bank of the Euphrates between Qurna and Suq ash-Shuyukh burst, turning what had been marsh-land into a large lake (Roux 1960:30–1). If this story is correct, then it marked the end of what was known in the Middle Ages as the 'Great Swamp', an area some 80 x 320 km which extended virtually from Kufa to Basra (Fig. I.18). The early Islamic historian al-Baladhuri ascribed the for-mation of the Great Swamp to a series of floods which occurred during the Sasanian period, beginning in the reign of Kavadh I (AD 499–531) and continuing through the reign of Khusrau II (AD 590–628) when both the Tigris and the Euphrates burst their dykes at numerous points and 'the waters could in no wise be got back, and the swamps thus formed became permanent' (LeStrange 1905:26–7).

Problems of a similar sort continued to plague Iraq throughout subsequent centuries. The process of marsh and swamp formation was remarked on by G. Cressey in the 1950s, for the inadequate drainage of controlled irrigation water can create swamps and marshes. As Cressey noted, 'Since much of this irrigation water has no proper drainage channel through which to rejoin the main rivers, vast areas are waterlogged' (Cres-sey 1958:452). Indeed, an ancient association between canals and swamp or marsh formation was documented in the 1950s when an irrigation canal dug on the middle Tigris near Musaiyib revealed a 6 m deep stratigraphic sequence in which successive alluvial, canal and marsh bed deposits were exposed dating to between the Old Akkadian period and the medieval era (Harris and Adams 1957:161). Recently, marsh formation around ancient Borsippa has been the subject of a careful study which shows that, begin-ning in the seventh century BC, the site was surrounded by a large marsh (Cole 1994:81–109).

Finally, had the Gulf actually reached the area of Ur, Eridu or Tello, one must ask whether these sites could then have existed. W. Nützel has noted that the tidal pattern in the northern Gulf affects the waters of the Shatt al-Arab in that salt-water enters it at least as far as Abdul Khasib, *c.* 10 km east of Basra. This interchange of salt and sweet water would have made irrigation from such water impossible, for none of the staple cereals grown in antiquity would have been able to tolerate water with such a high salt content. Therefore, settlements must always have been situated outside the zone affected by such interchange. The very existence of sites like Ur, or for that matter, the mounds discussed above in the Hor al-Hammar district, Nützel argues, precludes the possibility that salt-water was present in close proximity to them (Nützel 1980:98–9).[18]

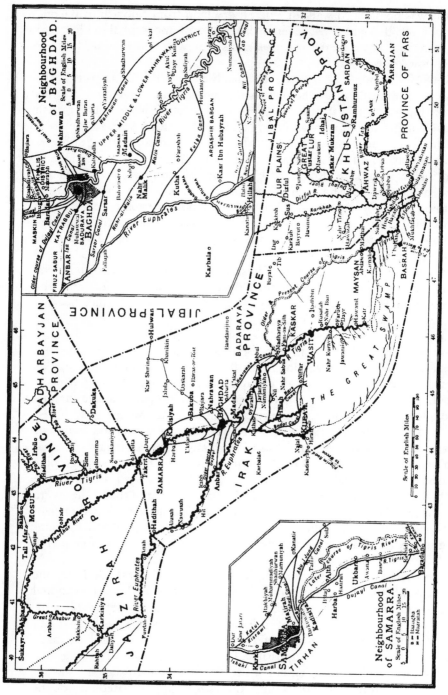

Figure I.18 Medieval Iraq, showing the location of the 'Great Swamp' (after LeStrange 1905: Map II)

CONCLUSION

The study of ancient Mesopotamian climate and environment is far from complete, and many unresolved problems remain to be addressed by coming generations of scholars. One thing is certain, however. Mesopotamia was *made* by the Tigris and Euphrates. It would not exist without the silt and salts brought south and deposited each year. The management of those two great rivers was of paramount concern in antiquity, as it remains today. None of the achievements of Mesopotamian production in the realm of agriculture, animal husbandry, or related industries (textiles, leatherworking, boat-building) can be understood except in reference to the very specific river regimes and soil conditions of the alluvium. These were fundamental to the very existence of the ancient Mesopotamian population and underlay all of their creative efforts.

NOTES

1 In fact there is considerable disagreement over the exact timespan covered by this Holocene moist phase. For some of the contending suggestions, see Potts 1985:680 and 1990:19–21.

2 E.g. in Jerusalem where records are available going back to 1861. Plotting annual rainfall against mean winter temperatures between December and March, Neumann and Sigrist clearly show that with a mean winter temperature between 7–8°C, rainfall was over 800 mm, while rainfall dropped to only 300 mm in years with a mean temperature of just over 12°C for the same period. See Neumann and Sigrist 1978:242, Fig. 1.

3 This consists of a receptacle such as a bucket on the end of a long, horizontal pole which is mounted on an upright stand. The bucket and pole are dipped down to collect water and then raised with the aid of a counter-weight on the opposite end. The *shaduf* may be attested in the myth 'Gilgamesh and Agga'. See Butz 1983:481.

4 Discussions of the regimes of the rivers can be found in many sources. See, *inter alia*, Ionides 1937; Brice 1966; Gibson 1972; Oates and Oates 1977; Adams 1981; Charles 1988.

5 E.g. Lipit-Ishtar of Isin (1931–1924 BC); Gungunum (1932–1906 BC), Abisare (1905–1895 BC), Sumuel (1894–1866 BC), Sin-iddinam (1849–1843 BC), Urdukuga (1830–1828 BC), Warad-Sin (1834–1823 BC) and Rim-Sin (1822–1763 BC) of Larsa; and Sumulael (1880–1845 BC), Sabium (1844–1831 BC), Apil-Sin (1830–1813 BC), Sin-muballit (1812–1793 BC), and Hammurapi (1792–1750 BC) of Babylon. See Edzard 1957:112–116. Cf. Renger 1990a:31–46.

6 J. Renger, on the other hand, considers the allusion in the date formula of Hammurapi's thirty-third year to the king having 'made it possible for the inhabitants of [the lands] Sumer and Akkad, who had been scattered, to return to their settlements' to reflect a situation in which the people had been made refugees through war. See Renger 1990a:34.

7 Although Cole 1994:95, n. 80, says she is 'usually identified as Naqia/Zakutu, the mother of Esarhaddon', most scholars are of the opinion

that she represents Adadguppi, mother of Nabonidus, since Nitokris' son is said to have been Labynetos, an apparently corrupt form of Nabonidus. See Lewy 1952; Röllig 1979:141; Black et al. 1987:24. The account is generally thought to reflect construction undertaken by Nebuchadrezzar II (604–562 BC).

8 Thus, Delattre 1888:459–60 believes that Xenophon must have been mistaken, whereas Mason 1920:472 believes it 'is quite possible at this point'.

9 The identity of the Pallacopas/Pallacottas with the *nār Pal-lu-kat* seems to have been first recognized by Delattre 1888:495 in an article of which Meissner 1896:8 was unaware when he suggested the same thing eight years later.

10 For the sources on the Iturungal see Edzard 1976–1980:223. Heimpel 1990:213 argues that the Iturungal was in fact the Tigris, and not an eastern arm of the Euphrates system.

11 But to this we can add one more toponym, namely Dilmun, which occurs in a lexical text (Archaic Lú) of Uruk IV date. Dilmun, a name which signified the northeast Arabian mainland and Bahrain islands, is the most distant region from Uruk mentioned in these texts. See Englund 1983:35–7; Cf. Nissen 1985:230.

12 Likewise published in *The London and Edinburgh Philosophical Magazine and Journal of Science*, 3rd ser. 5 (1835):244–52. I have not been able to consult either Beke or Carter in the original.

13 Remains of burnt fish offerings are known from Eridu, Ur, Uruk, Tello and Tell Asmar, but the species of fish recovered has not been specified. Cf. van Buren 1948:103–4.

14 For some recently published texts dealing with the fishermen responsible for 'the procurement of fish for offerings at major temples and administrative households of Umma', see Englund 1992:87–8.

15 For a recent overview of these messengers, see Sigrist 1986:51–63.

16 The Iraqi Dept. of Antiquities map of sites indicates Early Dynastic through Ur III occupation at Tell al-Lahm and Tell Judaida (also in the Hor al-Hammar district). See Waetzoldt 1981:162. I have not been able to check this map myself.

17 Edzard 1993:2, distinguishes between Sum. *a-ab-ba*, as a navigable waterway, and *ambar*, as a dense reed marsh.

18 P. Sanlaville has pointed to the existence of brackish lakes (e.g. Kurais el-Melah) with salinity levels of 15–20 per cent in March near the southwest border of the Hor al-Hammar. See Sanlaville 1989:9.

II *The Aboriginal Population of Southern Mesopotamia*

INTRODUCTION

It is commonplace in archaeology to find scholars searching for 'origins', be they of a category of material culture (e.g. pottery, a particular type of weapon, a motif), a technology, a domesticate, a culture, a people or even an entire civilization. The implication of such an exercise is that, at a certain point in time, the entity in question did not exist. Traditionally, indeed almost exclusively, origins have been attributed either to a fusion and mutation of old elements already present into something demonstrably new, on analogy with biological mutation and natural selection, or else to the arrival of something new and unrelated from outside the local area. The interaction of both processes, the fusion of new, extraneous elements with older 'ingredients' already present, represents a third possibility. For well over a century considerable debate has surrounded the question of when and whence came the earliest settlers of the southern Mesopotamian alluvium, few scholars believing that people had always (i.e. let us say from the Palaeolithic onwards) inhabited the area of what is today southern Iraq. This debate is made more complicated by the linguistically unique nature of the language spoken by the earliest historically tangible inhabitants of the region, the Sumerians, which belongs to none of the language families found in the neighbouring regions of Eurasia. In this chapter we shall examine some of the principal aspects of the 'Sumerian Problem' and consider the evidence for the earliest settlement of southern Mesopotamia.

THE 'SUMERIAN PROBLEM'

The Babylonians and Assyrians were never 'lost' to Western memory, principally because both peoples, and a number of their rulers, figure in various books of the Bible. The earlier inhabitants of southern Mesopotamia, however, are another matter. References to the land of *Shinar* in the Books of Genesis, Isaiah and Daniel have been identified conventionally with *Sumer*, a natural enough assumption given the fact that Babylon, Uruk, and Akkad were said to be in Shinar (Gen. 10, 10), as was the tower of Babel (Gen. 14, 2).[1] It has recently been shown, however, that Shinar is derived not from Sumer but from Shanhara, the name given to Babylonia during the Kassite period (*c.* 1400–1155 BC) by the population living west of the Euphrates (Zadok 1984:244). Indeed the Sumerians were almost completely unknown in the West until the remarkable discoveries made at Tello beginning in 1877 by the French Vice-Consul at Basra, Ernest de

Sarzec (Hilprecht 1896:63). It is necessary to say 'almost' in this connection for, while Tello provided the first archaeological demonstration of the Sumerians' existence, the title 'king of Sumer and Akkad' had already been identified in Akkadian cuneiform sources, leading the French Orientalist Jules Oppert to suggest in 1869 that an early people he termed 'Sumerian', speaking a non-Semitic language, had lived in southern Mesopotamia at one time. This conclusion, which we now know to have been correct, confirmed the suspicions of Edward Hincks, voiced as early as 1850, that the creators of the cuneiform writing system were neither the Assyrians nor the Babylonians, but a then unidentified people (Kramer 1963:19–21).

The fact that Sumerian and the Semitic dialects of Akkadian belonged to unrelated language families naturally caused early speculation concerning the affinities or lack thereof between the two 'peoples' identified as Akkadians and Sumerians. We can discount much of the earliest speculation, such as that of Rawlinson and Loftus who saw the earliest 'Chaldaeans', or Akkadian-speakers, originating without doubt in Ethiopia, or Baldwin who linked them with Arabia (Baldwin 1869:192–3). Once the Sumerians had been 'discovered', attention turned to the question of their origins, and we find Hilprecht, for instance, characterizing the earliest inhabitants of southern Mesopotamia as 'native Sumerians' in contrast to the 'invading Semites' (Hilprecht 1896:71) or Akkadian-speaking population. Flawed as this view may have been, it at least served to highlight the question, how native were the 'native Sumerians'? Were they indeed the indigenous, aboriginal population of the alluvial plain?

Opinions on this question have always been divided and continue so to this day. In 1920 the German Assyriologist Bruno Meissner wrote that the question of whether the Sumerians were indigenous to what is now southern Iraq, or came from some other region, would probably never be settled (Meissner 1920:15). Ten years later, however, a linguistic problem was identified which bore heavily on this question. In 1930 E.A. Speiser suggested that some of the oldest settlements in southern Mesopotamia attested in cuneiform sources bore non-Sumerian names. Speiser concluded that this was evidence of a pre-Sumerian occupation of the alluvium antedating the entry of the Sumerians into the region (Speiser 1930:38ff.). Although many of the details of Speiser's reasoning are spurious, in particular the arguments which he advanced concerning the ethnic affiliation of the bearers of the Jamdat Nasr 'culture' (c. 3100–2900 BC), the thesis has continued to attract followers to this day, and was subsequently elaborated with greater rigour by B. Landsberger (see below).

The date of the Sumerians' entry into southern Mesopotamia and the question of whether or not they were the region's first inhabitants were the subjects of a communication made in early September 1931 before the 18th Orientalist Congress in Leiden (Frankfort 1932:62–3) by the art historian Henri Frankfort. Frankfort set out to review recent archaeological work in southern Mesopotamia in an effort to determine the answer to what had by then been christened the 'Sumerian Problem'. The Leiden lecture was subsequently expanded into one of his most famous monographs, *Archaeology and the Sumerian Problem*, which appeared in 1932. Frankfort began with a review of the Early Dynastic period (*c.* 2900–2350 BC), since this was the era when, according to cuneiform sources, a population speaking and writing Sumerian was unequivocally present and apparently dominant in southern Mesopotamia. From the Early Dynastic period Frankfort worked his way back in time in an effort to determine whether the Sumerian-ness of that era was or was not recognizable in earlier times. Looking at the Jamdat Nasr period, Frankfort found features of human physiognomy in statuary and on reliefs which were, he argued, indistinguishable from those of the subsequent period and were therefore 'Sumerian'. He also considered the semi-pictographic texts from Jamdat Nasr and period III at Uruk to be 'definitely Sumerian', and thus argued for continuity in the southern Mesopotamian population between the Early Dynastic and Jamdat Nasr periods.

Frankfort's investigations yielded a similar result when he examined the evidence from the Uruk period (*c.* 3800–3100 BC). Focusing again on human, largely male, representations, Frankfort was struck by similarities between the long skirts, beards, shaved upper lips, knots of hair at the back of the head, and in some cases shaved heads and beards on statuary, in glyptic and in reliefs from the Uruk and and later periods. He also noted continuity in the use of stamp and cylinder seals, and in mudbrick architecture, and concluded that the congruence was sufficient to argue that the Sumerians were in southern Mesopotamia during the Uruk period. This brought Frankfort square up against the question of whether the Sumerians arrived in Mesopotamia at the beginning of the Uruk period, or whether they were there from the very beginning of settled life in the region at the start of the Ubaid period (*c.* 6000/5500–3800 BC).

Frankfort drew on the work of the German architect W. Andrae (Andrae 1930), who adduced parallels between the earliest buildings of the Ubaid horizon at Ur and elements of Sumerian and later Babylonian architectural tradition. Further, following the excavator of Uruk, J. Jordan, whose 'discovery of male figurines belonging to this period which show the long beard, shaved upper lip, and knot of hair at the back of the head' was seen as providing a decisive link with the later periods, Frankfort wrote, 'Since we have found them to be Sumerians in the early dynastic period, we must take them to be Sumerians in the earlier periods also' (Frankfort 1932:21). As to Speiser's objection based on non-Sumerian place-names, Frankfort tried to deflect what he admitted was a 'brilliantly defended thesis' by suggesting that non-Sumerian place-names in southern Mesopotamia need not be pre-Sumerian (Frankfort 1932:21–2, n. 4), and indeed he believed that if some of the names in question turned out to be Elamite (which is not, however, the case), this would lend further credence to his own view, based on ceramic styles but now largely discredited (Oates 1991:23–6), that the ultimate origins of the Ubaid culture were to be sought in southwestern Iran. Thus, Frankfort concluded his study by declaring emphatically that the Sumerians were not only 'the main authors of the civilization of the valley of the Two Rivers, but also . . . its earliest occupants' (Frankfort 1932:46), and in 1936 his colleague Seton Lloyd claimed that this was an opinion which was then shared by 'the majority of his archaeological colleagues' (Lloyd 1936:61).

In fact, it is clear that Lloyd's judgement was much too sweeping, for both in Europe and America there remained serious doubts as to the Sumerian-ness of the entire pre-Early Dynastic sequence of southern Mesopotamia. In 1944 the German Assyriologist B. Landsberger, living in exile in Ankara, published an important article on the Sumerians in which he took up the line argued by Speiser, identifying many of the names of the most important settlements of southern Mesopotamia, including Ur, Uruk, Larsa, Adab, Nippur and Sippar, as non-Sumerian. Landsberger went further, however, and claimed that many common cultural terms such as farmer (*engar*), herdsman (*udul*), fisherman (*ŠU.HA*), plough (*apin*), furrow (*absin*), palm (*gišimmar*), date (*zulum*), metalworker (*tibira*), smith (*simug*), carpenter (*nagar*), basketmaker (*ad.KID*), weaver (*ušbar*), leatherworker (*ašgab*), potter (*bahar*), mason (*šitim*), and possibly merchant (*damgar*) were also non-Sumerian. Landsberger called the speakers of the hypothetical sub-stratum language to which these words belonged 'Proto-Euphrateans' (Landsberger 1974).

One year later Anton Moortgat accredited what he perceived as a break between the Ubaid and Uruk periods to the activity of the Sumerians, but he was cautious enough to note that whether they were already there in the Uruk period, or whether they came in from outside, could not be answered on the basis of the evidence then available (Moortgat 1945:60). In 1945, with World War II not yet over, Moortgat would certainly have been unaware of Landsberger's study. For all the wrong reasons, Moortgat eschewed the use of coarse approximations of skull shape as practised by Frankfort, because of a perceived conflict between physical anthropological metric measurements of Sumerian skulls and his own simple art historical observations. Indeed, Moortgat found that the physical anthropological evidence was unusable since anthropologists classified the cranial index of Sumerian skulls as 'überlangschädelig', which we would call 'dolicocephalic' (narrow- or long-headed) in English, whereas this stood in stark contrast to the type of skull found in Sumerian sculpture (!), and thus one could not be sure that the skeletons in question were those of 'real' Sumerians, as opposed to Semites or a yet earlier sub-population in the region ('älteren Bevölkerungsteil des Zweistromlandes'). Moortgat concluded that the search for the origins and date of the earliest Sumerian population was naturally of great interest, but was unlikely ever to be resolved (Moortgat 1945:93).

In 1948–9 Frankfort delivered the lectures at Indiana University which were subsequently published in 1956 as *The Birth of Civilization in the Ancient Near East,* without doubt one of the most widely read popular books on Mesopotamian civilization ever written. While still maintaining that the Ubaid culture of southern Mesopotamia had an Iranian origin (this time on the Iranian Plateau rather than in lowland Khuzistan) (Frankfort 1956:43), Frankfort was forced to admit, 'We cannot say for certain whether its bearers were the Sumerians . . . But no decisive proof for a later arrival of the Sumerians has been offered, and the continuity in cult and architecture support the view that they were the dominant element in the Al Ubaid period, as they remained throughout the third millennium in the south of the country' (Frankfort 1956:48, n. 51). As 'positive proof for a later arrival of the Sumerians', Frankfort was obviously unwilling to admit Landsberger's arguments.

Not all scholars, however, continued to share Frankfort's optimism. The non-Sumerian nature of many important Mesopotamian place-names was a view shared by another giant of German Assyriology, Adam Falkenstein (Falkenstein 1959:14), who eschewed the question of when and whence the Sumerians had appeared, but felt that, in view of the place-names adduced by Landsberger, they were certainly not the first people to inhabit the region, even if they were just as certainly the 'creators' of the first urban civilization in the area. The American Sumerologist Samuel Noah Kramer concurred with Falkenstein and Landsberger, stating, 'It is reasonably certain that the first settlers in Sumer were not the Sumerians' (Kramer 1963:40). Kramer staunchly identified Landsberger's Proto-Euphrateans with the southern Mesopotamian population of the Ubaid period, and believed that the Sumerians only arrived sometime in the second half of the fourth millennium (3500–3000 BC), during the Late Uruk period (c. 3400–3100 BC) when writing first appears (Kramer 1963:41–2). These views notwithstanding, Kramer's opinion that the Sumerian 'homeland' should be sought somewhere near the Caspian Sea because of an alleged affinity between Sumerian and the Ural-Altaic languages is no longer taken seriously.

ARCHAEOLOGY AND EARLY SETTLEMENT

While philologists in the 1940s and 1950s were increasingly ready to accept the Sumerian versus non-Sumerian distinction in place-names as the decisive argument in the 'Sumerian Problem' debate, archaeologists began to take a different view of the matter. Although her results were not widely known until the appearance of the Woolley memorial volume in 1960, Joan Oates' 1953 Cambridge PhD dissertation (Oates 1960:44–5), in which all of the available Ubaid material from southern Mesopotamia was investigated, came out strongly in favour of continuity in southern Mesopotamian material culture from the early Ubaid period into Sumerian times, specifically in the realm of ceramics and architecture, but with the benefit of much more early material than had been available to Frankfort in 1932. In an effort to emphasize continuity in the sequence as observed in the lower levels of Eridu (Ubaid 1), Hajji Muhammad (Ubaid 2), Ur and al-Ubaid (Ubaid 3–4), Oates renamed the four phases of Ubaid occupation then attested in the south Ubaid 1–4. Commenting on the remarkable sequence of superimposed temples excavated at Eridu, she wrote, 'It is extremely difficult to believe that the location of the temple, its cult, and even its architecture would have continued in an unbroken tradition from al 'Ubaid to Sumerian times if there had been during this period any major change in the character of the population' (Oates 1960:46). Furthermore, Oates went on to stress that Lees' and Falcon's work (discussed in Chapter I) made the likelihood of 'a physical environment not greatly different from that which exists today, and particularly in the marshes' highly probable, suggesting that 'there were probably communities which gained as profitable a livelihood from hunting and fishing as did their neighbours from herding or primitive agriculture. In fact, we should be prepared to find traces, in pre-'Ubaid or pre-'Eridu' times, of more than one type of indigenous community, differing from one another in material culture and perhaps even in physical type and in language, although the second point will be difficult and the last impossible to verify' (Oates 1960:49).

In the event, Oates' expectation of pre-Ubaid occupation in southern Mesopotamia was long frustrated by the heavy build-up of alluvial sediment which blanketed all but a few earlier settlements (Fig. II.1). As dis-

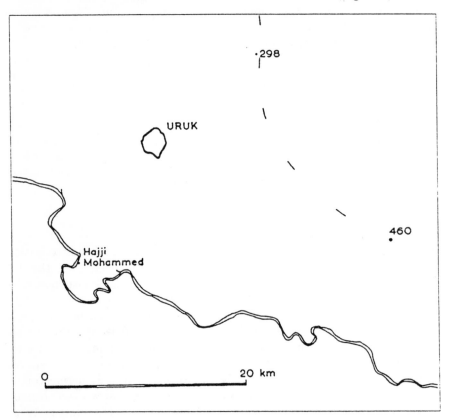

Figure II.1 Some of the principal early Ubaid sites in southern Mesopotamia (after Adams and Nissen 1972: Fig. 2)

cussed in Chapter I, the southern Mesopotamian plain is estimated, in places, to have risen by as much as 6–8 m during the past 6000 years, and at the Ubaid 2 type-site, Hajji Muhammad, for example, the latest occupational levels are concealed by 2.5 m of alluvial deposit (Huot 1989:24). Nevertheless, indications of pre-Ubaid sites have been detected sporadically over the years at sites like WS 298, a low, small mound located *c*. 10 km northeast of Uruk, where Adams and Nissen discovered painted pottery showing affinities to the Samarran and Choga Mami assemblages of central and eastern Mesopotamia (Adams and Nissen 1972:174–5). In 1983, a deep sounding by the French expedition at Tell Oueili (WS 460, where it appears as 'Tell Awayli'), near Larsa, uncovered more than 5 m of what is now called Ubaid 0 (Huot 1989: 29, Fig. 2; cf. Calvet 1989: 129–51), i.e. pre-Eridu, remains above the water-table (Fig. II.2), showing beyond doubt that the early occupation of southern Mesopotamia substantially precedes what was formerly taken to be the 'first' settlement of Ubaid 1 date. The early Oueili material is sure to excite debate for some time, but it is already clear that it shows close affinities to material from a number of other sites in eastern, central and northern Mesopotamia (Oates 1987:199–200), and is already being regarded by its excavators as the earliest evidence yet discovered for human occupation in the alluvium, but by no means the first (Huot 1989:39).

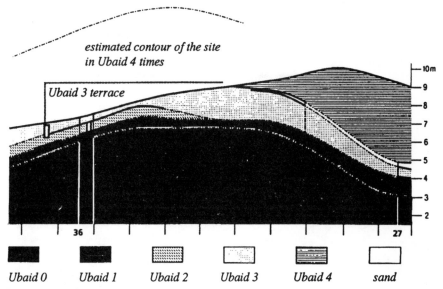

Figure II.2 Schematic section through Tell Oueili showing the disposition of Ubaid 0-4 deposits (after Huot 1989: Fig. 2)

In particular the so-called 'Choga Mami Transitional' (CMT), described by J. Oates as 'an "interface" style that itself, i.e. in its combined form, is one component of a particular assemblage in the Mandali region and perhaps elsewhere along the eastern edge of the alluvium' (Oates 1987:205), is generally seen now as having the closest affinities to the Ubaid 0 material (Fig. II.3). Indeed, this was already hinted at by the discovery of a few sherds of CMT in the 1981 sondage in area Y 27 at Tell Oueili by Yves Calvet (Calvet 1989:129), and two years later in X 36 where a 4 x 4 m sondage down to the water-table (1.57 m above mean sea-level) was taken down 6 m and levels 9–20 (20 was under water) were excavated which, in Joan Oates' opinion, 'represent an occupation contemporary at the latest with Eridu 19-16 [Ubaid 1] and in all likelihood extending much earlier' (Oates 1987:199).These levels are characterized not only by CMT sherds, but also by cigar-shaped bricks comparable to those known from Choga Mami and the Samarran site of Tell es-Sawwan in central Babylonia.

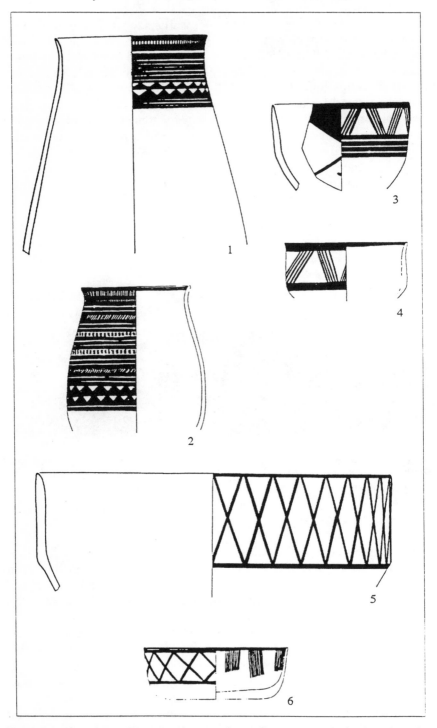

Figure II.3 Choga Mami Transitional pottery from Choga Mami and Ubaid o pottery from Tell Oueili. 1. Tell Oueili, level 10 (after Calvet 1987: Pl. 7.94); 2. Choga Mami (after Oates 1987: Fig. 7.59); 3. Tell Oueili, level 12 (after Calvet 1987: Pl. 9.9); 4. Choga Mami (after Oates 1987: Fig. 3.12); 5. Tell Oueili, level 12 (after Calvet 1987: Pl. 9.16bis); 6. Choga Mami (after Oates 1987: Fig. 4.18)

ENVIRONMENTAL CONSTRAINTS

The significance of an apparent link to the eastern piedmont area and Choga Mami at the 'beginning' of the occupational history of the alluvial plain lies in the fact that, to date, investigations at Choga Mami have yielded the earliest evidence in greater Mesopotamia for canal irrigation (at roughly 6000 BC) (Oates and Oates 1977:128–33), and it is believed by some authorities that, without irrigation technology, the southern alluvium could not have been 'colonized' by its earliest inhabitants. Hence, the apparent tie between Choga Mami and Tell Oueili fits in well with the hypothesized necessity of irrigation technology as a *sine qua non* for the earliest peopling of southern Mesopotamia. Before discussing this hypothesis in detail, however, we should consider more generally the various arguments put forward on the environmental level to explain the origins of the aboriginal population of southern Mesopotamia.

If we revert once more to *Archaeology and the Sumerian Problem*, we find that in 1932 Frankfort viewed the original colonization of the alluvium as an arrival by 'immigrants who settled in the valley of the Two Rivers *when it had dried sufficiently to become inhabitable*' (Frankfort 1932:18, my italics). Precisely what did Frankfort mean by this? Like many of his contemporaries, Frankfort was a believer both in de Morgan's reconstruction of an ancient Mesopotamian coastline which was much further north than it is today (cf. Fig. I.15), and in the theory of progradation outlined in Chapter I. In 1949 Ann Perkins (1949: 73 and n.212), one of his students at the University of Chicago, nicely summed up the view held by Frankfort and others like him in these words:

> While the Halaf culture flourished in the North the southern part of the Land of the Two Rivers may still have been completely under water or, as the land was built up by alluvial deposits carried downstream by the Tigris and Euphrates, a vast marsh in which human beings could find no suitable habitation. Gradually, as the process of deposition continued, the great swamp began to dry up. Points of land emerged from the marsh and became habitable. The earliest remains at all the sites which have been excavated to virgin soil are just above water-laid sand or black organic soil composed of river silt and decayed vegetable matter; certainly in the Ubaid period the region was still very wet.

As discussed in Chapter I, the same views can be found much later in the work of Adams and Nissen. Recently, Nissen has suggested that sea-levels upwards of 2.75 m higher than today existed during the Ubaid period, and that it was only a recession of sea-level *c.* 3500 BC which removed the bulk of the surface water from lower Babylonia. For Nissen, the Ubaid period was one of 'dispersed settlements in a largely water-covered area', and it is only after the retreat of the Gulf in the Uruk period that we find a significant expansion of settlement (Nissen 1988a:41–2; cf. Adams and Nissen 1972:9–11). In fact, essentially the same view was expressed forty years earlier by Charles Watelin (Watelin 1931:265–72) who suggested that the discovery of microlithic stone tools at Kish, and their absence at Ur, might be explained 'by the hypothesis that here and there islands existed and were perhaps inhabited before the valley as a whole became dry' (Frankfort 1932:18).

Oates has criticized Nissen's view that the south was largely uninhabitable until *c.* 3500 BC due to high sea-levels and higher precipitation, as well as his view that 'a change in climate made the water retreat into the Persian Gulf . . . [such that] large parts of the inundated Babylonian plain gradually emerged from the water and became habitable for the first time' (Nissen 1988b:145). We have reviewed the evidence for sea-level change in Chapter I, and seen that, in the opinion of Paul Sanlaville, sea-levels were, if anything, far lower in the Ubaid period than they are today. Thus, sea-level cannot be invoked as an explanation for the once perceived absence of early settlement on the southern Mesopotamian plain. However, it is important to stress that climatic conditions must be taken into account as much as sea-levels, and when this is done a different view of early Mesopotamian colonization is possible.

As noted in Chapter I, the climatic evidence for a relatively wet phase *c.* 6000/5500–3500 BC coincides largely with the Ubaid period. While Nissen has characterized water as a hindrance to early settlement, Joan Oates had already indicated in 1960 that conditions in the south could be viewed in quite a different way. As her statement quoted above shows, Oates saw the hunting and fishing potential of southernmost Mesopotamia as an attraction for early non-agricultural colonists, and she was 'prepared to find traces, in pre-'Ubaid or pre-'Eridu' times, of more than one type of indigenous community, differing from one another in material culture and perhaps even in physical type and in language' (Oates 1960:49). The early- mid-Holocene northward displacement of the summer monsoon, described in Chapter I, is likely to have made southern Mesopotamia periodically wetter and richer in game and plant resources during the seventh to fourth millennium BC than was subsequently the case. Rich in a variety of water fowl, mammalian fauna and exploitable flora, southern Mesopotamia is certain to have attracted elements of the hunting-gathering-herding population attested throughout northern Arabia in much less favourable ecological niches. The western desert regions of Iraq contain sites, associated for the most part with the main wadi systems (Wadis Farukh, Ghadaf, Ubaidh and Khirr) which drain into the Euphrates basin, which have yielded flint tools characteristic of the late pre-pottery Neolithic and early pottery Neolithic in the Levant, suggesting an eastward infiltration of hunters and pastoralists from at least 6000 BC (Zarins 1990:49-50). The Holocene playa lakes in the Rub al-Khali of Saudi Arabia, like most of northeastern Arabia, are characterized during the fifth and fourth millennia BC by a flint industry known as the Arabian bifacial tradition, the hallmark of which is the barbed and/or tanged bifacially flaked arrowhead (Potts 1990, I: 37-54). The population which used this stone tool technology practised a mixed economy herding sheep and goat, hunting small game, gathering and processing locally available grasses and perhaps cultivating cereals as well (Potts 1993:173–7; cf. 1994:236–7). It was widespread throughout northern Arabia (Zarins 1992:48–49) and certainly infiltrated southern Mesopotamia, where identical finds have long been known if not always recognized as part of a much wider phenomenon. This is true of the so-called 'Middle Palaeolithic' finds from the southern desert of Iraq (Voute 1957:135–56; Wright 1967:101–4, 1981:323) which, like the mis-identified Middle Palaeolithic finds from Qatar, are of Holocene date (Zarins 1992:65). Woolley found identical, bifacially flaked material, including tanged and non-tanged arrowheads, at Ur (Woolley 1955:Pls. 12a, 13), while Henry Wright picked up similar flint tools while he was surveying the area of Eridu.[2] Bifacially retouched lithics are also known from both Tell Oueili[3] (Fig. II.4) and Tello (Cauvin 1979:193–206), and they are sure to be present at many more sites as well.

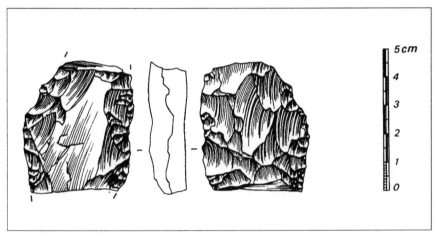

Figure II.4 Bifacially retouched flint tool from Tell Oueili (after Inizan and Tixier 1983: Fig. 2.7)

But if the climatic optimum in northern Arabia induced the movement of peoples into southern Mesopotamia from the surrounding desert regions, it is just as likely to have made the region attractive to other groups as well. That this was the case has already been demonstrated by the presence of CMT pottery at Tell Oueili and several of the Uruk survey sites, suggesting an influx of people from the Mandali district. There are, furthermore, indications of other links to the north and northeast which are suggestive of still more population elements amongst the earliest colonists of southern Mesopotamia as well. J.-L. Huot, for example, has remarked on the presence of a handful of very smooth, yellow-brown sherds from the basal levels at Tell Oueili, two of which L. Courtois and B. Velde describe as 'Soft Ware' (Courtois and Velde 1989:152) reminiscent of Hassuna pottery from northern Iraq. These could be dismissed as a result of exchange, signifying a movement of goods, not people. Yet an indication of a more significant relationship with the north, perhaps involving people as well as goods, is provided by the appearance of einkorn (*Triticum boeoticum*) in the same early Tell Oueili contexts. Einkorn can thrive with or without irrigation, but it is not a very salt tolerant cereal and requires an extra step in processing as it is a hulled rather than a naked wheat whose glume has to be removed before it can be ground (Neef 1989:158). More importantly, einkorn is traditionally considered at home in the dry-farming, more mountainous or piedmont zone of northern Mesopotamia (Huot 1989:41).

Joan Oates has also pointed out that given some of the apparent links between the pottery of Tell Oueili and the Samarran assemblage at Tell es-Sawwan in central Mesopotamia, and taking account of Halaf material reported at the latter site, one might posit a series of contacts linking the north Mesopotamian *Jazirah* with central Mesopotamia (Tell es-Sawwan) and eventually Tell Oueili (Oates 1987:203). In this regard, she is also somewhat persuaded by J.-D. Forest's argument that the CMT style represents an acculturation of Samarrans from central Mesopotamia who moved south under pressure from their Halaf neighbours to the north (cf. the signs of Late Halaf pottery in the Hamrin and Mandali areas), bringing with them the technology of irrigation, attested at Tell es-Sawwan, along with the Samarran ceramic tradition which, modified through contact with the earliest Ubaid settlers, appears as CMT (Oates 1987:203).

Still another avenue to explore is suggested by the discovery of Tell Rihan III in the Hamrin, a pre-ceramic site with circular, semi-subterranean houses, dating to *c.* 6500 BC, and the contemporary site of Choga Banut in Khuzistan (Aurenche 1987: 85–6). Olivier Aurenche suggests that if the eastern part of the Mesopotamian alluvium, modern day Khuzistan, and its piedmont fringes, like the Hamrin, were settled continuously from the aceramic Neolithic onwards, then it is logical to assume that a similar situation obtained in the western part of the alluvium, even if the earliest evidence of occupation is the later, ceramic Ubaid 0 occupation at Tell Oueili. For Aurenche the evidence from Tell Rihan III and Choga Banut convince him that there was a pre-ceramic non-Ubaid tradition already present in southern Mesopotamia before the appearance of the Ubaid tradition.[4] Sceptical of drawing ceramic comparisons with the northern Hassuna and Samarra traditions, Aurenche prefers to see sites like Tell Rihan III in the Hamrin basin of northeastern Iraq as a link between the 'Neolithic' heartland of the Iranian Zagros and the southern alluvium, while acknowledging that there is no direct connection, as well as an apparent chronological gap, between Tell Rihan III and Ubaid 0 at Tell Oueili. This, he feels, is due more to the state of research at this point in time than to a real lack of contact, and suggests that a process of colonization may have occurred linking the Zagros with southern Mesopotamia via the Hamrin, similar to what we know took place between the Zagros, the Deh Luran plain and Susiana.

CONCLUSION

In sum, the climatic optimum in the Arabian peninsula which resulted from the northward displacement of the summer monsoon is certain to have been at least partially responsible for the increased rainfall detectable in Mesopotamia during the early to mid-Holocene. Judging by the evidence just reviewed, hunter-gatherers from the north Arabian desert penetrated the area at about the same time as the earliest agriculturalists, some of

whom, armed with CMT pottery and a rudimentary knowledge of irrigation, may have entered the region from the east, while others, perhaps
bearing einkorn and Hassuna pottery, came from the north. To return to
Joan Oates' statement cited earlier, we should be prepared to imagine the
co-existence of a number of different ethnic groups, speaking different
languages and following different subsistence strategies – hunting and
gathering for some, agriculture supplemented by hunting and gathering for
others – in the earliest period of Mesopotamian settlement. The linguistic
problem of Sumerian versus non-Sumerian place-names in southern Mesopotamia may easily be accounted for by the diversity of the original population, drawn from a number of surrounding regions and speaking in some
cases wholly unrelated languages. A sea-level recession is unnecessary to
explain the impetus for the earliest settlement, and indeed agricultural
settlers, using primitive irrigation techniques, probably comprised but one
element in the original population. As early as 1949 Ann Perkins wrote, 'At
all sites so far investigated in the South the Ubaid remains rest directly on
virgin soil, and there seems little doubt that the people who bore this
culture were the first settlers on the alluvium of whom we have any trace',
but, she added, in a footnote, 'that a people whose mode of living was like
that of the modern Marsh Arabs might have preceded them has been suggested by Professor Frankfort' (Perkins 1949:73). That people, we suggest,
is most probably represented by the bifacially retouched stone tools described above, who are likely to have been drawn to the region by the rich
game resources of the area. The alluvial build-up which characterizes
southern Mesopotamia is such that we will probably never find traces of all
the early groups which might have contributed to the original peopling of
the southern alluvium. Nevertheless, the aim here has been to show that
conditions which were conducive to irrigation agriculture, and indeed irrigation technology, provide only part of the answer to the question of
where the earliest, aboriginal population of southern Mesopotamia
originated.

NOTES

1 Cf. the early American poetess Anne Bradstreet (1613–72) who, in 'The
  Foure Monarchies', wrote: 'On Shinar plain, by the Euphratan flood
  /This wonder of the world, this Babell stood' (ll. 128–129).

2 H.T. Wright commented as follows on these (in Frifelt 1989: 416): 'I
  think in my notes on the Eridu collection I have drawings of some of
  these types of points on this tabular chert of Saudi origin'.

3 Inizan and Tixier 1983: 164, suggested, 'Certain de ces formes (cordi-
  forme, piriforme) se retrouvent dans des sites riverains du Golfe associées à de la poterie d'Obeid, sans présence de houes en Arabie Saoud-
  ite, à Qatar, mais par contre associées à des houes dans certains sites
  d'Obeid (Tello)'.

4 Aurenche 1987: 86, 'Il semble donc bien que l'évolution ait eu lieu sur
  place, et que la tradition Obeid la plus ancienne s'enracine dans une
  population déjà présente'.

III Agriculture and Diet

There are at least four main ways of approaching ancient Mesopotamian diet and nutrition. Moving from the general to the specific, the first is to consider the basic requirements of human nutrition – the essential amino acids, fatty acids, vitamins and minerals needed by the human body – and then to look at the foods available in southern Mesopotamia which, in theory, could have provided them in antiquity. A second approach is to consider the foodstuffs mentioned in cuneiform sources. The lexical lists, a mixture of theoretical and pragmatic information, as well as a wide range of economic, historical, royal and cultic texts contain references to a variety of foods consumed in ancient Mesopotamia. A third option, little explored due to poor conditions of preservation and a lack of attention by archaeologists, particularly those concerned with the historical periods, is to consider the archaeobotanical evidence of foodstuffs. Floral and faunal remains have been recovered both in habitation quarters and in graves, where they sometimes occur as offerings. Finally, where human skeletal remains have been recovered in sufficiently good condition from graves, the categories of foodstuffs consumed by an individual can, to a certain extent, be reconstructed on the basis of trace element, stable carbon and nitrogen isotope analysis of human bone. The variable concentrations of elements in different sorts of plants and in the animals which consume them leave detectable traces in bone. These permit anthropologists to discriminate between diets based predominantly on cereals, meat or fish, and more narrowly within those categories between classes of plant and animal types. Elemental and isotopic studies, certainly one of the most exciting areas today in biological anthropology, have yet to be applied to skeletal material from Mesopotamia, which means it is to the other three approaches noted above that we must turn if we are to reconstruct early Mesopotamian diet.

NUTRITION AND DIET

The requirements of human nutrition are today sufficiently well understood (Scrimshaw and Young 1976:62–4) to enable us to sketch an outline of what it is the body needs and how those needs could have been met in ancient Mesopotamia. Each major category of foodstuffs available in Mesopotamia, be it cereals, legumes, vegetables, fruits, meat, fish, milk products or oils, provides some complement of essential amino acids, fatty acids, vitamins and minerals needed by the body. Our appreciation of an individual's intake is badly skewed by the nature of our sources. Lexical lists may give us a plethora of names of different foodstuffs theoretically grown, prepared and consumed in Mesopotamia, but we cannot be certain where actual consumption ends and the lexicographer's delight in words begins. Ration texts reveal only a very limited range of foodstuffs, suggesting that, unless the ration-receiving population was perpetually in a state of malnutrition, they must have been in receipt of other foodstuffs, no doubt from family plots, the produce from which never entered the central book-keeping machinery. Isotopic analyses, as noted above, have not yet been undertaken, and archaeological samples of foodstuffs are few and far between. The principal foodstuffs can, at any rate, be identified even if we are uncertain in all instances how those foods entered the diet of the inhabitants. We begin with the cereals.

CEREAL CULTIVATION

Barley

All species of barley are diploid (i.e. 2 × 7 chromosomes). In principal, there are two varieties which concern us, so-called 2-row and 6-row barley (Fig. III.1). The main difference between the varieties lies in the number of fertile florets on each spikelet. Both naked (*Hordeum distichum* var. *nudum*; *Hordeum vulgare* var. *coeleste*) and hulled (*Hordeum distichum*; *Hordeum vulgare*) forms, the latter requiring an extra step in processing to remove the hull or 'glume' (usually parching followed by pounding) which serves to hold the grain in the spikelet (Charles 1984:25), are known. While there is only a small genetic difference between the 2-row and 6-row varieties of barley, archaeobotanical studies by H. Helbaek in the 1950s and 1960s suggested that their cultivation took place in geographically distinct zones, for it appeared that 2-row barley was cultivated almost exclusively in upland, dry-farming situations, whereas 6-row barley was most commonly grown in lower-lying, alluvial areas with the aid of irrigation (Charles

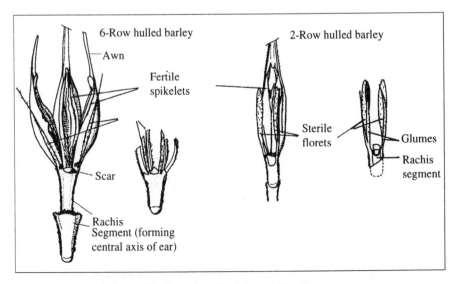

Figure III.1 Morphology of barley (after Charles 1984: Fig. 5)

1984:27). Further, he suggested that hulled 6-row barley developed by mutation from hulled 2-row barley after the latter had been brought from the uplands, where it was originally cultivated under dry-farming conditions, to the lowlands where it was grown with the aid of irrigation (Helbaek 1969:421 and Fig. 143). This dichotomy, however, is not entirely borne out by newer archaeobotanical evidence. Moving from earliest to latest, the distribution (Fig. III.2) of 2-row barley in northern and southern Mesopotamia is as follows: Yarim Tepe II (Halaf), Tell es-Sawwan, Choga Mami (Samarran, Early Dynastic), Tell Chragh (late Ubaid), Tell Bazmosian (Isin-Larsa/Old Babylonian, Middle Babylonian) and Nimrud (Neo-Assyrian, Hellenistic). Naked 6-row barley is present at Yarim Tepe I and II, Umm Dabaghiyah, Tell es-Sawwan and Choga Mami in early contexts, after which it disappears (Charles 1984:30), while hulled 6-row barley is attested at Tell Madhhur (Ubaid) in the piedmont (Hamrin basin), at Uruk (Uruk period) and Ur (Early Dynastic) in the southern alluvium, and at Yarim Tepe I and II, Tell Taya (Old Akkadian) and Nimrud (Middle and Neo-Assyrian) in the north (Renfrew 1984:39; for the evidence from Yarim Tepe I and II, see Bakhteyev and Yanushevich 1980:167–78). From

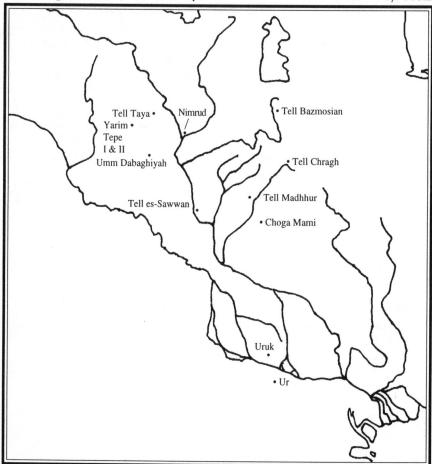

Figure III.2 Archaeobotanical evidence of barley

this it is apparent that 2-row barley is indeed limited to the northern sites, whereas 6-row barley appears in both northern *and* southern Mesopotamia.

The question is, how significant are the finds of 6-row barley in the north? At Umm Dabaghiyah the evidence consists of a single impression of a lemma, part of the barley floret. The evidence from Nimrud consists of but a few grains of hulled 6-row barley, leaving Tell Taya, near Mosul, as the sole northern site at which 6-row (hulled) barley was actually considered 'common' in the archaeobotanical remains (Renfrew 1984:36–7). Were the rare examples of 6-row barley in northern Mesopotamia imports from the south, rather than cultivars actually grown in the north? The answer to this question remains elusive, and expert opinion is divided. J. Renfrew, following Helbaek, believes that 'the hulled and naked forms of six-row barley evolved in cultivation from the wild two-rowed ancestor *Hordeum spontaneum* shortly after the first establishment of agriculture in Iraq, and that in some places they became the chief forms of cultivated barley' (Renfrew 1984:38). On the other hand, the presence of both hulled and naked 6-row barley at Yarim Tepe I and II has led Russian archaeobotanists to challenge Helbaek's hypothesis of the development of 6-row out of 2-row barley after the advent of irrigation agriculture in the lower-lying regions of Mesopotamia. Rather, they suggest that both 2-row and 6-row barley arose together in northern Mesopotamia from a common wild progenitor (*Hordeum spontaneum*) (Bakhteyev and Yanushevich 1980:177).

Judging by the cuneiform evidence, barley (Sum. *še*, Akk. *uṭṭatu/uṭṭetu*) was without doubt the most important cereal crop in southern Mesopotamia, so much so that the Sumerian word *še* came to be used generally for all 'grain', comparable to 'corn' in British English. Yet while the cereals section of the twenty-fourth tablet of the lexical series ur_5-*ra* = *hubullu* contains roughly sixty entries under *še*, most of the terms listed refer to grain or barley in the different forms in which it could be prepared (Powell 1984:49). Thus, the ancient classification is in no way comparable to our Linnaean botanical tradition of species differentiation, and we cannot, for instance, distinguish naked from hulled or 2-row from 6-row barley in the Sumerian terminology.[1]

The marked preference for barley over wheat in the south has generally been taken as a reflection of its greater salt tolerance and higher yields, and indeed a perceived increase in the ratio of barley to wheat has been interpreted as a sign of progressive salinization in southern Mesopotamia (Jacobsen 1982:16, 55). This trend is clearly illustrated in the so-called 'seed-and-fodder texts' from Telloh (ancient Girsu) which date to the Ur III period (*c.* 2100–2000 BC). These texts were drawn up just prior to sowing as a means of calculating the quantities of seed to be expended in cultivating the state fields, fodder required for the draught animals pulling the plough, fodder for animals too young to be put to work yet (presumably the offspring of the draught animals) and wages for workers. According to TuT 5, a Girsu seed-and-fodder text, barley accounted for over 98 per cent of the cereal cultivated in the year Shulgi 47 (Maekawa 1984:90).

Powell, however, has shown that the Mesopotamian preference for barley over wheat may be due to factors other than salinity tolerance. The same preference is historically attested in the rain-fed agriculture of Attica, for instance, where barley accounted for 90.3 per cent of the total cereal production in 329/8 BC (Powell 1985:13). The evidence from Greece seems to suggest that barley yield per hectare was higher than that of wheat, and indeed nowadays 'barley generally out-produces all the wheats, especially on poor and marginal land and with limited water supplies' (Powell 1985:16). In addition, as noted by a number of authorities, barley generally ripens 'two to three weeks earlier than wheat, enabling it to avoid rust' (Powell 1985:16). Moreover, as far as the salinity tolerance of barley goes, it is interesting to note that, because of its low rate of evapotranspiration, barley actually tends to *raise* the salinity level in the surface soil. Thus, even though barley is 'a relatively salt tolerant crop, due to its low irrigation requirements, it tends to *increase* soil salinity by the end of the growing season' (Butz 1979:262, n. 13).

Wheat

Wheats belong to the genus *Triticum*. Species are classified according to the number of chromosomes present as follows (van Zeist 1984:8-15). Diploid wheats are characterized by fourteen chromosomes in two sets of seven, whereas tetraploid wheats have four sets and hexaploid wheats six sets of seven chromosomes. All of these are hulled. Domesticated emmer wheat (*Triticum dicoccum*), one of the tetraploid wheats, is a hearty, drought resistant crop capable of producing excellent yields when irrigated (Charles 1984:25), and is certainly the best represented of all wheat species known in ancient Mesopotamia (Fig. III.3). Archaeologically, emmer is attested (Fig. III.4) at Early Neolithic Jarmo and Umm Dabaghiyah, Hassuna and Halaf period Yarim Tepe I and II, Samarran Tell es-Sawwan and Choga Mami, Ubaid period Ur and Tell Chragh, Early Dynastic Choga Mami, Isin-Larsa and Old Babylonian Tell Bazmosian, Qurtass, Tell Harmal, Tell Ischali, Khafajah and ed-Der, Middle Babylonian Tell Bazmosian and Neo-Assyrian Nimrud (Renfrew 1984:39).

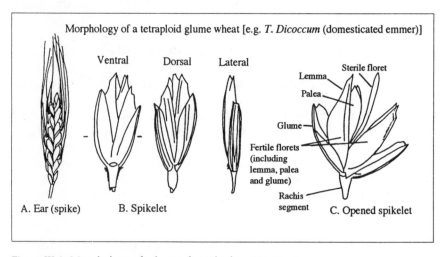

Morphology of a tetraploid glume wheat [e.g. *T. Dicoccum* (domesticated emmer)]

Ventral   Dorsal   Lateral   Sterile floret

Lemma
Palea
Glume
Fertile florets (including lemma, palea and glume)
Rachis segment

A. Ear (spike)   B. Spikelet   C. Opened spikelet

Figure III.3 Morphology of wheat (after Charles 1984: Fig. 1)

Figure III.4 Archaeobotanical evidence of wheat

Naked or free-threshing hexaploid wheats, such as bread wheat (*Triticum aestivum*) and club wheat (*compactum*), are also attested in ancient Mesopotamia. These are characterized by grains which 'are held quite loosely in the spikelet by the glumes...thus as the name implies, the grains thresh free of the ear quite easily, greatly reducing the amount of time required to produce clean grain from the harvested crop' (Charles 1984:25). Naked wheats have been found at Yarim Tepe II (Halaf), Tell es-Sawwan and Choga Mami (Samarran), Jamdat Nasr (Jamdat Nasr), Ur (Early Dynastic), Tell Taya (Old Akkadian), Tell Bazmosian, Tell Qurtass and ed-Der (Isin-Larsa/Old Babylonian) and Nimrud (Neo-Assyrian). Archaeobotanist Jane Renfrew has queried why, when the free-threshing wheats were known at quite an early date, the hulled varieties such as emmer and einkorn (more common in the north, cf. Chapter II) continued to be used. She suggests that the hulled wheats, although requiring more processing time and labour, were better for storage or 'less liable to bird or storm damage when standing in the fields?' (Renfrew 1984:35).

Given the various reasons why barley was preferred to wheat in antiquity discussed above, it is not surprising that wheat was scarcely cultivated in southern Mesopotamia. According to TuT 5, for example, only 1.7 per cent of the land cultivated at Girsu in the year Shulgi 47 was given over to emmer (Maekawa 1984:90) (Sum. *zíz*, Akk. *kunāšum* or *zīzum/zizzum*) (Powell 1984:51–6). As for the free-threshing wheats, if they are represented at all in the cuneiform record, as they probably should be given their presence on the sites listed above, then they might be subsumed under a generic term for 'wheat' (Sum. gig, Akk. *kibtu*) (Powell 1984:56). If we look again at TuT 5, however, we find that only 0.15 per cent of the land cultivated at Girsu was given over to gig in the year Shulgi 47 (Maekawa 1984:90).

Einkorn

Both wild (*Triticum boeoticum*) and domesticated (*Triticum monococcum* L.) einkorn are diploid, hulled wheats. Although it may seem very late to find wild cereals still in use, the Samarran and Ubaid levels (*c.* 6000–4000 BC) at Choga Mami have yielded wild einkorn, as have much earlier contexts at Jarmo (*c.* 6700 BC) (Renfrew 1984:39). This is probably due to the fact that wild einkorn was locally available and therefore exploitable, and indeed during the Choga Mami excavations in 1967–8 archaeobotanist H. Helbaek found stands of both wild einkorn and wild barley in the Zagros piedmont to the north and east of the site (Helbaek 1973:35–48).

As noted in Chapter II, domesticated einkorn (*Triticum monococcum* L.), or small spelt as it is also known, was generally confined to the northern, dry-farming areas of Mesopotamia, and is thought not to have been very well adapted to irrigated cultivation in the southern alluvium (Renfrew 1984:32). Einkorn produces a lower yield than the free-threshing wheats and is thus not particularly suited to an intensive agricultural regime. On the other hand, it is very drought resistant, and does well in poor soils, providing a yield where other species of wheats will not grow at all (Charles 1984:25). Archaeologically einkorn is attested in the seventh and sixth millennia BC at Jarmo and Umm Dabaghiyah, in the Samarran period at Tell es-Sawwan and Choga Mami, in Ubaid 0 contexts at Tell Oueili, in the Jamdat Nasr period at the type-site of Jamdat Nasr, in the Early Dynastic period at Choga Mami and in the Isin-Larsa/Old Babylonian period at Tell Harmal (Renfrew 1984:39). The late occurrence of einkorn at Jamdat Nasr and Tell Harmal is particularly interesting in light of its early presence in the south at Tell Oueili (cf. Chapter II). Thus far, the identification of einkorn in the cuneiform record has eluded experts like M. Powell and K. Maekawa.

LEGUMES

The legumes cultivated in southern Mesopotamian included lentil, garden pea, chickpea, and broad bean, all of which may be eaten as green vegetables, raw or cooked, or used as dried seeds. Other legumes, such as bitter and common vetch and, from Neo-Assyrian times onward, alfalfa (lucerne) (Heyer 1981:83–6), were cultivated as animal fodder. Legumes are especially important as nitrogen-fixing plants which enrich the soil (Charles 1985:40), thereby ensuring future yields, and as such represent an essential element in crop rotation schemes. In addition, they have been used successfully in land reclamation projects on heavily salinized land (Charles 1985:40). In describing cultivation at Lagash, Gudea (*c.* 2100 BC) referred to *gig, zíz* and *gú-gú*, or 'wheat, emmer and various pulses/legumes', showing that legume cultivation was of some general importance in ancient Mesopotamian agriculture (Stol 1985:127).

The lentil (*Lens esculenta*) is attested amongst the earliest cultivars in Western Asia. In greater Mesopotamia it is attested in the ceramic Neolithic period at Jarmo, in the Samarran period at Choga Mami, in the Late Uruk period at Tell Chragh, in the Old Akkadian period at Tell Taya, in the Isin-Larsa/Old Babylonian period at Tells Qurtass, Bazmosian, Yelkhi and ed-Der, in the Middle Babylonian period at Tell Bazmosian and in the Neo-Assyrian period at Nimrud (Renfrew 1985:67). The lentil is high in protein and able to withstand a fair amount of heat and drought, but generally speaking it is not very hardy and is sensitive to excess soil moisture (Renfrew 1985:67).

The common or field pea (*Pisum sativum* ssp. *arvense* (L.) Poir.) is attested in late prehistory at both Jarmo and Choga Mami. Later it appears as a food offering in the Royal Cemetery at Ur (Pu-Abi's grave), in Early Dynastic and Old Akkadian levels at Tell Taya and at Old Babylonian Tell ed-Der. A winter crop capable of growing in areas of low rainfall and mild winters, the field pea is greatly improved by irrigation (Renfrew 1985:68). Two texts from Tell Shemshara in northeastern Iraq contain what is probably a list of all the legumes grown in the area. The 'small pulse' (Sum. *gú-tur*, Akk. *kakkû*) may be either the field pea or perhaps the lentil (Eidem 1985:141–3; cf. Maekawa 1985:99, who expresses doubt about an identification with the lentil).

The grass pea (*Lathryus sativus*) is known at prehistoric Jarmo and Choga Mami, Old Akkadian Tell Taya, Old Babylonian Tell Bazmosian and Tell Yelkhi (?), Middle Babylonian Tell Bazmosian and Neo-Assyrian Nimrud. The grass pea is a hardy legume which is drought resistant and tolerant of waterlogging. In certain parts of the world it has proven itself to be a famine crop which will survive when cereals fail, but overeating causes lathyrism (Stol 1985:132).

Impressions of the chickpea (*Cicer arietinum*) were found in Pu-abi's grave in the Royal Cemetery at Ur, while carbonized examples are known from Middle Babylonian Tell Bazmosian and Neo-Assyrian Nimrud. An extremely salt tolerant plant, the chickpea is intolerant of frost. It may be eaten and prepared in a variety of ways and can be eaten raw, boiled, roasted, salted, sugared, in soup or puréed.

To date the broad bean (*Vicia faba*) is attested by only one seed from Old Akkadian Tell Taya, after which it appears in Islamic contexts in Iraq. It is the least drought resistant of all the legumes, and benefits greatly from irrigation. The 'big pulse' (Sum. *gú-gal*, Akk. *hallūrum*) is probably the broad bean, and not, as generally assumed, the chickpea (Stol 1985:127; cf. Maekawa 1985:99).

VEGETABLES

When we turn to the subject of vegetables we find abundant information on garlic, leeks and onions in the cuneiform sources (Waetzoldt 1987:23–56; Stol 1987:57–80; Farber 1991:234–42). Cucumbers (cf. Chapter XII) are also attested (Stol 1987:81–92), as are several minor vegetables (Postgate 1987:93–100). We shall look briefly at the most important of these.

In Mesopotamia the Sumerian term *sum* combined with another sign stood for a variety of members of the genus *Allium* including onion, leek and shallot while *sum* on its own generally meant garlic (Stol 1987:59). As is often the case in Mesopotamian lexicography, there are many more *sum* entries in the Early Dynastic lexical lists (no fewer than twenty-three as opposed to seven in the Archaic plant list from Uruk; Englund and Nissen 1993:121–2) than in the economic texts of the pre-Sargonic and later periods (Waetzoldt 1987:39), and while no fewer than sixteen varieties occur in third-millennium economic documents, some of these may refer to one and the same type of *Allium*. Often, onion (Sum. *sum-sikil*, Akk. *šamaškillum*) varieties were designated according to geographical criteria, thus 'Marhashi onion', 'Dilmun onion' (*sum-dilmun*) (Stol 1987:59), as in our term 'Brussels sprout', although 'date-palm onions' (*sum-gišimmar*), 'light onions' (*sum-babbar*), and 'spring onions' (*sum-GUD*), to name but a few varieties, are also attested (Waetzoldt 1987:30–8). That these onions were not imported from the countries from which their names were derived, but were grown locally in Mesopotamia is, however, clear. Onions, leeks and garlic were all grown in garden plots (*ki-sum-ma*) intercropped amongst date palms which, in Akkadian, were designated *terīqtum*, literally 'spaces left free' (Stol 1987:65). The cultivation period was the same as that of cereals (see below), with seeding most commonly taking place between September and December, and harvest in April/May (Waetzoldt 1987:24). Yields varied according to onion type, the average lying generally between six and eight litres per 100 sq.m (Waetzoldt 1987:25). That some of the varieties were certainly small-headed, more like our shallots or spring onions, is clear from the quantities harvested and their volumetric dimensions. Thus, texts mention, for example, 39,600 bundles of *gaz*-onions, each comprising 0.10 l, or 19,800 bundles of *zaha-tin* onions, each of which comprised *c.* 0.06 l (Waetzoldt 1987: 29).

From the reign of the Old Akkadian monarch Sharkalisharri comes an interesting archive of just over 100 texts known as the 'onion archive' which was discovered at Nippur in 1899 (Westenholz 1987:87–183). These texts document not only the cultivation of varieties of *sum* by a particular band of 'men of the vegetables' (*lú-sar-ra*), recording seed disbursement and harvest results, but also record the disbursement of onions by a man named Lugal-nì-BE-du$_{10}$, in charge of the 'Onion Office', to various people and institutions. Recipients of onions, which Westenholz says 'were considered something of a luxury item in the Mesopotamian diet', included the palace, the *ensi*'s (governor's) table, the god Ninurta, participants in Enlil's new year's festival, the steward, the cup-bearer, travellers to Umma, Akkade and Urú, and visitors from Adab and Marhashi (Westenholz 1987:92). Over 350 cloves of garlic were discovered by the Belgian expedition at Old Babylonian Tell ed-Der, the first time they have been recovered from an archaeological context in Western Asia (Renfrew 1987:162).

The Sumerian term *úkuš* or *kuš* denoted generally all of the Cucurbitaceae (members of the cucumber family) in ancient Mesopotamia, but these seem never to have been as important economically or dietarily as the members of the genus *Allium* (onions, garlic) as shown by the fact that most of the extant names occur only in the lexical sources and not in economic texts (Stol 1987:82). In addition to the cucumber, various types of melon, somewhat disguised under the rubric 'ripe cucumber', and gourds are attested. Two cucumber seeds were discovered at Neo-Assyrian Nimrud in a context well dated to *c.* 617-600 BC, while ten seeds of an unidentified Cucurbit were recovered on an Old Akkadian floor at Tell Taya (Renfrew 1987:162).

An interesting source for the use of a wide variety of garden vegetables is afforded by a unique tablet in the British Museum bearing two columns of entries on either side in which the Akkadian names of no fewer than sixty-one plants grown in the garden of Merodach-Baladan are enumerated. Assyrian sources from the reign of Sargon II (709–705 BC) report extensively on the rebellious Chaldaean chieftain Marduk-apal-iddina II, better known to us in the biblical form of his name as Merodach-Baladan. When the Assyrian king Shalmaneser V died in 722 BC Merodach-Baladan attempted to throw off the yoke of Assyrian domination in Babylonia, effectively controlling Babylonia for the next twelve years until 710 when Sargon marched south from Dur-Sharruken to hunt down the insurgent ruler. Column I on the obverse of the text opens with garlic, followed by onion and leek, and moves on to mention lettuce (*Lactuca sativa*, Akk. *hassu*), beet (*Brassica rapa*, Akk. *laptu*), cucumber and radish (*Raptanus sativus*, Akk. *puglu*) as well as a number of herbs and spices (discussed below) and many plants for which no identifications can be proposed. In this regard it is interesting to note that both lettuce and radish appear much earlier in Egypt, which may have been the ultimate source of their introduction into Mesopotamia (Potts 1994: 250, 255).

HERBS AND SPICES

English words such as 'herb', 'spice' or 'condiment' are scarcely able to convey the range of culinary, medicinal and magical uses to which a wide variety of plant seeds, petals, roots, resin, twigs or bark, were put in their fresh, dried, coarse ground and pulverized forms in ancient Mesopotamia. The complexity of this subject is apparent in the large number of Sumerian and Akkadian terms for which adequate translations elude us. This should not surprise us, however, for an area like modern Pakistan today boasts roughly 400 such plants (Turchetta 1989:17–36). In Sumerian such plants were termed *mun-gazi*, which Landsberger considered 'a generic term for spices', and were cultivated in plots of land called *ki mun-gazi* (Maekawa 1985:98). Some of the *mun-gazi* plants which have been tentatively identified (unless otherwise stated, all identifications are after Maekawa 1985:99) are listed below along with the uses to which they are put according to recent ethnobotanical studies in Baluchistan (this information is drawn from Turchetta 1989:24–30).

- coriander (*Coriandrum sativum*, Sum. *še-lú*, Akk. *kisibirru*); added to rice, vegetable and meat dishes
- cress and cress seed (*Erucaria aleppica*, *Lepidium sativum*, or *Nasturtium officinale*? (Stol 1983–84:28), Sum. *zà-hi-li*, Akk. *sahlû*)[2]
- black cumin (*Cuminum cyminum*, Sum. *zi-zi-bí-a-núm*, Akk. *zibiānu*); added to rice
- fennel (*Foeniculum vulgare*, Akk. *an/ddahšû*) (Farber 1991:234–42); 'chewed or drunk with water against stomach-ache'

Additionally, there are many such plants (or their seeds, etc.) for which translations differ, most notably Sum. *gazi*/Akk. *kasû*, for which scholars have suggested such divergent meanings as mustard, beet, cassia and licorice (Maekawa 1985:98);[3] *šurmēnu*, possibly juniper berries and *ninû*, thought to be mint (Bottéro 1987:13–14). During the mid-second millennium the cultivation of herbs and spices was well attested at Nuzi in northeastern Iraq, where they were employed medicinally by the physician Zizza (Zaccagnini 1979:128–9). Finally, one of the most interesting sources on ancient Mesopotamian herbs and spices is the list of plants grown in the gardens of Merodach-Baladan cited above. In addition to the vegetables already mentioned, the text lists dill (*Anethum graveolens*, Akk. *šibētum*), mint (*ninû*), safflower or 'bastard saffron' (*Carthamus tinctorius*, Akk. *az/supiru*), coriander (*kisibirru*), thyme (*Thymus*, Akk. *zambūru*), hyssop (*Hyssopus*, Akk. *zūpu*), and asafoetida (*Ferula asafoetida*, Akk. *surbi*) as well as many plants for which no identifications can be proposed (Meissner 1891: 292–6). The use of herbs and spices in cooking is well documented by the so-called 'culinary tablets' in the Yale Babylonian Collection (Bottéro 1987:11–20).

OIL PLANTS

While all plants contain oil, some contain greater amounts of it than others, usually stored in the roots or seeds. Mesopotamia's warm springs, hot, dry summers and great number of annual hours of sunshine are conducive to seed development and make this region one in which oil yield from seeds is generally high (Charles 1985:46). The uses of plant oils are many, ranging from an edible additive on food (e.g. in salad), to an important cooking ingredient, a component of paints and varnishes, a lubricant, a softening agent for leather, a medicine or component thereof, an ingredient in perfume, a preservative and anti-fouling agent on wood, a constituent of soap and a substance which can be burnt to provide light (Charles 1985:53–4).

Archaeologically speaking, the best-represented of all oil plants in Mesopotamia is certainly flax (*Linum usitatissimum*), the seeds of which have been found in late prehistoric contexts at Tell es-Sawwan, Choga Mami, Arpachiyah and Ur, in the Old Babylonian period at Khafajah and in the

Neo-Assyrian period at Nimrud (Renfrew 1985:63). It should not be forgotten, however, that flax fibres are used to manufacture linen (cf. Chapter IV). Indeed, Waetzoldt finds no cuneiform evidence whatsoever in either Sumerian or Akkadian sources for the use of linseed oil in third-millennium Mesopotamia, nor is it likely to have been used for human consumption because of the fact that it becomes rancid so quickly (Waetzoldt 1985:77, 86).

Sesame (*Sesamum indicum*), on the other hand, another important oil plant, while well attested in the written sources, is completely absent in the archaeological record of Mesopotamia.[4] Beginning in the Old Akkadian period around the time of Naram-Sin (2254–2218 BC), the sesame plant (Sum. *giš-i*) and its seeds (*še-giš-i*), as well as sesame fields (*ki-giš-i*) and cultivators (*engar-giš-i*), are all mentioned in the sources and Waetzoldt has suggested that the term *giš-i*, which literally means 'tree oil', was a loan from Eblaite (the language of Ebla in Syria) where the same term was used to describe olive oil (Waetzoldt 1985:79). Scholars are divided over the question of whether the plant itself is of African origin, as has long been assumed (Grigg 1974:17; Nayar 1976:232), or is an Indian domesticate descended from the wild *Sesamum orientale* var. *malabaricum* Nar. which can still be found in India today (Bedigian 1985:162; Bedigian and Harlan 1986:137–54). The resolution of this issue is important, for its arrival in Mesopotamia cannot otherwise be understood.

Let us consider the Indian hypothesis first. Because sesame is present at Harappa in the Mature Harappan period (Allchin 1969:323–9), and absent in Mesopotamian cuneiform sources prior to the Akkadian era, Postgate has suggested that, 'This strongly suggests that the plant was newly introduced at this time, probably from the Indus, where it is attested archaeologically, in the course of the lively trade between the two areas' (Postgate 1994:171) which had begun already in the pre-Sargonic era (Chakrabarti 1993:265–70). The fact is, however, that sesame only became important in greater India within the context of Hinduism, and the 'lump of charred sesame' from M.S. Vats' excavations at Harappa, which is virtually impossible to date precisely within the Mature Harappan period (*c.* 2500–2000 BC) (Shaffer 1992, II:429)[5] but which could as easily post-date as pre-date the attestation of sesame in Mesopotamian cuneiform sources, is completely unique in the Indo-Pakistani region at that time (Vishnu-Mittre and Savithri 1993:206 and 216 for the use of sesame in Hindu religion).

While an Indian origin for Mesopotamian sesame is certainly attractive within the overall context of Indus-Mesopotamian contact, as Postgate has noted, an African origin cannot be ruled out, particularly in view of recent analyses which have demonstrated that a stone pendant from Early Dynastic Tell Asmar in the Diyala region dating to *c.* 2500–2400 BC is in fact made of east African copal, a fossil resin not unlike amber which occurs on Zanzibar, Madagascar and around Mozambique (Meyer, Todd and Beck 1991:289). This point is intriguing when it is realized that, in the Ur III period, the city of Karhar, generally located somewhere between the Diyala and the area of modern Kirkuk, was an important producer of sesame, just as Nuzi (southwest of Kirkuk) was in the mid-second millennium BC

(Waetzoldt 1985:80). The mid-third-millennium east African connection at Tell Asmar in the Diyala, and the later abundance of sesame in the same general region may not be entirely unrelated. Finally, Waetzoldt suggests that, as sesame is attested at Ebla *c.* 2500 BC, and as the Sumerian term for it may be a loan-word from Eblaite, sesame may have been introduced into Mesopotamia from Syria, perhaps as a result of Akkadian campaigns in the area by Sargon and his successors (Waetzoldt 1985:80). If so, one might also suggest that Ebla, which is known to have had ties with Egypt (Scandone-Matthiae 1982:125–30), provides the link to Africa via Egypt which resulted in the appearance of both copal and sesame in eastern Mesopotamia.[6]

Unlike most of the other crops discussed here, including flax, sesame is today a summer crop in Iraq as it was in antiquity. This is borne out by the fact, noted by Waetzoldt, that most of the texts from the province of Lagash which mention the harvest of sesame are dated to the fifth month of the year, i.e. August/September, and as the growing period is usually about three months, the crop must have been sown in May/June (Waetzoldt 1985:81).[7] Indeed this is one of the strongest arguments for the identification of *giš-ì* with sesame (Waetzoldt 1985:87). Obviously sesame could only grow in southern Mesopotamia with the aid of irrigation, nor is it a salt tolerant plant (Charles 1985:49). Waetzoldt has shown that oil yield in the Ur III period was on the order of 20–22 per cent, i.e. the ratio between sesame seed and oil yield stood at roughly 5:1. This compares favourably with early nineteenth century sources from Germany which calculate a yield of 22.2–25 per cent (Waetzoldt 1985:81). The quantities involved could, moreover, be enormous. An Ur III text from Ur (UET III 1129 rv. 11+13) records no less than 470 *gur* 3.6 *sila* or *c.* 141,003.6 l of oil (Waetzoldt 1985:80), while an Old Babylonian text from Larsa (YOS V 153) notes sesame oil in the amount of 335 *gur, c.* 100,500 l (Butz 1979:383).

Aside from its industrial uses (for textile, leather and woodworking), sesame oil was definitely used in cooking and baking in ancient Mesopotamia (Waetzoldt 1985:82, 84), and indeed Herodotus says (*Hist.* I 193) that sesame oil was the only oil used in Babylonia. Furthermore, in late antiquity, and possibly earlier, sesame oil was burned in lamps. A discussion between Rabbis Tryphon and Jochanan ben Nuri, recorded in the Babylonian Talmud (Megilla 7b and Baba Kamma 58b) and thought to have taken place sometime between AD 80 and 135, runs as follows: 'Rabbi Tryphon said: "One may only burn olive oil [on the Sabbath and on holidays]". Rabbi Jochanan ben Nuri stood opposite him and asked: "What should the people of Babylonia do, who have nothing but sesame oil?" ' (Hauser 1993:390).

Finally, before leaving the subject of oil plants, mention should be made of the recovery of either mustard (*Brassica* sp.) or radish (*Sinapis* sp.) seeds in the temple oval at Khafajah in contexts dating to *c.* 3000 BC The seeds of either of these plants could have been used to make oil for cooking (Bedigian 1985:161).

FRUIT

The final category of vegetal food to be considered is fruit. This includes, first and foremost dates, as well as figs, grapes, pomegranates, apples and additionally pear, quince and plum in Assyria (Postgate 1987:115–44). We begin by considering dates.

At the end of the XIth tablet of the Sumerian *Epic of Gilgamesh* the eponymous hero, Gilgamesh, turns to Ur-shanabi, the boatman, and tells him to 'Go up on to the wall of Uruk . . . and walk around'. Surveying the ancient city in the early third millennium BC, Gilgamesh boasts, 'One *sar* (square mile) is city, 1 *sar* gardens, 1 *sar* claypits, as well as the open ground of Ishtar's temple. Three square miles and the open ground comprise Uruk' (Dalley 1989:51). The 'garden' in southern Mesopotamia was, first and foremost, a plantation of date palms (*Phoenix dactylifera*, Sum. ^{giš}*gišimmar*). As noted in our discussion of soils in Chapter I, date palms were routinely planted along the river and canal levees. Date palms are eminently suited to the Mesopotamian alluvium, for no other crop in the sub-tropical zone is as salt tolerant as the date palm (Dowson 1949:37; Charles 1987:1). No less important than the dates which it provided for human consumption as well as the wood for all manner of furniture, door-frames or roof-beams, the fibre for the manufacture of rope, or the fronds for the construction of houses, mats, baskets, etc. (Landsberger 1967; cf. Van De Mieroop 1992: 158), was the shade which it afforded, permitting the cultivation of most of the legumes and vegetables discussed above, as well as smaller fruit trees.

Gardens such as these were organized according to the principle of 'storeys', on analogy with the levels of a multi-storey building. The upper storey comprised the date palms themselves, the tallest trees in the garden and those which provided shade for everything growing beneath them; the middle storey comprised fruit trees of varying types which we shall discuss shortly; and the lowest story comprised cultivated plots of cereals, vegetables, legumes or a combination of all three. This is the same principle expressed today by the Arabic term *bustan*, which is used specifically of a multi-tiered palm-garden with inter-cropping of the sort just described (Charles 1990:58). It is scarcely surprising, therefore, that in the pre-Sargonic timber-and tree-plantation texts from Girsu (Powell 1992:102–3) the date palms, the *sine qua non* of the garden plantations, are themselves never said to have been cut down. Clearly the shade they provided was all important. As Powell notes in commenting on these texts, 'a mixed pattern of cultivation seems implicit, and certainly these trees must have been planted with an eye toward creating optimum conditions for light, shade, screening, etc.' (Powell 1992:107).

As for the fruit itself, dates are an important source of carbohydrates and calcium, as well as vitamins A, B and D (Dowson 1949:39). As the flesh of the date is 75 per cent sugar, the date is an important source of energy and may be eaten in its fresh (Sum. *uhin*, Akk. *uhinnu*) or dried (Sum. *zulum*, Akk. *suluppū*) form (Postgate 1987:117). Moreover, dates are particularly useful because of their ability to be preserved, stored and transported (Charles 1987:1). The date palm has been domesticated at least since the Ubaid period, for dates were recovered in Ubaid period contexts at Eridu and Tell Oueili (Huot 1989:26),[8] while later finds of dates and/or date stones have been recorded at Nippur, Tell ed-Der (Old Babylonian), Nimrud (Neo-Assyrian) (Renfrew 1987:158) and Larsa (Isin-Larsa and Hellenistic) (Neef 1989:151, 154). Carbonized date stones were also recovered in one of the private graves (PG 296) in the Royal Cemetery at Ur (Ellison, Renfrew, Brothwell and Seeley 1978:168). In the Old Babylonian period the management of date-palm gardens often presents us with a complicated picture of leasing, rental, documents assessing responsibility, payment in terms of expected yield and assignment of trees to military officers as a kind of prebend (Renger 1982:290–7).[9]

Deliveries of dates were often included with those of other fruits, most probably grown within the same garden or plantation (Sum. *kiri₆*, Akk. *kirûm*) area. Thus, pomegranates (Sum. *nurma*, Akk. *nurmû, lurimtu*), figs (Sum. *pèš(še)*, Akk. *tittu*), apples (Sum. *hašhur*, Akk. *hašhūru*) and grapes (Sum. *geštin*, Akk. *karānu*) all seem to have been inter-cropped with date palms (Postgate 1987:122). Other fruits which are likely to have grown in southern Mesopotamia include mulberries,[10] plums (Sum. *šennur*, Akk. *šallūru*), pears (Akk. *kamiššaru, angašu?*), quinces (Akk. *supurgillu/ šapargillu*) and a variety of berries (Sum. *gi-rim*) (Powell 1987:146–50). Cuneiform sources attest that both apples and figs were dried and strung (Postgate 1987:119), and indeed strings of sliced apple were discovered on a dish in PG 1054 in the Royal Cemetery at Ur (Ellison, Renfrew, Brothwell and Seeley 1978:172). As with dates, Sumerian fruits were often dried and packed in reed baskets, ceramic jars or wooden boxes for storage and transport. Postgate has noted that pre-Sargonic texts from Girsu routinely list four of the fruits mentioned above – dates, figs, apples and grapes – in regular sequence, much of which was destined for temple offerings and festivals. Deliveries for the king's table are known in the Old Akkadian period, but while there are some records concerning private merchants during the Ur III period, fruits, with the exception of the date, virtually disappear from the cuneiform record after 2000 BC. It would seem, therefore, that fruit consumption during the third millennium was largely, if not exclusively, restricted to temple and palatial contexts, and that the absence of fruit in the lists of food provided for the king at Mari during the Old Babylonian period represents a real contraction of fruit production. Postgate suggests that disturbances at the end of the Ur III period may have undone the cultivation of fruit trees which were much less hearty than their immediate neighbour, the date palm (Postgate 1987:125–7).

FIELD PREPARATION AND PLOUGHING

In his widely read *History Begins at Sumer*, the late Samuel Noah Kramer devoted a short chapter to what he called 'The First "Farmer's Almanac" ', a 111-line text consisting of 'a series of instructions addressed by a farmer to his son for the purpose of guiding him throughout his yearly agricultural activities' (Kramer 1959:65). Often called the Sumerian *Georgica* (e.g. by Kramer 1963:340–2; Salonen 1968:202–12; Oates and Oates 1977:119; Jacobsen 1982; Butz 1983:477–86; Hruška 1990:105–14), a new edition by

Miguel Civil of this important work, best referred to by its first words (*u₄-uluru^ru dumu-ni na mu-un-de₅-ga-àm*, 'in days of yore a ploughman gave his son advice'), has recently appeared (Civil 1994). Rather than seeing this as an agricultural 'handbook', the late Kilian Butz considered it a poetic account of the essential points to be aware of in the planting of a field (Butz 1983:477). Marvin Powell has emphasized that, 'Like the works of Hesiod, Cato, Varro, Vergil and Columella, it is not a manual on the order of *How to Keep Your Volkswagen Alive for the Compleat Idiot* ... but presumes a complex knowledge of agricultural practices, equipment, animals, metrology, economy and social relationships deriving from actual experience that we do not, and by the nature of things cannot, have' (Powell 1984:53). Moreover, as Powell goes on to stress (1984:57):

> There is nothing in this composition that suggests innovation. Agricultural history is characterized by conservatism, for the very good reason that no one wants to starve to death as the result of a bright idea, and it may be assumed that the author of the Georgica had no wish to make a fool of himself by recommending something unusual or by failing to note some tried and proven practice ... One may assume that ordinary farmers followed the system enshrined in the Georgica – not because it was recommended by some Babylonian Vergil, but because this was simply the way things were done.

There are many points of similarity between traditional, pre-mechanized agriculture in Iraq, the agricultural cycle as reflected in economic texts and the recommendations found in *The Farmer's Instructions*. In traditional, twentieth-century Iraqi agriculture, the so-called 'Niren-Niren' system was followed, leaving 50 per cent of the fields fallow while the other 50 per cent were cropped (Charles 1990:47). Studies of the agricultural texts from pre-Sargonic Girsu show that an identical two-year cropping-fallow cycle was most probably followed there in the late Early Dynastic period (LaPlaca and Powell 1990:75, 78), and the same distinction is implied in *The Farmer's Instructions* where the opening forty lines are thought to deal with the treatment of virgin land, i.e. the renewed cropping of previously fallow land, while the rest of the composition is devoted to advice applicable to ground which has already been brought under cultivation (Butz 1983:477).

Generally speaking, the treatment of previously fallow land followed the pattern flooding-leaching (spring-summer), ploughing-sowing (autumn-winter), while cultivated fields followed the pattern harvesting-threshing (spring-summer), fallowing (fall-winter) (LaPlaca and Powell 1990:82). Given the salinity of the Tigris and Euphrates (cf. Chapter I), it is hardly surprising that *The Farmer's Instructions* opens with a warning about leaching (Kramer 1963:340):

> When you are about to take hold of your field [for cultivation], keep a sharp eye on the opening of the dikes, ditches and mounds (so that) when you flood the field the water will not rise too high in it. When you have emptied it of water, watch the field's water-soaked ground that it stay 'virile' ground for you.

As K. Butz pointed out, this is a classic description of leaching, 'washing' the earth to remove the salt (Butz 1983:478), followed by the equally important step of drainage. In discussing the evidence from pre-Sargonic Lagash, LaPlaca and Powell concur that 'leaching out the accumulated salts' and 'softening up the soil after a year's fallow' were the primary purposes of the flooding recommended here (LaPlaca and Powell 1990:80). The flooding/leaching process was performed when the Euphrates was in spate, and LaPlaca and Powell have suggested that it 'may have been a sort of accidental by-product of flooding, and perhaps the practice of flooding itself goes back originally to flood control . . . used as an effective means for diverting water out of the canal system and away from the fields being harvested' (LaPlaca and Powell 1990:80). Hartmut Waetzoldt, on the other hand, has argued that the Sumerian verb used in the opening of *The Farmer's Instructions*, *a-dé*, meaning 'to flood (a field)', pertains in this and related contexts to flood control (Waetzoldt 1990:11). In this case, he suggests, it must relate to an emergency measure designed to prevent flood during times when the river was in spate or a canal close to overflowing, to the emptying of a canal if repairs had to be carried out on it or to the saturation of a field so that it would support some limited summer growth, suitable for grazing, and at the same time be easier to plough (due to the increased dampness) once the ploughing season began (see below). One must question, however, whether the first two of these justifications, both of which must certainly have applied in different circumstances, lie behind the opening injunction of *The Farmer's Instructions* to his son. Surely the context there would make either leaching or the softening of the ground prior to ploughing the more likely reason for opening the text with this particular injunction.

After drying out, the flooded or 'wet ground' (*ki-duru$_5$*) was surveyed and then handed over to ploughmen for the ploughing and harrowing which often began in the summer. Different designations also existed for 'ploughed' (*uru$_4$-lá*), 'harrowed' (*tab-ba*), and 'ploughed and harrowed' (*ku$_5$-rá*) land (Hruška 1985a). After ploughing, the fields were sown and then re-surveyed in the autumn in order to estimate the productivity of each field. In the spring, when the crop was mature, a survey was again made prior to harvesting. Harvesting was followed by threshing and the draught animals were probably grazed on the harvested fields shortly thereafter. Dikes and other elements of the irrigation system would have required maintenance in the winter so that accidental floods did not occur when the river was in spate, and the flooding of the fields could proceed in a controlled manner (LaPlaca and Powell 1990:76).

Differences in the agricultural year certainly existed in space and time throughout Mesopotamia, but it is certain that both ploughing and harvesting took many months each and in a very real sense shaped the Mesopotamian conception of the calendrical year. It might seem logical to assume that the year 'began' with the inception of ploughing and ended sometime after the harvest, but this was not the case. In fact, it was the other way around. At pre-Sargonic Girsu, where the year began roughly between 21 March and 17 April, the harvest normally started sometime after the middle of April and the 'first' month of the year was called 'Barley Eating Festival of Nanshe' while the fourth month was the '[month in which] the grain-pile is heaped up' (LaPlaca and Powell 1990:78–9). Texts from the Ur III period suggest that the harvest was carried out during the 'first' six months of the year (March/April-July/August), the first three of which were devoted to actual reaping, the last three to threshing, transport and storage (Hruška 1990:105). As LaPlaca and Powell conclude, 'On the whole, we believe these dates agree with the optimal sowing season of modern times, and we see no reason to believe this was radically different in antiquity' (LaPlaca and Powell 1990:80).

In traditional Iraqi agriculture, 'Ploughing did not usually commence until the first rains or until very humid conditions had softened the soil; ploughing while it was still moist could help to improve soil structure' (Charles 1990:50). At pre-Sargonic Girsu, on the other hand, ploughing may have begun even earlier, during the fourth month, and was finished by the end of the eighth month, which was called '[month when] the plough is taken apart [and stored away]' (LaPlaca and Powell 1990:80). If this were the case, however, some steps must have been taken to moisten the ground for no rain could be expected at this time of the year. An answer to the problem may be provided by a text from the Neo-Babylonian period, in which it is stated that fields, hardened and dried by the extreme heat of summer, were artificially irrigated during the fifth month (July-August) in order to soften them up for ploughing (van Driel 1990:21). As noted above, this is also one of the suggested rationales for the flooding prescribed in *The Farmer's Intructions* (Waetzoldt 1990:11). The stages in the agricultural calendar, as reconstructed by B. Hruška, are shown in Table III.1 (after Hruška 1990:105–14).[11]

Draught Animals and the Use of the Ard

After describing the leaching process, *The Farmer's Instructions* recommends that 'shod oxen' be allowed to trample the field. Weeds should then be removed, the field levelled, the ground broken up with a hoe and the clods of earth crushed. Warnings are given that care be taken about the yoke and other parts of the draught-animal apparatus. For every pair of oxen the ploughman should have an extra animal, and for every plough a spare one. Ploughing serves a variety of purposes. Not only does it condition the soil, prepare the ground for the seed and control weeds, all of which are necessary (Charles 1990:50), but ploughing with draught animals produces a roughly 400 per cent increase in productivity as against land which is tilled simply by human labour (Hruška 1984:151, n. 3). The plough type in question (Fig. III.5) is a shallow 'ard' or 'sliding plough' (Latin *aratrum*, French *araire*, German *Hakenpflug* or *Umbruchpflug*) (Potts 1994a:162). The 'true' plough (French *charrue*, German *Pflug*) is wheeled, has a 'coulter' that cuts the furrow which the ploughshare then widens, and a mould-board which pushes aside the furrow. Deep ploughing in an arid area like Mesopotamia would cause soil damage by exposing the more fragile B-horizon of the soil to the sun, in turn causing it to dry out and erode. While the ard does not turn the ground, loosening only the

Month		Conditions		Agricultural Operations	
Girsu	Gregorian	Max/Min °C	Av. Rainfall (mm)	Cultivation Year	Harvest-Fallow Year
I	Mar–Apr	29°/12°	10	last irrigation; harvest begins in optimal years	flooding (leaching)
II	Apr–May	34°/19°	2	harvest	surveying of wet fields
III	May–June	40°/21°	0	harvest continues; cutting, drying, stacking	inactivity
IV	Jun–Jul	42°/24°	0	harvest continues; transport and storage of grain	inactivity
V	Jul–Aug	44°/24°	0	harvest ends	inactivity
VI	Aug–Sep	40°/21°	0	beginning of ploughing; sowing begins in optimal years	inactivity
VII	Sep–Oct	36°/18°	2	ploughing; early sowing	inactivity
VIII	Oct–Nov	27°/11°	21	late sowing; end of ploughing	inactivity
IX	Nov–Dec	19°/6°	27	late sowing	inactivity
X	Dec–Jan	16°/5°	24	inactivity; end of late sowing of cereals	preparation of fields
XI	Jan–Feb	19°/6°	25	first seedlings appear; irrigation	preparation of fields
XII	Feb–Mar	20°/8°	29	irrigation	inactivity

Table III.1 *Stages in the Mesopotamian agricultural calendar*

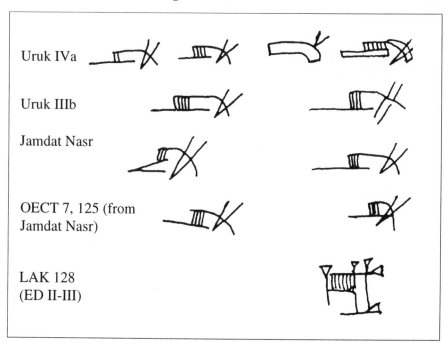

Uruk IVa		
Uruk IIIb		
Jamdat Nasr		
OECT 7, 125 (from Jamdat Nasr)		
LAK 128 (ED II-III)		

Figure III.5 The sign for *APIN* from the Late Uruk to the Early Dynastic II (Fara) period (after Hruška 1985: Abb, 5)

upper 15–20 cm (Hruška 1985:50) of topsoil, it effectively breaks the capillary network through which soil moisture could be lost. This makes it ideally suited to ploughing in arid areas. Finally, the ard is light and easily carried on the shoulders, and is affordable by even the poorest farmers, which explains its wide distribution throughout Eurasia from prehistoric times to the present day (Potts 1994a: 162–4).

The use of the plough and draught animals is thought by many authorities to represent a 'second' Agricultural Revolution (Sherratt 1981:261; cf. Hruška 1984:151), of equal importance to the beginnings of domestication itself (Grigg 1974:15). David and Joan Oates suggest that the ard has been used in Mesopotamia at least since the Samarran period, when an increase in the number of sites suggests that more extensive areas were being brought under cultivation (Oates and Oates 1977:119; cf. Hruška 1985:47. n. 4). By the Late Uruk and Jamdat Nasr periods the sign ZATU 2: 33 (= ATU 1: 214) is clearly recognizable in the Archaic Texts from Uruk as *APIN*, the plough (Green and Nissen 1987) (Fig. III.5).

In conjunction with those examples of ards which have been collected throughout Eurasia, the Archaic signs for *APIN* allow us to reconstruct with reasonable accuracy the main features of the ancient Mesopotamian ard. The ard consisted of a long, wooden beam (*sag-apin*) which was often composite, the front section mortised and bound with rope or cord to the rear part. This seems to be what is shown on the Archaic *APIN* signs, where a series of two or more vertical lines link the front (straight) with the rear (curving) part of the beam. While the front end of the beam slotted into the

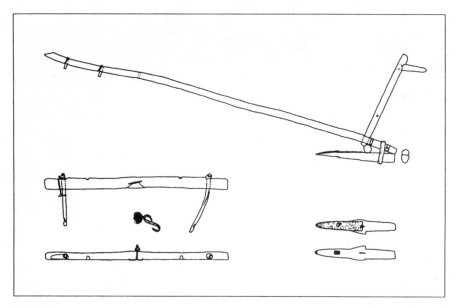

Figure III.6 A type of ard used in Kerman province, Iran, in the 1960s (after Lerche and Steensberg 1983: Fig. 10)

yoke of the draught animals, the rear end was attached to the wooden stilt or stilts (*giš*á-apin, *giš*da-pa), shown as a more or less upright V in the *APIN* signs, which were held by the ploughman, and to the sole (*giš*dam-apin, *giš*PI-apin), that piece of wood on which the actual ardshare was mounted. Sumerian sources use two terms in reference to the ardshare, *eme*, meaning 'tongue', and *giš*zú, meaning 'tooth' (Hruška 1985b:52). These were clearly separate pieces of equipment. Looking at traditional ards from Iran (Fig. III.6), we find some on which the ardshare is shaped like a socketed, flattened, triangular spearhead which slipped directly over the sole, and this may be what is meant by the 'tooth', whereas other examples show a small wooden beam, one part of which slots into the upright part of the sole, while the other end slots into a socket at the end of the actual ardshare (Lerche and Steensberg 1983:Figs. 33, 35). This is perhaps what is meant by 'tongue'. In later periods as in the modern era the pointed ardshare of the socketed, triangular type was often made of bronze or iron (Potts 1994a:163–4), but in Mesopotamia, where the determinative for wood, *giš*, precedes all components of the ard, it is clear that, at least originally, these were made of wood. An Ur III text from Umma dealing with wood and timbering refers to the delivery of forty *giš*eme *giš*apin-šè, perhaps the 'tongue' referred to above, which were certainly made of wood (Steinkeller 1987:93 and 111, s.v. 45). The wooden nature of the essential, earth-breaking parts of the ard is interesting in light of the Sumerian literary work known as the *Disputation between the Hoe and the Plough* (sic, ard) in which the obsolescence of the ard 'tooth' is contrasted with the fact that the hoe sharpens and renews itself through use. The ard's 'tooth' breaks and has to be replaced, a hoe lasts twelve months but an ard only four and the repair of an ard takes twice as long as its work life (Hruška 1985b:53, and n. 28). Although never stated, it is probably permissible to conclude from this that hoe-blades were typically made of a more durable material, and indeed flaked stone hoe-blades (Fig. III.7) are a feature of the Ubaid (Kozlowski 1987:Figs. 8–9; Inizan and Tixier 1983:Figs. 1, 3.2) and

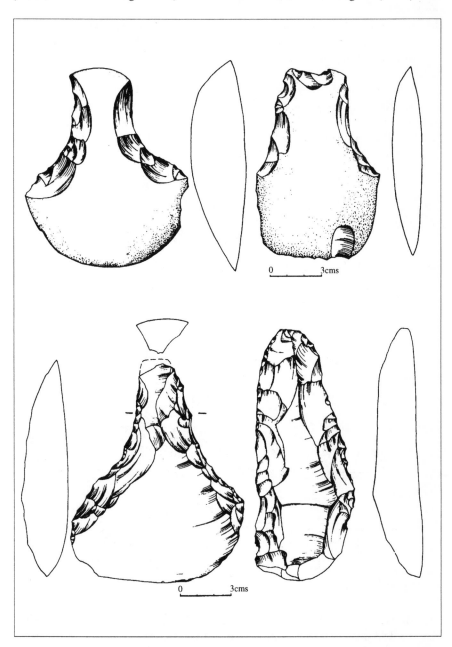

Figure III.7 Flaked stone hoe-blades from Tell el-Saadiya in the Hamrin district of eastern Iraq (after Kozlowski 1987: Figs. 8–9).

pre-Ubaid periods in greater Mesopotamia (Cauvin 1979:193–206), although here again one should note that the Sumerian term ^{giš}*al-zú sì-ga* (Akk. *allu*), denoting 'hoe', which is preceded by the determinative for wood, *giš*, is certainly amongst the wooden objects produced at Umma in the Ur III period (Steinkeller 1987:93 and 107, s.v. 35).

The Seeder Plough

Although Armas Salonen identified the Archaic *APIN* sign discussed above as the 'seeding plough', on the basis of the similarity between Akk. *epinnu* and Sumerian *apin*, these are not attested before the Early Dynastic period (Hruška 1985b:51, and n. 18 with refs. to many illustrations on seals) when several representations of seed ploughs appear in Mesopotamian glyptic art (Fig. III.8). A well-known representation of a seeding plough is also known from the Kassite period (Fig. III.9), as is a Neo-Assyrian depiction (Fig. III.10) on a *kudurru*, or boundary stele, from the reign of Esarhaddon (680–669 BC) (Hruška 1988b:Abb. 3–4).

Figure III.8 Early Dynastic glyptic representations of the seeder plough (after Amiet 1961: Pl. 106.1402 (Ur), 1403 (Fara), and 1404 (no provenience, Louvre)

Figure III.9 Kassite representation of a seeder plough (after Hruška 1988: Abb. 3)

In many respects the seeding plough, called ^{giš}*numun-gar* in Sumerian (Hruška 1985b:51–2), was arguably the most important piece of technology ever developed in Mesopotamia. As the Kassite representation (Fig. III.9) shows particularly clearly, the use of the seeding plough was

Figure III.10 Neo-Assyrian representation of a seeder plough (after Hruška 1988: Abb. 4)

labour-intensive, requiring at least two if not three men to work on each plough team: one to drive, one to sow, and one to turn the animals (Maekawa 1984:82; cf. Halstead 1990:189). Nevertheless, labour was readily available in ancient Mesopotamia and the seeding plough was undoubtedly the key to the exceptionally high yields recorded there.

Lines 46–54 of *The Farmer's Instructions* specify precisely how the seeding plough is to be used to sow the seed (Jacobsen 1982:59):

On each *nindan* [= 6 m] draw 8 furrows [*ab-sín*]; closely ranged furrows strangle their barley plants. When you seed-plough the field keep an eye on your man who drops the seed, let him drop the barley-goddess [i.e. the single seed-corn] each 2 'fingers' (= 3 1/3 cm).[12] Have him drop 1 *gín* [= 1/60 l.] to each *nindan* [= 6 m]. If the seed does not penetrate [?] into the womb [of the furrow] replace the peg of the tongue of your plough [i.e. adjust it to go deeper], if the 'tail' is loose make the 'tail' smaller [meaning not clear].

As Marvin Powell has noted, the so-called 'two finger rule' may well go back to a time when the ard was still used and Mesopotamian sowers planted individual seeds by hand with a space of two fingers' width between them (Powell 1984:54). That this was no longer the case once the seeding plough was developed is clear, but with the new technology came the requirement for the farmer to make sure that the man feeding the seeding plough's hopper took care to drop the seed properly.

In order to understand the metrology used in *The Farmer's Instructions* it is necessary to have an understanding of some basic Sumerian weights and measures (Powell 1990). The most relevant ones are given below:

Weights
 1 Sum. *še*/Akk. *uṭṭetu* = 'barleycorn' = 0.04–0.05 g
 1 Sum. *gín*/Akk. *šiqlu* = 'axe' (English: shekel) = 180 *še* = *c.* 8.33g
 1 Sum. *ma-na*/Akk. *manû* = 60 *gín* = 10,800 *še* = *c.* 500 g
 1 Sum. *gú(n)*/Akk. *biltu* = 'load' (English: talent from Gr. *talanton*, cf. Lat. *tollo*) = 60 *ma-na* = 'counter' (English: mina) = *c.* 30 kg

Volume Measures
   1 Sum. *sìla* = 10,800 *še* or barleycorns = *c*.1 l
   10 *sìla* = 1 *bán* = 10 l
   60 *sìla* = 6 *bán* = 1 *bariga* = 60 l
   300 *sìla* = 30 *bán* = 5 *bariga* = 1 *gur* = 300 l

Area Measures
   1 *sar* = 36 sq.m
   100 *sar* = 1 *iku* = 3600 sq.m
   600 *sar* = 6 *iku* = 1 *eše* = 21,600 sq.m
   1800 *sar* = 18 *iku* = 3 *eše* = 1 *bùr* = 64,800 sq.m = 6.48 ha

The Farmer's Instructions calls for eight furrows per six-metre-width of field, or furrows which are 75 cm apart. It further instructs the reader to use 1 *gín* (1/60 *sìla* = 0.016 l) of seed per *nindan*, i.e. per six-metre-length of furrow. If we project this onto a field the size of the standard Sumerian surface measure, the 6.48-ha *bùr*, we then arrive at the following seeding rate per *bùr*: 1/60 *sìla* × 8 (furrows) × 1800 (*nindan* = 1 *bùr*) = 240 *sìla*. As Powell has noted, the 240 *sìla* per *bùr* rate is widely attested in the cuneiform sources. It appears as a standard, modal figure in an Old Babylonian mathematical text; it was the basis for the pre-Sargonic *gur* at Fara; and it lies at the origin of the earliest Babylonian definititions of surface area measured in seed, first found in the late Kassite period but possibly of much earlier, Old Babylonian ancestry (Powell 1985:23, 1984: 35). That this 'modal' rate was not always observed, however, has been shown by Maekawa, who finds that at both Umma and Girsu during the Ur III period, fields with eight, ten or twelve furrows per *nindan* are recorded. Thus, when ten furrows were present, the seeding rate rose to 300 l (1 *gur*) per *bùr* (6.48 ha) (Maekawa 1990:125).

Sowing Rates and Yields
When, in the nineteenth century, the seeding plough was introduced for the first time into Britain, it is estimated to have resulted in a 50 per cent saving on the expenditure of seed as compared to broadcast sowing by hand over a ploughed field (Halstead 1990:187). Herein lies the explanation for Mesopotamia's fabled yields. By way of comparison, let us first consider the yields achieved in traditional Iraqi agriculture.

   Given the insignificance of the wheats in southern Mesopotamian agriculture, our discussion of yields will focus exclusively on barley. Twentieth-century studies of 'traditional agriculture' and Iraqi government estimates of expected yields vary considerably. In the Diyala region, Adams found 'the average yield from 77 randomly sampled fields of barley in the area served by gravity-flow canals emanating from the Diyala weir was 1,396 ± 67.5 [kg] per hectare' (Adams 1965:17). David and John Oates cite Iraqi government figures of 800 kg/ha for rain-fed and 1000 kg/ha for irrigated barley. Taking into account soil salinity as well as the variable quality of the land being cultivated, the Dutch agronomist A.P.G. Poyck preferred a more conservative figure of *c*. 720

kg/ha for irrigated barley grown on small-holdings (Oates and Oates 1977:120).

Modern data suggest that a family of six needs 6 ha of irrigated land for sustenance at subsistence level, half of which lies fallow at any given time. Yields will, of course, vary depending on irrigation conditions, while the total amount of land which can be brought under cultivation will also vary depending on whether it is tilled by hand using a hoe or ploughed with draught animals. The Oates suggest, 'With a minimum acceptable cereal yield of 550 kg per hectare on a simple fallow system of one to four years, and a diet supplemented by hunting, fishing and gathering such as the evidence from all early village farming sites attests, the land requirement would be about one and a half hectares of cultivable land per head of population' (Oates and Oates 1977:120). A six-person family would probably consume no more than 600 kg in a year which would leave plenty left over for seed and spoilage, even using the Oates' ultra-conservative estimate of 550 kg/ha, Poyck's mildly conservative figure of 720 kg/ha, the Iraqi government figure of 800 kg/ha, or Adams' very high Diyala yields of almost 1400 kg/ha.

It must be emphasized, however, that most of the agriculture which concerns us in southern Mesopotamia was significantly more efficient than that which has been practised by individual families in recent years, since the figures available to us in the seed-and-fodder texts from sites like Telloh concern large estates with hundreds and thousands of acres under cultivation, not small-holdings cultivated by peasant farmers in the third millennium BC. Individual families in southern Mesopotamia certainly did have the opportunity to cultivate plots with which they were able to supplement their rations, but this sort of cultivation is not recorded by the official texts of state and temple estates. The key to the productivity of ancient Mesopotamian agriculture as compared to its modern or pre-modern counterpart in Iraq was without doubt the seeding plough.

If we consider yields during the very well-documented Ur III period, we find that the average yield was 30 *gur* (9000 l) per *bùr* (6.48 ha) or 1388 l per ha (Maekawa 1984:85). Actual as opposed to projected yields (i.e. those based on pre-harvest surveys) varied greatly, coming in at 104 per cent, 61 per cent, and 94 per cent of expected yield based on RTC 407, a text from Tello which covers six calendar years (i.e. three harvests because half the land was in fallow) (Pettinato and Waetzoldt 1975:259–90). If we round up the 1388 l. per ha. yield cited above to 1400 l, and if we recall the amount of seed required per *bùr*, then a 1400 l yield per ha represents a yield of 1:30 (1400 *sìla*/ha = *c.* 1000 kg/ha), and even higher yields (up to 1:76) are attested in the pre-Sargonic era (Maekawa 1984:85). Some years ago Butz and Schröder (Butz 1983:470–86; Butz and Schröder 1985:165–209) contested this, suggesting that yields of this sort were impossible without modern methods of fertilization, and arguing that the figures given might reflect productivity over a number of years, as in a seven year cycle. Postgate, however, countered this by saying there was no evidence for such a cycle (Postgate 1984:97–102). A solution to this important problem seems now to have been provided by Paul Halstead.

Halstead has recently observed that we must interpret these yields not so much as a reflection of astonishing productivity, but as a reflection of the small amount of seed expended, and this is directly attributable to the fact that the Sumerians used the seeding plough. Thus, they were able to seed much less in relation to the amount grown than in most other pre-modern societies where broadcast sowing was the norm. For example, where the seed sown was 1 *gur* per *bùr*, this represents 46 *sìla*/l or *c.* 32 kg per ha. If we compare this with broadcast barley sowing in modern Iraq, we find that anywhere from 50 to 128 kg of seed are expended on every hectare sown, or roughly 1.5–4 times as much as the Ur III figure. Thus, only 25–64 per cent of the modern Iraqi figure for barley seed per ha was expended in ancient Mespotamia, and this fact lies at the heart of the extraordinary yields recorded in antiquity there (Halstead 1990:187).

The Plough Team

Alongside the seeding plough, the systematic use of draught animals must be credited with contributing greatly to the productivity of ancient Meso-potamian agriculture. The ancient Mesopotamian plough was normally drawn by oxen, and it is clear that, in terms of agricultural costs and benefits, there is a very close relationship between the size of the area cultivated and the fodder requirements of the plough team. Unlike sheep and goats, cattle do not graze on the steppe in Iraq today, nor did they in antiquity. Thus, for all practical purposes their feeding, and hence part of their cost, must be subtracted from the food produced for feeding the human population. Food for draught oxen came from the same source as food for people, namely the large tracts of land devoted to cereal cultiva-tion. Draught animals were given rations (Fig. III.11) and, when not in their stalls or working, could only be pastured on cultivated land. Therefore, as Renger notes (1990:267):

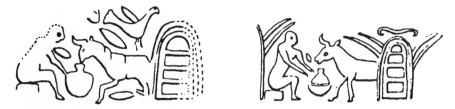

Figure III.11 Cattle being fed. The impressions are from SIS 4 at Ur which dates to the early ED I period (Porada et al. 1992:104) (after Amiet 1961: Pl. 58.791 and 793)

We are faced with a situation in which a balance has to be struck be-tween a maximum possible acreage for cereal production and a min-imum acreage necessary for pasturing the animals required for working the cereal land. Thus the relation between acreage used for cereal pro-duction stands in direct relation to the number of animals needed for draught purposes during the planting season.

For purposes of cost accounting, ancient Mesopotamian scribes normally totalled seed and fodder together to arrive at the total investment in a field in comparison with the expected or realized yield. A pre-Sargonic text from Girsu (VS 14.184, year Lugalanda 6) for example, states that for the initial ploughing (see below) of 8 *bùr* 3 *iku* of land, i.e. 51.84 + 1.08 ha = 52.92 ha, 12.25 *gur-sag-gál* or 1764 *sìla*/l seed (1 *gur-sag-gál* = 144 *sìla*) and 3528 *sìla*/l fodder were required. Both here and in later Ur III texts we see a seed:fodder ratio of 1:2 which is extremely high and therefore costly, perhaps because the parcels of land in question were difficult to work (Hruška 1984:154). Powell suggests that the 'normal' relation between seed, feed and labour rations was 60:60:36 *sìla*, or approximately 1:1 seed to fodder (Powell 1984:47). Even so, when one realizes that the costs of seed are roughly the same as the costs of feed, it becomes clear how expensive and vital a component the plough team represented. Powell suggests that a team of four draught oxen routinely received 30 *sìla*/l of feed, and certainly not less than six *sìla* each, per day (Powell 1984:51, n. 65).

An important question to detemine, however, is the exact number of animals involved, since the speed of ploughing depends naturally on the efficiency of the plough team (Fig. III.12) which is itself dependent on the

Figure III.12 Harnessing an ox, from a cylinder seal of the Jamdat Nasr period (?) in the British Museum (after Amiet 1961: Pl. 40.612)

number of draught animals used. Salonen suggested that a 'normal' plough team consisted of two pairs of oxen, each in a double yoke, one in front of the other (Hruška 1985b:54). Studies in sub-Saharan Africa have shown, however, that the use of a second team of draught oxen brings about a reduction in speed on the part of the aggregate team from e.g. 2.2 km/hour to 1.8 km/hour. On the other hand, the length of the working day can be extended by up to 20 per cent when using two pairs of oxen as opposed to one. Three pair, on the other hand, is less economical since it results in an increase of only another 5 per cent more work time per day, while adding substantially to fodder costs.

The use of two pairs of oxen for ploughing is well attested in cuneiform texts, where the four oxen in a team are identified as first and second front, and first and second rear. The distinction between the two pairs is, moreover, clear in §242 of the Laws of Hammurapi according to which a higher rent was charged for the two front oxen than for those in the rear (Renger 1990:275). The importance of ancient Mesopotamian draught animals is also clearly shown by the so-called 'Ox Laws', for which parallels exist in most of the famous Mesopotamian law codes, including the Laws of Hammurapi, the Laws of Lipit-Ishtar and the Hittite laws. These contain stipulations such as the following (Roth 1980:129–30):

> §1 If [the renter] has [destroyed] the eye of the ox, he shall pay one-half of its value; §2 If [the renter] has broken the horn of the ox, he shall pay one-third of its value; §3 If [the renter] has cut [?] the hoof tendon of the ox, he shall pay one-fourth of its value; §4 If [the renter] has broken the tail of the ox, [he shall pay one-. . . of its value]; §5 If [the renter] has injured the . . . of the ox, he shall pay one-fourth of its value; §6 If an ox, while crossing a river has drowned [lit. died], he [i.e. the renter] shall pay according to its full value; §7 If a lion has killed a yoked ox drawing [a plough or wagon], he [i.e. the renter] shall not have to replace [the ox].

Concern for the welfare of the draught animals is also clear. An Ur III text concerned with leather goods (BM 111759) mentions twenty-eight sheep-skins for the yokes of seven oxen (Sigrist 1981:185, 188). Clearly injury to a draught team could mean substantial losses in agricultural productivity.

Use of the Plough

It is clear both from traditional agricultural practice and the variety of cuneiform *termini technici* that different types of ploughing were performed in ancient Mesopotamia, involving both the ard and the seeding plough. Pre-Sargonic texts such as VS 14.184 (Girsu, Lugalanda 6) mention a number of ploughing functions (the discussion here follows Hruška 1984:153–4). Specific terms (e.g. LAK 483-*si* or LAK 483-*si-ga*) denoted the first ploughing (German *Umbruchpflügen*), in which new land was brought under cultivation for the first time or fallow land was brought back under cultivation. The function of this was to plough under the already present vegetation, destroying weeds and stray remainders from the last cultivation of the particular plot of land. It also served to break up the ground so that the newly seeded plants could better spread their roots, and affected the field's hydrology by interrupting capillary action so that the nutrients in the soil (minerals and organic remains) were loosened and more easily absorbed. For the purpose of breaking the soil in this manner, it is most probable that the ard was employed, and indeed this is what is described in *The Farmer's Instructions*, ll. 30–32, where the use of the 'soil-breaker-plough' to break up the field, followed by harrowing, is distinguished from ll. 41-58 where the seeding plough is described (Jacobsen 1982:58–9).

Another pre-Sargonic term (*numun-gar*) may refer to normal seed ploughing in autumn, or perhaps to a kind of ploughing prior to a test planting (*numun-na sì-ga*) following several years of fallow. After the harvest the ground was ploughed (*ku₅-rá*, lit. '[earth] cut') in the direction opposite to that in which it was planted, and gone over several times with a harrow in order to plough under the stubble of the last harvest. In a situation where both the irrigation water and the soil were saline, the repeated harrowing of fields was beneficial (Hruška 1984:153-154, n. 13), in order to enhance drainage and prevent salinization (Butz 1983:478).

The Farmer's Instructions (ll. 26-27) tell us that the ard was able to plough 18 *iku*, i.e. 1 *bùr* (6.48 ha) of ground without, however, specifying the time required to do so (Hruška 1988b:151, 1990:106).[13] Ur III texts show that a plough team of oxen at Girsu could plough between 1.2 *iku* (0.43 ha) and 2.25 *iku* (0.81 ha) per day, while a standard rate of 2 *iku* (0.72 ha) per day was the norm at Umma. The variation in ploughing capacity at Girsu is thought to reflect the variability in number of furrows per *nindan* discussed above which could be as little as eight or as much as twelve (Maekawa 1990:125). Powell suggests that the notional Ur III rate amounted to the standard *danna* of 1800 *nindan*, which equates to 1.8 *iku* (0.648 ha) per day (Powell 1984:53). If this is so, then 18 *iku* mentioned in *The Farmer's Instructions* would have taken ten days to plough.

These figures are much higher than ethnographic studies of ploughing in traditional Western Asiatic agriculture. Thus, for example, studies of ard use in Iran have shown that an estimated 500 sq.m (0.05 ha) can be ploughed in a day, at which rate it would take 129.6 days or *c*. 4 months to plough 18 *iku* (6.48 ha) (Hruška 1990:106). Such differences, of course, must relate to the number of draught animals employed and equally to the number of furrows to be ploughed. In this context it becomes clear that the variability in Ur III seeding patterns is nothing short of dramatic, since twelve furrows per *nindan* represents a 50 per cent increase in terrain to be ploughed over eight furrows per *nindan*. When calculated over the course of 18 *iku* (6.48 ha), an increase from eight to twelve furrows per *nindan* means that an extra 43.2 km must be covered by the plough team (Powell 1984:47).

Assuming for a moment that a hypothetical 18 *iku* (1 *bùr*) field of 64,800 sq.m is perfectly square, this would mean that the field measured 254.55844 m, or 42.426406 *nindan* on a side. If each *nindan* has eight furrows, that means there are 339.41124 furrows to plough. If this is done over the distance of 254 m (the length of the field) then a single ploughing amounts to 86.21 km to be covered by the plough team. If cross-ploughing is done, then we have to double this to 172.42 km. If we reckon with a speed of 2.3 km/hour for a team of oxen, this will take 74.96 hours to plough. Working six hours per day (Hruška 1990:112, n.17) it will take 12.49 work days to do the cross ploughing. In 'normal' agricultural circumstances we can assume cross-ploughing of the entire area twice (258.63 km), plus seed ploughing once (86.21) for a total of 344.84 km to travel. This translates into 149.93 hours of ploughing which, at six hours of ploughing per day, amounts to 24.98 days of work.

The overwhelming magnitude of the labour involved in ancient Mesopotamian agriculture in one of its most developed phases, the Ur III period, is clearly shown by a text from Girsu (BM 18060) which covers the ten-year period from the year Shulgi 42 to Amar-Sin 3 (*c*. 2053–2044 BC). In this decade no less than 35,365 *bùr* 16 *iku* (= 229,165.2 + 5.76 ha) were under cultivation amounting to a total of 229,170.96 ha This means that, on average, 22,917 ha were under cultivation each year, and indeed this figure compares well with TuT 5 from the year Shulgi 47 which says that 3,744 *bùr* 14.5 *iku* were to be sown under control of the governor of Girsu, amounting to *c.* 24,266 ha Quite clearly, in terms of human and animal labour, equipment and time, Mesopotamian agriculture of this sort was carried out on a grand scale.

Although the supposition of perfectly square fields of a given size is fine for calculating work per day, it is rare to find perfectly square fields in any traditional agricultural regime, and indeed for the later third millennium, Neo-Babylonian and Achaemenid periods we have a considerable fund of information on the shape of fields. The variation in field size is undoubtedly, at least in part, a reflection of the degree to which agriculture was or was not state-run in any given period. Thus while the average size of Ur III fields (Fig. III.13) is *c.* 100 *iku* or 36 ha, fields in the Old Akkadian period were only 4–10 *iku* (Liverani 1990:158). In actual shape ancient Mesopotamian fields were most often strips of land, their length exceeding their width by a factor of ten on average. Mario Liverani suggests that the elongated shape is a natural response to two constraints. On the one hand, long narrow fields probably arise from the exigencies of getting water out of canals onto the field. On the other hand, the difficulty of using the seeding plough with two pair of oxen, which were no doubt difficult to turn, may underlie a preference for furrows of maximum length requiring fewer turns of the plough team, particularly at Girsu (Liverani 1990:171). Interestingly, the long strip-like fields of the third millennium are strikingly reminiscent of fields on the Middle Tigris which were documented in the 1950s and discussed recently by Nicholas Postgate (Postgate 1990:Figs. 3a–b).

MEAT AND MILK PRODUCTS

The basic triad of sheep (*Ovis aries*), goat (*Capra hircus*) and cattle (*Bos taurus*) predominated in southern Mesopotamia (Figs. III.14–16). In addition, the pig (*Sus domesticus*), often thought to be of less importance (Postgate 1994:166), was actively herded from at least the Late Uruk through the Ur III period. The Archaic lexical list W 12139, formerly thought to be a list of terms for 'dog', has now been identified as a list of swine, while Archaic economic texts (e.g. W 23948) show that swine were herded and classed administratively according to age just as sheep and goats were (Englund 1988:147–8 and n. 147). During the Ur III period pigs were given up to 3.6 *sila*/l of barley per day in order to fatten them (Englund 1988:143, n. 16). Faunal remains of domesticated pig, usually slaughtered when young, are known from a number of sites, such as Tell Oueili (Ubaid 4) (Desse 1983:194, 196, Tables 1–2) and Uruk (Late Uruk, Early Dynastic, Old Babylonian) (Boessneck, von den Driesch and Steger 1984:153–63, 176; cf. Boessneck 1992:267–70). Wild boar (*Sus scrofa*), moreover, were hunted in the marshes (Fig. III.17), as numerous depictions in the glyptic of various periods attest (e.g. Amiet 1961:Pls. 39.604, 607; 40.609). Remains of wild boar have also been uncovered in archaeological

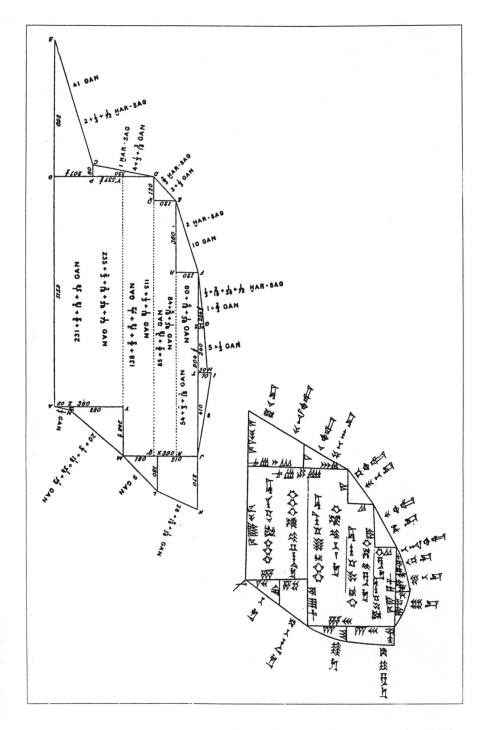

Figure III.13 Ur III field plan (upper right) with a schematic transliteration showing the individual fields to the left (after Liverani 1990: Fig. 1)

Figure III.14 Sheep as depicted in Late Uruk or Jamdat Nasr glyptic (after Amiet 1961: Pl. 41.618)

Figure III.15 Goat as depicted in Early Dynastic glyptic (after Amiet 1961: Pl. 100.1328 (Ur) and Pl. 87.1143 (Khafajah, IIIa))

Figure III.16 Cattle as depicted in glyptic of the Jamdat Nasr period (after Amiet 1961: Pl. 42.629A (Khafajah, Sin Temple II))

Figure III.17 Wild boar being hunted in the marshes (after Amiet 1961: Pl. 40.609 (no provenience)

contexts, e.g. at Uruk (Late Uruk, Jamdat Nasr (?)) (Boessneck, von den Driesch and Steger 1984:154, 178; cf. Boessneck 1992:267–70), and some (e.g. *šah₂-ᵍⁱˢgi*) seem to have been kept for breeding as well (Englund

1988:142). Without entering into all of the problems surrounding livestock in ancient Mesopotamia, the question must, however, be asked, to what extent did meat and milk products figure in the ancient inhabitants' diet?

The basic answer to this is a short 'not very much'. In essence, none of these animals were normally consumed as part of the regular diet because of the fact that their secondary products and labour were much too valuable for the animal itself to be slaughtered. As discussed above, cattle were employed consistently as draught animals for ploughing and were therefore well tended. Indeed, in spite of some explicit representations of cattle herds in Late Uruk glyptic and Early Dynastic inlay scenes of milking (Gouin 1993:Figs. 1, 3; cf. Stol 1993:100) (cf. Chapter VI), 'official accounts from Ur (from either a palace or a temple) suggest that dairy productivity was poor and, although recorded, was not of paramount importance' (Postgate 1994:164).

Sheep and goats, on the other hand, were kept principally for the fleece and hair they provided for the textile industry (Van De Mieroop 1993:161–82) and only secondarily for their skins (Sigrist 1981:141–90) (cf. Chapter IV). Secondary products, such as cheese and ghee (clarified butter), were made from goat's and cow's milk, whereas sheep's milk is only known to have been used for the manufacture of cheese for the Achaemenid prince Arsham who was active at Sippar in the reign of Darius II (423-405 BC) (Stol 1993:109). One of the apparently principal products derived from pigs, on the other hand, was fat or grease (Postgate 1994:166) (for pork placed in graves as offerrings, cf. Chapter X). As for meat consumption, at Old Babylonian Ur sheep and goat meat appears only as an offering to the temple and on the occasion of special festivities (Van De Mieroop 1993:171). Likewise during the Neo-Babylonian period, although older sheep at Uruk and Sippar were fattened systematically for a short period in the *bīt urê* and then slaughtered, their meat was generally destined as food offerings to deities, and eventual consumption by temple staff (van Driel 1993:239, 242). How such meat was prepared and, when it was eaten, is indicated by a small number of so-called 'culinary tablets', such as those in the Yale Babylonian Collection, which contain recipes for the preparation of meat stews. These involve legs of mutton, as well as wild fowl such as pigeon and 'small birds' which may have been ducklings or sparrows (Bottéro 1987:11–20).

CONCLUSION

For many years the agricultural regime and cultivars of southern Mesopotamia were neglected subjects, but over the course of the past two decades great strides have been made in illuminating this all-important area of study. The scale and scope of the agricultural activities conducted in Mesopotamia, the immensity of the yields achieved, and the all-pervasive nature of fundamental production touched all members of society. Apart from the very soil and water of the southern alluvium, the agricultural productivity on which Mesopotamia's inhabitants depended for their livelihood must rank as the foundation of Mesopotamian civilization.

NOTES

1 Although one wonders whether the rare *še kur-ra*, 'mountain grain/barley' might refer to an upland variety, such as 2-row barley, which was scarcely attested in the south in the historic era?

2 According to Xenophon (*Cyropaedia* I 2.8, 11), the Persian king and army ate cress ('cardamum'), perhaps because it makes the body retain water, an advantage in a hot climate. See Sancisi-Weerdenburg 1993.

3 Cf. Steinkeller 1987:92, who stresses that it 'grew wild in Southern Babylonia, excluding identification with either cassia or mustard, both of which are foreign to the flora of Southern Iraq'. According to sources cited by Steinkeller, wild licorice (*Glycirrhiza glabra*) is common in many parts of the riverine area of southern Iraq where licorice has been used in medicines and for firewood.

4 Renfrew 1985:64, notes finds of sesame seeds at the Urartian site of Karmir Blur in Armenia, Harappa in Pakistan, Shortugai in Afghanistan and Ch'ien Shan Yang in China. In fact, Shortugai should be removed from this list, for the only oil plant represented there is flax, attested by impressions in baked brick. See Willcox 1989:182.

5 Kenoyer 1991:32–5 discusses Vats' excavations, noting (32) that 'the proposed dates [of Vats] are no longer valid' and further (50), that all of the 'Early to Intermediate strata identified by Vats', in which group the Trench V, Mound F, Stratum III locus of the sesame would fall, belong to the Mature Harappan period, and not, as Vats suggested and Bedigian 1985:162 believes, to the second half of the fourth millennium BC.

6 Given what has just been said, it is not clear how one should interpret the isolated recovery of a single grain of sesame pollen in seventh millennium BC Ali Kosh on the Deh Luran plain of northern Khuzistan. See van Zeist 1985:37; Bedigian 1985:171.

7 For more detail on this question, and for the instances of 'early' sesame, see Stol 1985:119.

8 Cf. Moorey and Postgate 1992:197. Palm wood, as opposed to date stones, has been found at other sites, including Nuzi, Abu Qubur and Uruk.

9 A prebend in this sense refers to a perquisite, stipend or benefit conferred on an individual. It was often paid out of the holdings of an estate, usually a temple, and could be bought and sold, somewhat like an annuity.

10 The suggested identification with *ÚRxA.NA* made in Postgate 1987:120, was withdrawn in Postgate 1992:186.

11 For traditional Iraq see Charles 1990:47–64; and, for *The Farmer's Instructions*, discussions in, e.g. Butz 1983:477ff. It should be noted that the stages differ in some details from the reconstruction of LaPlaca and Powell discussed here.

12 Powell 1984:53, n. 68 translates, 'Ašnan [the barleycorn] should be dropped [or should fall] every two fingers, so that one gín of barley is planted for you every nindan [of furrow length]'.

13 The figure, according to Civil's new edition, is certainly not 180 *iku*, or 10 *bùr*, as stated in Jacobsen 1982:58, and rebutted in Powell 1984:50.

IV Inedible Natural Resources

INTRODUCTION

The prevailing view in most general works on Mesopotamia is that the region was essentially devoid of any natural resources other than water, clay and reeds. Traditionally, this extreme resource poverty was considered a spur to the development of a bureaucracy which organized, alongside local production, the import of all other necessary raw materials. In fact, while the import of a wide range of foreign goods did occur, few studies of Mesopotamia have taken the trouble to accurately document the far from insignificant local natural resources which were exploited in antiquity. As we have seen, even the predominantly infertile soil and saline water, when properly managed, were capable of producing a vast agricultural surplus. In this chapter we shall examine those other inedible resources which contributed so significantly to the ancient Mesoptamian economy. The most important resources have been arranged here under the rubrics 'animal, mineral, vegetable', and it is in this order that we shall treat them.

ANIMAL PRODUCTS

Textiles

The vast herds of sheep which constituted such a large segment of the herding sector in the ancient Mesopotamian economy provided the bulk of the raw material needed for the textile industry. Because of generally unfavourable conditions of preservation in most parts of the world, archaeological evidence of textiles (outside of Egypt) is always meagre. Where textiles are preserved, however, this is often due to the biocidal effects of contact with the corrosion products found on metals (Reade and Potts 1993:101), a situation most often encountered in graves. Nevertheless, poor conditions of preservation combined with less than meticulous excavation have meant that very few remains of textiles have been found outside of the late pre-Islamic period in Iraq (Fujii 1980). In the entire Royal Cemetery at Ur, for example, only five textile fragments were recovered, one of which was linen (from PG 357, 800 and 1237). Uruk has yielded twenty fragments, one of which was undatable, two of which came from Parthian period contexts, and the rest of which were discovered in Neo-Babylonian double-jar burials (van Ess and Pedde 1992:258–9).[1] Some of the Early Dynastic cylinder sealings from Fara, on the other hand, bear clear textile impressions (Waetzoldt 1972:xix-xx).

In contrast to this relatively unpromising situation, a wealth of information exists in cuneiform sources on the Mesopotamian textile industry during the Ur III period (Waetzoldt 1972). With linen playing a quantitatively small if élite role (Waetzoldt 1983:583–94) (see below), and cotton unknown until the late periods (cf. Chapter XII), wool was by far the most important material used for the manufacture of textiles in Mesopotamia. If clothing the population was second in importance only to feeding it, then one can understand why H. Waetzoldt considers sheep-shearing, or more accurately sheep-plucking,[2] the main event of the Sumerian agricultural calendar after the cereal harvest (Waetzoldt 1972:10). The significance accorded wool-plucking is clearly shown by the fact that the month in which it occurred was named the month of the 'sheep-plucking shed' in the pre-Sargonic calendars at Girsu and Adab (Waetzoldt 1972:10; Cohen 1993:61).

Five classes, ranging from first (royal) to fifth (normal), in addition to coarse, unclassed wool, were recognised in the Ur III period (Waetzoldt 1972:47–8).[3] Judging by the economic texts the overwhelming majority of wool produced in Mesopotamia was of the poorer quality but the percentage of wool belonging to each of the qualitative classes varied greatly within a flock of sheep and between different cities (Waetzoldt 1972:62–3). Moreover, wool quality varied according to sheep breed, as did the quantity of wool produced per animal. Thus, the fat-tailed sheep (*udu-gukkal*) produced wool of high quality (first and second classes), an individual animal yielding on average 1.4 minas (*c.* 0.7 kg) of wool. The territory of Lagash was the centre of its husbandry, and in the year Shulgi 36 (2089/88 BC) a total of 66,095 fat-tailed sheep were registered there according to a text (Lau 161) from Telloh (Waetzoldt 1972:5). In contrast, the 'highland/ mountain sheep' (*udu-kur-ra*), kept mainly around Umma though present at Drehem and Lagash as well, only rarely produced third-class and yielded mainly fourth- and fifth-class wool. The most common sheep of the Ur III period, called *udu-uli-gi*, was found throughout southern Mesopotamia, although its centre was Drehem. This breed produced *gi*-wool at the rate of between 1.5 and 2.24 minas (0.75–1.12 kg) per animal. *Gi*-wool was coarse and only rarely entered the fourth and fifth classes. More often it was unclassed and used for general wool rations and the manufacture of coarse garments.

The estimation of wool yield is difficult, particularly as it depends not only on the breed of sheep but on the age of the individual animal. A text from Girsu (CT X 41) records 1388 talents $1\frac{5}{6}$ minas as the total wool production from fat-tailed sheep in the year Shulgi 35. If we combine this with the text cited above from the following year which puts the total fat-tailed sheep population of Lagash at 66,095 sheep, dividing the number in the latter text by the amount of fleece listed in the former, then we arrive at a yield of 1.32 minas or 0.66 kg per animal. This figure is certainly too low since the total sheep population included lambs which would not have been plucked. By way of comparison, one should not look to the highly bred merinos of the modern day which yield 7–10 kg of fleece per animal. A figure of 0.78-0.907 kg is recorded for adult sheep in fourteenth-century England (Waetzoldt 1972:17), while the average in pre-1930 Palestine was 0.96 kg per animal. A 1.3–1.49 kg yield in Turkey, and a 1.59 kg yield in Iraq in 1947 have been recorded for fat-tailed sheep. The figures cited above for Ur III sheep, which range from 0.7 to 1.12 kg per animal, are perfectly respectable in comparison with other pre-modern data.

In contrast to both the present day and the Old Babylonian period when shearing is and was mainly a male occupation, the plucking of sheep fleece in the Ur III period was done exclusively by female workers (*géme*). One text from Girsu (TuT 164:19:11) mentions 816 female workers under a single inspector, while other texts from Ur record groups of 60 and 90 women. From Mari in the Old Babylonian period comes a request for an extra 300–400 men because the 150 men already mustered were insufficient, and a text from the time of Hammurapi says that 1000 men were not enough to carry out the annual fleece plucking (Waetzoldt 1972:14). It is difficult to say just what the significance of the change in gender roles from the Ur III to the Old Babylonian period signifies, and why the activity of fleece plucking should have been, apparently, such a gender-specific occupation in each period. To adequately understand the problem, however, would undoubtedly require a much broader look at gender roles across a range of professions in ancient Mesopotamia through time.

The texts which record fleece plucking give an indication of both wool yield and herd size. One Ur III text (HSS IV 37 rv. 15ff)) mentions 2259 sheep plucked in a single day (Waetzoldt 1972:14). If this is projected over a three-month period of plucking it would mean that a total of some 203,310 sheep were plucked in a season. This is by no means an unreasonable figure since a text from Ur (UET III 1504) records 12,500 talents (375,000 kg) of fat-tailed sheep wool which, based on the average yield per animal cited above (1.4 minas = 0.7 kg), implies the existence of roughly 535,714 animals.

The actual numbers of animals recorded are, however, much lower. A text from Drehem covering a four-year period mentions 347,394 sheep, which yields an average of 85,076 sheep annually. This figure, in fact, far exceeds the 66,095 fat-tailed sheep cited earlier (Lau 161), the 52,406 fat-tailed + 22,381 *gi*-sheep (total: 74,787) in TuT 27 or the 55,220 cited in ITT IV 7002, all of which come from Girsu. This variability in numbers of sheep is also a reflection of the size of the textile industry in different cities. Texts giving annual totals of fleece produced reflect the same variability. Thus, texts from Drehem (SET* 200) and Lagash (CT X 41) list over 1200 talents (36,000 kg) and 1377 talents (41,310 kg) of wool, respectively. In contrast, a text from Ur (UET III 1504) records no less than *c.* 13,900 talents (417,000 kg), suggesting that the textile industry there, or at least the standing herds of sheep, were more than ten times as large as those of Drehem and Lagash.

That these differences were real is borne out by marked differences in the amount of rations given out to employees of the textile industry. One text from Ur (UET III 1504) lists 1148 talents (34,440 kg) of wool which were distributed as rations to male and female dependents/workers (temple functionaries, agricultural workers, fishermen, shepherds, messengers) of the Nanna-Ningal temple complex. Working on the premise that the standard annual wool ration was 4 minas (2 kg) per person (Gelb 1965:235), this means that *c.* 17,220 people were given wool rations. Although not all of these individuals were involved in textile production, it is clear that the flock management, the plucking and treatment of the fleece and the eventual weaving implied by the tons of fleece produced annually presupposes textile production on an industrial scale in the Ur III period.

Textile factories are attested in cuneiform sources in seven cities during the Ur III period, including Alsharraki, Lagash, Nippur, Puzrish-Dagan (Drehem), Umma, Ur and Uruk. Their personnel included an inspector in overall charge of the operation, followed by foremen in charge of each category of labourer and finally by the weavers, fullers, basket-makers, bearers, scribes and attendants/servants of the weavers. The weavers themselves (Fig. IV.1) made up the largest group of labourers. These were exclusively females, supplemented by children. Texts from Girsu listing the size of the weaving establishment there mention 1097 female weavers and 626 children in the year Shulgi 48, 1051 weavers in the following year, Amar-Sin 1 and 1019 weavers and 686 children in the year Amar-Sin 9 (Waetzoldt 1972:93). The women who made up this labour force were a mixture of prisoners-of-war (Gelb 1973:70–98), slaves and free persons. Some were *arua* (Gelb 1972:1–32), i.e. people 'given' or dedicated to a temple as a human votive offering by a complete cross-section of society which, in this case, included fishermen, fullers, Amorites, silversmiths, merchants, prefects and even the city governor. In addition to actual weaving, weavers were expected to perform additional tasks such as fleece plucking, field and canal work, towing boats and transporting reeds.

Figure IV.1 Depiction of women weaving (?) on a cylinder seal of Late Uruk or Jamdat Nasr date (after Amiet 1961: Pl. 19.319)

Without doubt the largest weaving mill in the territory of Lagash was the one at Guabba where, according to one text (HSS IV 3) 4272 female weavers and over 1800 children were employed. When we add to this the other personnel of the textile factory, principally the foremen, fullers, basket-makers and attendants, then it becomes clear that well over 6200 people were employed in one establishment. This deduction, moreover, is borne out by the amounts of barley received by the supervisor, 680 and 475 *gur* on two different occasions (total: 204,000 l + 142,500 l = 346,500 l), which would have provided monthly barley rations for thousands of women and children. If we use an average monthly ration of 30 l of barley per adult female worker, and 15 l per child, then the number of workers listed above in HSS IV 3 required 128,160 l for the women (4272 workers) and 27,000 l for the children (1800 workers), for a total of 155,160 l of barley or just over 517 *gur*. All in all Waetzoldt estimates that over 15,000 people worked in textile factories in the territory of Lagash alone (Waetzoldt 1972:99). This figure is comparable only to that attested at the capital

Ur itself during the Ur III period when an estimated 13,200 weavers under 60 foremen are attested (Waetzoldt 1972:99).

Texts dealing with actual weaving show that pieces up to 4.5 m wide and 20 m long could be woven in the Ur III textile factories, as compared with a maximum breadth of 1.8 m in Egypt (Waetzoldt 1972:131). An indication of the output of finished textiles is provided by two broken summary texts from Ur which list the amount of finished textiles delivered to the fullers, i.e. those whose job it was to tread and beat the woven cloth in order to clean and thicken it. This amounts to 5800 pieces of *c.* 155 talents (4650 kgs) total weight, but as over half of the text is lost, one can probably reckon with a total of *c.* 10–12,000 pieces. This figure, however, should probably be doubled again as the text concerns only two overseers, whereas the names of at least two more are known.

Finally, one should not underestimate the labour and raw material requirements of the fullers who cleaned the finished cloth after it had been woven. It is estimated that roughly 7.7 work days were required by the fullers to treat each kilogram of finished cloth. Depending on the type of cloth being treated, greater or lesser amounts of oil and alkali were needed, varying somewhat in ratio from 1:5.5 to 1:4 (i.e. oil: alkali) per kilogram of cloth (Waetzoldt 1972:159). Considering the fact, as noted above, that annual textile production in individual cities ran to tens of tons, it should be clear that enormous quantities of oil and alkali were consumed in the textile factories of southern Mesopotamia.

Leather

Outside of Egypt, leather is rarely preserved on archaeological sites in Western Asia, although the remains of small leather bags, discovered in Neo-Babylonian double-jar burials at Uruk, have recently been published, and a similar practice is attested in roughly contemporary, post-Assyrian graves at Assur (van Ess and Pedde 1992:223). In contrast to the dearth of archaeological evidence, however, a considerable amount of information is available on the tanning of hides in cuneiform sources, particularly during the Ur III and Isin-Larsa periods. This has been studied by a number of scholars. Sources from Isin have been analysed by the late Vaughn Crawford (Crawford 1948) and Marc Van De Mieroop (Van De Mieroop 1987); material from Umma and Drehem has been collected by Marcel Sigrist (Sigrist 1981:141–90; 1992:396–8), while Marten Stol has written an overview of the leather industry in all periods (Stol 1983:527–43).

Sheep, goat, cattle and ass/donkey provided the bulk of the hides tanned in ancient Mesopotamia, followed by pig. Among the rarer hides used were wild boar, buck (?) and gazelle. Deer, mountain goat, aurochs and bear hides are never mentioned, although the animals themselves are. The animals which provided the hides had sometimes died accidentally or been attacked by wild dogs. In some cases, however, they had been intentionally slaughtered for their skins. Generally speaking, the number of hides referred to in the cuneiform texts seems low. Composite records of deliveries of skins from cattle herders, shepherds and farmers, summarized on a single tablet, suggest an annual intake of *c.* 2150 skins from a single agricultural sector at Umma but Sigrist suspects that this is well below the real total in any given year (Sigrist 1981:151).

As is to be expected from the complexity of the tanning process, the tanner (Sum. *ašgab*, Akk. *aškapum*) in Mesopotamia was a specialized craftsman. During the Old Babylonian period the leatherworker was often attached to a particular palace, though he sometimes made goods for private individuals as well (Renger 1984:88). Some of the late lexical sources name specialists such as the 'tanner for shields', 'tanner for doors', 'whip maker', and 'shoe-maker' (Stol 1983:529). Traditionally, tanning in preindustrial societies was performed in three ways: by the addition of minerals, such as alum or potassium, using oils or by employing vegetable matter, such as gall nuts which are rich in tannin. According to ethnohistoric and ancient sources, two methods have been traditionally favoured in Western Asia. The so-called 'primitive' method involves using salt, sour milk or flour to remove the hair, and pomegranate skins or plant roots to perform the actual tanning. The 'industrial' method uses calcium to take off the hair and gall nuts, oak bark, sumac or alum for tanning. Several ritual texts give recipes for tanning goat and cattle hides. In treating goat hides, the hair was removed using milk and flour. Oil and fat were then rubbed into the skin, followed by alum dissolved in grape juice. In treating cattle hides, the hide was put in flour and then bathed alternately in water, beer and wine. It was then placed in a mixture of ghee (clarified butter), aromatic plants and flour. Finally, it was dyed with alum (Stol 1983:530). As anyone who has been near a tannery knows, tanning is an industry which makes its presence felt in the environs through some oftentimes fearsome odours. For that reason, as well as for reasons of economic expediency, tanning is often concentrated in particular quarters and we know from cuneiform sources that in the Achaemenid period there were tanning quarters in both Uruk and Nippur. In fact, there must have been tanning quarters in many if not all of the major cities.

Leather goods were destined for a wide variety of uses in Mesopotamian society. At Umma during the Ur III period leather products as well as other edible and inedible goods were offered to deities as part of the so-called *sattukkum* system (cf. Chapter VIII). This consisted of presenting offerings first to the deity and thereafter redistributing them to high-ranking members of the community, e.g. to the governor of the city (*šakkanakkum*), to two temples for use in several doors, to the *ensí* for his chariots, to the head of the tanning establishment and to several other people of seemingly high rank (Sigrist 1981:179). Three interesting summary texts covering, in two cases, twelve months and in the third case five months in the years Shulgi 37, 39 and 40 record the distribution of 1155, 563 and 1146 skins, respectively, to over a dozen deities at Umma. These were most probably redistributed thereafter to temple officials, just as food offerings to deities were (cf. Chapter VIII).

Functionally speaking, tanned leather was used in the manufacture and decoration of boats, chariots, doors, chairs, thrones, harnesses and reins (Sigrist 1981:184), protective padding on the yoke of oxen (cf. Chapter III) in order to protect them from injury, transport and storage sacks for water, wine, salt, seed, flour, spices or herbs (*mun-gazi*) and shoes, sandals and boots (Stol 1983:536, 542). Messengers, much used during the Ur III period (Sigrist 1986:51–63), were given a standard issue of leather sandals, boots and water bags before embarking on a journey, as were caravans.

Bone

Animal bone was used throughout the Old World for making a wide variety of tools and non-utilitarian objects from the Palaeolithic era onwards. It is surely not correct to say, as has sometimes been implied, that bone objects were of little importance in Mesopotamia after the third millennium BC, with the exception of mid-second millennium Nuzi (Liebowitz 1980–1983:43). This impression is undoubtedly the result of several biases. The contexts excavated have not always been those in which bone objects might be expected to occur; techniques of recovery have not favoured the recovery of small, fragile objects of bone; and publication of one of the largest bodies of evidence, that of Uruk, has only just occurred. While it is not correct to say that all periods are equally well represented in the corpus, bone objects do occur throughout Mesopotamian history.

For the most part studies of bone objects in Mesopotamia give no indication of which animals were most exploited. However, it is most likely that sheep/goat, followed by cattle, equids and swine provided the bulk of the bone used to fashion implements and decorative fixtures.[4] At Uruk, from which perhaps the largest collection of bone objects in southern Mesopotamia has been recovered (Fig. IV.2), bone was used for decorative inlays (Jamdat Nasr, Early Dynastic, Neo-Babylonian, Seleucid-Parthian periods), figurines (Parthian period), needles (Ubaid, Uruk, Early Dynastic, Parthian periods), spindles (Uruk, Seleucid-Parthian period), spindle whorls (Neo-Babylonian, Seleucid-Parthian period), spatulas (Seleucid-Parthian period), dagger handles (Neo-Babylonian period), combs (Seleucid-Parthian period), rings (Kassite period) and dice (Old Babylonian (?), Seleucid-Parthian periods) (van Ess and Pedde 1992:187–219). Knucklebones (*astragali*) were also used to play a game which was probably ancestral to those played widely through Western Asia to this day (van Ess and Pedde 1992:187–8; cf. Boehmer and Wrede 1985:399–404).

MINERAL PRODUCTS

Clay

As shown in Chapter I, clay is a major constituent of the sediment deposited whenever the Tigris and Euphrates flood their banks. In Chapter VI the dominant clay-based industry in ancient Mesopotamia, pottery production, will be discussed separately. Here, however, it should be noted that in addition to pottery, a wide range of other utilitarian items, including spindle whorls, sling balls, mullers, hammers, hoes, axes and sickles (Anderson-Gerfaud 1983:177–91; Benco 1992:119), as well as figurines (both anthropomorphic and zoomorphic), beads and cones for wall decoration were made of clay.

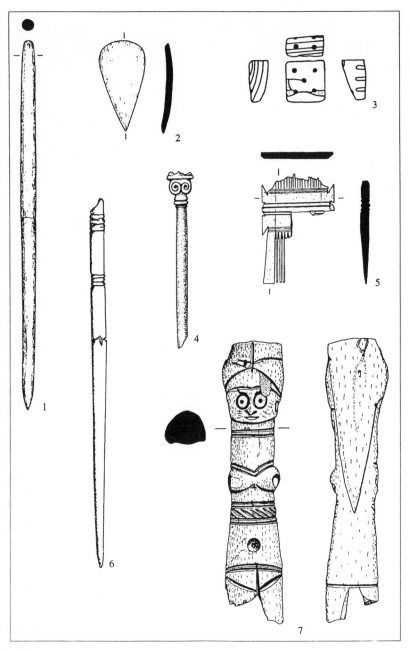

Figure IV.2 A selection of bone objects from Uruk. 1. needle, Ubaid period, 16.4 cm long, 0.7 cm dia. (after Lindemeyer and Martin 1993: Taf. 106.1740); 2. tear-drop shaped spatula (?), Ubaid period, 4 cm long, 2.3 cm max. width, 0.3 cm thick (after Lindemeyer and Martin 1993: Taf. 109.1778); 3. die, Old Babylonian (?), 1.9 cm on a side (after van Ess and Pedde 1992: Taf. 126.1524); 4. pin with Ionic capital head, Achaemenid/Seleucid, 7.8 cm long, 0.58 cm dia. (after van Ess and Pedde 1992: Taf. 127.1536); 5. comb, Seleucid/Parthian, 4.6 x 3.5 x 0.4 cm (after van Ess and Pedde 1992: Taf. 126.1517); 6. needle, Seleucid/Parthian, 16.5 cm long, 0.7 cm dia. (after van Ess and Pedde 1992: Taf. 124.1493); 7. figurine, Parthian, 12.7 cm long, 3 cm wide (after van Ess and Pedde 1992: Taf. 119.1437)

Bitumen

Alongside baked mudbrick and limestone (see below), the most durable material available in ancient Mesopotamia was without doubt bitumen or asphalt (Sum. *esír*, Akk. *ittû* (unrefined), *kupru* (dry), *qīru* (fresh)) (Schmid 1981:116). Various sources of bitumen were exploited in antiquity, principally in the area of modern Khuzistan on either side of the Karun river, in the east Tigris region heading towards the Zagros mountains, around Ur, near Mosul and in the Hit-Ramadi area on the Middle Euphrates. The bitumen used in the recent past in southern Mesopotamia has traditionally been gathered at bitumen seeps near Hit (Fig. IV.3; cf. the Akkadian word for bitumen, *ittû*),[5] attested in the Middle Assyrian annals of Tukulti-

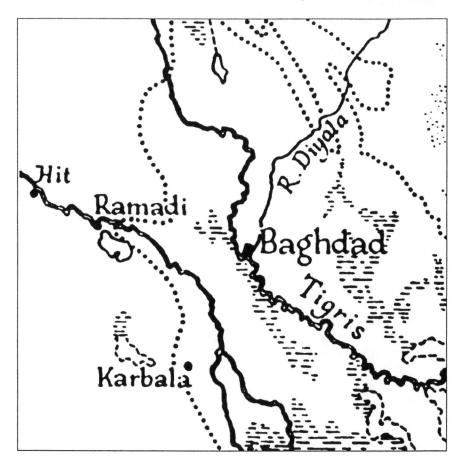

Figure IV.3 Map showing the location of Hit (after Lees and Falcon 1952: Fig. 1)

Ninurta as 'The town of *Id*, at the bitumen spring' (RGTC 5), and in Greek as *Is*, the source which Herodotus cites in describing the construction of the city wall of Babylon. According to Herodotus (*Hist.* I 179; Obermayer 1929:49ff.), the wall was constructed

> using throughout for their cement hot bitumen, and interposing a layer of wattled reeds at every thirtieth course of the bricks . . . The bitumen

used in the work was brought to Babylon from the Is, a small stream which flows into the Euphrates at the point where the city of the same name stands, eight days' journey from Babylon. Lumps of bitumen are found in great abundance in this river.

The river of bitumen, one assumes, was in fact a seep, and it is interesting that the excavations of the ziggurat of Babylon, the famous 'tower of Babel', have indeed confirmed the use of layers of bitumen up to 12 cm thick, apparently employed to hinder rising damp in a structure, the foundations of which were actually below the level of the surrounding water-table (Schmid 1981:101, 116).

Various designations exist for the sorts of bitumen which were used in different contexts, and a basic distinction seems to have obtained between 'dry bitumen' (*esír-HI.A*), measured by weight in *gú* or talents (30 kg) and types such as 'house bitumen' (*esír-é-a*), measured volumetrically in *gur* (300 *sìla/l*) (Powell 1990:497; Gelb 1982:589; Sollberger 1966:117). This distinction reflects the real difference between various forms of naturally occurring bitumen, which may be found as a solid, brittle lump, or thick fluid. In addition to its use in brickwork, bitumen was employed in a wide variety of other ways. According to cuneiform texts, figurines were made of it, doors were coated with it, boats and ships were caulked with it, baskets were waterproofed with it, stone masonry blocks were set in it, magic rituals employed it and medical ointments sometimes contained it (CAD I/J: 310-311, s.v. *ittû* A). Considerable quantities were used in the leather industry for waterproofing or at least coating sandals, and texts mentioning up to 290 *gur* (87,000 l) of bitumen destined for leatherworking factories are attested (Sigrist 1981:161). Many archaeological finds of bitumen from Uruk have been published, particularly from Uruk period contexts, when bitumen was employed for a wide variety of objects of uncertain function in geometric shapes, for bullae and jar stoppers and for maceheads (van Ess and Pedde 1992:127–33; cf. Lindemeyer and Martin 1993:241–52).

One of the domains for which we have the most information concerns the use of bitumen in boatbuilding and repair. Given the importance of water transport in an area like southern Mesopotamia this is certainly one of the most significant contexts in which bitumen was put to use. We shall discuss the use of bitumen for caulking watercraft in Chapter V.

Limestone

One of the most widely held beliefs about the southern Mesopotamian landscape is that it was entirely devoid of stone of any kind. It is commonplace to consider all objects of stone discovered on archaeological sites in southern Mesopotamia as imports from one of its neighbours, whether Anatolia, Iran or more distant regions such as Oman, Central Asia or the Indian subcontinent. In the case of limestone, however, this has now been recognized as a false presumption.

A wide variety of pendants, seals, beads, vessels and architectural elements were made of limestone throughout southern Mesopotamia's long history. During the Uruk and Jamdat Nasr periods most of the important religious buildings at Uruk, including the Limestone Temple (*Kalksteintempel*), the Stone Cone Temple (*Steinstifttempel*), the *Riemchengebäude*, Temple-Palace E and the Stone Building (*Steingebäude*) incorporated important elements of white, grey-white and yellow-white limestone in their fabric (Boehmer 1984:142). Some of these buildings were constructed on a limestone socle of blocks *c.* 10 cm thick and up to 60–80 cm in length. Although early excavators, such as Julius Jordan, assumed that all of the limestone used at Uruk must have come from hundreds of kilometres away in the Zagros mountains of Iran, the brilliant architectural historian Ernst Heinrich had observed as early as 1934 that the light grey limestone of the Late Uruk period temples was available at an outcrop only 60 km away from Uruk, and further that the same sort of distinctively coloured limestone had been used at Ur, a site considerably closer to the source (Heinrich 1934:46).

In 1962 another of the Uruk excavators, Heinrich Lenzen, noted that the large cement factories in southern Iraq at Samawa and Iskanderia quarried limestone from outcrops just beneath the alluvial deposits by the banks of the Euphrates near Samawa and el-Khidr. Finally, in 1983 R.M. Boehmer visited these outcrops (Fig. IV.4) for the first time and was immediately struck by the visual similarity between the stone visible at an outcrop called Ummayad some 25 km southwest of Samawa and that used at Uruk in the fourth millennium BC. The outcrop itself is only *c.* 50 km from Uruk, while

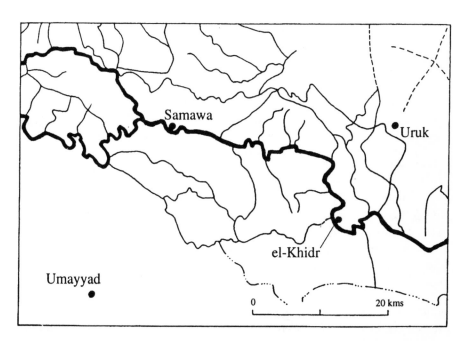

Figure IV.4 Map showing the location of the limestone outcrop at Umayyad in relation to Uruk (after Boehmer 1984: Abb. 1)

other sources are even closer. Moreover, the stone could have been transported by river back to Uruk, a far more likely means of carrying large slabs than overland transport from the Zagros mountains. Finally, petrographic analysis has shown that the stone from Ummayad is generally comparable to the limestone used in the Uruk temples, and there seems little doubt therefore that this was one of the sources used in antiquity for the limestone employed at Uruk (Boehmer 1984:146).[6] Although no signs of ancient stone quarrying have been identified, it is unlikely, given the activities of more recent stone quarriers, that such could be found at Ummayad.

Glassy Quartz (Rock Crystal)

One of the more neglected aspects in the study of the Bronze Age societies of Western Asia has been their lithic industries. Traditionally, when ceramics and metals came to be used extensively, less use was made of stone tools and prehistorians interested in lithics have not unnaturally tended to focus on those earlier societies with a greater abundance of material. As in the case of all other minerals, it has generally been assumed that whatever raw materials were used for stone tool manufacture in southern Mesopotamia must have been imported from outside the region. In the case of certain materials such as the volcanic glass known as obsidian (Inizan 1987:305–15) this is certainly true. Sometimes circumstantial evidence exists which, apart from the presumed provenience of the raw material itself, suggests that tool production was not local. One recent example of this is the Ubaid 3–4 site of Tell el-Saadiya in the Hamrin basin of northeastern Iraq, where the absence of all but two cores, the preponderance of already retouched blade blanks and the lack of any flint knapping areas, suggests to the excavators that the stone used there (overwhelmingly flint, small amounts of obsidian and rare instances of jasper) was all imported, some of it in finished or semi-finished form (Kozlowski 1987:281).

What was locally available at Tell el-Saadiya, however, was quartzite. Used exclusively for the quantitatively rare choppers and chopping tools, quartzite occurs 'in massive quantities on the low terrace of the Diyala in the vicinity of the site' (Kozlowski 1987:278). A similar situation, moreover, seems to have obtained at Tell Oueili in the south. In 1981, M-L. Inizan and J. Tixier discovered a workshop area *c.* 45 m in diameter on the northwest edge of the site where glassy quartz had been worked. Numerous pebbles, cores and débitage (waste flakes) were recovered along with finished, semi-finished and broken blades (Fig. IV.5). Contrary to the expectations of most scholars, Inizan and Tixier believe that the quartz used at Tell Oueili, and the flint as well, was picked up locally in the nearby alluvial deposits. Obsidian, also found at the site, was apparently the only imported material used in the lithic industry (Inizan and Tixier 1983:164–75). The examples of Tell el-Saadiya and Tell Oueili clearly show that, while the bulk of the stone used for the chipped stone industry in southern Mesopotamia may have been imported, whether in raw, semi-finished or finished form, locally available quartz and quartzite was used, at least in the Ubaid period, for the manufacture of stone tools.

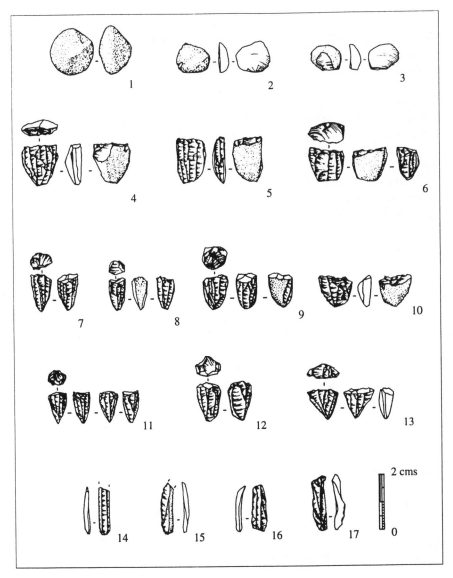

Figure IV.5 Glassy quartz pebbles, flakes, cores and blades from Tell Oueili (after Inizan and Tixier 1983: Fig. 6)

Salt

Of all the minerals available in the natural environment few have such serious dietary implications as salt (Sum. *mun*, Akk. *ṭābtu*).[7] Nevertheless, the acquisition of salt has generally been overlooked in studies of ancient Mesopotamian diet and economy. It is often assumed that free salt intake is unnecessary for hunting and gathering populations, and that it only becomes an issue once people have adopted an agricultural existence. Even so, experts disagree on the daily salt requirement of agriculturalists, estimates varying between 2 and 15 g per day.

Salt occurs naturally in various forms. It may be found in its crystalline form as rock salt, in a dissolved form in briny lakes or marshes (salines) or contained within certain halophytic plants. The processing of halophytic plants for the extraction of salt for human consumption is well documented in Africa, but is labour-intensive. Moreover, despite the fact that the Tigris and Euphrates carry large amounts of dissolved salt (cf. Chapter I), its extraction requires much more work than the removal of salt from the many salines which are found throughout Iraq (Fig. IV.6) for the simple reason that the intense summer heat reduces the brine in them by making the water evaporate, leaving only the salt behind. At this point, the salt can literally be 'harvested' (Potts 1984:253, n. 85). During the late nineteenth century salt was a state monopoly within the Ottoman Empire and, thanks to the records of the so-called Ottoman Public Debt Administration, the precise locations of all of the economically important salines in Mesopotamia along with their average annual yield in kg are known.

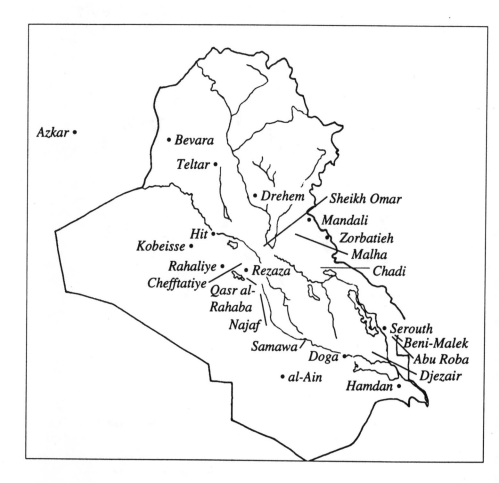

Figure IV.6 Salines in Mesopotamia exploited during the nineteenth century by Arab tribes on behalf of the Ottomans (after Potts 1984: Map 1)

In pre-Sargonic sources from Fara we find the profession of 'salt gatherer' (*mun-ur₄*) and in lexical sources an entry for the 'salt man' (*lú-mun*) occurs. Nevertheless, the relative infrequency of references to salt procurement in cuneiform texts suggests that, as in more recent times, salt was often gathered at salines by nomads who 'farmed' it and used it as a cash crop to sell or exchange for other goods which they lacked but which they could procure from town- and city-dwellers (Potts 1983:205–15). The 'salt bricks' mentioned in an Ur III text from Ur (UET III 1021) were probably brick-shaped blocks of salt cut from the salt beds at the saline of Samawa, one of the most important salines in the neighbourhood of Ur.

During the Ur III period the disbursement of leather bags to Amorites, at least some of whom may have continued to live as nomads on the western fringes of the Mesopotamian alluvium,[8] the occurrence of a variety of salt known as 'Amorite salt' and the existence of a lexical term for 'leather bag for salt' all suggest that nomadic groups may also have been employed by the Ur III state to gather salt. This is particularly interesting in that the Ottomans are known to have employed bedouin tribes at eight salines in Iraq to gather salt annually for the state monopoly system. Apparently, both states hit upon the same manpower solution to the problem of how to get salt from the salines to the state storehouses.

As for the uses of salt in ancient Mesopotamia, salt appears in a variety of medical prescriptions, religious rituals and cult meals. UET III 1498, an account of goods held in a goldsmith's workshop at Ur during the Ur III period, mentions 20 *sila*/l of salt, suggesting that cupellation was performed already at this early date. Cupellation is a technique of separating gold from silver whereby silver chloride is formed when the salt attacks the silver. The silver chloride is then absorbed into the walls of a crucible leaving only the gold behind. Salt was also employed in the tanning of hides and for the preservation of fish.

But it is as an additive to the human diet, particularly in an arid environment where salt loss through perspiration is a serious problem, that salt is most important. In this regard the texts which discuss the Old Akkadian reconstruction of the *é-kur* shrine at Nippur are particularly interesting (Westenholz 1987:24–7).[9] Some of these texts record the rations given to skilled and unskilled workmen, hundreds of whom were employed, including goldsmiths, sculptors, joiners, metalsmiths, inscription masons, common workmen and their foremen. According to these texts monthly rations of barley, dried fish and salt were given out in the amount of 0.5 *sila*/l of salt, 5 *sila*/l dried fish, and an illegible amount of barley for the workmen, and double that amount (1 *sila*/l salt, 10 *sila*/l dried fish) for the foremen. According to one text (OSP 2:9) 28,350 l of barley, 1820 l of dried fish, and 182 l of salt were received for 'the work camp' in the 'Month of [the] Early Hot Season'. Using the ration rates just mentioned, this would have been sufficient to 'pay' 364 workmen at the lower rate of 0.5 l of salt per person, although realistically some of the allotment would have been destined for foremen and superintendents of higher rank. Another, related text (OSP 2:11) lists 6 royal scribes, 35 foremen, 397 workmen and soldiers and at least 2 superintendents. The numbers of 'draft officers' and 'superintendents' mentioned at the end and beginning, respectively, are lost, as are about fifteen lines in the middle of the text. Of the men listed in the text, 397 received 0.5 l of salt, while 43 foremen and superintendents received 1 l of salt per person, thus requiring a total of 241.5 l of salt for the monthly ration allowance.

Some idea of daily intake can be gained by considering this quantity in light of modern recommended requirements. Nowadays a 1 kg bag of refined salt amounts to 0.8 l of dry volume, so that the amount in question, 241.5 l, represents *c.* 301.875 kg of salt. Thus, a 0.5 l ration would have weighed 0.625 kg, while a l l ration would have equalled 1.25 kg. Assuming a 30-day month, these figures imply daily free salt intake averaging 20.83 and 41.66 g, respectively for the workmen and their supervisors. As these figures far exceed the 12–15 g currently recommended for an adult with a mixed diet, however, it might also be suggested that the salt rations were intended for the entire family of the workman who received them.[10] The fact that the ration texts date to the 'Month of (the) Early Hot Season' might also help explain why these salt rations were so high.

Minor Minerals

In addition to salt and limestone numerous other minor minerals were employed for industrial purposes in southern Mesopotamia, though whether all of these originated locally is difficult to ascertain. Among these we may mention *annuharum*,[11] a 'mineral dye' or mordant used to produce white colour in both the tanning (Sigrist 1981:157) and textile industries (Waetzoldt 1972:174, n. 128). Eventually, this seems to have been replaced by *gabûm*, generally identified with alum (Levey 1958:166–9; Stol 1983:534). Another substance used in large quantities in textile factories as a cleansing agent was *im-babbar$_x$* (lit. 'white earth') probably identical to fuller's earth. Ur III records of deliveries list quantities of between 5 and 16 talents (150–480 kg), and it is estimated that roughly 0.154 kg of this substance was needed to clean 1 kg of fabric (Waetzoldt 1972:173). Unfortunately, none of the cuneiform sources give us any indication of where these substances originated. Fuller's earth is a montmorillonite clay with low aluminium content which absorbs oil and has traditionally been used to degrease fleeces, and was undoubtedly locally available, for the clays of southern Mesopotamia are, by and large, of the montmorillonite variety (Jacobs 1992:132).

VEGETABLE PRODUCTS

Timber

Given the nature of the environment of southern Mesopotamia, it is hardly surprising that wood has only rarely been preserved in archaeological contexts. Indeed the wood varieties attested on archaeological sites (Table IV.1)[12] are limited and irregularly represented both in space and time. Nevertheless, at the time of writing over a dozen species have been identified archaeologically, although it is still difficult in most cases to link the names of trees attested in the cuneiform sources with those of modern tree

Common Name	Species Identification	Sum./Akk. names[1]	Site	Period
ash	*Fraxinus syriaca*	uncertain	Larsa	Hell.
box	*Buxus sempervirens*	ᵍⁱˢ*taškarin, taškarinnum?*	Nuzi	Middle Bab.
cedar	*Cedrus libani*	ᵍⁱˢ*eren, erenum*	Nuzi[2]	Middle Bab.
Christ's thorn	*Ziziphus* cf. *spina-christi*	uncertain	Uruk	Ur III/Old Bab.
cypress	*Cupressus sempervirens*	ᵍⁱˢ*šu-úr-man, šurmīnum*	Ur	Neo-Bab.
fig	*Ficus sp.*	*pèš, tittum*	Uruk	Neo-Bab.
mulberry	*Morus alba*	uncertain[3]	Uruk	L. Uruk/JN
			Nimrud	Neo-Ass.
oak	*Quercus sp.*	ᵍⁱˢ*ha-lu-úb, haluppum?*	Jarmo	Neolithic
			Nimrud	Neo-Ass.
palm	*Phoenix dactylifera*	ᵍⁱˢ*gišimmar, gišimmarum*	Eridu[4]	Ubaid
			Tell Oueili	Ubaid
			Nippur	?
			Nuzi	Middle Bab.
			Larsa	Neo-Bab.
			Uruk	Neo/Late Bab.
			Abu Qubur	Ach.
pine	*Pinus sp.*	*asūhum*	Tel ed-Der	Old Bab.
			Nimrud	Neo-Ass.
			Ur	Neo-Bab.
poplar	*Populus sp.* (in some cases *Euphratica*)[5]	ᵍⁱˢ*asal, ṣarbatum*	Tell Oueili	Ubaid
			Tell Mefesh	Ubaid
			Abu Salabikh?	ED III
			Tell ed-Der	Old Bab.
			Nuzi	Middle Bab.
			Uruk	Neo-Bab.
			Larsa	Hell.
tamarisk	*Tamarix sp.*	ᵍⁱˢ*šinig, bīnum*	Arpachiyah	Halaf
			Tell Oueili	Ubaid
			Abu Salabikh	ED III
			Tell ed-Der	Old Bab.
			Larsa	Neo-Bab., Hell.
walnut	*Juglans regia*	uncertain[6]	Nimrud	Neo-Ass.
			Uruk	Neo-Bab.
willow	*Salix sp.*	ᵍⁱˢ*ma-nu, e'rum*[7] ᵍⁱˢ*šà-kal, šakkullum*	Tell Mefesh	Ubaid
			Abu Salabikh?	ED III

[1] After Van De Mieroop 1992:155–61.
[2] Unsubstantiated identifications have also been made on samples from fourth-millennium Uruk, and Neo-Assyrian Khorsabad and Nimrud.
[3] Postgate 1992:185–6.
[4] Unsubstantiated identifications have also been made on samples from Old Babylonian Uruk and Kassite Nippur.
[5] Taken as certain by Steinkeller 1987:91.
[6] Postgate 1992:185–6.
[7] Identification favoured by Steinkeller 1987:92.

Table IV.1 *Woods attested archaeologically in Mesopotamia*

species. Indeed economic texts (Table IV.2) contain many more names of tree types than we can posit sound identifications for, while lexical sources list the names of upwards of 550 trees and woody plants (Powell 1987:145–51).

Wood was employed for a wide variety of purposes in southern Mesopotamia. At Umma in the Ur III period logs, roof-beams, levers, pegs, pointed sticks, rungs, posts, rods for reed buckets, planks, boards, boat ribs, hoes,

Tree	Attestations	Species	Habitats: Forests (*tir*)	Plantations (*kiri₆*)	Edges of fields (*ašag_x*)
asal₂	38	*Populus euphratica?* (poplar)	15	14	–
gi gíd	9	?	–	9	–
gul-bu	14	?	–	11	–
hašhur	15	*Pyrus malus?* (apple)	–	11	–
ildag_x	9	a poplar?	–	9	–
še-du₁₀	13	?			
šinig	21	a tamarisk?	–	3	12
ù-suh₅	16	a pine?	–	7	–
giš bar₆-bar₆	3	'white tree'	–	–	–
gipar_x	3	?	–	–	–
GÍRgunû	2	?	–	–	–
giš gíd-gíd	1	?	–	–	–
gišimmar	2	*Phoenix dactylifera* (date palm)	–	–	–
ma-nu	1	a willow?	–	–	–
mes bar₆-bar₆	2	?	–	–	–
mes ha-lu-úb	4	?	–	–	–
taškarin	4	*Buxus?* (boxwood)	–	–	–

Table IV.2 *Trees in the pre-Sargonic 'timber' texts from Tello*

hoe blades, ploughshares, sickle handles and boat keels of wood are all attested (Steinkeller 1987:73–115). A wide range of functions is also found at pre-Sargonic Girsu (Table IV.3). Let us examine for a moment the use of wood for architectural/structural support in Mesopotamia.

Tree	Common Name	Wood Used For
asal₂	poplar	timber, firewood, parts of the plough, planks for boats, handles (e.g. for axes), ladder rungs, parts of wagons or carts, pestles (?), cabinets (?), yokes for oxen, steering oars
gi gíd	?	firewood, boards/beams, beds, spear shafts, steering oars, parts of boats
gul-bu	?	branches, firewood, ploughs, poles, spear shafts, beds, steering oars, carts, cabinets
hašhur	apple	trunks, branches, pegs of many kinds (e.g. for wagons or carts), ribs for carts
ildag_x	a poplar?	ploughs, beds, containers (?)
še-du₁₀	?	bows, pegs, cart poles
šinig	tamarisk?	–
ù-suh₅	a pine?	ship timbers, boats, planks, poles, steering oars, spear shafts
giš bar₆-bar₆	'white tree'	–
gipar_x	?	smeared with bitumen it was used as some sort of boat equipment
GÍRgunû	?	–
giš gíd-gíd	?	–
gišimmar	date palm	(fruit production, fibres)
ma-nu	a willow?	–
mes bar^{giš}-bar₆	?	–
mes ha-lu-úb	?	–
taškarin	boxwood	–

Table IV.3 *Uses of wood according to the pre-Sargonic 'timber' texts from Tello*

Wood was employed for roof-beams, uprights/pillars for support, balconies, doors, lintels, stairways, shelves and wainscoting (Margueron 1992:82). Given the size of some of the monumental temples and palaces excavated in Mesopotamia one must naturally ask how ancient builders managed to cope with the structural problems they must have encountered. For example, as J.-Cl. Margueron has noted, the central cella of the Late Uruk period Limestone Temple (Fig. IV.7) at Uruk is *c.* 11 m wide, a span which most probably surpasses the size of any available beams (Margueron 1992:87). In analysing the Old Babylonian Sinkashid palace at Uruk (Fig. IV.8), Margueron has classified the spaces which had to be spanned by bearers into different length categories. Taking the building as a whole, and allowing for a distance of 50 cm between beams, the numbers of beams required to roof the palace would have been as follows:

Beam Size (m)	Quantity Required	Total Number of Lineal Metres
4–5	520	2080–2600
5–7	550–600	2750–4200
7–9	300	2100–2700
10	50	500
12	190	2280
5 m elements	380	4680

This amounts to a maximum of 16,820 lineal m (16.82 km) of wood to roof the palace if the beams were 50 cm apart, or about half that amount if we extend the interval to 1 m, assuming of course that the building was only a single storey (Margueron 1992:92). Given the fact that Nur-Adad built a similarly sized palace at Larsa in the same period, Margueron wonders that the requisite timber existed in the region. He also notes that the Neo-Babylonian king Nabonidus says specifically that he *imported* 5000 cedar trunks for his reconstruction of the temple at Sippar (Margueron 1992:93), emphasizing the lack of any exotic woods such as this (which probably came from Lebanon) locally. The apparent resource-poverty of southern Mesopotamia, particularly with respect to wood, would suggest that all of the common wood employed in temples and palaces of this sort must have been imported, presumably from the Iranian highlands, with the more exotic woods coming from India, Anatolia, Lebanon, etc. Yet this is patently incorrect, as the cuneiform sources from pre-Sargonic Girsu and Ur III Umma clearly demonstrate.

Approximately 150 texts from Girsu deal with wood in one form or another (Powell 1992:99–122). Generally speaking, these texts fall into four categories. Some sixty-five deal with wood on hand or in storage, i.e. not freshly cut or growing; approximately forty texts concern 'wood newly cut from the marsh woodlands, from tree plantations ("gardens"), or from the dikes surrounding fields and farms' (Powell 1992:100); seven texts deal with 'wood counted where it grows (*or*: has grown)', called *giš ki mú-a-ba šid-da*; and another forty texts refer to tools, vehicles and other objects made of wood.

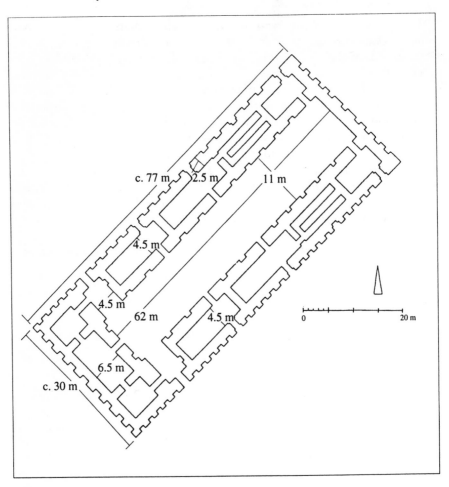

Figure IV.7 Plan of the Limestone Temple at Uruk, showing width spans of individual spaces, in metres (after Margueron 1992: Fig. 1)

It is clear from these texts that different types of trees were grown in different areas. Some were grown in forests/woods (*tir*) and in plantations/ gardens (*kiri$_6$*) ; others were grown along the sides of fields (*asag$_x$*) and in plantations (*kiri$_6$*); still others were grown only in plantations (*kiri$_6$*). The areas involved were often small in comparison with the large tracts of land devoted to cereal cultivation. Thus, three texts relating to three different years within a six-year time-span concern, on two occasions, the harvest of areas of 3 *iku* (1.08 ha) and on one occasion 0.5 *iku* (0.9 ha). Not surprisingly the forests produced the largest timbers, while most of the wood used for objects came from the plantations.

As Powell notes, 'Riverain woodlands were probably "wild" only in the sense that they were not planted, for those about which we have information were clearly the property of the state or temple, and we may assume that cutting timber was a prerogative that was just as jealously guarded in the Presargonic period as in Hammurabi's time, when unauthorized felling of trees could cost one one's life' (Ebeling 1932:439; cf. Powell 1992:120).[13]

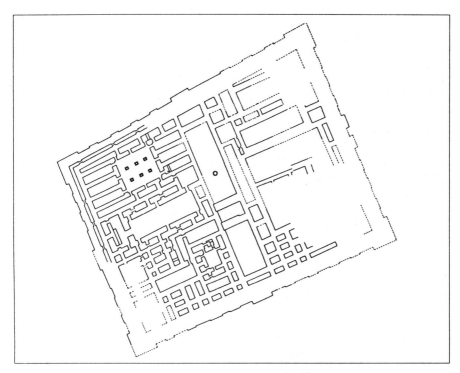

Figure IV.8 Plan of the palace of Sinkashid at Uruk (after Margueron 1992: Fig. 5)

This being the case, it is hardly surprising that the wooded stands around Girsu were managed by professional foresters, just as they were at Umma in the Ur III period. In general these specialists were called *lú tir*, literally 'forest man', although several tamarisk plantations along the dikes which separated the irrigation canals from the fields were managed by another set of specialists called *lú šinig*, literally 'tamarisk man'. While some of the foresters received land from the temple for use as prebends (i.e. as a sort of stipend), others seem to have been sharecroppers (Powell 1992:105). Texts dealing with soldiers show that the Girsu foresters were meant to perform military duty, while agricultural texts show that they were also called upon to participate in dike construction and harvesting. The Girsu foresters probably paid nominal taxes in the form of 'presents' brought to religious festivals.

It is obvious that all human settlements of whatever size have an insatiable capacity for consuming fuel and when industrial uses, such as ceramic production, ore reduction, and metals casting are added to normal household consumption for cooking and heating, the problem of fuel sources can become acute. This is especially the case in those arid portions of Western Asia which have little in the way of forest cover. In some cases, as we know from historical and palynological sources, deforestation has occurred in areas which were formerly well wooded (Brice 1978:141–7). In other instances it is likely that, where wood was scarce and/or expensive, animal dung cakes were burned in place of wood (Miller 1984:45–7; cf. Ochsenschlager 1993:37). Without denying that dung may have been widely used in ancient Mesopotamia as a source of fuel, it is clear from the Girsu texts that both 'large and small firewood', most of which seems to have been poplar, was harvested in the local vicinity of the site. Moreover, several texts refer to the stacking of wood in piles, sorted by length, for seasoning,[14] as well as to its transport by raft or boat.

Turning now to the Ur III material from Umma, P. Steinkeller has recently studied seventy-three texts detailing the activities of about sixty foresters (*lú tir*) working in the riverain thickets or copses near the site. These men belonged to a class called *erín*, meaning 'colonist' (both foreign and local), which constituted an important source of labour during the Ur III period. As at pre-Sargonic Girsu, the Umma foresters could be called upon to serve as soldiers when so required. Otherwise, they seem to have worked and received rations for part of the year, and held land allotments on a prebendary basis for the rest of the year (Steinkeller 1987:75).

A text from the last month of the year Amar-Sin 8 records an inspection under the authority of the governor of Umma, the purpose of which was 'assessment of the foresters' manpower to determine the volumes of barley and wool needed to sustain them during the coming year' (Steinkeller 1987:76). This text reveals that there were thirty forests scattered throughout the province of Umma. Each was under the supervision of one overseer who in turn supervised three foremen in charge of ten gangs of workers. As Steinkeller writes (Steinkeller 1987:101):

> Although we know that the riverain thickets of Southern Iraq have been utilized, more or less haphazardly, from ancient through modern times, it is only in the Ur III period that one finds evidence for planned and organized exploitation of this ecological niche. The intricate nature of the organization and operation of the Umma forest sector and the existence of specific quotas of forest products which the foresters were required to collect demonstrate that we are dealing here with a highly purposeful and coordinated economic activity directed toward controlled exploitation of the resources in question.

The yield of the Umma forests was certainly substantial. One text (no. 60) covering a period of seven years (Amar-Sin 8-Shu-Sin 5) reveals that no less than 7390 talents (223 tons) of *ma-nu* wood was harvested in that time. Another (no. 12) concerns a single delivery of 88 talents (2.64 tons) of *ma-nu* wood. The purpose of the 10,800 pointed sticks mentioned in another pair of texts (nos. 9 and 12) is unknown. Were they used for fencing, or as weapons (Fig. IV.9)? As far as contributing to the boatbuilding industry at Umma, one text (no. 47) lists the delivery of 810 boat ribs and 59,290 pegs of *ma-nu* wood. Furthermore, in addition to wood the foresters of Umma were responsible for providing literally tons of grass cut as fodder. A single text (no. 55), for example, notes 60 talents (1.8 tons) of *ù-su-uš* grass (Steinkeller 1987:102–15 for text references).

From an archaeological point of view it is clear that both the Girsu and Umma wood and forestry texts reveal the existence of a rich and variegated material culture in wood, little of which has survived. Yet on a few points the written and archaeological sources are broadly comparable. Thus, at pre-Sargonic Girsu (Table IV.3) poplar was used for axe handles according to the cuneiform sources, while a slightly later Old Akkadian grave at Nuzi has yielded fragments of an adze handle identified as boxwood (Starr 1939:494). While the overwhelming majority of the surviving wood (and some of the charcoal) fragments from most sites in Mesopotamia, such as Ur, Nimrud, Nuzi, Larsa, Nippur, Abu Qubur and Abu Salabikh, represent structural, architectural elements (mainly roof-beams) (Moorey and Postgate 1992:197–8), Uruk has yielded an interesting inventory of wooden objects, mainly from Neo-Babylonian double-jar burials, which reveals something of the wide range of uses to which wood was put in ancient Mesopotamia (van Ess and Pedde 1992:177–86, Taf. 103–10). Alongside many small pieces of geometric and floral inlay, probably from boxes, are interesting examples of small figurines, vessel fragments, boxes, vessels and a dagger handle which terminates in a carefully carved bull's head (Fig. IV.10).

In conclusion, the texts discussed above should dispel once and for all the notion that southern Mesopotamia was bereft of any useful wood, or any building materials other than mudbrick, bitumen and reeds (see

Figure IV.9 Man with a pointed object (stick?) over his shoulder, from an early ED I seal impression found in SIS 4 at Ur (after Amiet 1961: Pl. 58.791)

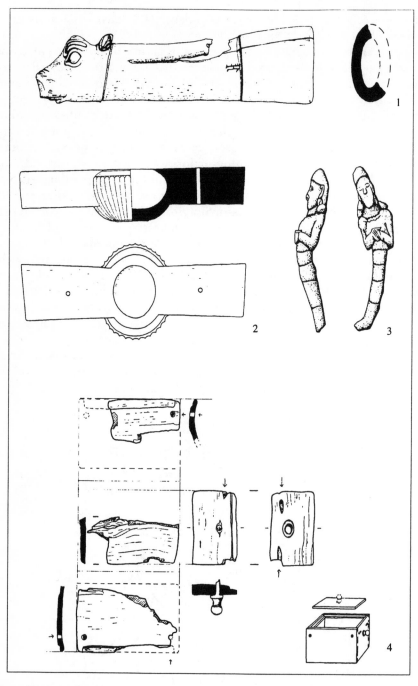

Figure IV.10 A selection of wooden objects from Neo-Babylonian Uruk. 1. dagger handle made of walnut with bull's head terminal, 17 cm long, 3 cm high (after van Ess and Pedde 1992: Taf. 103b-c); 2. two-handled bowl, species uncertain, 21.1 cm long, 7.5 cm max. width, 4.1 cm thick (after van Ess and Pedde 1992: Taf. 106.1333); 3. anthropomorphic figurine, species uncertain, 6 cm high, 1.8 cm max. width (after van Ess and Pedde 1992: Taf. 104.1330); 4. fragmentary, rectangular box made of pistachio, 6 x 4.3 x 3.3 cm (after van Ess and Pedde 1992: Taf. 108.1335)

below). The fact that the most durable objects of antiquity – brick buildings, stone cylinder seals, beads, vessels and statuary or figurines and tablets of baked clay – have been found in superabundance on sites in Mesopotamia should not blind us to the fact that wood, like textiles, leather, reeds and other perishable materials, played an important role in the material life of the region.

Reeds

As H.St.J.B. Philby wrote of his sojourn amongst the Marsh Arabs in southern Mesopotamia in 1917, 'Their staple product was, however, the reeds of the marshes, always in great demand among the tribes themselves . . . an easy crop requiring no more than the cutting and bundling, and renewing itself each year without human attention' (Philby 1959:66–7). The marshes of southern Mesopotamia are rich in the common reed (*Phragmites australis*) (Hepper 1992:193), and this was without doubt the basic reed (Sum. *gi*) exploited in antiquity (Waetzoldt 1992:125). Reed was used extensively for fodder, for the manufacture of baskets and mats (Goetze 1948:165–202), in house, canal and boat construction, and as fuel. Microwear studies of Ubaid period clay sickles from Tell Oueili have suggested that these common tools could have been used for cutting reeds (Anderson-Gerfaud 1983:177–91), and a new study of their distribution in southern Mesopotamia suggests that this may indeed have been their primary function, rather than having been used to harvest cereals as was long assumed (Benco 1992:119–34). Clay sickles virtually identical to their Ubaid forerunners were in use during the Late Uruk period as well (Fig. IV.11) (Finkbeiner 1985:37). Later, during the Old Babylonian period, reeds were cut with a bronze or copper tool (*urudu ha-bu-da*) (Waetzoldt 1992:128).

Like forestry, reed cutting was organised and controlled by institutions such as the state during the Ur III period (Waetzoldt 1992:125–46) and the Nanna-Ningal temple complex at Ur in the Old Babylonian era (Van De Mieroop 1992:147–53). Overseers, foremen and common workmen were employed to cut bundles (*sa-gi*) which were then amassed into loads (*gú gi*) or bales (*gu-kilib*). Although reed was usually referred to without further specification, some distinctive types are mentioned, such as 'green' or 'fodder' (*gi-zi*) and 'split' (*šid*) reed. 'Fodder' reed is so called because of its extensive use as sheep fodder (Waetzoldt 1992:129; van Driel 1992:171),[15] while 'split' reed was the most important material used for baskets, mats, doors, posts, etc., and was never used for fodder or fuel. Its price was markedly higher than that of other types of reed, costing 1 shekel (8.33 g) of silver per 300 bundles.

In an Ur III text (CT 7: 31) describing the bitumen needed to caulk the Magan boats (cf. Chapter V) 4260 bundles (*sa*) of *šid*-reed and 12,384 bundles of *izi*-reed are cited. As the unit of weight *gú*, weighing 30 kg, was sometimes used for reed, and each load consisted of between ten and twenty bundles,[16] Waetzoldt estimates that each bundle weighed c. 1.5–3 kg (Waetzoldt 1992:128). This being the case, the amount of *šid*-reed required in CT 7: 31 was between 6.39–12.78 tons, while the quantity of *izi*-reed was

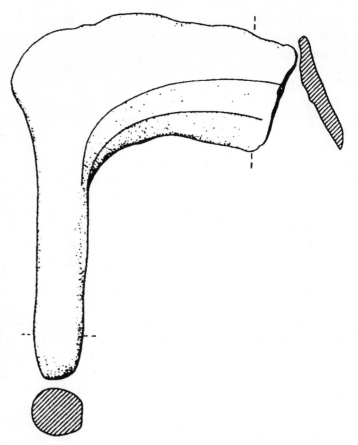

Figure IV.11 Fragmentary Late Uruk period clay sickle from the surface of Uruk. The narrow, vertical part is the handle; the wider, bevelled area is the blade (after Finkbeiner 1985: Abb. 11.23)

no less than 18.576–37.152 tons. That these were not exceptional amounts is borne out by an Old Babylonian text from Ur which records the delivery in three instalments of 26,230 bundles of reed, which represents between 39.345 and 78.69 tons (Van De Mieroop 1992:148).

Such enormous quantities are explicable when one sees how much reed is required to construct even a relatively small object. Thus, according to one Ur III text (MVN 14: 229, 4ff.) the manufacture of thirty, 50-cm-high baskets for holding tablets required 140 bundles (210-420 kg) of *sid*-reed, as well as 60 palm fronds, 60 palm ribs, and 180 boxwood branches. The manufacture of a 60-l basket for transporting or storing grain required 1 bundle (1.5–3 kg) of reed, 1 l bitumen, and 1/3 palm rib, and took 1/3 of a work day (Waetzoldt 1992:131).

The magnificent reed houses (*mudhif*) of the modern Marsh Arabs (Ochsenschlager 1992:54–8) have long been recognized as the lineal descendants of the beautiful reed structures shown on Late Uruk limestone basins and glyptic (Fig. III.16), and on the carved soft-stone vessels found on sites of the Early Dynastic era like Khafajah (Delougaz 1960:90–5) and Uruk (Lindemeyer and Martin 1993: Taf. 62.770, 63.797 and 69.1105) (Fig. IV.12). But it should also be realized that reed houses are attested in north Babylonian cities like Babylon and Borsippa during the Neo-Babylonian and Achaemenid periods (van Driel 1992:174), and stands of usable reed were by no means limited to the far south of Mesopotamia (Cole 1994:81–109).[17] Reed houses undoubtedly formed a more important part of the urban and rural landscape than has generally been recognized by scholars, who have tended to assume that all of the population in Mesopotamia lived in mudbrick dwellings.

Flax

In Chapter III flax (*Linum usitatissimum*, Sum. *gu*) was discussed in the context of potential sources of vegetable oil used in ancient Mesopotamia. As noted already, there is little evidence for the manufacture and use of linseed oil at any time in Mesopotamian history, even if it was so employed elsewhere in prehistory (Helbaek 1959:103–20). Linen, however, a textile made from the fibres of the flax plant, is widely attested throughout Western Asia, beginning around 7000 BC at Çayönü in southeastern Turkey

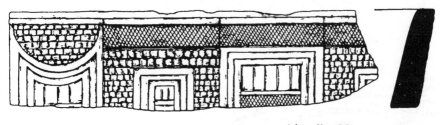

(rim dia. 23 cm)

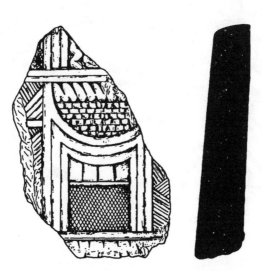

Figure IV.12 Architectural façades on carved soft-stone vessel fragments from Uruk (after Lindemeyer, and Martin 1993: Taf. 63.797 and 69.1105)

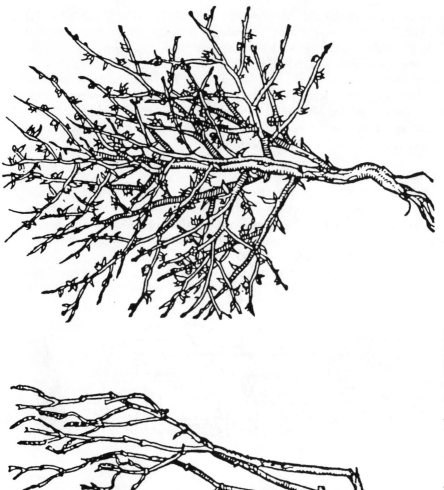

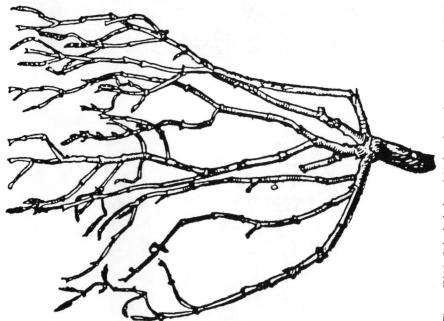

Figure IV.13 *Salsola kali and Haloxylon salicornicum* (after Butz 1984: 281)

(Potts and Reade 1993). In Mesopotamia, although not nearly so import-ant a part of the textile industry as wool, linen (Sum. *gada*) accounted for approximately 10 per cent of the total textile production during the Ur III period, the principal centres of its manufacture being Ur and Lagash (Waetzoldt 1983:585).

Flax reaches maturity in about a hundred days, but so strips the soil of nutrients that the fields in which it is grown must lie fallow for several years thereafter. In order to manufacture linen, flax requires a completely unique preparation treatment. After harvesting by hand, the bundles gathered must be dried, their seed capsules removed with a comb, and their stalks put into water in order to separate the woody parts of the plant from the fibre. After drying, the fibres are then beaten with a hammer or special tool and all remaining woody parts are removed. At this point the flax fibres are sent to the weaving workshops where they are combed and eventually spun. In all, the process was very labour-intensive. Waetzoldt estimates that one fifth-class piece of linen required over 20 balls of thread, 4–5 l of alkali, and 130–150 work days (Waetzoldt 1983:586), nor does this take into account other steps which may be necessary, including washing, bleaching and dyeing.

For these reasons linen was always quite rare in Mesopotamia and was considered a luxury item, according to the cuneiform sources. Linen was worn by high-ranking individuals, including the king of Mari and various city governors. Ur-Nammu (2112–2095 BC) boasts of having hung a linen hanging in the Gipar at Ur. Statues of deities were draped in linen, and priests wore it as well. Linen cloths were used for the tables, thrones and beds of the élite, and medical bandages are known to have been made of it (Waetzoldt 1983:592–3). In short, linen was probably the most exclusive indigenous textile known in ancient Mesopotamia.

Alkali

A substance called *naga* was used in Mesopotamia in the baking of bread and in the manufacture of soap used on textiles, leather and the human body (Waetzoldt 1972:172; Sigrist 1981:159–60; cf. Stol 1983:529). Possibly derived from the ashes of *Salsola kali* and/or *Haloxylon salicornicum* (Fig. IV.13), *naga* seems to have been a generic term for soda (N_2CO_3) (Butz 1984:281ff.). The supply of *naga* was important and must have been well organized, although little or no information is available on its extraction. On the basis of the Ur III leatherworking texts from Umma, M. Sigrist estimates that one cowhide or ten sheepskins required 1 *sìla*/l of *naga* for tanning, and deliveries of 4 *gur* (1200 l) are attested (Sigrist 1981:160). Similar amounts of *naga* are recorded in Ur III texts from Umma, Ur and Lagash which record the deliveries of chemical supplies to the weaving establishments there. In all cases it was used as a bleaching agent (Waet-zoldt 1972:172).

CONCLUSION

This review of animal, mineral and vegetable products locally available in southern Mesopotamia should have gone some way towards dispelling the illusion that the region was totally devoid of any natural resources apart from water, clay and reeds. Admittedly, most of the information reviewed here comes from cuneiform rather than archaeological sources, but it is an important corrective to our often distorted image of the material culture of an area so famed for its monumental architecture, durable ceramics and fine stone statuary and seals. Perishable goods made of wood, leather, reeds and textiles have clearly been lost to archaeologists in all but the most exceptional circumstances, while the local provenience of important minerals such as limestone, quartz and salt has too quickly been overlooked. Mesopotamia's import of metals and stones is undeniable, but its local resource base was far greater than has often been recognized.

NOTES

1 The only fragment for which an identification is available is W 21594,1, a fragment of cotton fabric (cf. Chapter XII).

2 Shearing in the sense of trimming the fleece of an animal with a pair of shears is not attested in the cuneiform sources. In nineteenth-century Palestine sheep were plucked after they had been made to fast for three days. Apparently this made it easier to pull their fleece out. See Waetzoldt 1972:11.

3 The system of classification was reformed in the year Shulgi 27.

4 Cf. Boessneck, von den Driesch and Steger 1984:170, Tab. 2, for the distribution of fauna by weight of animal bone recovered between the Uruk IV and Achaemenid periods.

5 According to Bauer, Landsberger and von Soden 1933:226, n.2, and Leemans 1960:218 and n. 1, the Akkadian word for bitumen, *ittû*, was derived from the name of the source at Hit.

6 Cf. Potts (T.F) 1989:123, n. 2, who cites further references to these outcrops and to others upstream from Baghdad.

7 Unless otherwise referenced, all information is drawn from Potts 1984:225–71. For a detailed discussion of the various varieties of salt in Sumerian and Akkadian terminology, see Butz 1984:272–316.

8 Amorites also settled in Mesopotamia proper and lived further west in the area of modern Syria and north Arabia.

9 The Nippur texts published by Westenholz are referred to here using the abbreviation OSP 2.

10 This remains, of course, pure speculation.

11 For a discussion of *annuharum*, see Butz 1984:283 with no clear identification, however.

12 Adapted from Moorey and Postgate 1992:197–9, with additions on Uruk from Engel and Kürschner 1992:271–4. For the species present, see Willcox 1987:101–6 and 1992:1–31.

13 Van De Mieroop 1992:157, notes that an Old Babylonian text from Uruk refers to a gardener who was fined half a mina of silver (250 g)

'for cutting down an *ašūhu*-tree in another man's garden. This penalty corresponds to the punishment prescribed for such an offence in the Laws of Lipit-Ishtar (§ 10) and Hammurabi (§ 59)'. Cf. Sanati-Müller 1990:193.

14 Willcox 1992:4, emphasizes that; 'Wood is usable as fuel after one year of drying; when green it smokes excessively and burns poorly. Where high temperatures were required this period may have been extended'. Obviously this does not apply to dead wood gathered for use as firewood.

15 Ochsenschlager 1992: 54 notes that in the recent past the Marsh Arabs have harvested reeds during the day to feed to their water buffalo at night.

16 This compares well with van Driel 1992:175, who discusses a Neo-Babylonian text from Sippar which implies that a load or bale consisted of fifteen bundles.

17 Obviously the ecological conditions existed in many parts of Mesopotamia for the growth of exploitable stands of reeds. For example, in central Iraq reeds 'grow in vast profusion in lagoons around Samarra' (J. Black, pers. comm.).

V Watercraft

INTRODUCTION

In Chapter I we saw that southern Mesopotamia was a land dominated not only by the Euphrates and its branches, but by a substantial number of artificial canals as well, many of which were navigable. Not surprisingly, therefore, a great deal of travel, transport and communcation was water-borne, and indeed some scholars consider the facilitation of trade and transport by Mesopotamia's canals (whether so intended or not) to have been as important a role as irrigation (Sauren 1966:36). In Chapter IV the principal locally available raw materials were introduced and, as has already been indicated, many of these were put to good use in the construction of watercraft. These will be discussed in greater detail below when we examine the different sorts of watercraft used in the region.

MATERIALS USED FOR THE WATERCRAFT OF SOUTHERN MESOPOTAMIA

In the Sumerian literary composition known as *Nanna-Suen's Journey to Nippur* the moon deity Nanna-Suen sends men out to collect the materials necessary for the construction of his Magur-boat (Ferrara 1973:ll. 37–58). The Magur-boat was said to resemble the moon in its crescent phase when, seen above the night skies of Iraq, it lies on its convex side, resembling a boat with a high, curving prow and stern at either end. Among the materials needed for the Magur-boat were mats, reeds, bitumen, wooden ribbing, a stern-plank and other elements of cedar (not local!) and juniper. The silver boat models from the Royal Cemetery at Ur may give us some idea of what Nanna-Suen's Magur-boat may have looked like, but it should be apparent even to non-sailors that the types of vessels ascribed to deities in literary texts undoubtedly differed from those used on the canals and rivers of southern Mesopotamia, while these, in turn, were probably different from those which went out into the Gulf on long-distance trading journeys. Even within the confines of Mesopotamia itself, different functional categories of vessels existed, serving different purposes.

Perhaps one of the simplest ways of approaching a classification of the watercraft of southern Mesopotamia lies in distinguishing between the two most dominant materials used for construction, reeds and wood. As discussed in the last chapter, reeds were an important economic resource in southern Mesopotamia. Although reed vessels may be identified on the basis of sets of parallel lines or striations, representing the reed bundles of which they were made and the seams where the reed boats were sewn together (Casson 1971:22–3), such unequivocal depictions are relatively rare in Mesopotamian glyptic (Fig. V.1). Flat-bottomed barges with high, upturned prow and stern, commonly shown in Late Uruk and Early Dyn-

Figure V.1 Sewn reed boats in Early Dynastic and Old Akkadian glyptic. 1. Khafajah, Early Dynastic (after Amiet 1961: Pl. 91.1211); 2. provenience unknown, stylistically Early Dynastic, Allard Pierson Museum (after Amiet 1961: Pl. 86.1131); 3. Tell Asmar, late Akkadian (after Amiet 1961: Pl. 113.1505)

astic glyptic, generally lack the striations which make an identification of reed construction assured. Nevertheless, the curved and flexible nature of their ends suggests that these, too, were made of reeds, and it was perhaps the shallowness of the hull, doubtless a reflection of how little of it actually protruded above the water line, which caused the seal-cutters of the period to represent these boats without any striations (Fig. V.2). Paul Johnstone, moreover, suggested that the caulking of reed vessels with bitumen created a smooth exterior which would explain why many vessels never show the striations characteristic of reed bundles and their lashings (Johnstone 1980:10).

An Old Babylonian text from the year Rim-Sin 16 (UET V 645) lists a boatbuilder as a recipient of reeds (Van de Mieroop 1992:148) and numerous Ur III texts specify the use of reeds for boatbuilding (Waetzoldt 1992:128 and n. 34). In addition to the craft itself, ropes (Sum. *gilim, dur*) used in boating were made of 'split' reed (*gi-šid*). According to an Ur III

Figure V.2 Smooth (bitumen-covered?) reed boats on Jamdat Nasr and Early Dynastic glyptic. 1. Uruk, Uruk III (after Amiet 1961: Pl. 46.655); 2. Ur, ED I (after Amiet 1961: Pl. 61.827); 3. Tell Agrab, ED I or II (after Amiet 1961: Pl. 62.829); 4. Khafajah, ED III (Pl. 86.1135); 5. Fara, ED II (after Amiet 1961: Pl. 86.1130)

text the manufacture of a 27-m-long rope took 1.5 days and required 16.25 reed bundles (24.375–48.75 kg of reeds), giving an average consumption of 0.6 of a bundle (0.9–1.8 kg) per metre of rope (Waetzoldt 1992:132–4). Punting poles (*gi muš*) made of *ù-suh₅* wood (pine? Powell 1992:117)[1] and known to reach lengths of up to 6 m are attested in both pre-Sargonic and Old Babylonian sources (Van de Mieroop 1992:160; Powell 1992:117–8). In the more recent past, reeds have sometimes been used as punting poles by the Marsh Arabs, although these are said to have broken easily (Ochsenschlager 1992:53, 68). We shall discuss below the use of bitumen for caulking and it is likely, as noted above, that bitumen was employed on reed as well as wooden plank boats. The bundled reed boats used until recently by the Marsh Arabs of southern Iraq were coated on the exterior with bitumen, but are said to have 'seldom lasted as long as a year' (Ochsenschlager 1992:67).

In 1977/8 Thor Heyerdahl sailed a reed boat from Iraq to Karachi in Pakistan and then across the Indian Ocean to Djibouti at the mouth of the Red Sea. The 18-m-long *Tigris* had a crew of eleven and part of Heyerdahl's justification for the journey was to challenge A. Salonen's claim that the reed craft of southern Mesopotamia were suited only to river and canal navigation (Heyerdahl 1986:30). Indeed, as Heyerdahl and his crew showed, the *Tigris* was perfectly seaworthy and 'with its double hull and extraordinary buoyancy a reed ship could sail right up into the shallows . . . where no keeled vessel could get in, and remain standing dry on the bottom without capsizing when the tide went out, ready for loading and departure with the next high tide' (Heyerdahl 1986:34). This point is surely important in considering the exigencies of loading and unloading cargo in ancient Mesopotamia where few traces of what could be called docks or port facilities have ever been found (see below), although references to the quay of a canal or river (Akk. *karum*) where goods were presumably off-loaded, bought and sold, abound (Röllig 1976:292ff). As a matter of interest it should be noted that the *Tigris* had 'a maximum rate of 4 knots in moderate winds and an average speed of 2.5 knots during the whole journey' (Soitzek 1986:229).

Wooden, plank-built boats were probably used in prehistoric Mesopotamia from an early date. Ubaid period boat models of clay are known from several sites, including Eridu and Tell Mashnaqa in Syria where an example closely resembling the Eridu model was recently discovered (Thuesen n.d.).[2] These are generally deep-keeled vessels with pointed, upturned prow and stern. As their sides are relatively high and smooth they would seem to represent wooden, rather than reed, boats. An interesting fragment of a boat model was picked up on the surface of one of the Warka survey sites and is thought to belonging to the Ur III or Old Babylonian period. The fragment (Fig. V.3) from the prow of the boat, is divided across the broken end by an internal, vertical wall. H.J. Nissen estimates that, originally, the model would have measured at least 60 cm long, and suggests that this is a representation of a cargo vessel, clearly different from those vessels (probably of reed) which have an upward curving prow and stern (Adams and Nissen 1972:214).

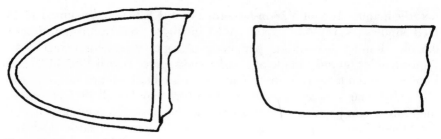

Figure V.3 Boat model from the surface of a Warka survey site (after Adams and Nissen 1972: 214, no scale)

The construction of boats using locally available wood is well attested in the cuneiform sources. One Ur III boatbuilding text (Amherst 66 rev. 11ff.) refers to 11,787 pieces of wood, stipulating in most cases what part of the ship they were destined to be used for (Waetzoldt 1992:140, n. 56). An Old Babylonian text from Ur (UET V 468) attests to the use of the date-palm midrib (?) (Van De Mieroop 1992:159–60) in boat construction, three hundred of which were delivered by twenty-five workers (Landsberger 1967:27). M. Powell has noted a number of wooden elements used in boat construction amongst the pre-Sargonic 'timber' texts from Girsu. Planks of *asal*₂ (*Populus* sp. (*euphratica*?)) for short or deep-draft boats are attested, as are the handles of steering oars (Powell 1992:109–10). Both *gi gíd* and *gul-bu* (unidentified) were probably used for steering oar handles as well. Ships' timbers were made of *ù-suh₅* (pine?), as were steering oars, punting poles and elements of the mooring apparatus (Powell 1992:117–18). As noted in Chapter IV, an Ur III text from Umma lists the delivery of 810 boat ribs of *ma-nu* wood (willow?).

Palm-fibre and palm-leaf ropes (Sum. *šu-sar*, Akk. *pitiltum*) of differing thicknesses and weights were made by 'twisting' (Akk. *patālum*). Old Babylonian texts from Ur (e.g. UET V 468) show no fewer than 186 labourers employed in this sort of rope manufacture, and texts relating to the distribution of ropes for the outfitting of boats reveal that enormous quantities of such rope were employed. The Ur III text cited earlier (cf. Chapter IV) in the context of reed use in the construction of Magan ships (CT 7: 31a) lists no less than 276 talents (8.28 tons) of palm-fibre rope (*šu-sar KAxSA*) and 34 talents (1.02 tons) of palm-leaf rope (*šu-sar peš*) (Landsberger 1967:7; cf. Postgate 1994:218; Tosi and Cleuziou 1994:746).

The tons of palm-fibre rope called for in this text suggest that some of the watercraft of the Ur III period must have been sewn or stitched vessels, a possibility to which scant attention has ever been paid in the literature on Mesopotamian watercraft.[3] Sewn plank boats are an important and well-studied phenomenon in northern Europe, the Mediterranean, the Indian Ocean, South Asia and Southeast Asia (McGrail and Kentley 1985). The sewn vessels of the Gulf, Red Sea and Indian Ocean are justly famous in nautical literature and have been commented on by European observers for almost two millennia. In the mid-first century AD the anonymous author of the *Periplus Maris Erythraei*, a commercial mariner's handbook containing information on travel between Egypt and India, noted 'boats sewed together . . . known as *madarata*' (Schoff 1912:§ 36) on the southern coast of Arabia. In 1890 the great Austrian Orientalist and South Arabian explorer Eduard Glaser suggested that the word rendered *madarata* in Greek by the author of the *Periplus* was undoubtedly the same as Arabic *muddarra'at* or *madra'at*, a vessel fastened with palm-fibre (Glaser 1890:190). In his chronicle of the Sasanian wars, Procopius (*c*. AD 500–560+) wrote of the ships in the Red Sea and in India as follows: 'Nor indeed are the planks fastened together by iron nails going through and through, but they are bound together with a kind of cording' (*On the Persian War* I xix 23–24). The tenth-century Persian writer Abu Zaid Hasan of Siraf, on the Gulf coast of Iran, described Omani shipbuilders who travelled to the Maldive and Laccadive islands off the Indian coast where they felled coconut palms, 'and with the bark of the tree they spin a yarn, wherewith they sew the planks together, and so build a ship' (Anonymous 1979:107). At the end of the thirteenth century Marco Polo observed the use of coconut palm-fibre by the inhabitants of Hormuz, near Minab in southern Iran, noting 'and from that they spin twine, and with this stitch the planks of the ship together' (Anonymous 1979:108). James Bruce, who described boats on the Red Sea near Quseir in the late eighteenth century, felt that sewing the hull gave it an elasticity which made it more resistant to damage than one fastened with iron nails. 'The planks of the vessel', he noted, 'were sewed together and there was not a nail nor a piece of iron in the whole ship; so that when you struck upon a rock, seldom any damage ensued' (after Hornell 1942:14). The use of palm-fibre cordage in the Gulf was observed in 1828 by G.B. Kempthorne (after Bowen 1949:107) and specifically on Bahrain in the 1890s by S.M. Zwemer (after Schoff 1912:156).

Given the fact that the Ur III texts express the quantity of palm-fibre rope used by Mesopotamian shipwrights in terms of weight, one can be impressed by the sheer tonnage involved, but it is difficult to get an accurate impression of quantity which, for a commodity like rope or cord, is more easily understood by length. Some impression can perhaps be gained by considering the Fourth Dynasty royal ship of Cheops found near the Great Pyramid at Giza. This vessel, 43.63 m long and 5.6 m wide, is said to have needed 5000 m (5 km) of cordage (Lipke 1985:27). The structurally very different *Sohar*, a 23-m-long, 6.2-m-wide replica of the type of sewn-plank boat thought to have been sailed in the early medieval era, used no less than 400 miles (640 km) of coconut palm-fibre rope (coir) (Severin 1985:280). The 207 talents (6210 kg or 6.21 tons) of fish oil mentioned in CT 7:31a along with the tons of rope or cord probably represent an anti-fouling agent used on the rope (see below) as opposed to the wooden hull itself which was caulked with bitumen.

In reviewing the uses of wood (cf. Chapter IV), mention was made of a text attesting to the provision of 59,290 wooden pegs for the boatyards of Umma during the Ur III period (Steinkeller 1987:106, s.v. 27 and 112, s.v. 47). Had Paul Johnstone been aware of data such as this, he would have had a ready answer to the question which he posed in his posthumously published *Sea-craft of Prehistory*: 'Did any ancient shipbuilder in the Indian Ocean and Arabian Gulf . . . use tenons and dowels to keep planks in place?' (Johnstone 1980:179). The Ur III data is important, particularly in view of the fact that wooden, bamboo or cane pegs were traditionally used in combination with sewing or stitching throughout the Gulf/Indian Ocean region in the pre-modern era. As Gemelli Carreri observed at Kung island in the lower Gulf in the late seventeenth century, 'Instead of nails, which they are without, they use "chevilles" [pegs] of bamboo or cane, and further join the planks with "ficelles" [strings] made of rushes [probably coir or coconut fibre]' (after Stiffe 1899:296). Similarly, Marco Polo found 'wooden trenails' (i.e. 'nails' of wood) used in combination with the coco-nut palm-fibre cord mentioned above during his visit to Hormuz (after Schoff 1912:155).

Another justification for the use of so many pegs is provided by an account of the repair of a *ganja*, a large, ocean-going, traditional wooden vessel used on the Malabar coast of South India. Ship-worm (*Teredo*) had attacked the hull of a vessel, beginning to tunnel right through it and therefore calling for urgent treatment. As J. Hornell describes, 'the ship-wright had driven a long peg into every hole marking the beginning of a *teredo*'s tunnel. As there were hundreds of holes closely set, the hull below the waterline resembled the quill-armour of the fretful porcupine in angry mood. Later, when all holes had been plugged, the projecting ends were cut off level with the surface' after which the hull was freshly caulked (Hornell 1942:12). By way of comparison, it is interesting to note that in construct-ing a replica of a fourteenth-century Swedish boat measuring 22.5 m long, 3.4 m wide, and 0.9 m high, some 3000–4000 wooden nails and spikes were used (Varenius 1986:118).

Finally, it should be noted that among other, locally available raw ma-terials, leather appears in texts dealing with ship and boat outfitting. BM 105587 is an Ur III text in which the work of one man (*guruš*) for eight days is required to make something in leather for the king's boat. Copenhagen 30 concerns the construction of a wooden frame covered with leather in three different colors on the royal boat of Amar-Sin. The work took five *guruš* five days and involved eighty-five skins. Another text (*AnOr* 7: 366) concerns work done on the divine boat of Ninlil or Ninurta, at the behest of the *ensí*. Four skins and five days of work were required for one worker to decorate the boat (Sigrist 1981:181–2).

THE NATIVE TYPOLOGY OF WATERCRAFT

Turning to the native Mesopotamian typology for watercraft, although geographical distinctions such as 'Dilmun boat', 'Mari boat', or 'Assur boat' were often used, the generic Mesopotamian 'boat/ship' (*má*) was differentiated by size, i.e. volumetric capacity, rather than provenience or appearance. Thus, for example, during the Ur III period ships of 60, 50, 40, 30, 20 and 10 *gur* size were in use at Umma, and it is clear that some of the canals around Umma were navigable only by small vessels (Sauren 1966:37–9). At the same time, contemporary texts from Ur (e.g. UET III 272) mention ships varying in size from 1 to 300 *gur*. Labour time for the repair (or construction?) of a 60 *gur* boat is reckoned in one case (WMAH

3) at 602 person-days, and in another (TCL V 5673) at 900 (Sauren 1971:170).

This variation in size is particularly interesting in view of the observations made of traditional seacraft in the Indian Ocean at the beginning of the present century. As W.B. Huddleston noted in describing the situation in India, 'The character of the coast and its harbours calls everywhere for different types of boats and vessels . . . sailing vessels on the coast are mainly from ten to three hundred tons' (Huddleston 1928:342). It is clear that a fairly similar range of vessel size obtained in southern Mesopotamia.

While figures such as these clearly reflect the holding capacity of ancient watercraft, some scholars have rather simplistically equated this designation of size or volume with absolute carrying capacity, suggesting for instance that a 60 *gur* vessel, literally an '18,000 l' craft, had an 18,000 l capacity (e.g. Gelb 1982:589, who suggested that a 60 *gur* boat could have transported 18,000 one-*sila*/l ceramic vessels). In fact, however, we do not know that this was the case, and some allowance must surely be made for the crew and their belongings. As T. Gomi has recently pointed out, 'no clue is offered by these texts to estimate the relationship between the size of a ship and the amount of cargo on board. In other words we do not know whether a ship of 180 *gur* could carry 180 *gur* (ca. 54,000 l)' (Gomi 1993:41). H. Sauren has pointed out that WMAH 3, an Ur III shipbuilding text from Lagash, refers to a 60 *gur* ship loaded with 150 talents (4500 kg) of bitumen (Sauren 1971:165).[4] This ratio, if broadly applied, means that an average 2.5 talents (75 kg) of cargo could be transported per *gur* of ship's capacity. On the other hand, in discussing the transport of wine at Mari, A. Finet calculated that a boat with 300 10 *qa* (= 10 l) jars, each weighing 20 kg, comprised a load of 6000 kg or 6 tons, and suggested that this represented the normal capacity of a 20 *gur* vessel (Finet 1974–1977:122–31). In studying the royal ship of Cheops mentioned earlier, P. Lipke observed, 'An MIT computer hydrostatics program projected a total hull weight of 38.5 long tons, full load displacement of 92.4 long tons for a maximum capacity of 53.9 long tons with a draft of 0.96 m from these offsets' (Lipke 1985:30). It is clearly no easy matter to calculate actual carrying capacity from the very general rubrics of volumetric size used to describe ancient Mesopotamian watercraft.

Another way of approaching actual carrying capacity is to examine some of the examples of ship rental. Rental costs depended very much on what was being transported, but some indication of carriage possibilities are contained within the extant rental documents. Thus, for example, at Umma during the Ur III period a 60 *gur* ship normally rented for 10–20 *sila* of barley per day, a 40 *gur* ship for 15 *sila* per day; and a 20 *gur* ship for 5–6 *sila* per day. A boat rented for 30 *sila* of barley to transport goods from Apisala to Umma (MCS 6, 82 H 7165:1–18) carried 30 *gur* barley, 20 *gur* dates and 2 *gur* 140 *sila* wheat. The rent was notionally broken down as follows: 15 *sila* barley was the rent for carriage of the barley, and 15 *sila* barley for the dates (when handling of the goods is included, the price is normally increased further). Judging from the rent paid, this ought to have been somewhat larger than a 60 *gur* boat, whereas the barley, dates and wheat carried amounted to a total of just under 57.5 *gur*. Recently, R.K. Englund has suggested that a regular formula existed for figuring boat rental in the Ur III period which factored in distance and load. The formula amounted to a charge of 1 *sila*/l of barley 'per loaded *gur* per *danna* [one double-hour, i.e. the distance travelled in two hours]' so that, for instance, 'a barge transporting 20 *gur* of barley over a distance of 20 *danna* would result in a rental fee of 20 × 20 = 400 *sila*' (Englund 1988:167–8, n. 40).

CAULKING

As for caulking wooden plank boats with bitumen, it may be appropriate to begin with an ethnohistoric account of boat repair in the area of al-Hiba (Lagash) (Ochsenschlager 1992:52):

> New bitumen, which is said to come from Hit, can be purchased in Chabaish or Basra (about 80 kilos for one dinar), but it is not often needed in large quantities for bitumen can be used again and again and is usually salvaged from an old boat (as are most of the wooden boards) to build a new one. If a boat is leaking from small cracks and the bitumen coating is still in good condition, the cracks can sometimes be sealed by heating them with a length of burning reeds and then rolling the area with a short section of reed. Ordinarily a boat is stripped of its bitumen with a hammer and chisel every year and its hull is repaired . . . The old bitumen, with whatever new bitumen is necessary, is heated to liquid consistency and stirred occasionally with a stick . . . A shovel full of liquid bitumen is distributed over its [an oil drum's] surface like a large pancake and carried to the repaired boats. One or two workmen spread the bitumen evenly over the surface with *sobay*, wooden rollers with conical ends. They frequently moisten the rollers with water and pick out lumps of extraneous material or unmelted bitumen. The exterior of the boat is coated in sections, the bottom first, next one side, then the other. Two or more layers are usually applied until the protective coating is ca. one to three cm. thick. One man quickly spreads wet mud from the canal bank over each section as it is finished, while another throws cans of water over the mud to keep it moist and pliable. The mud, according to informants, fuses to the bitumen and gives the coating extra strength. When the bottom and sides are completed the boat is turned upright and layers of bitumen are spread over the decks, the top of the prow and stern, and the edges of the boat's sides. The final stage is packing the bitumen in the interior rib joins or wherever a large crack in the wood or a poor joint seems to require it. The boat is usually allowed to dry overnight before launching.

There are a number of Ur III shipbuilding texts from Lagash (WMAH 3) and Umma (TCL V 5673, Or 47/49: 249), as well as several Old Babylonian texts from Larsa (YOS V 90, 231, 234, and 239) and a Neo-Babylonian text from Uruk (UCP 9 90 no. 24:21) which list amounts of bitumen used in shipbuilding. Thus, YOS V 231: 5 mentions 'bitumen for caulking', while YOS V 234: 6 speaks of 'a bitumen smear [to be used] on boats', and UCP 9

90 mentions *esír-hád-a ša pahê ša elippēti* 'bitumen for caulking boats' (CAD I/J: 310; CAD K: 555). H. Sauren has summarized the quantitative data contained in the Umma and Lagash texts relating amounts of bitumen of different sorts to the caulking of vessels of varying sizes (Sauren 1971:168). From his data I have extracted the figures given in TCL V 5673 and put these into Table V.1. As I.J. Gelb showed that 1 *sìla*/l of dry bitumen weighed 1 mina (500 g) (Gelb 1982:589, based on TCL V 5680), we have been able to calculate the total amounts of bitumen used in caulking in TCL V 5673 and thereby work out the rate of bitumen use per *gur* capacity.

It would seem logical to assume that the amount of bitumen used to caulk a boat was proportional to its size, and indeed Table V.1 shows that the amount of bitumen needed to caulk a ship increased with the size of the ship. At the same time, the amount of bitumen used was inversely proportional to their *gur* of capacity. As Sauren stressed, the Umma text is a one-year summary account of daily disbursements for the construction and maintenance of watercraft. As such, we cannot be absolutely certain of the specific amounts required for the caulking of individual ships. The Old Babylonian text YOS V 231 from Larsa (Rim Sin 12, or *c.* 1810 BC), is a record of bitumen (*esír* and *esír-has₅-rá*) allotments for two 20 *gur* (6000 l) ships.[5] In addition to mentioning 4 *gur* (1200 l)[6] of *esír* per ship, it lists 150 *sìla*/l of *esír-has₅-rá* for coating the interior and exterior of the two vessels. This 1350 l of bitumen equates to 675 kg, giving a per *gur* capacity ratio of only 33.75, well below the figures cited in Table V.1. That these figures should not be applied to all Mesopotamian watercraft is suggested by another Old Babylonian text where we find that a 20 *gur* boat required 8 *gur* (2400 l = 1200 kg) of bitumen for caulking, which represents a ratio of 150 kg of bitumen for caulking per *gur* capacity (Leemans 1960:219). Undoubtedly there was a significant degree of variation depending on the age of the vessel, how badly it was in need of caulking, whether the entire hull needed treatment, and whether or not the vessel was used only on the canals or on the open waters of the Gulf.

Another text which raises the question of how much bitumen was needed for the caulking of an individual boat/ship, and the scale of the

Boat Tonnage	Equivalence in sìla/litres	Bitumen required to caulk such a ship	Bitumen total in kg	Bitumen use per gur capacity
60 *gur*	18,000	131 *gú* (3930 kg) *esír-hád* ('dry') 1 *gur* (300 l) *esír-é-a* ('house') 8.80 *gú* (264 kg) *esír-gul-gul* ('broken')	4080	68 kg
30 *gur*	9000	90 *gú* (2700 kg) *esír-hád* ('dry') 150 *sìla* (150 l) *esír-é-a* ('house') 4 *gú* (120 kg) *esír-apin* ('plough?')	2895	96.5 kg
10 *gur*	3000	15.5 *gú* (465 kg) *esír-hád* ('dry') 50 *sìla* (50 l) *esír-é-a* ('house') 33 *gú* (990 kg) *esír-gul-gul* ('broken') 3.5 *gú* (105 kg) *esír-apin* ('plough?')	1585	158.5 kg

Table V.1 *Amounts and types of bitumen used to caulk boats according to TCL V 5673*

bitumen-provisioning industry in ancient Mesopotamia is CT 7:31, an Ur III text from Girsu (cf. now Tosi and Cleuziou 1994). In addition to specifying large quantities of timber, palm-fibre rope, reeds and fish-oil for the construction of an unspecified number of vessels, 3170 *gur* bitumen (*esír-luh*) 'for caulking Magan boats' (*má-má-gan du₈-dè*) is mentioned. The amount of asphalt/bitumen involved is problematic. If we use the standard Akkadian to Old Babylonian *gur* of 300 *sila* ≈ 300 l (Powell 1990:497) then we are faced with the staggering figure of 951,000 l of bitumen[7] which clearly represents massive exploitation of bitumen seeps. If one works on the basis of the figures cited in Table V.1, converting the 951,000 l to 475,500 kg of bitumen, then this amount would have sufficed to caulk 116.5 60 *gur* boats, 164 30 *gur* boats, or 300 10 *gur* boats. Of course, these figures may be well under the size of seagoing boats sent to Magan, and given the fact that vessels of up to 300 gur capacity are attested in Ur III records, as noted above, considerably fewer large vessels may be implied by this text.

TRAFFIC AND THE LEGAL RAMIFICATIONS OF WATER TRAVEL

When the cuneiform sources from a specific site are examined it becomes clear that many canal names can be associated with specific cities, such as Apisala, Babylon, Dilbat, Kish, Lagash, Nippur, Sippar, Umma and Uruk (Stol 1980:362). Often, however, Assyriologists can do little more than compile lists of their names. With the exception of rare cases such as Umma, where the local topography has been carefully studied (Fig. V.4), we often have difficulties in interpreting itineraries between specific places mentioned in texts, even though it is clear that they are travelling up and down canals. Nor is it generally an easy matter to use the archaeological evidence of specific canals visible on the ground to help elucidate the cuneiform sources, although attempts have been and must be made.[8] Distances are often given between the point of origin and the destination (cf. the discussion of the *a-ab-ba* in Chapter I), however, and this is of considerable interest in helping to roughly estimate the locations of unidentified towns and cities.

With all of the travel and transport which we know took place on the rivers and canals of southern Mesopotamia – and mention has not even been made here of simple punting, rowing or towing – there were bound to be accidents and infractions. Indeed, these are well documented in the cuneiform literature, and not infrequently involve the arrest of the ship's captain or the rentor of a ship for damages to the ship or its cargo in consequence of an original rental agreement, as well as arrests for damages arising from accidents involving more than one vessel. The latter difficulty is in fact covered by §240 of the Laws of Hammurapi. When one ship going upstream collided with another coming downstream, 'the captain of the upstream travelling ship rammed and sunk by a downstream travelling ship, the captain of the more maneuverable downstream travelling ship must replace the other ship as well as the lost goods. These latter must be specified under oath by the wronged ship's captain before the god'. A similar

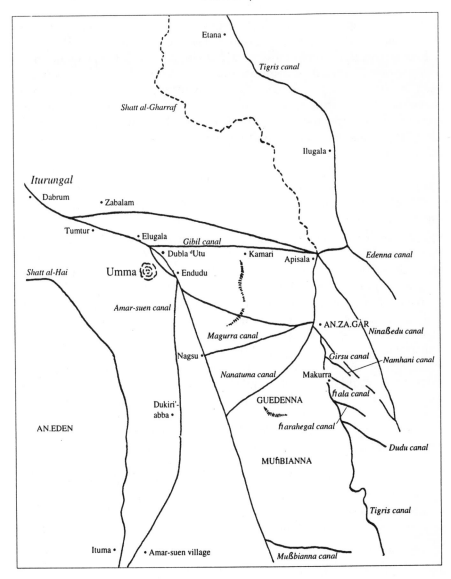

Figure V.4 Reconstruction of the canal system around Umma (after Sauren 1966)

statement occurs several centuries later in the Middle Assyrian laws (Pet-schow 1972–1975:234). In §236 of the Laws of Hammurapi the liability of the rentor of a vessel who had been negligent, banked or sunk the boat is stipulated as the replacement of the damaged vessel and any goods lost. In fact, the same attitude towards 'negligence' is already found in the earlier Laws of Eshnunna where a negligent captain is responsible for restoring not only the lost goods but also the ship to its owner (§ 38). According to §238 of Hammurapi's laws, however, if the renting captain raised the sunken vessel, he owed only half of its price to the owner. This concern, moreover, is mirrored in the boat rental contracts of both the pre-and post-Hammurapi era, in which the rentor was bound to return 'a healthy ship to the quay/harbour of its master' (Petschow 1972–1975:235).

Recent investigations at the Old Babylonian site of Mashkan-Shapir have uncovered a building complex adjacent to a canal which seems to have been involved in the storage and disbursement of goods coming in by boat. An economic text from the building 'lists a number of boats, the days they were used and the names of those responsible' (Stone and Zimansky 1992:215). This may well represent a typical Old Babylonian quayside storehouse.

THE CHARACTER OF WATERCRAFT IN SOUTHERN MESOPOTAMIA AND THE SURROUNDING AREA

Regardless of the fact that reed boats and sewn plank-built vessels can be found in many parts of the world, there is no denying that these show as many differences cross-culturally as other categories of material culture, such as ceramics. Thus, while certain common techniques and solutions to problems may appear in widely differing regions, their cultural expression and the materials used vary enough for the end product to have a distinctive appearance vis-à-vis others of its type. The late nautical archaeology specialist, Paul Johnstone, suggested that by examining the representations of watercraft on the stamp seals of Bahrain and Failaka in the Gulf (ancient Dilmun), it would be possible to gain at least a partial understanding of the sorts of ships which must have sailed between Mesopotamia and the Indus Valley in the late third and early second millennia BC

A close examination of all of the early iconography of sailing vessels from Harappan sites (Fig. V.5), the Oman peninsula and the Gulf region (Fig. V.6), however, shows clearly that each differed from the other in many points of detail and overall form (Potts 1995), as indeed Egyptian vessels differed from Mesopotamian ones (Boehmer 1974:15–40). Double-ended vessels, i.e. those in which 'the fore end of the hull is always sharp and pointed, usually with a long and tapered overhang' and 'the stern has a

Figure V.5 Harappan sailing vessel depicted on a stone stamp seal from Mohenjo-Daro (after Potts 1995: Fig. 1)

Figure V.6 Early second-millennium BC Gulf watercraft depicted on a stamp seal from Failaka, Kuwait (after Potts 1995: Fig. 11)

similar though less pronounced form' (Hornell 1942:22), made of both reed and wood, are known in the Gulf and the Indus Valley, while square-sterned vessels are attested in Oman and the Indus Valley. When the founder of the Old Akkadian empire, Sargon of Akkad, boasted that 'ships from Meluhha, Magan and Dilmun made fast at the dock of Akkad' (Gelb and Kienast 1990:166), it was probably no difficult matter to distinguish them by their outward appearance. For a start, ethnohistoric sources show that, in the Gulf region and Oman, bitumen has never been used extensively as a caulking material, whereas fish, shark or whale oil mixed with lime made from ground-up shell, has been the preferred caulking medium for the past few centuries (Potts 1995). We must always beware, moreover, that the representations of Mesopotamian watercraft on cylinder seals generally suggest craft used on the rivers and canals, whereas vessels for open-water sailing must have been quite different.

CONCLUSION

The subject of watercraft in ancient Mesopotamia, although studied for some time now, is one in which much remains to be done by scholars with an understanding of technical, nautical terminology, available materials and traditional boatbuilding techniques around the world. In concluding this chapter it remains to comment on a very general perception which appears from time to time in the literature of early watercraft.

Over the years, several scholars have suggested that the watercraft of antiquity were probably similar to traditional Arab seacraft. Specifically, plank-built vessels shown on early second-millennium BC stamp seals from Failaka (Kuwait) have been deemed 'exactly similar' to a Gulf Arab *bum* (a type of doubled-ended vessel, Fig. V.7) of the recent past (Alster 1983:51).

Figure V.7 Scale drawing of an Arab *bum* (after Bowen 1949: Fig. 4)

These latter vessels are generally measure 12–36 m long, 6–7.6 m wide, 2.6–4 m deep and 60–200 tons in weight, and are thought to represent 'the least changed of the old-time Arab type of trading vessel' (Hornell 1942:23). Yet it would be naive to believe in the similarity of pre-modern Arab seacraft and ancient Mesopotamian vessels without careful scrutiny of the problem. 'Traditional' technologies which appear 'changeless' are often far more dynamic than the average observer might suspect. In this particular case, it has long been recognized by maritime historians that, 'European influence – Portuguese, English, French and Dutch . . . led to the gradual introduction of far-reaching modifications in the build of the larger vessels engaged in trade or warfare' in the Gulf region (Hornell 1942:22). T.M. Johnstone and J. Muir showed many years ago that Portuguese influence on the Arab *bum* had been considerable (Johnstone and Muir 1962:58–63), both directly and through the intermediary of Portuguese-influenced, Indian watercraft. This is indicated clearly by the many technical, nautical terms in Gulf Arabic which are loan-words from Portuguese, including Arabic *burd*, 'board', from *bordo*, *brinda*, 'shifting stay or runner' from *brandal*, *balīma*, 'butt tackle', from *balima*, *bindēra*, 'flag', from *bandeira*, *durmēt*, 'sleeping shelf', from *dormente*, *zabdara*, 'gunwale', from *cevadeira*, *chāwiya*, 'clench', from *cavilha*, *kabirt*, 'deck', from *coberta*, *kashtīl*, 'castle', from *castelo* and *kalfat*, 'to caulk', from *calafeto/calafate* (Johnstone and Muir 1964: 299–332).

    Given the fact that many of these terms are essential structural elements of the Arab *bum*, it is clear that the vessels seen in the recent past and those of the pre-sixteenth century AD must have differed considerably in outward appearance. As a window on the past, therefore, the 'traditional' watercraft of the region must be used with great caution, and this applies, no doubt, to the reed boats of the southern Iraqi marshes as well. Culture change can be subtle and yet far-reaching. In nautical architecture it is not restricted to such obvious changes as outboard motors and satellite navigators. A proper understanding of ancient Mesopotamian watercraft requires a careful study of the indigenous sources, both written and archaeological.

NOTES

1 This identification seems unlikely to me, since pine is not indigenous to southern Mesopotamia. See Willcox 1992:7–8.

2 J.S. Madsen, who studied the Mashnaqa model, believes it represents a bitumen-coated reed boat rather than a wooden plank boat.

3 It is, to my knowledge, nowhere mentioned by any authority prior to de Graeve 1981:100, who says only, 'joints might also have been reinforced by cord lashings, although there is in fact no direct evidence'. Neither Casson 1971 nor Johnstone 1980 seems to have ever considered the possibility, nor did Landsberger, who seems not to have asked himself what a shipyard would do with almost 10 tons of palm-fibre and palm-leaf rope or cord.

4 Casson 1971:26, n. 5, assumed that the entire *gur* capacity of a vessel was equivalent to its carrying capacity and attempted to convert *gur* to litres to pounds, based on the equation of 1 litre of grain = 1.7 lb (*c.* 850 g). At this rate a 60 *gur* ship would be able to carry 15,300 kg of cargo. Of course we do not know that the ship mentioned in WMAH 3 was necessarily full when it was loaded with its cargo of 150 talents of bitumen.

5 Treated differently in Leemans 1960:218–21; and Heimpel 1987:38 and 86.

6 Leemans calculated the value of the Old Babylonian *gur* of bitumen in the YOS V texts at 120 l. See Leemans 1960:219.

7 Cf. Powell 1990:498–9, where variant *gur* of 120 *sila* at Mari and during the Kassite to Neo-Babylonian periods are discussed. There is nothing to suggest, however, that the standard Old Akkadian-Old Babylonian *gur* of 300 *sila*/l would not have been used in the Girsu text.

8 For some recent examples, see e.g. van Driel 1988:124–8 and map 3; or Frayne 1991:399–400, n. 126.

VI Pottery Production

INTRODUCTION

Clay (Sum. *im*, Akk. *ṭiṭṭu*) (Barrelet 1968:28–30), the basic ingredient in pottery production, is one of the most ubiquitous natural resources in southern Mesopotamia. All of the clay used in antiquity for local pottery manufacture was the calcium-rich, montmorillonite clay (Jacobs 1992:132) deposited by the Tigris and Euphrates in the course of periodic flooding (cf. Chapter I). Over the millennia vast amounts of pottery were produced in Mesopotamia, much of which lies in broken form on the surfaces of sites of all periods (post-6000 BC). William Kennet Loftus is generally considered the first person to have recognized a practical use for the millions of sherds found scattered on the archaeological sites of Mesopotamia when he wrote in 1857, 'The invention of the potter appears to have been racked in designing new forms, and their endless variety throughout Chaldaea may eventually prove of much use in determining the age of the ruins where each occurs' (quoted in Delougaz 1952:1, n. 1). This realization encapsulates to a large degree the purpose to which pottery study has been dedicated until more recently developed techniques of physico-chemical analysis gave archaeologists and ceramicists the power to answer questions relating to production technology and clay provenience.

Even today, it is probably fair to say that the first priority for most Mesopotamian archaeologists studying pottery is to be able to situate specific forms, ceramic fabrics, techniques of manufacture and types of surface treatment in particular spatial and chronological contexts. Together, the contemporary ceramic forms in use at any given point in time represent an *assemblage*. This is analogous to a cultural fingerprint which changes through time. Collectively, that series of assemblages by which a site or region is characterized constitute the building blocks of a ceramic *typology*. Once a typology has been delineated in a given area, individual sherds or vessels found on the surfaces of sites, in excavations or in museums (and with no known provenience) can be slotted into it, the typology serving as a tool for ordering otherwise undatable archaeological deposits.

To readers unfamiliar with the archaeological literature this must seem a narrow, reductionist view of ceramics and their significance, as indeed it is. Judging the age and origin of a piece of ancient pottery may be of great utility to an archaeologist nowadays, but that would hardly have been the first reaction of an inhabitant of southern Mesopotamia upon looking at a vessel. Users of pottery who were not particularly antiquarian were probably oblivious to the question of a vessel's age (perhaps less so to its origin if the piece were patently foreign) and much more concerned with its function within the spectrum of daily chores performed in a household and the choices to be made from a household's ceramic repertoire. Was a vessel to be used for mixing, serving, cooking, eating from, drinking out of, storage, etc.? Presumably considerations such as these determined human selection and attitudes towards domestic ceramics, just as functional requirements dictated what forms potters manufactured and in what sizes. The gulf is indeed great between traditional, archaeological concerns with ceramic assemblages and typologies based on form and decoration which have a specific cultural and chronological dimension, useful in dating and characterizing archaeological deposits, and what one might call a 'native' view of ceramic forms as a response to a range of functional demands. The problem is, how is one to arrive at a native, functional understanding of Mesopotamian ceramics?

CERAMIC FORM AND FUNCTION

An interest in ceramic function rather than form and decoration alone is not altogether new in Mesopotamian archaeology. Early in this century several scholars put forward functional typologies. The 'typologies' of the German prehistorian Viktor Christian (Ebeling and Calmeyer 1957–1971:182–3) or the French Assyriologist H. de Genouillac (de Genouillac 1934:vff.) were, however, simply an imposition of German and French household/functional terms, comparable to English notions like 'beaker', 'bowl', 'cup', 'jar', 'vat', etc., on Mesopotamian shapes. These were assigned to Mesopotamian forms on the basis of intuitive European notions of ceramic proportions (e.g. the ratio between vessel height and mouth diameter) and attributes (e.g. spouts, handles) and the designations thereby implied. Thus, a bowl should be broad and open at the mouth, not constricted like a jar. A cup should be taller than it is broad, and should be holdable in the hand, as for drinking. A vat must be large, not something one would serve tea in, and so forth. In publishing his excavations at Nuzi in northeastern Iraq, R.F.S. Starr proposed similarly 'intuitive' definitions for jars and pots. He wrote, 'The term jar is applied throughout to the deep, large vessels having no neck and little or no shoulder. Pots are those definitely constricted at the top, having a clearly defined shoulder and neck' (Starr 1939:387, n. 3).

Attributions such as these, while attempting to divine the function of a particular ceramic form, are wholly ethnocentric. The modern European conception of what it is or is not appropriate to drink from, eat off, prepare food in, etc., need have little or no relation to ancient perceptions. Nor is it possible to rely on physico-chemical testing for residues, a costly and time-consuming procedure which is scarcely applicable to more than a few selected samples of ceramics in any given project, as a means for identifying the ancient uses to which a particular vessel may have been put.

An alternative approach which has curiously been overlooked by virtually all archaeologists concerned with Mesopotamian ceramics is to examine the written information available on native categories of ceramic classification. In this regard Mesopotamia is unique amongst ancient Western Asiatic regions in possessing a rich lexicon of names for ceramic vessels. Numerous scholars, including Albright (Albright 1919:173–94), Schroeder

(Schroeder 1930–31:111–12), Meier (Meier 1935–36:365–6), Landsberger (Landsberger 1937–1939:136–40), Deimel (Deimel 1944:324–5) and Salonen (Salonen 1966) have investigated specific terms used for individual vessels. Yet these often concern very unusual types, such as cult vases, rather than the mass of pottery used in everyday situations. The lexical material, while not without its difficulties (for general orientation, cf. Civil 1975; Nissen 1981:99–108), is more promising, as are several Ur III texts which concern ceramic production at Umma. Let us briefly examine each of these bodies of evidence.

The Lexical Sources

The series ur_5-ra = *hubullu* is a set of some twenty-four bilingual Sumerian and Akkadian tablets. With over 9700 entries it has been described as a Mesopotamian 'inventory of material culture' (Civil 1975:125). Tablet X of the series (Landsberger 1959) is a list of over 350 names for ceramic vessels (Sum. *dug*, Akk. *karpatum*). As such, it is of prime importance in any attempt to understand native Mesopotamian ceramic categories. Apart from some very general designations, such as 'storage jar' (Hh X: 11), 'libation vessel' (14–16), 'suspension vessel' (39), 'small', 'perforated', 'new', 'old', 'damaged', 'large' (41–59), 'cracked' (100) and 'painted' vessels (105), vessels 'bound with rope' (106), 'ostrich egg-shaped' (110), 'sprinkling' (173) and 'drinking' vessels (176), there is a recurrent constellation of ten vessel designations which re-appears five times in variant forms and runs as follows: vessel for water (*a*), beer (*kaš*), milk (*ga*), oil (*i*), sesame oil (*i-giš*), ghee (*i-nun-na*), lard (*i-šah*), fine (sesame) oil (*i-dùg-ga*), wine (*geštin*) and honey (*làl*) (112–121; 131–140; 153–162; 182–191; 226–235). In addition, there are a number of other liquid-specific terms such as vessels for 'beer-mash' (*gakkul, nam-tar, dúr-bùr*) (211–213), and those used in the preparation of beer (*a-nag*) (305). The only apparently inedible liquid for which a vessel designation exists is some kind of salve (*tur*) (130). Otherwise, there are only a very few terms for vessels used to hold dry goods, although some of the more general terms like *karpatum* could hold flour, barley, groats or malt (Oppenheim 1937–39:357).

From a native, Mesopotamian point of view then, it would seem that the most significant cluster of liquids and their containers, judging by the lexical literature, is the list of ten commodities given above. It may come as a surprise that this should be so, particularly for archaeologists who are not used to classifying ceramics by their putative function or the materials contained within them. Nevertheless, it is important to consider the native categories of classification and to see how far these can be exploited in conjunction with other written and archaeological sources of information. To that end we shall briefly examine some of the principal liquids[1] and their containers.

Beer

In his monumental study of the ceramics discovered by the Chicago expedition on sites in the Diyala region of northeastern Iraq, P. Delougaz noted the large number of spouted vessels in Protoliterate (Late Uruk and Jamdat

Nasr) levels dating to *c.* 3400–2900 BC which clearly resembled the proto-cuneiform signs for milk, beer, oil, etc. in the Archaic texts,[2] and indeed the tradition of generally similar, tall spouted forms continued right through the Early Dynastic period (Fig. VI.1). Thus, from the standpoint of native typology, it is interesting to see that the original signs which stood for particular liquids were graphic representations of the containers which held them and in many cases these necessarily had spouts so that the liquid could be decanted, flat bases so that the vessel could sit comfortably and high shoulders tapering to a slender base, perhaps so that the vessel could easily be held in both arms when pouring. After water, beer was certainly one of the most important liquid beverages in ancient Mesopotamia (Röllig 1970, Stol 1971:167–71).

The sign for beer (*kaš*) in the Archaic texts (Fig. VI.2) is very obviously a straight-spouted vessel,[3] and over the years several scholars have investigated the variation in vessel forms illustrated in the Archaic texts (Szarzynska 1969:16–24) as well as on Late Uruk and Jamdat Nasr cylinder seals (Baudot 1978–79:5–67). Recently, A.R. Millard has suggested that Late Uruk jars with curving and drooping spouts (Fig. VI.3) may also have been beer jars, contending that the curvature of the spout would 'impede the access of oxygen because carbon dioxide released by the fermentation of the beer within would form a barrier in the spout' (Millard 1988:55). While this is an interesting point, the fact remains that the Archaic sign for beer has a straight spout running almost vertically off the shoulder of a narrow-necked jar, not a drooping spout.

The lexical sources contain a variety of words within the semantic field of beer, including beer vat (6–8, 12–13), jug (9–10), vessel for beer-mash[4] (73, 211–213), mug (76–78, 85–86) and large (83–84b) and small brewing vessel (214). Are we dealing with a large variety of vessels which could be differentiated visually by the ancient Mesopotamians or by modern archaeologists on the basis of form (and possibly decoration?), or is this plethora of names the result of scribal delight in words? It is virtually certain that many of the extant beer vessel terms identified functionally distinct containers used in the brewing process, and not just a range of vessels for drinking. Ur III economic texts contain a variety of technical terms for the different sorts of vessels which held the dough used in so-called beer-bread,[5] herbs or spices (*dug-kur-KU.D Ù*), and the finished beer (*[dug]utúl*). While these latter vessels came in various sizes (examples of 10 and 60 *sila*/l capacity are known, see Table 1), the vats used presumably for the storage of beer (*dug-lahtan*) are known in sizes ranging from 15 to *c.* 603 *sila*/l (Waetzoldt 1970–1971:18, n. 115). Were these storage vessels all similar in shape and proportions, differing only in size, or was the single term applied because the function only was the same in each case, allowing for a wide range of formal variation? If we believe the lexical sources, a particular type of potter called the *lú-[dug]lahtan* was specifically engaged in the manufacture of these vats. Certainly economic texts show that potters were attached to brewing establishments (*é-bappir*) in the Ur III period (Waetzoldt 1970–1971:9, 18).

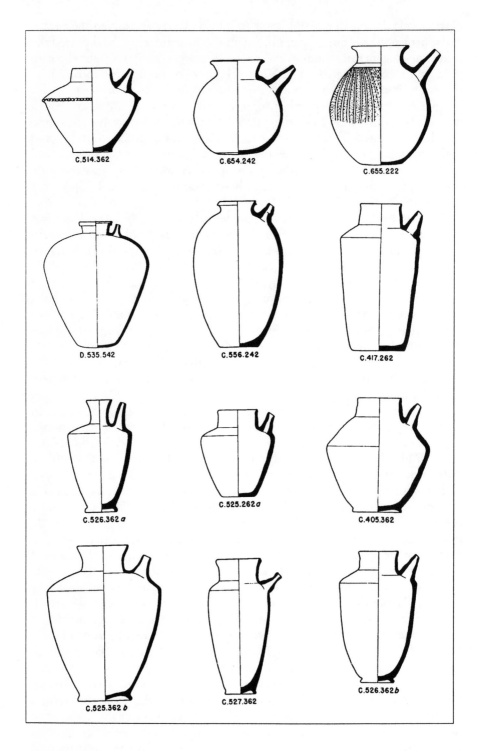

Figure VI.1 Spouted forms of Jamdat Nasr through ED III date from the Diyala region (after Delougaz 1952)

Figure VI.2 Lager, bitter or ale? Three varieties of Archaic signs for beer (after Nissen, Damerow and Englund 1990: various figs.)

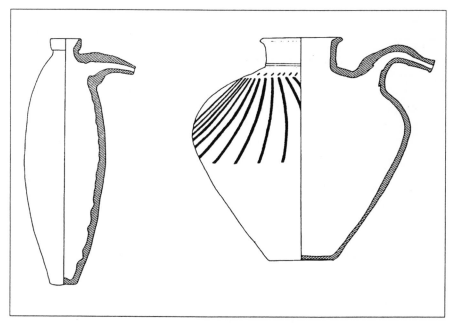

Figure VI.3 Late Uruk vessels with drooping spouts from Habuba Kabira in Syria (after Sürenhagen 1978: Tab. 17.102, 12.76)

Milk and its By-products

Unlike beer, milkfat is generally represented in the Archaic texts (Fig. VI.4) by a straight-necked vessel without a spout (Nissen, Damerow and Englund 1990:136, 178; cf. Deimel 1944:324–5; Englund 1991:101–4), although one of the signs used for it may include either a spout or a strap handle (?). A famous inlaid panel from the Ninhursag temple at Tell al-'Ubaid which dates to the late Early Dynastic period shows a scene (Fig. VI.5) of milk being poured from a large, short-necked vessel with pointed base through a strainer and into a squat, spouted vessel (Gouin 1993:136, Partie B2 and Fig. 2e). In spite of the fact that the proto-cuneiform sign for milkfat is obviously a stylization, it most closely resembles the vessel out of which the milk is being poured on the Tell al-'Ubaid relief.

The consumption of milk and its by-products in antiquity has been examined in recent years both from a physiological and an archaeological point of view. The extent to which it was an important dietary component

Figure VI.4 Three varieties of Archaic signs for milkfat (after Nissen, Damerow and Englund 1990: various figs.)

four or five thousand years ago is by no means self-evident. To begin with, however, it is necessary to review several points about milk and milk products.

Milk supplies the amino acid lysine, otherwise absent in a diet based largely on cereals, as well as providing the body with fat, protein, sugar and calcium (Simoons 1971:431–9, 1980:83–92).[6] Milk is extremely versatile, and can be converted into a variety of products such as cheese, yoghurt and ghee (clarified butter) which can be stored in an arid climate where raw milk would otherwise spoil. It is important to realize, however, that animals not intentionally bred for milk production produce very little of it (cf. Chapter III). Moreover, human populations are not physiologically well adapted for the consumption of milk. This is especially true of adults who, with the exception of Euro-Americans, have difficulty in digesting milk because of a lack of the enzyme lactase which breaks down lactose. In fact, lactase production ceases in all humans after the age of about 4 years, and even though most Euro-American juveniles, sub-adults and adults continue to drink milk thereafter they do not produce any more lactase. Lactose tolerance is, moreover, a recent genetic development, and adult milk consumption is, in general, a recent and geographically restricted feature of the human diet. Fermented products such as cheese and yoghurt are thus important, not only because they can be stored and kept over longer periods of time than raw milk, but also because these have a lower lactose content.

As a close examination of the archaeological evidence by A. Sherratt showed some years ago (Sherratt 1981:261–305; cf. Gouin 1993:135–45),

Figure VI.5 Detail of the milk-pouring scene from the Ninhursag temple at Tell al-'Ubaid (after Gouin 1993: Fig. 1)

milk production through selective herding and milk consumption on a large scale were part of a 'secondary Neolithic revolution' which occurred throughout the Eurasian steppe corridor and arid north Africa (including Western Asia and thus Mesopotamia) beginning around 4000 BC. Ceramically, it is marked by a whole new series of closed pottery vessels, including butter churns, which appear in the Chalcolithic (e.g. in Ghassulian contexts in Palestine) and Neolithic societies of Eurasia. It is in this context that the appearance of cattle scenes with milk vessels in Late Uruk glyptic along with actual scenes of milking in the Early Dynastic period (Fig. VI.6), signs for milk and its by-products in the Archaic texts and the relief from the Ninhursag temple at Tell al-ʿUbaid must be seen. They are not part of a system of milk production and consumption which was already ancient by the end of the fourth millennium. Rather, they are some of the earliest and clearest representations of milk usage in Western Asia.

Among the Archaic texts from Uruk is a small group of approximately eight documents which, with one exception, 'seem to record exclusively measures of liquid goods, in all likelihood animal fats and milk products' (Englund 1991:101–4), most probably clarified butter or 'ghee'. If we examine the written sources from the later periods in Mesopotamia then we find a wide range of names applied to vessels associated with milk, including Akk. *nakrimu* (a leather container for milk or beer), *namāṣu* (a churn), *sakirru* (a churn?),[7] *matqanu ša šizbu,* (a tripod, often wooden, for

Figure VI.6 Glyptic representations of 1. cattle and calves with milk vessels (?) in their byres (after Sherratt 1981: Fig. 10.12); 2. a cow being milked on an Early Dynastic seal in the Louvre (after Amiet 1961: Pl. 87.1148) 3. a goat (?) being milked on an Early Dynastic seal in a private collection (after Amiet 1961: Pl. 87.1146)

supporting milk vessels with pointed bases), *karpatu* (a pot for milk), *kūtu* (a clay, metal or rarely wooden container, often with a spout, for the storage or serving of liquids), *hallu* (a ceramic container for milk) and *lahannu* (a 'bottle' for milk). As in the case of beer, it is difficult to know how form-specific the notion of a milk container was. Certainly one of the Archaic signs which has been identified with Sum. *ga*, 'milk' (Green and Nissen 1987; cf. Szarzynska 1969:19, no. 9), bears a striking resemblance to two-handled, Central European vessels used in milk processing and indeed occurs visually on Late Uruk glyptic as well (Fig. VI.7) (Sherratt 1981:281, third row down, far left).

Figure VI.7 Archaic sign *ga*, 'milk' (after Szarzynska 1969: 19), compared with a two-handled, late prehistoric Central European churn (after Sherratt 1981: 281), and a Late Uruk seal impression from Uruk on which the same sign clearly appears in the upper portion of the scene (after Brandes 1979: Taf. 30)

Oil

The Sumerian term ^{dug}*šagan* denoted a pointed vessel which was mainly used to hold oil (Waetzoldt 1970–1971:22, n. 161). Often these were transported in a kind of net-or basket-like support which was suspended from a pole, as shown clearly on Early Dynastic limestone wall reliefs and glyptic (Fig. VI.8). The same type of large vessel seen on the Khafajah relief is well known in the contemporary corpus of pottery from sites like Ur (Woolley 1934:Type 61) and Tell al-'Ubaid (Hall and Woolley 1927:Pls. LIII, LVII). Moreover, smaller examples have appeared as far away as Umm an-Nar island off the coast of Abu Dhabi (Frifelt 1991:Figs. 86–90, 125–128, 137, 179–181, 207) (Fig. VI.9) where, as analyses have confirmed, the vessels in question were Mesopotamian in origin (Mynors 1983:377–87). This is particularly interesting in view of the fact that, as Ur III texts attest (e.g. UET III 1511), fine sesame oil was one of the commodities exchanged for copper from Magan (the Oman peninsula) by Mesopotamian merchants in the

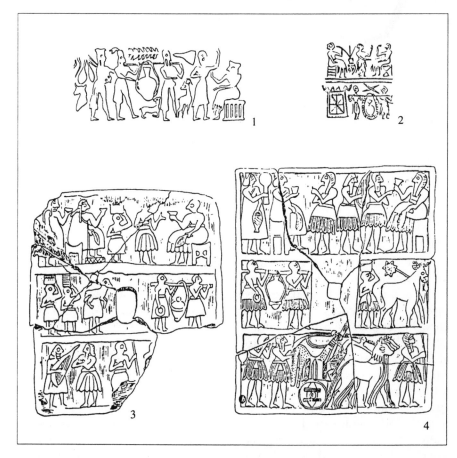

Figure VI.8 Early Dynastic representations of large (oil?) jars being carried by a support suspended from a pole. 1. ED II seal from Fara (after Amiet 1961: Pl. 100.1317; 2. ED IIIa, Royal Cemetery of Ur (after Amiet 1961: Pl. 90.1191); 3. late ED II/early ED III, Sin Temple IX, Khafajah (after Amiet 1961: Pl. 93.1222); 4. ED II, House D, Temple Oval at Khafajah and Ur, lower left fragment (after Amiet 1961: Pl. 93.1223)

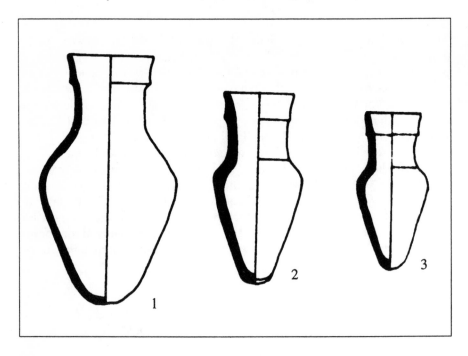

Figure VI.9 Comparable ceramic vessels from 1. Umm an-Nar; 2. Ur; and 3. Tell al-'Ubaid (after Potts 1986: Fig. 7.6-8 not to scale)

reign of Ibbi-Sin (cf. Potts 1993:425). It is logical to suppose that oil may have been shipped in containers such as these.

Wine

Tablet X of ur_5-*ra* = *hubullu* contains a wide variety of terms for wine vessels (generally *dug-geštin* but other variants occur, e.g. entries 120, 139, 161, 190, 234, 325–326), and as we saw in Chapter III, grapes were certainly cultivated in southern Mesopotamia in antiquity, where red wine seems to have been the norm. The god Ningishzida appears as a god of wine and the grape in a text which speaks of his shedding red tears, while elsewhere, in mystical texts identifying parts of deities' bodies with non-biological elements, his eyeball is equated with a grape (Lambert 1990:127). There is, nevertheless, little direct archaeological or philological information available from the region, most of it coming instead from sites like Mari on the Middle Euphrates or Nimrud in Assyria. From the point of view of ceramics it is interesting to note that, at Mari, wine was sold not according to specified amounts in liquid measures, but by the jar, and the same applied to grain, oil, and honey (Finet 1974–1977:122–31). This suggests the use of standard measures (and by extension ceramic forms?) which were recognized, if not necessarily stated explicitly, and A. Finet suggests that the 10 *qa*/l jar was the common unit of measurement for wine at Mari.

The discovery of drinking tubes (the ancient equivalent of straws for imbibing liquids) in the Royal Cemetery at Ur (Woolley 1934), and the frequency of banquet scenes in Mesopotamian glyptic (Selz 1983) (Fig.

Figure VI.10 Two banquet scenes showing drinking through tubes. 1. Early Dynastic, Khafajah (after Amiet 1961: Pl. 89.1171); 2. ED IIIa, Royal Cemetery of Ur (after Amiet 1961: Pl. 90.1190)

VI.10) showing the consumption of beverages, need not point exclusively to wine drinking but could equally apply to beer. Indeed the term for a drinking tube used for beer is well attested (Sum. *gi-níg-kaš-šur-ra*, Akk. *qan kuninnāti*). Nevertheless, it is likely that wine was drunk, not as we know it today in individual beakers or cups out of a bottle, but out of large vats, similar to the Greek *krater* or mixing vessel. In the Achaemenid period Xenophon described the drinking of barley wine through drinking tubes in Armenia. The wine, he says, was set out in large bowls, with barley floating on surface (*Anab.* IV 5). By this time, too, wine-sets of Greek or Mediterranean inspiration had begun to appear in greater Mesopotamia, as shown by their discovery at Deve Höyük near Carchemish and Qalat al-Bahrain on Bahrain island (Moorey 1980:181–97). This mode of mixing and drinking wine introduced a different, non-Mesopotamian set of vessel forms, often of metal, and has no bearing on the earlier periods of wine consumption in the region.

Honey

There exists no monographic study of honey (Sum. *làl*, Akk. *dišpu*) in ancient Mesopotamia (for orientation see CAD D: 161–163, s.v. *dišpu*; and Lambert 1972–1975:469). Honey was measured by the *sìla*/l and names for honey vessels appear, as noted above, in Hh X (121, 140, 235). Judging from the extensive use of honey in medical prescriptions, honey vessels must have been part of the household stock of all healers. On the other hand, numerous religious texts concerning offerings to the gods as well as texts concerned with the consecration of new buildings involve the use of honey, often mixed with oil. Judging from the variety of designations attested to for types of honey, e.g. 'dark honey', 'red honey', 'white honey', 'mountain honey', 'date honey' and 'grape honey', the ancient Mesopotamians knew nearly as many different types as we do today. Nothing suggests, however, that it was ever a commodity for common consumption. How advanced apiculture was in southern Mesopotamia is unclear, but in a Neo-Assyrian period text Shamash-resh-usur, the governor of Suhi on the Middle Euphrates (near the modern Haditha region of western Iraq), boasts as follows (CAD D: 163):

> I have brought down from the mountain of the Habha-people the bees that collect honey [which none of my forefathers had ever seen or brought down to the land of Suhi], and established them in the gardens of the town GN – [there] they [now] collect honey and wax, I [also] know how to [separate] honey and wax by melting [the combs] and [my] gardeners know it too [and should somebody appear later on and ask the old people of the country] "Is it true that Shamash-resh-usur, the governor of Suhi, has introduced honey bees into Suhi?"

Although we are given no indication of what may have been used as a hive in southern Mesopotamia, hollowed-out date-palm trunks, used historically as beehives in both Yemen and Oman, would have been a readily available resource.

Mass-Production, Professionalisation, and Standardisation

The question may legitimately be asked, does the existence of a wide-ranging lexical field covering ceramics necessarily presuppose an organized, industrial mode of pottery production, or is such a range of terms equally compatible with household, domestic production for individual, familial use? The existence of complex folk taxonomies of other categories of material culture throughout the world (for orientation, see Conklin 1980) would suggest that detailed taxonomic classification and intensity of production are by no means linked in a systemic fashion. What is important to note, however, is the existence of the professional title for 'potter' (*bahar*) already in the Archaic professions and titles list of the Late Uruk and Jamdat Nasr periods (Nissen, Damerow and Englund 1990:156). This is a clear indication that the division of labour had proceeded to the extent that potting had become a profession which was conducted by specialists on more than just a household basis. While the evidence for the industrial organization of ceramic specialization during the Ur III period is clear (see below), there is important archaeological evidence which proves that a high degree of organized ceramic production, involving both standardization of shapes and specialization of labour, was well entrenched in southern Mesopotamia by the Late Uruk period.

In 1968 H.J. Nissen published the results of his soundings in area K/L XII at Uruk. There he presented, for the first time, his views on ceramic mass production in ancient Mesopotamia (Nissen 1970:101–91; cf. Adams and Nissen 1972:99, 'The early mass-produced pottery types'). Nissen was struck by the fact that, of *c.* 6000 sherds recovered, roughly 80% were from either bevel-rim bowls or conical cups, followed by the solid-footed goblets of the Early Dynastic I period (Fig. VI.11). This material, he noted, differed completely from the rest of the ceramics of the late fourth and early third millennia BC and was, judged metrically, visually or in terms of paste and surface treatment, clearly mass-produced. Unsatisfied with previous suggestions that these vessels had served to hold votive offerings, as simple household vessels or for manufacturing yoghurt, Nissen pointed to a formal similarity between bevel-rim bowls and the sign for 'cereal ration' (*ninda*) in the Archaic texts and to the presence of the same sign as part of the pictogram GU_7 meaning 'ration/distribution' (Nissen 1970:137; cf. Nissen, Damerow and Englund 1990:51) (Fig. VI.12). The notion of mass production of the cheapest product possible to serve as a ration-container accounted for the coarseness of the paste of these vessels, their crudeness in general and their great uniformity in appearance.

Nissen's suggestion was later investigated by G.A. Johnson who presented a geometric model for measuring the internal volume of a bevel-rim bowl (Fig. VI.13), the principal mass-produced type of the Late Uruk and, to a less extent, Jamdat Nasr period (Johnson 1973:135, Fig. 30). After measuring hundreds of complete profiles Johnson found that volumes seemed to cluster around three modes, averaging 0.922, 0.647 and 0.465 l, respectively. He then compared this with cuneiform data on barley rations to see if these corresponded with known ration amounts. This is difficult, however, given that rations for men, women and children differed from period to period and their size in the Late Uruk period is, in any case, unknown. Monthly rates were sometimes as high as 96 *sila*/l (pre-Sargonic) or as low as 40 *sila*/l for men (Ur III), as high as 36 *sila*/l (pre-Sargonic) or as low as 18 *sila*/l for women (pre-Sargonic) and as high as 20 *sila*/l for boys (Old Akkadian) or as low as 10 *sila*/l for girls (Ur III) (Ellison 1981:40–1, Table 3). Undaunted by the uncertainty surrounding the putative rations which were thought to have been dispensed in the bevel-rim bowls, Johnson rounded his figures up to standard units of 1, 0.72 and 0.50 l, suggesting 'the existence of a standard volume measure, and the production of bevel-rim bowls with volumes proportionate to this standard measure' (Johnson

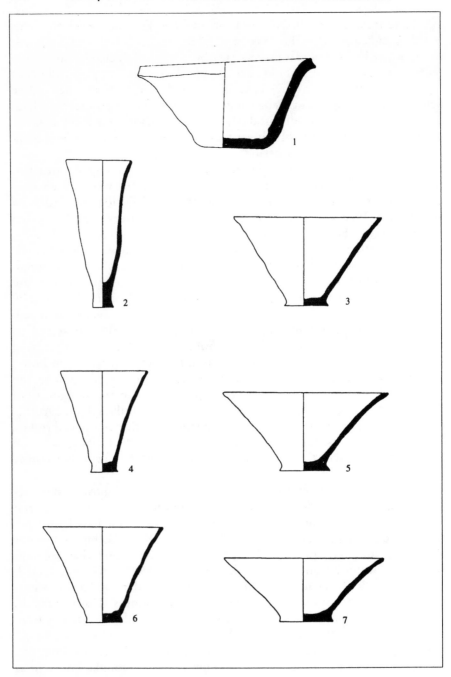

Figure VI.11 Late Uruk, Jamdat Nasr and ED I mass-produced types from Uruk. 1. bevel-rim bowl; 2. solid-footed goblet; 3-7. conical cups (after Pongratz-Leisten 1988: 275, 301)

1973:135). In 1978 T.W. Beale criticized Johnson's defence of Nissen's theory, showing that the modal distribution was more apparent than real, and suggesting that the bevel-rim bowls were home-made votive containers brought to the temple (Beale 1978:289–313). Since then, several other

Figure VI.12 Archaic signs, based on the bevel-rim bowl (1. Uruk IV; 2. Uruk III), for 'cereal ration' and the sign for 'ration/redistribution', made up of a sign for the bowl and a human head (after Nissen, Damerow and Englund 1990: Abb. 17s)

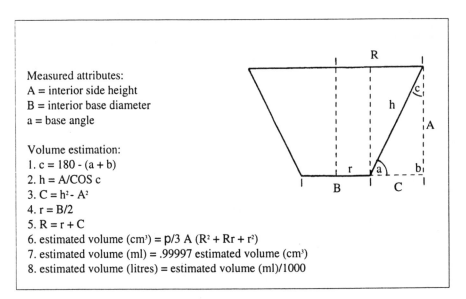

Measured attributes:
A = interior side height
B = interior base diameter
a = base angle

Volume estimation:
1. c = 180 - (a + b)
2. h = A/COS c
3. C = h² - A²
4. r = B/2
5. R = r + C
6. estimated volume (cm³) = p/3 A (R² + Rr + r²)
7. estimated volume (ml) = .99997 estimated volume (cm³)
8. estimated volume (litres) = estimated volume (ml)/1000

Figure VI.13 How to estimate the volume of a bevel-rim bowl (after Johnson 1973: Fig. 30)

scholars have attacked Nissen's theory, most recently A.R. Millard, who suggested that bevel-rim bowls functioned as bread moulds (Millard 1988:49–57).

At issue here is not so much the function of bevel-rim bowls and the other mass-produced types identified by Nissen, as the fact of their mass production. Beale's suggestion that they were home-made can be rejected out of hand. They were, as anyone who has ever studied them carefully can see, mass-produced and so uniform in appearance that household production by thousands of individual potters cannot be entertained as a serious possibility (Millard 1988:54, while contesting the ration-container thesis, accepts that they were mass-produced). Moreover, the sophistication of most of the Late Uruk pottery repertoire and the difficulty of achieving many of the forms by which it is characterized, such as composite vessels (Fig. VI.14) with high, carinated shoulders, nose-lugs, spouts and strap handles, not to mention the use of the wheel[8] (Fig. VI.15), argue strongly against the possibility of large-scale household production in southern Mesopotamia at this date.[9]

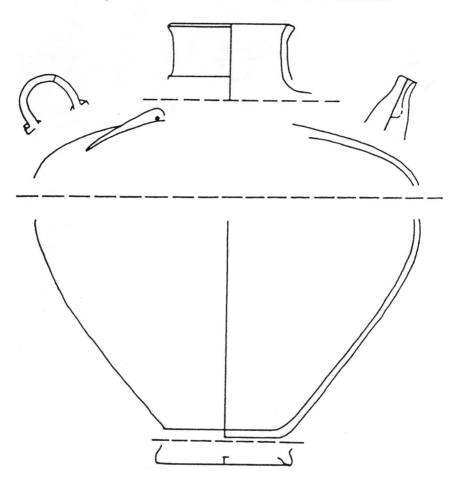

Figure VI.14 Drawing showing the composite nature of a large, spouted Late Uruk vessel with separately constructed ring base, lower body, shoulder, spout, nose-lugs, strap handle and neck (after Sürenhagen 1978: Fig. 49)

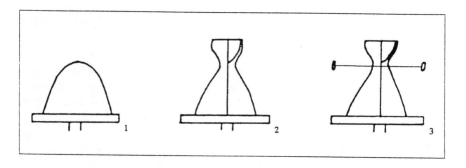

Figure VI.15 Diagram showing the use of the wheel for mass-producing small vessels 'off the hump', i.e. from a large lump of clay (1) off which individual vessels are successively thrown (2) and then cut with a string across their base (3) (after Sürenhagen 1978: Fig. 48). This was the technique used to throw conical cups and solid-footed goblets

Evidence from Umma

Two Ur III texts from Umma (MW 124 and 125) (Waetzoldt 1970–1971:7–41) are long-term ledgers concerning the work of two large pottery workshops over the course of a year. Both texts follow the standardized accounting procedures[10] (Fig. VI.16) introduced during the middle of Shulgi's reign (2094–2047 BC) whereby the amount of labour (usually converted into time, i.e. working days) and materials 'loaned' by the state to the foreman in charge is reported as a 'debit'. This is followed by an enumeration of 'credits', i.e. real production during the year. The texts conclude with a balance posting either a deficit if the labour and raw materials on hand at the beginning of the reporting period exceeded production, or a surplus if they were under the work unit's actual performance.[11]

Generally speaking, potters during the Ur III period worked in teams of from two to ten men[12] under a supervisor, although in some cases they worked alone. As professional craftsmen they were attached to all sorts of establishments where the need for ceramics and presumably breakage were constant, including state kitchens (*é-muhaldim*), breweries (*é-bappir*), mills

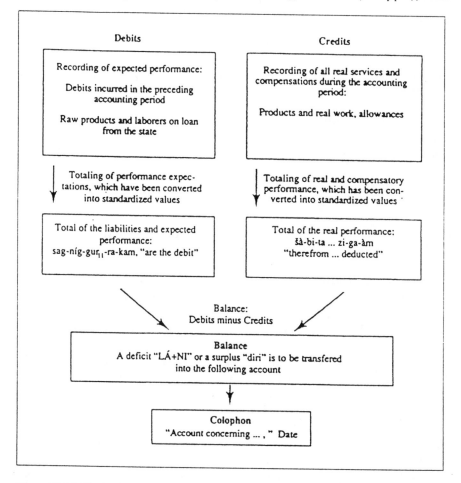

Figure VI.16 The basic structure of Ur III balanced accounts (after Englund 1991: Fig. 1)

(*é-HAR.HAR*), various temples, and the houses or palaces of high-ranking individuals including Shulgi himself (Waetzoldt 1970–1971:9–10). The rations given to potters were similar to those apportioned to most other craftsmen, varying between 30 and 60 *sila*/l of barley per month and 3–4 minas of wool per year. Additionally, their children received 10–20 *sila*/l of barley per month and 1–1.5 minas of wool per year.

The importance of the Umma texts for an understanding of late third-millennium ceramics in southern Mesopotamia is twofold. On the one hand, they present us with an assemblage from the middle of the Ur III period[13] consisting of no fewer than forty-six different vessel types which, in contrast to the 'theoretical' typology of the lexical literature, is no mere amalgam of names from chronologically disparate sources assembled by a scribe. On the other hand, these texts record precisely the amount of time required to manufacture each specific category of vessel. In terms of real performance, MW 124 records the manufacture of nearly 2000 vessels and 12 other clay objects, representing a total of 3604.38+ workdays, while text MW 125 records the manufacture of 66,711 + vessels along with 40 other clay objects, representing some 7206.2 workdays. As Table VI.1 shows, the Ur III timekeepers were extraordinarily punctilious in reckoning precisely how long it took to make ceramic vessels of varying size, although the surprising length of time involved for individual vessels (e.g. 1 work day of 12 hours[14] for a 30-*sila*/l vessel) suggests that in calculating labour-time all of the steps up to the actual throwing, that is, collecting the clay, treatment of clay (washing, sieving, mixing with temper), etc. were included. Whether these calculations also took into account firing time and/or the time necessary to fire up the kiln is not clear (Waetzoldt 1970–1971:11). The fact that 60 talents (1800 kg) of reeds are noted in the 'debit' section of MW 124, ostensibly as fuel for the ceramic kilns, is perhaps an indirect indication that firing time and costs were calculated into the total production cost of a given vessel type.

The principal difference immediately discernible between the nomenclature of ceramics in the lexical tradition and that found in the Umma texts is the frequency of volumetric qualifications in the latter case. Thus, generic words for 'vessel' (*dug, dug-GAR*) may be accompanied by a qualifier such as 1, 2, 5, 10, 15, 20, 30 or 60 *sila*/l. This concern with the volume of a given vessel is reflected in the not insignificant number of southern Mesopotamian sherds and complete vessels which bear a short notation, incised before firing, of their actual *sila* capacity. In this regard, an Old Babylonian mathematical text published by F. Thureau-Dangin in 1932 is important in stating the relationship between the dry capacity in grain of a ceramic vessel and its circumference and depth (Gelb 1982:588). The high number of 1-*sila*/l vessels in MW 125, no fewer than 60,217 of which are mentioned, is striking. Nor is this figure without precedent. No less than 75,652 1-*sila*/l vessels are booked in another Ur III text from Girsu (RTC 307 IX 7). With regard to the discussion of the disbursement of barley rations in ceramic containers mentioned above, I.J. Gelb, the godfather of all studies on the ancient Mesopotamian ration system, cited these texts as evidence in favour of Nissen's ration bowl hypothesis (Gelb 1982:589).

Vessel Name	Meaning	Capacity	Production Time	Total Production
dug-10 (-sìla)	10-*sìla* vessel	10 l	0.3 day	120
dug-15-sìla	15-*sìla* vessel	15 l	0.5 day	85
dug-20 (sìla)	20-*sìla* vessel	20 l	—	60+
dug-30 (-sìla)	30-*sìla* vessel	30 l	1 day	170
dug-am-am-am-da-dù	. . . . vessel	*c.* 1 l?	0.1 day	38
dug-dúr-bala	upright vessel for pouring	*c.* 10 l?	1 day	12
dug-dúr-bùr	filter vessel	*c.* 10 l?	0.5 day	15
dug-ga-10 (-sìla)	10-*sìla* vessel	10 l	0.3 day	25
dug-gal	large vessel	20 l	—	60+
dug-GAM.GAM.HU	. . . . vessel	*c.* 1 l?	0.2 day	1
dug-GAR	(storage vessel for bread, flour, water?)			
dug-GAR-a-šu-DI	. . . . vessel	*c.* 2 l	0.16 day	30
dug-GAR-ka-dagal	. . . . vessel with a wide mouth	25–30 l	1–1.25 days	374
dug-GAR.NÌ-a-SU.SU	. . . . vessel	-10 l	0.3 day	9
dug-GAR-1-sìla	. . . . 1-*sìla* vessel	1 l	0.25 day	[351]
dug-GAR-2-sìla	. . . . 2-*sìla* vessel	2 l	?	[ ]
dug-GAR-5-sìla vessel	5 l	0.3 day	1128	
dug-gur-túl	drawing/ladling vessel	20 l	1 day?	31
dug-kur-KU.DÙ-1-gur	*kurKUDU* storage jar of 1 gur (for oil, beer, spices, cereals, clay?, honey)	300 l	10 days	3
dug lahtanx-1-gur	*lahtan*-jar of 300 l for beer-bread dough or oil	300 l	10 days	6
dug lam-ri6	*lam-ri6*-vat	*c.* 10–15 l	0.5 day	12
dug ma-al-tum-tur	small bowl	?	0.16 day	300
dug ma-an-hara4	*namhāru*-jug	10 l (3–20 l)	0.66 day	15
dug-nì-luh	wash basin (bronze, silver)	5–10 l	0.25 day	13
dug-NIGÍN-d[a]	. . . . vessel	*c.* 10 l	0.5 day	[298]
dug-sag-gá	. . . . vessel	*c.* 10 l	0.5 day	60
dug sìla-bàn-da	. . . .-*sìla*-vessel	10 l	1 day	122
dug sìla-gal	large *sìla*-vessel	*c.* 1 l	0.1 day	[144]
dug sìla-KU.DÙ	*sìla*-vessel in the form of a KU.DÙ-vessel	*c.* 1 l	0.066 day	2400
dug sìla-sá-du11	*sìla*-vessel in the form of a *sá-du11*-vessel	*c.* 1 l	0.066 day	61,047+
dug sìla-sag-gá	*sìla*-vessel in the form of a *sag-gá*-vessel	*c.* 1 l	0.1 day	33
dug sìla-zà-HAR	. . . .-*sìla*-vessel	*c.* 1 l	—	6+
dug sìla-zà-LI	. . . .-*sìla*-vessel	1 l+	0.25 day	780
dug-šà-gub	beer-mash vat	10 l	—	120
dug šagan	pointed vessel	0.3–12 l	5.5–6 days for 110–120 l vessels	49
dug tá-bil-tum	carring/transport vessel	1–3 l	0.5 day	185
dug-ubur-imin	vessel with 7 teats/nipples	*c.* 10 l	1.5 days	12
dug utúl-10-(-sìla)	10-*sìla* basin	10 l	0.5 day	4
dug utúl-60-(-sìla)	60-*sìla* basin	60 l	2 days	[2]
dug utúl-gal	large basin	*c.* 30 sìla/l	1.5 days	204
dug utúl-murux	medium basin	*c.* 30 sìla/l	1 day	120
dug utúl-tur	small basin	*c.* 5 sìla/l	0.25 day	40
dug za-hum-ì	. . . . vessel for oil	*c.* 1 sìla/l	0.1 day	30
dug zí-tu-ru-um	. . . . vessel	*c.* 1 sìla/l	0.16 day	195
dug-x [ ]	. . . . vessel	1–5 sìla	0.16 day	4

Table VI.1 *Ceramic typology at Umma during the Ur III period according to MW124 and 125*

Aside from the volumetric designations found in the Umma ceramic terminology, we find a variety of vessels identified by the commodities they were meant to hold, such as milk, beer-bread, beer-mash and oil. If we had access to living Mesopotamian informants it would, of course, be fascinating to see them identify the vessel types named in the Umma texts with contemporary Ur III ceramic forms found in archaeological excavations. While this is obviously impossible, a list of some thirty-five vessel forms used in the Diyala during the Ur III period has been drawn up, along with illustrations which give some idea of the range of ceramic variation in this period (Table VI.2, Figs. VI.17–VI.18). Certain types, known from the Umma texts, are obviously missing in the Diyala collection, however, the most obvious ones being the two different vessels of 1 *gur* (300 l.) capacity which must have been enormous, and the *dug-ubur-imin*, or 'vessel with 7 teats/nipples'.

In conclusion, there can be no doubt that specialization (i.e. craft production by specialists); standardization (i.e. 'reduction in variability' as expressed in a high 'degree of homogeneity') and mass production characterized the Ur III ceramic industry, as indeed they characterised pottery production from at least the Late Uruk period onwards in Mesopotamia. Considering the wealth of data contained in them, it is surprising that the Umma documents seem to have gone unnoticed by most archaeologists

Category	Description	Type Numbers	Comments
bowl	open conical	B.002.200b	only 1 example
	thick-walled	B.032.200b	popular
	thick-walled, shallow	B.031.200	
	open	C.042.200,	last one most common bowl
		B.043.200a-b, B.123.210,	form
		B.151.210	
	miniature	A.151.210	not illustrated
	large, with ring base	C.111.310a	
	large, with flat base	C.111.210	surface find
	large, spouted	C.544.312	only 1 example
lid		B.061.210	
cup	crude with flaring top	B.256.200	attested earlier
	thin-walled	B.706.360	new type continuing later
	miniature	A.026.200	
jar	wide-mouthed, flat-based	B.184.220a, B.573.240	
	'with pinched pouring lip'	B.536.224	
	small, spouted	B.545.222b	
	small, flat-based, narrow mouth	B.536.240b	
	tall, flaring-necked	B.546.222, C.657.242	
	tall, wide-necked	B.645.540a	close parallels elsewhere
	lidded	C.555.440	
	miniature	A.055.100, A.545.360	
	medium-sized storage	C.555.510	
	large storage	D.556.640	
bottle	squat with convex base	B.663.570b, B.663.520	
	miniature	A.653.540	
'household'	medium-sized	C.466.470	survival from earlier periods
brazier	large shallow	D.201.201a-b	
tub	oval	D.800.102	
lamp		B.813.522	new type continuing later

Table VI.2 *Common pottery types of the Ur III period in the Diyala region*

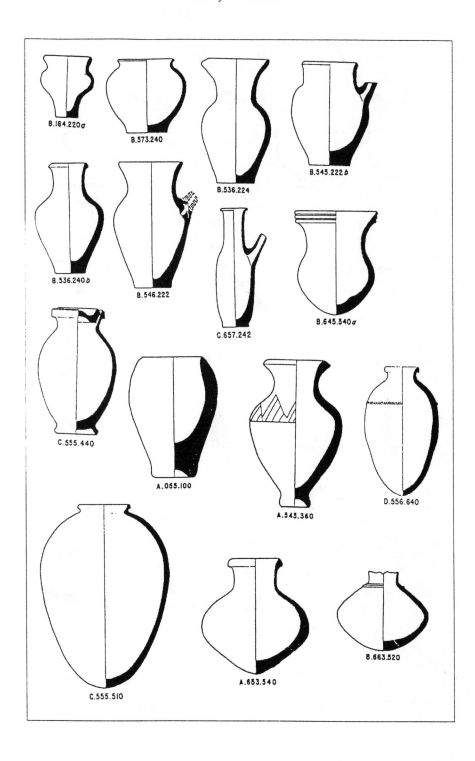

Figure VI.17 Ur III jars and bottles (after Delougaz 1952)

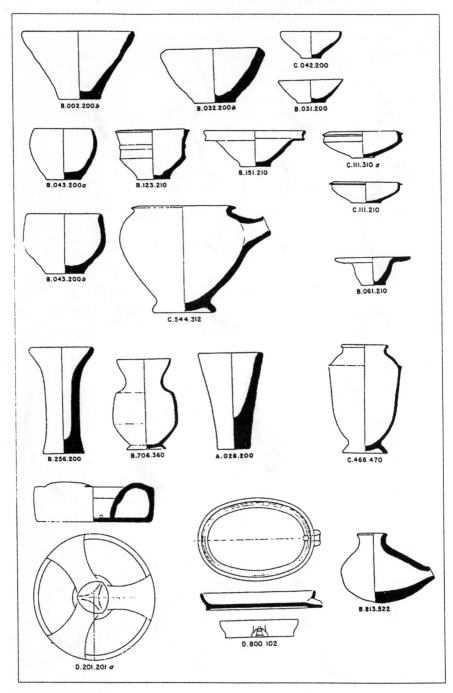

Figure VI.18 Ur III bowls, cups, lid, brazier, tub and lamp (after Delougaz 1952)

discussing these issues in the archaeology of greater Mesopotamia (e.g. Blackman, Stein and Vandiver 1993).

The question may be asked, to what extent does the pattern of ceramic production in the fourth and third millennia BC continue into the later periods? While there are no Old Babylonian texts which contain the level of detail found in the Ur III texts just considered, the evidence of the ceramics themselves must argue conclusively against the notion of a diminution in professionalization or specialization. J. Renger has cited a pair of texts from Sippar, one of which records the delivery of 1380 vessels by a potter, while the other contains a remark to the effect that 100 vessels were 'still in the hands of the potters' (Renger 1984:88–9). In addition, an Old Babylonian text (YOS V 253) records an agreement regarding the apprenticeship of an individual to a potter. Nevertheless, Renger suggests that, during the Old Babylonian period, 'pottery generally was made by individual members of a household, mostly the women, using their own hearth, an open fire, or perhaps a common kiln to fire their pottery' (Renger 1984:89). This belief, however, is at complete variance with the nature of the ceramics themselves. There seems no question, when the ceramics themselves[15] are examined, that we are dealing with the same level of industrial production as earlier. The use of the fast wheel, the complete uniformity in clay preparation and the massive amounts of sherds reflecting identical shapes, all argue for a level of professionalization, specialization and standardization as great in this as in all other periods of the historic era in Mesopotamia. This is not to deny that, as at Habuba Kabira, a small, statistically insignificant portion of the pottery used in the region may have been handmade, but this level of local production was never comparable to that achieved in the workshops of the major towns and cities of the area.

At first glance, the monumental quantities of pottery found on sites in Mesopotamia seem to be at variance with the relatively rare occurrence of positively identified potter's kilns (Sum. *udun*, Akk. *utûnu*). Yet this is quite clearly a product of excavation in areas unlikely to have housed industrial establishments. For whereas solitary examples have been excavated at a number of sites, such as Jamdat Nasr and Early Dynastic Uruk (Pongratz-Leisten 1988:267ff., in Area Md XV 4–5), Early Dynastic III Abu Salabikh (Moorey 1994:146), Old Akkadian Tell Yelkhi (Bergamini, Saporetti, Costantini, Costantini Biasini and Masiero 1985:45 and photograph p. 157) in the Hamrin basin, Isin-Larsa period Tell Asmar in the Diyala (Delougaz 1952:122, n. 197) and Kassite Tell Kesaran in the Hamrin (Valtz 1985:69 and photograph p. 167), some five hundred or more kilns have been reported from Umm al-Hafriyat, a small site near Nippur (Adams 1981:no. 1188), while seven areas of pottery production have been identified on the surface of Al-Hiba (ancient Lagash) and at least ten kilns have been excavated at the Ubaid period site of Tell Abada in the Hamrin basin of northeastern Iraq (Jasim 1989:86; cf. Moorey 1994:143–6). More recently, concentrations of 'slag heaps and kiln wasters', found near two small canals running through the Old Babylonian site of Mashkan-Shapir, have been interpreted as evidence of ceramic workshops (Stone and Zimansky 1992:214). It is thought, however, that this was not a unique find, and there seems to be evidence of 'ceramic manufacture in all parts of the site . . . every neighborhood probably had its own potter' (Stone and Zimansky 1992:217). At Ur, on the other hand, I.M. Diakonoff has interpreted the heavy concentration of terracottas found at nearby Diqdiqah as evidence of 'a village of potters' (Diakonoff 1985:52, n. 14).

CONCLUSION

In this discussion of ceramics more emphasis has been placed on function and content than is usually the case in studies of Mesopotamian pottery. This approach represents a clear departure from standard archaeological approaches to the definition of ceramic assemblages, and is aimed at defining the viewpoint of the users of ceramics rather more than is normally the case in archaeological studies of ceramics.

Moreover, this sort of study has implications for an understanding of typological change through time. Once we begin to think of form and size in relation to function, then changes in the ceramic repertoire take on added significance. No longer are they merely seen as reflections of changing fashions. Rather, the disappearance of old forms and the introduction of new ones may imply the introduction of new foods and drinks, techniques of food and drink preparation and approaches to storage. Moreover, new forms may be adopted, whether to serve old needs or as part of the equipment needed to service new ones, as a result of contact with a foreign group. This is not meant to be a reversion to late nineteenth- and early twentieth-century diffusionism in which successive prehistoric ceramic assemblages were interpreted as the results of the appearance of new populations. Rather it is meant to call attention to the fact that ceramic production, like many categories of technology, is inherently conservative and any significant changes should be scrutinized with a view to determining what functional consequences are implied by formal variation. In order to examine this subject in more concrete terms, we shall return to the subject of ceramics in Chapter XIII, where the changes which took place in the ceramic repertoire of southern Mesopotamia following its conquest by Alexander the Great are examined.

NOTES

1 For general orientation on liquids consumed in ancient Mesopotamia, see Bottéro 1957–1971:302–6.

2 Delougaz 1952:135, noting the similarity between ATU 136 and vessel shape B.003.200b; ATU 139 and C.536.270; ATU 153 and C.665.222; and ATU 140 and a spouted vessel from Fara (*MJ* XXII: Pl. XXV.3).

3 Note that whenever signs are illustrated from the Archaic texts these have been rotated 90° to the right so that they appear in their upright position. On the tablets themselves, they appear as though lying horizontally on their sides. My justification for altering their position is simply to make comparison with pottery drawings easier.

4 'Dough which was lightly baked before being crumbled in water to form the mash which would ferment'. See Millard 1988:55.

5 This was a confection of unmalted grain and spices, made in an oven, which was combined with beer-mash, made with malted grain, in the making of bread.

6 The discussion of milk and the problems surrounding its digestion is drawn from Simoons' work.

7 Dr Jeremy Black (pers. comm.) has pointed out to me that in the Sumerian literary composition known as *Dumuzi's Dream*, 'it is a *topos* that the "churns" lie overturned at Dumuzi's farmstead after the demons have carried Dumuzi away to the underworld'.

8 Sürenhagen 1978:89–90, and 95 where fifteen basic forms, along with other factors including clay preparation, the use of the wheel and the use of slips, lead Sürenhagen to the conclusion that most of the ceramic production at Habuba Kabira was the work of professional potters.

9 Sürenhagen 1978:95 found some evidence for small-scale, hand-made, local production by non-professionals. In such cases the clay used was poorly prepared and fired at low temperature (*c.* 350–500°C).

10 For this type of text in general, see Englund 1991:256ff.

11 For the mechanics of timekeeping in these and other Ur III accounts, see Englund 1988:169ff.

12 Female potters are not attested at this time. It is a general rule in Western Asia, though undoubtedly not true all of the time, that household production of pottery in antiquity was most commonly carried out by women, while industrial-scale production was predominantly performed by men.

13 MW 124 is probably to be dated to the year Amar-Sin 4, i.e. 2043/2042 BC. See Waetzoldt 1970–1971:31, n. 205.

14 For the 12–hour workday see Englund 1988:169.

15 For an archaeometric study of Old Babylonian pottery from Old Babylonian Der see Jacobs 1992:121–36.

VII Metal Production

INTRODUCTION

Ever since the systematic study of prehistory began in the nineteenth century countless scholars have commented on the impact of metalworking on the early societies of Europe and Western Asia. As a popular writer and, at the same time, an influential academic, the Australian-born prehistorian V. Gordon Childe (1892–1957) was probably more responsible for emphasizing that impact than any other English-speaking author of the twentieth century. One can scarcely pick up a work by Childe without finding references to the 'relatively large amount of social labour' expended in 'the extraction and distribution of copper and tin', the possession of which, in the form of bronze weaponry, 'consolidated the positions of war-chiefs and conquering aristocracies' (Childe 1941:133), or 'the opportunities for immense improvements in human equipment' provided by copper and bronze, the realization of which was only 'restricted by the relative scarcity of the materials and the cost of transport from the metalliferous mountain regions to the fertile valleys where population naturally congregated' (Childe 1944b:34). Childe emphasized 'the dependence of riverine societies on imported raw materials' (Childe 1937:20), a view which, as noted in Chapter IV, has often been exaggerated with respect to southern Mesopotamia, but at the same time he was well aware of early experiments with flint and bronze sickles by the Danish agricultural historian Axel Steensberg which showed conclusively 'that the saving effected by merely translating a flint sickle into bronze is considerably less than might have been anticipated' (Childe 1944a:3). Steensberg had shown that bronze sickles were capable of harvesting in 60–66 minutes what flint sickles could achieve in 68–73 minutes, scarcely a huge difference in efficiency. As a result Childe had to admit that metal tools *per se* were not intrinsically superior to stone ones, except insofar as the obsidian or chert used for stone implements in southern Mesopotamia 'had to be imported and paid for from the social surplus. Under such circumstances copper tools that can be resharpened and remelted when worn out would come cheaper in the long run' (Childe 1952:116). This is a far cry from those nineteenth-century authorities who, expressing their unshakeable faith in 'progress', extolled the virtues of metal over stone tools without a sufficient understanding of their respective properties.

In southern Mesopotamia we are faced with a situation in which metal ores were completely lacking and yet, not only were jewellery, weaponry, tools, statuary and other cast fixtures made of metal, but units of metal came to be used as equivalency standards in the pre-monetary, Mesopotamian economy. The range of metals used in southern Mesopotamia was considerable. Moreover, the literature on metallurgy is vast and no attempt will be made here to repeat what is already well synthesized elsewhere.[1] The following discussion, therefore, is intended only for general orientation and is of necessity superficial.

COPPER

With the publication of J.D. Muhly's monumental *Copper and Tin* in 1973 (Muhly 1973:155–535; cf. 1976:77–136) an enormous amount of data on copper previously scattered throughout the scholarly literature became easily accessible. Since that time a great deal more work has gone into identifying the copper sources exploited in Western Asia, analysing objects with a view to determining the provenance of the copper from which they were manufactured, linking place-names mentioned in Sumerian and Akkadian literary and economic texts as sources and suppliers of copper with actual geographical regions, and disentangling the specific terms used for different sorts of cuprous metal and ore to arrive at an accurate understanding of just what is meant by the various extant *termini technici*.

For decades it has been commonplace to think of Iran, Anatolia, Cyprus and Oman as sources of the copper used at different times in southern Mesopotamia, as indeed metallurgical, archaeological and Assyriological studies have confirmed. Yet it is less widely known that the area near the modern border between northern Iraq and southeastern Turkey (Fig. VII.1) was a source area which should be considered seriously as well. In 1845 Austen Henry Layard visited 'the Tiyari mountains, particularly in the heights above Lizan' on the Lesser Zab north of Mosul, where he found that, 'in the valley of Berwari, mines of iron, lead, copper, and other minerals abound. Both the Kurds and the Chaldaeans make their own weapons and implements of agriculture, and cast bullets for their rifles, – collecting the ores which are scattered on the declivities, or brought down by the torrents' (Layard 1849:223–4).[2] This discovery is particularly important in view of the fact that a number of very early copper finds have been made at sites in northern Iraq. These include a pendant from Shanidar cave which dates to the early ninth millennium BC (Solecki 1969:311–14; cf. Muhly 1983:350), a cold-hammered awl of native copper[3] from the aceramic site of Tell Maghzaliyah dating to the seventh millennium and seventeen pieces of copper ore from nearby Yarim Tepe I in sixth-millennium contexts (Müller-Karpe 1991:106). The copper sources described by Layard lie *c.* 130 km northeast of Tell Maghzaliyah and would have been easily accessible from the south via the Tigris and Lesser Zab. They would seem to provide a plausible and geographically closer alternative to the Anatolian mines at Ergani Maden which are usually considered (Muhly 1983:351) the source of the copper found at Shanidar, Maghzaliyah and Yarim Tepe[4] (Fig. VII.1).

Throughout Western Asia arsenical copper was one of the most important types of copper exploited in antiquity. Of those arsenic-rich copper sources closest to southern Mesopotamia, Anarak in central western Iran (Fig. VII.2), where the important Talmessi mine is located (Muhly 1973:232), is most likely to have been the source of the arsenical copper

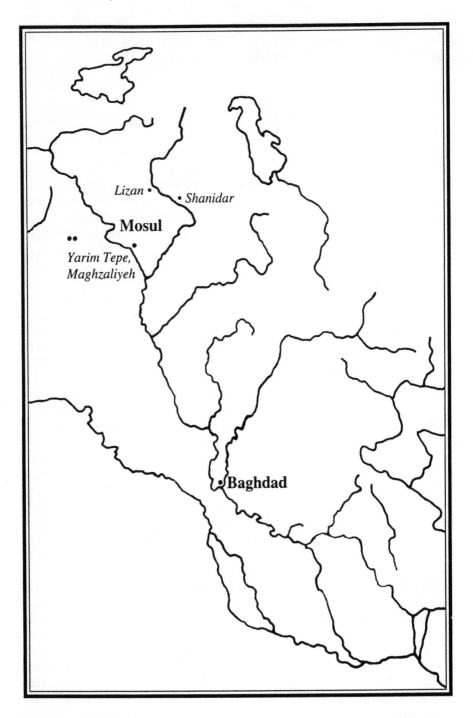

Figure VII.1 Map showing the location of the metalliferous region near Lizan first noted by Layard in 1845.

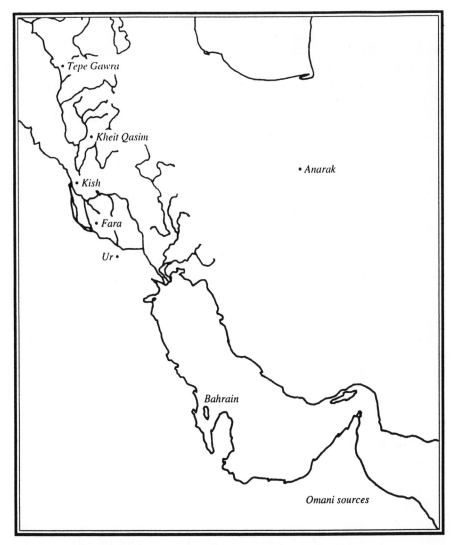

Figure VII.2 Map showing the location of the arsenic-rich copper sources at Anarak and sources of later importance in Oman, as well as sites in southern Mesopotamia with finds of arsenical copper and early tin-bronze.

which first appeared in southern Mesopotamia during the fourth millennium BC.[5] As recent studies have shown, the once alleged scarcity of arsenical copper in Mesopotamia (Muhly 1983:353) is beginning to appear more and more an artifact of insufficient analysis. Eight objects of Jamdat Nasr date from Fara were all found to be made of arsenical copper, as were eleven out of thirteen objects from levels XII–VIII (mid-fourth to early third millennium BC) at Tepe Gawra, and six out of thirteen objects analysed from the ED I cemetery at Kheit Qasim (Fig. VII.2) in the Hamrin basin (these had an average arsenic content of 2.7 per cent) (Muhly 1993:127). Moreover, arsenical copper continued to be important into ED IIIa times, as shown by the finds from the Royal Cemetery at Ur, where 42 per cent of the objects analysed by the University of Pennsylvania's *Meso-potamian Metals Project* were found to be made of arsenical copper (Muhly 1993:129).

Use of the Anarak source was probably never exclusive, and it is not unlikely that Mesopotamian traders, often employed by the temple or palace, brought copper into the country from a variety of sources in all periods. As early as the Jamdat Nasr period painted ceramics of Mesopotamian origin (Méry 1991:62 and Table 3) appeared in the Oman peninsula (Fig. VII.2) and it has often been suggested that this marked the beginning of a relationship between Mesopotamia and Magan, as the Oman peninsula was called, in part for the procurement of copper (Potts 1990, I:90), which was to last for well over a millennium. Much of the Magan copper, however, entered Mesopotamia via the intermediary Dilmun, identifiable in the late third and early second millennia with the modern islands of Bahrain (Potts 1990, I:219–226) (Fig. VII.2). By the middle of the eighteenth century BC, just as the cuneiform evidence for the import of Magan copper via Dilmun ended, copper from Cyprus (ancient Alashiya) made its first appearance in Mesopotamian cuneiform texts, and thereafter both Cypriot and Anatolian copper were to be important in Mesopotamian metallurgy.

Most of the copper deposits in Anatolia, Iran, Oman and Cyprus consist of sulphide ores, a point which is well known (Muhly 1973:171; Hauptmann 1985:25) yet largely unappreciated by archaeologists and Assyriologists interested in Mesopotamian metallurgy. The particular significance of this fact lies in the technical problems posed by the use of a sulphide ore. As J.D. Muhly explains (Muhly 1973:171–2):

> Technically, the ore must first be roasted in an oxidizing atmosphere, in order to produce a copper oxide. Then the copper oxide reacts with the copper sulphide to produce copper and sulphur dioxide. If the initial process is incomplete, thus producing a material known as *matte*, an impure mixture of copper and copper sulphide, this *matte* must be fully roasted to oxide and reduced with carbon, like a simple oxide ore, to produce pure copper. In practice, most early smelting of sulphide ores was probably aimed at a dead roast to oxide followed by a simple reduction with charcoal.

The nature of a sulphide ore thus often presupposes a two-stage smelting process – reduction of the raw ore to *matte*, followed by refining to a state in which the metal is pure enough to use.

As a general rule it can be assumed that smelting, the initial refining of copper ore, took place at or close to the source area in order to obviate the high cost of transporting raw ore. On the other hand, the fact that cuneiform texts consistently distinguish refined (*urudu-luh-ha*) from unrefined copper (*urudu*) strongly suggests that it was *matte* and not refined copper that was often imported into the country. Old Assyrian texts concerned with the import of copper from Anatolia distinguish *urudu* from *urudu-sig₅*, the latter term appearing when written phonetically as *dammuqum*, 'fine, good' (CAD D:180, s.v. *dummuqu*), and this suggests that it is not just 'fine quality' but actually 'refined' copper that is in question. A comparable concern with 'good' and 'bad' ingots appears in the Old Babylonian correspondence of the copper merchant Ea-nasir of Ur, probably the most well-known figure in the early second-millennium trade with Dilmun (Oppenheim 1954:10). It is only logical to assume that if 'good' ingots referred to already refined copper, these would have been more expensive to purchase than 'bad' or unrefined *matte* ingots. Moreover, the recognition that *matte* was being imported into Mesopotamia accounts for the otherwise inexplicable results of an analysis of a Neo-Assyrian ingot from Nimrud in the British Museum which was found to contain *c.* 15.5 per cent iron along with significant levels of antimony, bismuth, lead, silver and zinc. The team which undertook this analysis concluded, 'It demonstrates that copper was being transported and traded in a raw and unrefined state rather than being refined at or near to the mines' (Moorey, Curtis, Hook and Hughes 1988:47), but it seems more likely that a preliminary smelting resulting in the production of the ingot had taken place, for it was as an ingot and not as ore that the copper was sent to Nimrud. Moreover, the iron content of the Nimrud ingot is hardly surprising given the fact that iron-bearing sulphide ores are even more difficult to refine than ordinary sulphide ores (Muhly 1973:172). As part of the evidence for the distinction between refined and unrefined copper use in southern Mesopotamia derives from several 'recipe' texts which give instructions for the making of tin-bronze, it is best at this point to turn to the subject of tin.

TIN

In antiquity tin (Sum. *nagga [AN.NA]*, Akk. *annaku*) was important, not in its own right, but as an additive to copper in the production of the alloy bronze (Sum. *zabar*, Akk. *siparru*) (Joannès 1993:97–8). The exact proportions of tin required to make bronze were somewhat variable. In some cases, ancient recipes (see below) call for a ratio of tin to copper as high as 1:6 or 16.6 per cent, while other texts speak of a 1:8 ratio or 12.5 per cent (Joannès 1993:104). Muhly considers 'the classic ratio' about 1:9 or 11.11 per cent,[6] noting however that modern bronzes generally contain 10 per cent (and rarely exceed 15 per cent) tin.[7] This is not to say that ancient objects have not been analysed which contain much less tin, but pieces with a tin content of, for example, 1–4 per cent were probably not intentional alloys so much as the result of the uncontrolled melting down of tin-bronze together with copper objects in order to cast new pieces. In cases where copper objects formed the bulk of the material being reused, and no extra tin was added, the smiths produced copper with a smattering of residual tin, rather than intentional, low-tin bronzes. Whether a little tin was considered better than no tin at all we do not know.

In spite of new excavations and more analysis, it remains as true today as it did nearly twenty years ago that 'there is little or no tin bronze' in Western Asia before *c.* 3000 BC (Muhly 1977:76; cf. Muhly 1983:9). The presence of at least four tin-bronzes in the Early Dynastic I period (for the date, see Porada, Hansen, Dunham and Babcock 1992:110) Y-Cemetery at Kish signals the first appearance of tin-bronze in southern Mesopotamia, although one of the pieces analysed contained only 6.24 per cent tin, and Muhly feels 'this sporadic occurrence of bronze does not constitute a serious use of the new alloy' since, as noted above, arsenical copper continued in use at sites like Tepe Gawra, Fara, Kheit Qasim and Ur (Muhly 1993:129) (Fig. VII.2). By the time of the Royal Cemetery at Ur (Early Dynastic IIIa), according to M. Müller-Karpe, 'tin-bronze had become the dominant alloy' (Müller-Karpe 1991:111) in southern Mesopotamia. As evidence for this statement one can point to the fact that nine out of twelve objects analysed by Pernicka and Pászthory are tin-bronze, eight with a tin content of 2–10 per cent, and one with over 10 per cent. To these must be added two spearheads from PG 580 in the Royal Cemetery which have tin contents of 10.2 per cent and 11.3 per cent, a shaft-hole axe from PG 1751 with 10.3 per cent tin and a dagger from PG 49 with 9.6 per cent tin, all of which were analysed by the University of Pennsylvania's *Mesopotamian Metals Project* (Muhly 1993:129). Interestingly, some of these tin levels are in the range of the levels prescribed by later cuneiform texts which contain information on alloying (see below).

On the other hand, as noted above, 42 per cent of the metal objects from the Royal Cemetery analysed by the Pennsylvania project were made of arsenical copper, suggesting that if tin-bronze was beginning to take the lead in southern Mesopotamian metallurgy, it was certainly not by much. Part of the difficulty of judging such figures, however, lies in the fact that we are only speaking in terms of percentages of objects analysed without any appreciation of the size of the entire sample. Moreover, as Müller-Karpe has suggested, it is quite possible that different sites will be found to show different proportions of tin-bronze and arsenical copper in their metal inventories. Thus, at Ur the analysis of metal vessels seems to show a greater tendency to use tin-bronze, whereas metal vessels from the slightly later Cemetery A at Kish (ED IIIb) were predominantly made of arsenical copper. The decision to make an object out of tin-bronze or arsenical copper may have been dependent not just on the availability of tin as opposed to arsenical copper, but on the particular type of object being manufactured. Cast objects from the Royal Cemetery, such as weapons and tools, seem to be made of arsenical copper more often than tin-bronze, whereas metal vessels (Müller-Karpe 1993a, 1993b) exhibit just the opposite pattern. This is a somewhat unexpected observation, however, since metal vessels are normally hammered and not cast. Hammered vessels ought to have been easier to manufacture in arsenical copper than in tin-bronze, whereas tools and weaponry ought to have been easier to cast in tin-bronze rather than arsenical copper. Müller-Karpe suggests that the relative scarcity of tin and the difficulty of obtaining it may have given it a high status, thereby making its use in the manufacture of élite metal vessels more desirable than arsenical copper. Certainly the high cost of tin is readily visible when we compare the equivalency charts showing the amounts of tin and copper procurable for one shekel of silver (Tables VII.1–3). Finally, it might have been possible to produce thinner sheet

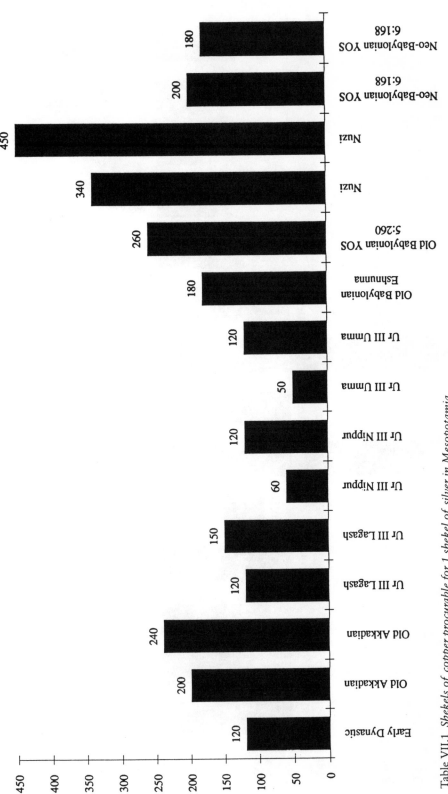

Table VII.1 *Shekels of copper procurable for 1 shekel of silver in Mesopotamia*

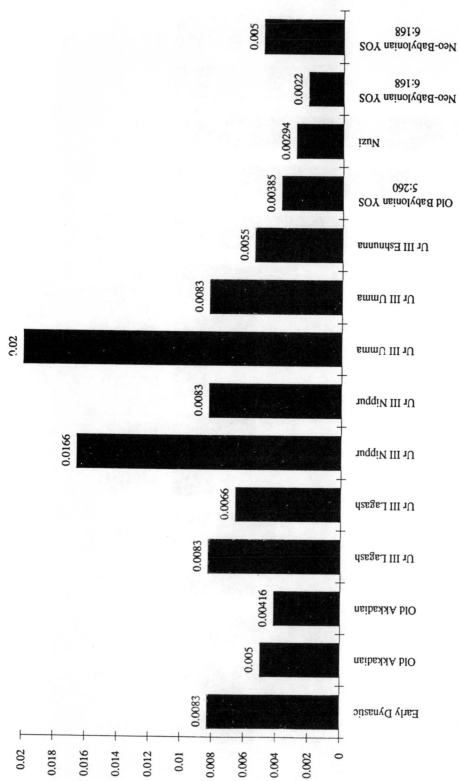

Table VII.2 *Cost of 1 shekel of copper in fractions of a shekel of silver (8.33 g)*

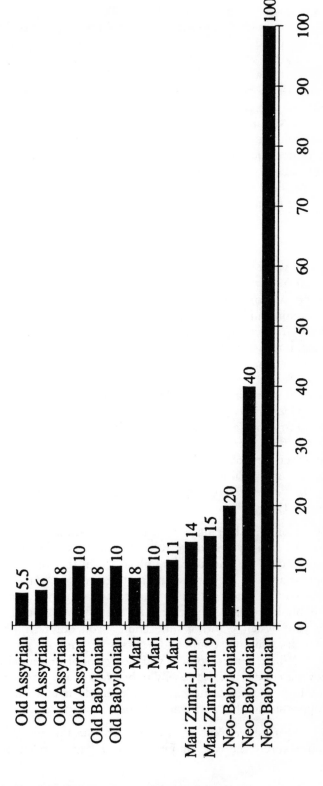

Table VII.3 *Shekels of tin procurable for 1 shekel of silver in Mesopotamia (the year Zimri-Lim 9 = 1768/7 BC)*

metal out of tin-bronze than arsenical copper and 'thus lighter and more elegant vessels' (Müller-Karpe 1991:112).

The sources of the tin used in southern Mesopotamia have been sought from Thailand in the east to Cornwall in the west. Most metallurgists believe that it was cassiterite (SnO_2), which occurs as 'bright black placer crystals' (for a convenient overview, see Wertime 1978:2) in certain rare alluvial deposits, that was exploited in antiquity, and not stannite (Cu_2FeSnS_4) (e.g. Charles 1978:27, 29). Gudea of Lagash says he received tin from Meluhha, generally identified with the Indus Valley, and in the Old Babylonian period it was imported to Mari from Elam. Thus, in spite of recent claims for ancient tin mines in Turkey (e.g. Yener 1989), the eastern origin of most of the tin used in southern Mesopotamia seems clear. We shall examine some recent work suggesting that tin reached Mesopotamia from Central Asian sources in Chapter XIII.

SILVER

A precious metal and therefore never as abundant as copper, silver (Sum. *kug, kù-babbar*, Akk. *kaspu*) (Joannès 1993:97–98) was well known in southern Mesopotamia, as shown by the fact that some 8.4 per cent of all extant third-millennium metal vessels were made of it (Müller-Karpe 1990:161). In antiquity it was not silver ore which was principally exploited, but rather argentiferous lead ores from which silver was extracted by a two-step method of smelting and cupellation (cf. Chapter IV on cupellation). While a variety of ancient lands are attested in literary texts as sources of silver, including Dilmun, Aratta, Elam, Marhashi and Meluhha, all of which are to the east or south of Mesopotamia, Sargon of Akkad referred to a locale in Anatolia as the 'Silver Mountain'. Moreover, as later Old Assyrian sources make clear, Anatolia was the source of Mesopotamian silver *par excellence* (Moorey 1985:110–111).[8]

In one of the Sumerian disputation texts, conventionally known as the *Dispute between Copper and Silver*, copper derides silver as follows (Kramer 1963:265):

> Silver, only in the palace do you find a station, that's the place to which you are assigned. If there were no palace, you would have no station; gone would be your dwelling place . . . In the [ordinary] home you are buried away in its darkest spots, its graves, its 'places of escape' [from this world]. When irrigation time comes, you don't supply man with the stubble-loosening copper mattock; that's why nobody pays any attention to you! When planting time comes, you don't supply man with the plough-fashioning copper adze; that's why nobody pays any attention to you! When winter comes, you don't supply man with the firewood-cutting copper ax; that's why nobody pays any attention to you! When the harvest time comes, you don't supply man with the grain-cutting copper sickle; that's why nobody pays any attention to you!

While the most well-known silver object from southern Mesopotamia ever found is surely the vase of Entemena of Lagash from Tello (Fig. VII.3),

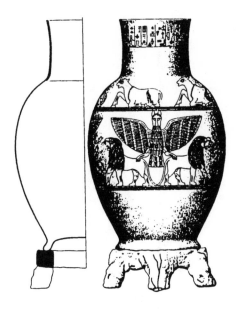

Figure VII.3 The silver vessel of Entemena from Tello (after Müller-Karpe 1990: Abb. 6–7)

silver was used for a wide variety of small objects from the Late Uruk period onwards (Moorey 1985:114–5). A unique and possibly experimental piece to which Müller–Karpe has drawn attention is a copper-silver arrow-head (Fig. VII.4) with no less than 25 per cent silver from the Late Uruk Riemchengebäude at Uruk (Müller-Karpe 1991:109).

An interesting mathematical text shows us some of the concrete problems involved in the working of silver, albeit with hypothetical values (Michel 1989:110). The exercise consists in determining the amount of silver necessary (by weight) for the manufacture of a piece of sheet silver of a particular length, breadth and surface area. We shall return to the subject of silver below when we examine the question of pre-monetary commodity equivalencies.

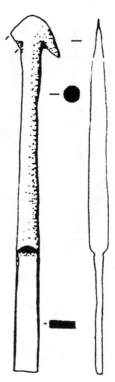

Figure VII.4 A Late Uruk, copper-silver arrowhead with 25 per cent silver from the Riem-chengebäude at Uruk (after van Ess and Pedde 1992: Taf. 83.974)

LEAD

As noted above, silver was normally obtained in antiquity by extracting it from lead ore, a circumstance which would lead one to expect a considerable degree of overlap in the distribution patterns of both metals. In fact, lead had already appeared by the seventh millennium BC in Anatolia but it took another three millennia before silver objects began to appear in any quantity. Lead (Sum. *a-gar₅*) (Joannès 1993:97–8) was put to a surprising variety of uses. It was employed to make beads, pendants, vessels, pipes, sheet coverings, cores of statuary and their bases, and weights (Moorey 1985:121–4). Indeed the use of lead to make metal vessels has been underrated. While Müller-Karpe estimates that only 3.4 per cent of the 1980 metal vessels from third-millennium Mesopotamia which he has catalogued were made of lead (Müller-Karpe 1990:161), that figure swells to 51.6 per cent if one considers only the Jamdat Nasr period, or 22 per cent if one looks just at the Early Dynastic era (Müller-Karpe 1993a:137). Clearly, therefore, lead was readily accessible and actively employed by late fourth- and early-third millennium metalsmiths, although by the end of the Early Dynastic period lead use for vessel manufacture had dropped off dramatically, and only 0.2 per cent of all known vessels attributable to the Early Dynastic III period were made of it.

Copper-lead alloys were relatively common at Susa in southwestern Iran during the late fourth and third millennia, and at least one piece from

Uruk, a small lion of Late Uruk or Jamdat Nasr date, was made of copper with 9 per cent lead (van Ess and Pedde 1992:13, Taf. 13.70). In view of the evidence from Susa this would not seem to have been the result of an aberrant experiment or accident of some kind (Müller-Karpe 1991:109). In fact, the piece in question may well have been imported from Susiana.

IRON

As Moorey has succinctly outlined, 'although iron was current in Mesopo-tamia for much of the Bronze Age, it was generally a rarity, valued as a curiosity and primarily used for small pieces of jewellery, for ornamenta-tion and for the blades of presentation weapons' (Moorey 1985:101). Thus, the economic and material importance of iron in the periods of greatest concern here, and in southern Mesopotamia as opposed to Assyria, was probably minimal, a point reinforced by the fact that there are no safely attested prices for iron in cuneiform texts prior to the first millennium BC (Bjorkman 1989:14).

In spite of this, it is interesting to note that iron (Sum. *anbar*, Akk. *parzillu*) (Joannès 1993:97–8) appears already in the Archaic texts from Uruk (Vaiman 1982:33–8). As the Archaic sign for iron, *an*, stood both for 'iron' and 'heaven', A.A. Vaiman has suggested that iron was perceived as the 'metal from the heavens', an association which he believes relates to the alleged meteoric origin of some of the earliest pieces of iron known from Uruk, Ur and Tell al-'Ubaid. The meteoric origin of these finds has been argued largely on the basis of their nickel content. As meteorites often contain around 7.5 per cent nickel, this has often been used to discriminate meteoric from terrestrial iron.[9] It may be legitimately asked, however, whether Mesopotamian observers, on seeing a meteor coursing through the sky, would have been able to find it after it had landed and would have realized its metallic properties and hence attempted to produce an object from it. In fact, as extraordinary as it may seem, examples do exist of meteorites which were observed to fall and then recovered. This was true in the case of Nejed 1, a 59.4 kg meteorite which was seen falling in 1863 near the Wadi Bani Khaled in the Rub al-Khali desert of what is today Saudi Arabia, and Jalandhar, a 2 kg meteorite which fell near the village of the same name in the Punjab district of India in 1621 and was later forged into several swords and knives (Buchwald 1975:1273, 1275, Fig. 1869).

GOLD

Gold (Sum. *kù-sig₁₇*, Akk. *hurāṣu*) occurs in southern Mesopotamia only sporadically prior to its explosive appearance in the Royal Cemetery at Ur (ED IIIa) (Maxwell-Hyslop 1971:1). Only a very few pieces, including a fragment of gold wire from the late Ubaid period at Ur, and a goat amulet from the Late Uruk period at Uruk (Moorey 1985:76–77), predate the lavish gold vessels, tools, weaponry and jewellery discovered by Woolley at Ur. Viewed in this light, the undisputed mastery of goldworking tech-niques illustrated by the material from the Royal Cemetery is all the more impressive. Evidence of gilding, chasing, inlaying, casting, filigree work, cloisonné, hard soldering and granulation attest to an extraordinarily high level of competence amongst the Early Dynastic jewellers of Ur (Alexander 1976:99–106).

Although the physical identification of an actual goldsmith's workshop area, long posited at Old Babylonian Larsa, seems highly unlikely (Bjorkman 1993:1–23), Old Babylonian texts from the palace of Sinkashid at Uruk[10] and Ur III texts (Van De Mieroop 1986:131–51) from the capital, Ur, throw light on the operations of a goldsmith's workshop. Texts such as those describing gold objects made for Shulgi to dedicate as temple offerings show clearly that gold supplies were carefully monitored in the royal workshops. Thus, in enumerating the weights of different gold objects, the amount of gold lost during production, expressed as 'loss during purification', 'loss during lamination', or more generally 'loss during work', was kept at the minuscule level of 0.27 per cent or 1/2 (0.02–0.025 g) grain per shekel (8.33 g) of gold (Van De Mieroop 1986:138–9). How were such precision measurements arrived at? Neo-Babylonian texts from Uruk dating to the reign of Nabonidus (555–539 BC) mention the weighing of gold in bulk using bronze weights of 3, 2 and 1 mina (i.e. 1.5, 1, and 0.5 kg) (Joannès 1987:2–3), whereas in the Old Babylonian Sinkashid palace texts haematite weights were used, as shown by text 90 where we read, 'The [quantity of the] gold was checked [and determined] by means of the set of weights of haematite belonging to Awilum' (Veenhof 1991:29). The highly refined weighing procedures used for precious metals in the palace at Mari during the Old Babylonian period have recently been studied in great detail by F. Joannès (Joannès 1989:113–52).

Twenty years ago scholars favoured the Pactolus area of western Anatolia (Fig. VII.5), whence the Lydian king Croesus derived his fabled wealth, as the likely source of southern Mesopotamia's gold supply. This, however, was based on the mistaken assumption that platiniridium inclusions in Pactolus gold made it readily distinguishable from that of other sources (Muhly 1981:146, 1983:1–14; Moorey 1985:74–5), and that the presence of such inclusions in objects from the Royal Cemetery thereby implied the use of Pactolus gold in their manufacture. It has since been shown that platiniridium occurs in gold from a number of sources (Maxwell-Hyslop 1977:83–6), and scholars today favour sources other than the Pactolus region for the third-millennium gold of Mesopotamia. According to the cuneiform sources, gold entered Mesopotamia at different times from a wide variety of neighbouring lands, including the mountain of Hahhum, perhaps near Malatya in eastern Turkey, Mardaman, near Mardin (?) in southeastern Turkey, Meluhha (the Indus Valley), Harali, somewhere in eastern Iran (?) and Egypt (Moorey 1985:73). The enormous quantities of gold discovered in recent years at Hellenistic period sites in ancient Bactria (northern Afghanistan/southern Uzbekistan), such as Tillya-tepe, might make one think that some of the gold of eastern provenance which reached Mesopotamia may have originated in this area, perhaps travelling westward together with lapis lazuli (Maxwell-Hyslop 1977:85–6). This was, after all, the main source of gold for the later Seleucid kings of

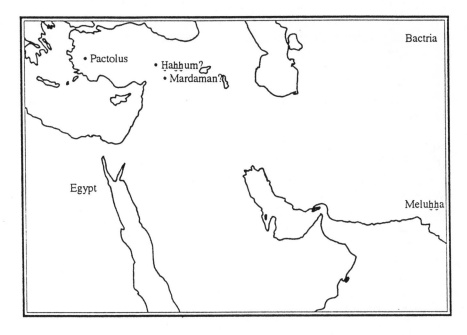

Figure VII.5 Some sources of Mesopotamian gold according to both literary and archaeological evidence

Mesopotamia (Sherwin-White and Kuhrt 1993:63) (cf. Chapter XIII). And yet it is important to realize that, like the copper of Dilmun or lapis of Meluhha, the gold called 'Bactrian' did not originate in that region, but further east, possibly in the mountains of Dardistan (Vogelsang 1989:169) to the north of Peshawar in modern Pakistan.

WORKSHOPS AND METALWORKING

The variety of metals in use in southern Mesopotamia naturally engendered a division of labour amongst metalworkers. Smiths (Sum. *simug*, Akk. *nappāhum*), responsible for (s)melting and casting, were distinguished from metalworkers (Sum. *tibira*, Akk. *gurgurrum*) who worked metal and created objects. These, on the other hand, were distinctly different from jewellers (Sum. *zadim*) and goldsmiths (Sum. *kù-dim/dím*, Akk. *kutimmum*). Given the large number of metal tools, weapons and vessels recovered from sites in southern Mesopotamia, there is, as with ceramics, a frustrating lack of excavated workshop facilities. The many claims for metalworking areas at Mari, Ur, Uruk, Khafajah, Kish and Tell Asmar can all be discounted (Moorey 1985:36–7), and until very recently only the Isin-Larsa period site of Tell edh-Dhiba'i – with its baked-clay pot-bellows, crucibles, baked clay moulds, model clay axehead and *tuyère* fragment – was considered a definite site of metalworking (Moorey 1985:37–8). Interestingly, no stone moulds were discovered at the site, although a roughly contemporary stone mould for a shaft-hole axe is known from Tell

Shemshara in northeastern Iraq (Maxwell-Hyslop 1971:73). More recently, concentrations of copper/bronze slag found throughout the Old Babylonian site of Mashkan-shapir have led to the suggestion that metalworking areas, although particularly prominent on the central mound, were probably scattered throughout all of the residential neighbourhoods there (Stone and Zimansky 1992: 216).

Aside from the archaeological evidence just mentioned, several texts contain valuable information on metal workshops. Thus, for example, an Ur III text from Ur (UET III 1498 rv. III 5ff.) lists the metal supplies of a smithy (*é-simug*) in the following order: tin (*nagga*), refined copper (*urudu-luh-dè*), unrefined copper (*urudu*), *sù-gan* (unidentified; see below), and lead (*a-gar₅*) (Waetzoldt and Bachmann 1984:5, n. 18). A pre-Sargonic text from Lagash (RTC 23 I 1ff.) is an important source on alloying. In it we read, '1 mina 15 shekels [i.e. 75 shekels] *urudu*[11] [the alloying rate] is 7 for the bronze[vessel?] of Kuli, x²-KAKA, the smith of Nanshe has weighed it. 1 1/3 minas [i.e. 80 shekels] refined copper [*urudu-luh-ha*] – the corresponding tin: 13 1/3 shekels – [came from] Urzababa' (Waetzoldt and Bachmann 1984:6). To understand this text we must consider the second half of it first. There we see that the smith began with 80 shekels of copper and 13.3 shekels of tin, or 93.3 shekels of metal. Out of this he fashioned a bronze vessel (?) of 75 shekels, implying that 18.3 shekels of metal (19.2 per cent of the total metal to begin with) were lost in the process. If we reckon the tin:copper ratio based on the amount of metal begun with, then the tin represented 14.25 per cent of the whole. On the other hand, if we reckon its percentage based on the weight of the finished product, then the end result was a 17.73 per cent tin-bronze. Neither method, undoubtedly, is correct as the 18.3 shekels of metal lost probably included tin as well as copper. What is important to emphasize, however, is the fact that only *urudu-luh-ha* was alloyed with tin to make bronze, thus showing that this term refers to refined or pure copper.

One substance which remains a mystery in metal recipe texts is *sù-gan*. In one text (*JCS* 15: 114) we read (Waetzoldt and Bachmann 1984:9):

1. 1 mina [60 shekels = 499.8 g] tin-bronze [*zabar*]
2. the corresponding [production] loss [*izi-kú-bi*]: 4 shekels [33.32 g]
3. the corresponding tin [*nagga-bi*]: 8 shekels [66.64 g]
4. the corresponding refined copper [*urudu-luh-ha*]: 5/6 of a mina and 6 shekels [= 56 shekels = 466.48 g]
5. the corresponding loss [through production] of the refined copper: 7.3 shekels 24 grains [= 7.433 shekels = 61.91689 g]
6. the [corresponding] *sù-[gan-bi]*: 0.5 shekel [4.165 g] 6 grains [0.033 g][=0.5039615 shekel = 4.198 g]

The text begins by naming the end-product, namely 60 shekels (499.8 g) of tin-bronze, before speaking of the raw materials used in its production (i.e. tin plus refined copper), and the loss incurred in refining the copper, even though this was necessarily the first step in the entire process. Thus, 56 shekels (item 4) of refined copper (= 466.48 g) were combined with 8 shekels (66.64 g) of tin (item 3) for a total of 64 shekels of metal (533.12 g), 4 shekels (33.32 g) of which were lost (item 2) in the manufacturing process. In the latter part of the text (item 5) we learn that in the production of the 56 shekels of refined copper 7.433 shekels of copper were lost along with 0.5039615 shekels of *sù-gan*. Waetzoldt suggests that *sù-gan* was a material which was added during the refining process but was then 'lost' and could not be accounted for further. It has been suggested that *sù-gan* might have been 'finely pulverized charcoal' (Waetzoldt and Bachmann 1984:13). However, as Waetzoldt has shown, *sù-gan* was sometimes two to five times as expensive as copper at Lagash and Nippur (Waetzoldt and Bachmann 1984:17), making it unlikely that it was a form of charcoal. Pernicka, on the other hand, has suggested that *sù-gan* may have been a flux (an additive used in the smelting process which bonds with impurities forming slag, which is drained from the smelting oven or crucible leaving the refined metal behind) such as borax, imported from Iran, Central Asia or Turkey and therefore very expensive (Waetzoldt and Bachmann 1984:18).

METALS-BASED EQUIVALENCY STANDARDS AND THEIR FLUCTUATIONS THROUGH TIME

Beginning in the early third millennium land sales were recorded on so-called *kudurrus*, stone stelae of varying shape with or without decoration in low relief. Equivalents of a given area of land were expressed in units of wool, oil, soup, copper and silver (Krecher 1980:503).

Metals were measured according to the following system (Powell 1990:510):

1 Sum. *še*/Akk. *uttetu* = 'barleycorn' = 0.04–.05 g
1 Sum. *gín*/Akk. *šiqlu* 'axe' (?) (English: shekel) = 180 *še* = *c.* 8.33g
1 Sum. *ma-na*/Akk. *manû* (English: mina) = 60 *gín* = 10,800 *še* = *c.* 500 g
1 *gú(n)*/Akk. *biltu* = 'load' (English: talent from Gr. *talanton*, cf. Lat. *tollo*) = 60 *ma-na* = *c.* 30 kg

Lexical sources give the names of *še* weights ranging from 0.3 to 0.4, 1, 2, 3, 4, 5, 10, 15, 20, 22.25, 30, 36, 45, 60, 90, and 120 *še*, although the actual weights which recur most frequently in economic texts are 15, 20, 30, 60, 90, and less commonly 10, 22.5 and 45 *še*. The smallest weight found in the Larsa hoards weighed 0.910 g, and is thought to represent 20 *še*. In the Parthian period, however, divisions of 1/12, 1/24 and even 1/48 *še* are attested (Mayer 1985:203–15). Weights of 10 shekels or less were normally made of haematite, examples of which, along with scales, have been found in a series of Old Babylonian graves at Ur (viz. LG/23, 199; LG/45, 204; LG/113, 205; LG/124, 208; LG/145, 210; LG/170, 212 and LG/193) (Veenhof 1991:29). Scales are rarely depicted in representational art, and apparently occur only once in glyptic art, on an Old Akkadian seal in the Moore collection (Joannès 1989:125, n. 56, referring to a seal illustrated in OIP 47: no. 42).

The early *kudurrus* follow the formula 'x *iku* of land, the field FN [i.e. 'field name']; x shekels of silver [to] the seller(s) was weighed out' (Gelb,

Steinkeller and Whiting 1991:199) and offer examples such as 7 *iku* of land for 12 shekels of silver (Gelb, Steinkeller and Whiting 1991:49, Chicago stone), i.e. 47.08 ha for 99.96 g of silver. Moreover, a 'statement of rate' is often included as well, e.g. 'on that day, 30 quarts of barley [were the equivalent of] [1] mina [of copper]', or 'on that day, 1 shekel of purified silver was [the equivalent of] 80 quarts of barley'.

Ur III documents in which movable goods were transferred, rather than land alone, were overwhelmingly reckoned in silver, however. When silver actually changed hands it was customary to have someone on hand with a balance, usually a smith (*simug*) goldsmith (*kù-dím*), jeweller (*zadim*) or merchant (*dam-gàr*) (Wilcke 1980:507). During the Kassite period gold became the dominant but not sole standard of reckoning, functioning alongside silver and lead in some instances (Müller 1982:270–8).

Throughout its long history, southern Mesopotamia was characterized by considerable equivalency fluctuations in the realm of metals. The extraordinary chronological span of the economic texts provides us with an unparalleled view of those fluctuations. Examples of equivalencies for copper, tin, silver and gold have been provided (Tables VII.1–4) to illustrate changes from the Early Dynastic to the Achaemenid periods. It is impossible to draw any general conclusions from these graphs, however, and glaring jumps or drops in prices can only be understood against the backdrop of contemporary political events and economic trends. Even within a fairly restricted period of time, such as that of the Third Dynasty of Ur, moreover, one would have to do a detailed study on a year-by-year basis and with full awareness of the political history of the era in order to properly interpret ancient Mesopotamian microeconomics.

Readers should note that, up to this point, the term 'price' has not been used. This has been deliberate for, as the economic historian Karl Polanyi observed, 'Equivalents as such are merely devices by which quantitative relations are set up between goods of different kinds . . . The usual rendering of such relations as "price" is misleading since . . . it tends to restrict the concept of equivalency to market exchange. Actually, the scope of equivalencies was by no means limited to situations of market exchange' (Polanyi 1977:63–4). Indeed, the essence of equivalency is the fact that, when goods of one sort are notionally substituted for those of another, this 'leaves the result unaffected with respect to a definite operation such as reciprocating, redistributing, or exchanging' (Polanyi 1977:64). Situations of commercial purchase certainly did exist in ancient Mesopotamia, but as Polanyi has shown, by thinking exclusively in terms of 'prices' we introduce a whole nexus of economistic conceptions into the ancient Mesopotamian situation which need to be demonstrated before they are assumed. For that reason, it is wiser to continue referring to equivalencies of commodities such as copper, silver and gold, rather than prices.

CONCLUSION

The inventory of metal objects found in graves of all periods in Mesopotamia, the commercial, military and diplomatic efforts expended on

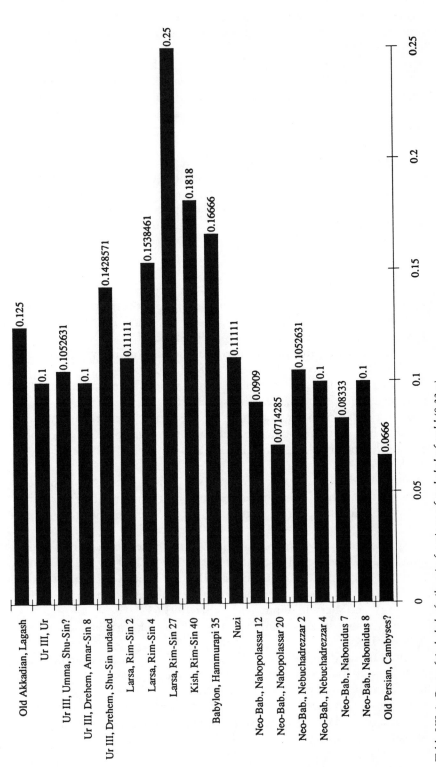

Table VII.4 *Cost of 1 shekel of silver in fractions of a shekel of gold (8.33 g)*

acquiring metals, and the technical expertise evinced by the end-products all justify our viewing the metallurgical industrial sector of southern Mesopotamia as one of primary importance from at least the fourth millennium onwards. With no metalliferous zones whatsoever within the borders of the area studied here, metal use and the energy devoted to the manufacture of metal goods are obviously inversely proportional to metal availability. A great deal of questions remain to be answered in this field, however. Where did tin come from? What was *sù-gan*? How directly did Mesopotamian appropriation of metal ores or ingots affect the societies in the source areas? What kinds of barriers to trade existed, why and for how long? One thing is for certain. Without the concerted collaboration of metallurgists, Assyriologists and archaeologists in this complex field, progress would be slow on the resolution of many of these issues. Happily, as the work of the Heidelberg and Philadelphia *Mesopotamian Metals Project* shows, this is an area in which interdisciplinary collaboration has already made some substantial gains.

NOTES

1 Probably the easiest reference to use for all metals is the excellent work of Moorey 1994:216–301.

2 I owe this reference to Müller-Karpe 1991:108.

3 On the problems surrounding the identification of native copper, see Maddin, Stech Wheeler and Muhly 1980:211–25.

4 For other early finds of copper on sixth- and fifth-millennium sites in northern Mesopotamia, see Muhly 1983:351.

5 Nothing suggests that metalsmiths of this period were themselves enriching their metal through the addition of free arsenic. See Waetzoldt and Bachmann 1984:8; Muhly 1993:119.

6 Muhly 1978:43.

7 Muhly 1973:244. By way of comparison it is interesting to note the extreme variability in the tin content of bronzes manufactured at Ebla in Syria. Figures there range from as low as 5 per cent up to 16.6 per cent. See Waetzoldt 1981:371, n. 44. None of these figures, however, compares with the extraordinary high-tin bronzes from Kerala which contain 20–25 per cent tin. See Srinivasan 1994.

8 In the Seleucid period (cf. Chapter XIII), the southwestern portion of Turkey known as Cilicia was the principal source of silver for the Seleucid kings. See Sherwin-White and Kuhrt 1993:63.

9 There is some disagreement over the validity of this distinction. See Moorey 1985:92.

10 Sanati-Müller 1990:131–213, esp. nos. 88–97 in which 'Mar-Bulalum and the gold- and silversmiths' receive specified quantities of gold, often for plating wooden objects such as thrones.

11 Pre-Sargonic and Old Akkadian texts, however, sometimes use *urudu* by itself instead of *zabar* when speaking of bronze, as is the case here. See Waetzoldt and Bachmann 1984:7.

VIII Some Material Correlates of Religious Life

INTRODUCTION

In spite of A.L. Oppenheim's famous views on 'why a "Mesopotamian religion" should not be written' (Oppenheim 1977:172ff.), this sphere of life cannot be sidestepped in a work of this sort for the simple reason that religious behaviour formed the active, functional context for a not inconsequential portion of the material culture (either excavated archaeologically or attested in literary texts) of ancient Mesopotamia. The difficulties inherent in any attempt to understand the vast, complex and fragmentary literary and material record of ancient Mesopotamian belief systems are certainly profound, but it would be unacceptable to ignore the religious sphere altogether and thereby strip many of the finds discussed in the literature of Mesopotamian art and archaeology of their context. To begin, a few words are necessary in order to convey something of the general principles of Mesopotamian religious behaviour.

MESOPOTAMIAN RELIGION

We begin with the *numinous*, a word used by historians of religion in describing the experience of human confrontation with the terrifying, awe-inspiring, fascinating and irresistible extra-human forces embodied in the natural phenomena of the physical world (Jacobsen 1976:3). At the risk of over-simplification, religion may be considered 'the positive human response' to those forces, i.e. to the numinous, 'in thought (myth and theology) and action (cult and worship)'. In an effort to 'capture' the qualities of those forces and to translate them into something which can be metaphorically grasped by humans, those qualities are concretized, crystallized and in some cases, as in Mesopotamia, anthropomorphized as individual 'deities'. Hence, Mesopotamian religion was necessarily a polytheistic one since the numinous was immanent in all natural phenomena (Jacobsen 1976:3, 11).

Deities were distinguished from other beings by the possession of *me*, which can be understood as those divine 'properties or powers of the gods which enable a whole host of activities central to civilised human life, especially religion, to take place' (Black and Green 1992:130). Some of those properties, such as the 'throne of kingship' or the 'temple drum' were indeed objectified, so that they may take on the meaning of a concrete emblem of the deity.[1] In Mesopotamia the 'great gods' possessed *me* and distributed it to the lesser gods and mortals. It was, in fact, the source of their divine power (van Dijk 1971:533). The term *me-lám*, on the other hand, signified the 'brilliant, visible glamour...exuded by gods, heroes, sometimes by kings, and also by temples of great holiness and by gods' symbols and emblems' which was 'terrifying, awe-inspiring' (Black and Green 1992:130), and likened to an 'awesome nimbus' (Jacobsen 1976:16) or 'radiant aura' (George 1994:26).

Individual deities in Mesopotamia were distinguished in writing by the sign *dingir* (Akk. *ilu*) (van Dijk 1971: 532–3; Lambert 1971:543–6), written as a determinative before divine names and divine objects, which included symbols and weapons to which sacrifices were made. Deities were hierarchically arranged under the supreme deity An (Akk. *Anu*, literally, 'heaven') but somehow An the great god was consistently overshadowed[2] by locally more important divinities in individual cities[3] whose power was exemplified by their possession of the 'creative word' (Sum. *inim*) and in their power to determine human fates. As an example of the creative word we may cite a Sumerian literary text concerning the moon god Nanna/Sin, in which we read: 'You, Sin, your word goes forth on earth; [and] plants and herbs grow' (van Dijk 1971:534). Here as always, the creative power of a particular god or goddess is the power of the natural phenomenon represented by that deity.

Once the separation of heaven and earth was effected, according to the Babylonian *Epic of Creation* (Dalley 1989),[4] An appears as the 'father' of the natural deities, with Ki (lit., 'earth') as the 'mother'. On analogy with human sexual procreation a whole series of 'male' and 'female' deities were then spawned (Lambert 1980–83:219). Thus, the daughters of An included such earthly vegetation deities as Nisaba, Baba, Gula and Ezinu, who are called *ki-sikil* and *ama-ki-sikil*, 'pure', or 'pure mothers', whereas heavenly phenomena such as Gibil (fire) and Ishkur (storm) were male 'sons' of heaven. 'Creation-deities', such as Enlil and Enki, were male sons of An, while 'mother goddesses' such as Ninhursag, Dingir-mah, Ninmah and Nintu were among his female daughters, differing however from the vegetation deities in that they played a role in human creation (van Dijk 1971:535).

Astral deities such as Nanna (the moon) and his daughters Utu (the sun) and Inanna (Venus) were created out of the underworld. Generally speaking we see a broad division into two divine realms, one of 'heavenly' deities, the other of 'earthly' ones. Some deities, however, had two forms, one heavenly, the other earthly (e.g. Geshtin and Geshtinanna; Nisaba and An-nisaba) (van Dijk 1971:536). Moreover, deities could take variant forms within one incarnation, usually expressed in terms of a temporal differentiation. Thus, for example, Utu could also be 'Utu of the Black Moon'.

DIVINE IMAGES

It follows from the anthropomorphic nature of Mesopotamian deities and their creation via patterns of human-like procreation, that the visual images of those deities would assume a more or less human form. It is necessary to use the qualifying phrase 'more or less' because, from the mid-third millennium BC (Early Dynastic II) onward, deities were distinguished from mortals in Mesopotamian iconography (on seals, reliefs and sculpture) by being shown wearing some sort of headgear with horns, usually resembling a cap, helmet or crown (Amiet 1961:161–2; Boehmer 1972–1975:431–4). How then are we to interpret the absence of anthropomorphs wearing the horned crown prior to the ED II period (Boehmer 1971:466–9, 1972–1975:431–4)?

Several possibilities spring to mind. The absence of the horned crown has been taken by some scholars to be an indication that the deities of the pre-Early Dynastic II era had not yet become fully anthropomorphized (Boehmer 1990:64–5, n. 24), the implication being that the horned crown was an essential, absolute marker of divinity which would necessarily be present on any anthropomorphic image if it was meant to represent a divinity. On the other hand, the absence of the horned crown at this early date could simply mean that the horned crown had not yet become enshrined as an attribute of divinity. One could indeed argue that at least some of the many small anthropomorphic clay figurines found on sites of Ubaid and Uruk date (e.g. Spycket 1968:54–60) represent deities and none of these, to my knowledge, shows the horned crown. Other attributes, such as the lizard-face seen on some female deities of the Ubaid period, sometimes interpreted as indications that these represent 'demons or other supernatural beings' (Perkins 1949:83), may have been used to differentiate the human from the anthropomorphized, divine form. Alternatively, one might suggest that the Mesopotamian world view of the late prehistoric and early historic periods differed so markedly from that of the ED II period that it recognized in concrete form no deities whatsoever, only the forces of nature. We know so little about early Sumerian religion, and obviously next to nothing about religion during the Ubaid and Uruk periods, that it would be dangerous at this point to rely overly on the symbolic use of the horned crown from 2500 BC onwards as a yardstick against which to measure the presence or absence of divine images five hundred or a thousand years earlier. Indeed, we know of some cases after ED II times when figures assumed to be divine but without horned crowns are thought to have been distinguished by their size. A case in point is provided by the over life-size anthropomorph on the Stele of the Vultures, generally identified as Ningirsu. Several centuries later Ningirsu's exaggerated size was well expressed by Gudea of Lagash when he said (Cylinder A IV 14ff.), speaking of the deity, 'there was a man [*lú*] who was so tall, that he stretched from the earth up to heaven' (van Dijk 1971:534).

The general problem of distinguishing representations of deities from those of mortals is not merely one of academic or art historical interest, however. It becomes important, for example, in trying to correctly interpret the many extant anthropomorphic statues found in temples. The famous hoard of anthropomorphic statuary found in the Abu temple at Tell Asmar is a case in point. Are the unusually large male and female figures (72 and 59 cm tall, respectively) with their over-sized eyes divine statues, as Henri Frankfort believed (Frankfort 1970:46), or are they, in view of the absence of horned crowns, representations of dedicants (cf. Chapter X), people who dedicated statues of themselves to a certain deity which might then be set up in his/her temple in order to represent that person in perpetual prayer before the deity (Seidl 1980–1983:315)? Are they, as W.W. Hallo has suggested, 'deceased royalty, and their kin', representing 'the human donor in votive guise' before the deity, set up 'to proffer prayer unceasingly in lieu and on behalf of the donor' (Hallo 1988:57, 58 and n. 25)? These are important issues if we are to avoid misinterpreting the anthropomorphic statuary which has survived from ancient Mesopotamia.

As for genuine divine images of deities in statuary, these, writes Beaulieu (1993:241):

> were more than just simple representations of deities. They were fash-ioned and repaired in the temple workshop[5] according to elaborate pre-scriptions which transformed their lifeless matter into the living incarna-tion of the deity. The divine presence was thereafter maintained in the statue through the daily performance of complex rituals and ceremonies which were probably borrowed, for the most part, from the ceremonial of the court on the model of which gods and their retinues were believed to lead their existence.

A song (*balag*, 'lyre', 'drum'?[6]) of Inanna the goddess which talks about her defilement by an enemy who enters her shrine gives us some indication of how such statues were draped. We read, 'That enemy laid his hands on me, he killed me with fright. I was terrified, he was not afraid of me. He tore my garments off me, he dressed his wife in them. That enemy cut off my lapis lazuli, he hung it on his daughter' (Black 1985:36, ll. 250–3). In this case the verb used in the last line means literally 'cut a string or thread', suggesting it was a necklace of lapis lazuli which was taken from the divine statue of Inanna. As this text shows, both clothing and jewellery formed part of the accoutrements which adorned divine images. As we know from a variety of sources, statues 'owned far more jewellery than they could conveniently "wear"' (Black 1985:53). Inventories of the divine jewellery and other precious objects belonging to specific deities are preserved, such as that of Adad, found at Tell Haddad (ancient Me-Turan), in the Hamrin district of northeastern Iraq (al-Rawi and Black 1983:137–43), or those of Nana and the 'Lady of Uruk' from the site of the same name (Sack 1979:41–6). Such jewellery has generally been interpreted as 'the sum of votive and other gifts made to the image by its worshippers' (al-Rawi and Black 1983:138). One famous Old Babylonian text (LB 1090) from an un-identified site somewhere in central Babylonia is an inventory of eighty old and thirty-five new items of jewellery and attire belonging to Ishtar of Lagaba. In it, the old items are described as 'all that, so much as is regis-tered, which lies in the reed chest; it is the old [belongings]', while other objects are listed as new additions to the chest (Edzard and Veenhof 1976–1980:137). As the Neo-Babylonian texts from Uruk show, thousands of gold rings, pendants, rosettes, stars and ornaments of other sorts, some of them sewn onto the garments of the deity, were kept in the temples of the major deities.

In keeping with the anthropomorphism of Mesopotamian divinities, the deities needed not only jewellery and clothing but food as well. At Uruk in the Neo-Babylonian period Eanna had three main offices dealing with food preparation for deities. These were the *tabihutu* ('activity/prebend of'), butchers/meat carvers who prepared meat offerings from sacrificial animals, the *sirasûtu* ('activity/prebend of'), brewers who made daily offerings of beer and the *nuhatimmutu*, bakers who made porridge, cakes and sweets. A standard opening statement in reports on the offerings to the deities runs as follows: 'The bread looks nice, the beer tastes good' (Beaulieu 1993:252). This was a way of saying that the deity was in his or her temple and 'all's right with the world'. It is important to recognize, however, that food prepared for deities was an essential part of the redistributive economy of the temple, at least for the priesthood and other temple personnel. Thus, after duly making offerings to the deity, the food itself would be redistributed to members of the temple staff as a kind of perquisite. In some cases, moreover, the king himself received a portion of the divine offerings (Beaulieu 1990:93).

One aspect in the 'life' of a divine image which we have not yet touched on is travel. The divine images of deities described above are known to have made journeys to sanctuaries outside of their own city, journeys which are described in a number of literary compositions, such as *Nanna-Suen's Journey to Nippur, Nininsina's Journey to Nippur, Ninurta's Journey to Eridu, Inanna's Journey to Eridu,* and *Enki's Journey to Eridu* (Sjöberg 1957–1971:480–3), as well as finding mention in letters and royal inscriptions. In many cases these journeys represented annual visitations to renew old cultic ties and achieve fertility, while in others they appear to have been unique visits for a particular, pragmatic purpose.

As an example of a divine journey related in a literary work we may consider *Nanna-Suen's Journey to Nippur*, a text of some three hundred lines dating in its present form to the Old Babylonian period but thought to have been composed in the Ur III period. The text begins by praising Nippur, the city of Enlil, Nanna-Suen's father. Nanna-Suen decides to visit his father. Consequently, he loads his boat with plants and various animals. During the journey he stops at various places including IM^{ki}, Larsa, Uruk, Shuruppak and another city (unreadable name), in each of which he is received by the main deities. Finally, Nanna-Suen arrives at Nippur, where he goes to the gate-keeper of the temple of Enlil (*é-kur*) and asks him to 'open the house', promising the gate-keeper that if he lets him in, he will give him the gifts which he has brought by boat. The gate-keeper happily opens the gate and Nanna-Suen enters. Enlil puts on a banquet, after which Nanna-Suen asks his father for a series of things: an early flood on the Euphrates so that he can return to Ur, late barley in the fields, fish in the river, reeds in the canebrake, honey and wine in the gardens and orchards, tamarisks on the steppe, wild boar in the forests and a long life in the palace, all of which Enlil gives to Nanna-Suen, upon which he returns to Ur (Ferrara 1973).

Similar journeys are also referred to in royal inscriptions. Gudea (Cylinder B III 5–11) speaks of the return of Ningirsu from Eridu, which he had visited on the occasion of the New Year's celebrations. Ningirsu is said to have been accompanied by streaming light, and Gudea tells us that he decorated the temple of the god with carnelian and lapis in order to receive him, as well as preparing a banquet for him. It is not certain whether this account describes what was a yearly event, or whether it was a unique one occasioned by the need to report to Enki (in Eridu) on the building and consecration of the Eninnu in Girsu which Gudea had constructed for Ningirsu. Since he later appears in the Old Babylonian period as the brother of Nanshe, daughter of Enki, Ningirsu must have been a son of Enki even though, in Gudea's time, he appears as the son of Enlil.

'Practical' journeys are also attested, particularly those of Nanna-Suen of Ur to Nippur. In one case Sin-iddinam, king of Larsa, went to Ur in order to give the city god Nanna-Suen gifts on the occasion of the New Year celebrations. From there Siniddinam and Nanna-Suen journeyed together to Nippur to ask Ninlil and Enlil to give the king a long life and reign. In another case Nanna-Suen went to Nippur to ask king Shulgi's permission to destroy an enemy land. Given what has been said above in Chapter V on the importance of the canal system of southern Mesopotamia, it stands to reason that much of the travel done by deities, i.e. by their divine images, was by boat. This is stated explicitly in *Nanna-Suen's Journey to Nippur.* Another illustration is provided by the lyric song of Inanna cited earlier, where we read, 'The treasure was . . . in the prow of the boat (245) I [Inana], the queen, was riding in the stern of the boat (246)' (Black 1985:36 and 11).

Divine images might be moved for reasons other than those just described. In time of war any threat to the anthropomorphic image of a deity was viewed with the greatest horror. Indeed, divine statues were particularly targeted by invading armies and might be carried off to the land of the victor in an effort 'to actualize the rupture between the god and his native land. This rupture was the result of the anger of the god who summoned the enemy to destroy the land and bring the statue to a foreign country already elected by the god himself as his new place of residence' (Beaulieu 1993:242). Examples of the removal of cult statues by a conquering king or of their restoration by a later monarch abound, a number of them concerning the statue or statues of Marduk kept in his temple, the Esagila at Babylon. Thus, in the mid-sixteenth century when the Hittites sacked Babylon they carried off a statue of Marduk which is said to have been later restored to the city by an early Kassite ruler named Agum (Foster 1993:273). After crushing the Kassite dynasty *c.* 1155 BC (Steve and Vallat 1989:228), the Elamite king Kudur-Nahhunte II removed the divine statue of Marduk from the Esagila of Babylon and carried it off to Susa along with Enlil-nadin-ahi, the last king of the Kassites (Brinkman 1968:89). Several decades later, according to an Akkadian poem, Nebuchadrezzar I (1124–1103 BC) beseeched Marduk in prayer, asking 'How long, oh lord of Babylon, will you dwell in the land of the enemy?' According to the text Marduk's answer, 'Take me from Elam to Babylon. I, lord of Babylon, will surely give you Elam', prompted Nebuchadrezzar's invasion of Elam resulting, among other things, in his recovery of a statue of Marduk (Foster 1993:301). Whether, in each case, the same statue of Marduk is meant, we do not know. Certainly when the Neo-Assyrian king Assurbanipal campaigned against Elam, he claims to have recovered a statue of the deity

Nanna at Susa where it had been, he says, for the previous 1635 years (Vallat 1993:25).

In fact, sources from the Neo-Assyrian (Fig. VIII.1) and Neo-Babylonian periods frequently refer to the removal of divine statues from temples when a city was conquered. In order to prevent this from happening, however, the besieged citizens of a city sometimes took their divine images and fled into hiding in the mountains or the marshes, or sent them to the safest place they could think of. Thus, when Merodach-Baladan II was confronted by the imminent invasion of his country by the Assyrian king Sargon II, he gathered all the gods of the Sealand (i.e. from all of the smaller temples and shrines throughout the region) together in his capital, Dur-Yakin. Sargon captured Dur-Yakin in 709 BC and two years later returned the gods to their shrines. As he says, 'I established the freedom of the cities of Ur, Eridu, Larsa, Kissik, and Nemed-Laguda, and I returned to their cult centers the gods who had been carried off, and I reinstated their regular offerings, which had been interrupted' (Beaulieu 1993:243).

Figure VIII.1 Transport of divine statues by Assyrian soldiers of Tiglath-Pileser III (after Seidl 1980–83: Abb. 1)

A similar situation occurred almost two centuries later. Fearing a takeover by the army of Cyrus the Great, founder of the Achaemenid empire, the last Neo-Babylonian king, Nabonidus, ordered 'a massive gathering of the gods of Sumer and Akkad into the capital' in 539 BC (Beaulieu 1993:242). The Neo-Babylonian Chronicle Series for his seventeenth year informs us that, '[. . .the gods] of Marad, Zababa and the gods of Kish, Ninlil [and the gods of] Hursagkalama [i.e. Kish] entered Babylon. Until the end of the month Ululu the gods of Akkad [. . .] which are above the wall and below the wall were entering Babylon. The gods of Borsippa, Kuthah, and Sippar did not enter [Babylon]'. These events are, moreover, confirmed by a number of letters from Uruk. Thus, in one letter (YOS 3 145) from Ri[mut] to two officials of Eanna at Uruk, we read, 'Send me one leather mat and five (inflatable) goatskins for the boat concerning the La[d]y of Eanna via the soldiers who will bring the boat parts to me, [so that] the Lady of the Eanna may go upstream to Babylon on the Euphrates' (Beaulieu

1993: 244). In another letter (YOS 19 194) one Bazuzu 'has brought a boat from Babylon . . . and he said thus: "I will take the barley for the regular offerings of the Lady-of-Uruk to Babylon' (Beaulieu 1993:245).

As Beaulieu has expressed it (1993:257):

> During the months preceding the Persian invasion, Babylon became a vast repository of cult statues attended to and cared for by hundreds, if not thousands, of members of their respective clergies. Emissaries went back and forth between the capital and provincial centers; shipments of foodstuffs and other commodities were sent by land and by water, increasing the confusion of a kingdom already at bay. Each sanctuary had its own rituals and practices sanctified by tradition and jealously guarded by a priestly college, which transmitted its knowledge to a restricted number of initiates. They could keep the divine representations alive only by performing the rituals properly, offering the right food, and handling the appropriate paraphernalia. In their absence, the statues would lose their divine substance and fall into neglect. The gods would leave their earthly abodes, abandoning their land to its fate.

Following the success of Cyrus and his triumphal entry into Babylon, the Neo-Babylonian Chronicle states tersely that 'From the month Kislimu to the month Addaru the gods of Akkad which Nabonidus had brought down to Babylon returned to their places'. Similar information, albeit with more flourish, is repeated for propagandistic purposes in the Cyrus Cylinder, where we read (Beaulieu 1993:243):

> As for the gods of Sumer and Akkad which Nabonidus, to the wrath of the lord of the gods, brought to Babylon, at the command of Marduk, the great lord, I [Cyrus] caused them to dwell in peace in their sanctuaries, [in] pleasing dwellings. May all the gods I brought [back] to their sancturaries plead daily before Bel and Nabu for the lengthening of my days, may they intercede favourably on my behalf.

Clearly, while Nabonidus may have had good reason for wanting to defend the cult statues of his realm from the Persian invaders, Cyrus was able to win the respect of the Babylonian population by restoring the very statues which some may have feared he would have stolen. In this way, his actions mirror very closely Sargon II's behaviour in 707 BC when he restored the divine images of Ur and the other cities of the south to their original temples (see above).

DIVINE SYMBOLS

In addition to being anthropomorphized, individual deities often possessed concrete material correlates in the form of specific objects or emblems (Sum. *su-nir*, Akk. *surinnum*). These might be made of silver[7] or gold encrusted with semi-precious stones. Texts record deliveries of sacrificial animals for the emblem of a deity. Such emblems are occasionally mentioned in written sources, for example in cases where a deity is compared to a specific object or an object appears in context together with a particular deity. Thus 'Nisaba, who holds the tablet of lapis-lazuli' (Krecher 1957–1971:495), and was the patron deity of scribes and writing, was symbolized by a tablet. Divine symbols also appear in oaths and legal texts where, in taking the oath, the oath-taker swears by the symbol of a particular deity (for instance, in Old Babylonian legal contexts, see van Lerberghe 1982:245). According to the Stele of the Vultures, Eannatum made his adversary, the 'man of Umma', swear by the net of Enlil (Edzard 1976:65; Grégoire 1991:351–2), so vividly depicted on the stele itself (Fig. VIII.2), albeit in the hands of Ningirsu.[8] Similarly, in an Old Babylonian text from Tell Sifr an individual 'hoists the [ritual] axe of the god Lugal-kidunna', and 'walks [with it] around [his] garden' as part of a real estate transaction (Krecher 1957–1971:495).

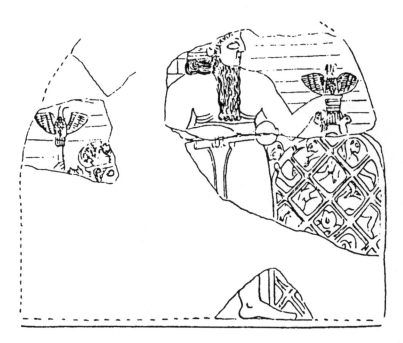

Figure VIII.2 The net of Enlil, shown on the Stele of the Vultures (after Amiet 1961: Pl. 103.1369)

Kudurrus, or boundary stones (Fig. VIII.3), such as those of Nazi-Maruttash (1307–1282 BC) or Melishihu (1188–1174 BC), sometimes contain written enumerations of divine symbols (Krecher 1957–1971:496). Moreover, symbols themselves often appear on stelae and *kudurrus* together with 'labels' or explanations of divine attributes, as on the Shamash-tablet of Nabuapplaidina (*c.* 900 BC) (Seidl 1957–1971:484–90, 1989; Gropp 1985:458). These are our main sources for the iconography of divine symbolism. Some of the main deities and their symbols are represented in Fig. VIII.4.[9]

Figure VIII.3 Drawing of a *kudurru* from Babylon (after Seidl 1989: Abb. 9).

THE HOUSE OF THE DEITY

As we have seen, anthropomorphized, natural phenomena were at the heart of the ancient Mesopotamian belief system. Harmful phenomena, such as disease, needed to be warded off and guarded against, whereas in the case of a beneficent phenomenon it was considered important 'to cleave to it and try to insure its presence' (Jacobsen 1976:13). There were several

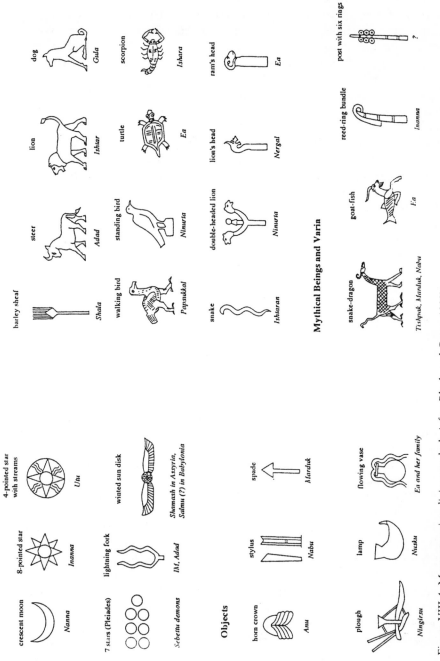

Figure VIII.4 Mesopotamian divine symbols (after Black and Green 1992)

ways in which a deity's presence could be guaranteed. These included the building of a house for the deity, the fashioning of images of the deity, the composition of religious works in praise of the deity and the enactment of cult dramas (Jacobsen 1975:65–97) for the deity. All of these mechanisms were material and ritual expressions of devotion. Let us begin by examining the building of a house for the deity.

Like any human being, a deity needed a house (Sum. *é*, Akk. *bîtum*). That house is what we generally refer to as a temple. Jacobsen suggests that, 'In some sense the temple, no less than the ritual drama and the cult image, was a representation of the form of the power that was meant to fill it' (Jacobsen 1976:16). The presence of the divine residence among the houses of the human community was a sign that the deity was 'present and available' in 'a holy abode' 'among the [creatures] in whom is breath of life' according to a hymn to Nanna (Jacobsen 1976:16). The salient difference between the house of a mortal and that of a deity was its sacredness, as expressed in its 'awesome aura' (*ní*) and 'awesome nimbus' (*me-lám*). Thus, the *é-kur* of Enlil at Nippur is described as 'the blue house, your [Enlil's] great seat, laden with awesomeness, its beams of awe and glory reach toward heaven, its shadow lies upon all lands'.

The daily routine in the deity's house was similar to that of a normal household. The deity had a staff of 'servants' (priests) who served the deity with 'daily meals, changing his clothes, cleaning his chambers, making his bed for him. Outside were lands belonging to the god and cultivated by other human servants, the god's retainers. Thus the god – because the temple was his home – was not only near and approachable, he was involved with the fortunes of the community and committed to maintaining it' (Jacobsen 1976:16). In the deity's private apartment stood his/her cult statue. This was called the 'dark room' (Sum. *itima*, Akk. *kissum*) which 'knows not daylight', its ritual vessels 'no eye is to see'. In the heavily Graeco-Roman-influenced terminology of temple features used in common archaeological parlance, this is the *cella*, comparable to the *sanctum sanctorum*, the 'holy of holies' wherein the Ark of the Covenant was kept in the Jewish temple.

In many cases the identities of the deity and the temple blended and merged, the latter becoming an architectural embodiment of the former, as for instance in the case of *é-anna* at Uruk, the 'house [of the] date clusters', referring to Inanna, 'lady [Nin] of the date clusters [*anna*]',[10] or *é-babbar*, 'house rising sun' of Utu/Shamash, also called Babbar, at Larsa and Sippar. As a result, an entire genre of literary compositions known as temple hymns, i.e. hymns 'addressed to temples' (e.g. Sjöberg and Bergmann 1969; Gragg 1969), grew up, a collection of which was made and dedicated by Enheduanna to her father, Sargon of Akkad. These hymns praise forty-two individual temples with vivid imagery. Thus the *é-babbar* of Shamash at Larsa is called the 'House which comes forth from heaven, visible in Kulaba [part of the city of Uruk, a neighbouring city], shrine Ebabbar, white purebred steer . . . Your brightness [is] . . ., pure [and lustrous like] lapis lazuli' (Sjöberg and Bergmann 1969:27). The temple of Inanna at Uruk is described as follows: 'Eanna, house with seven corners, lifting the 'seven fires' at night . . . Your princess is the pure horizon, Your queen [is] Inanna' (Sjöberg and Bergmann 1969:29), while the temple of Shamash at Sippar appears thus: 'Sippar, dais, upon which Utu sits daily (?), Sanctuary (?) of heaven, star of heaven, crown, borne by Ningal, House of Utu . . . When he, the lord reposes, the people repose [with him], When he arises, the people arise [with him]' (Sjöberg and Bergmann 1969:45).

Archaeologically speaking, the late prehistoric temples of the Ubaid period appear closely related to the houses of mortals, the only difference being that whereas both share a tripartite plan (Aurenche 1981:51) at the building's core (often flanked in private residences by other rooms), the residence of the deity is externally distinguished by the elaborate use of niches and buttresses (Fig. VIII.5). Otherwise, they are similar in most respects (Roaf 1984:80–90). With time their ground-plans evolved, and we are fortunate in possessing a number of architectural plans incised on clay tablets of Ur III to Neo-Babylonian date, some of which are thought to represent temples (Heinrich and Seidl 1957–1971:664–5) (Fig. VIII.6), as well as what is perhaps the most famous such plan of all, shown on the lap of Gudea, governor of Lagash, in one of his most celebrated seated statues, now in the Louvre (Statue B).

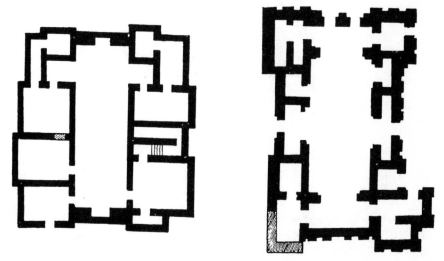

Figure VIII.5 Ubaid house (Tell Madhhur) and temple (Eridu VII) plans (after Margueron 1987: Figs. 1k and 3a)

Along with the architectural remains of many large temples from sites excavated all across southern Mesopotamia, and the temple plans just mentioned, we also have considerable iconographic information, much of it from Late Uruk seal impressions (Amiet 1975:144–9). Here we can iden-tify the temples of Inanna by the presence of her symbol, the reed-ring bundle (cf. Fig. VIII.4), most frequently represented at Uruk in the Late Uruk and Jamdat Nasr periods (Fig. VIII.7). A temple, in the form of a reed house, is moreover represented on a limestone basin from Uruk (Fig. VIII.8), while reed-ring bundles are also shown on the Warka Vase (Fig. VIII.9). The widespread association of horns with divinity (see below)

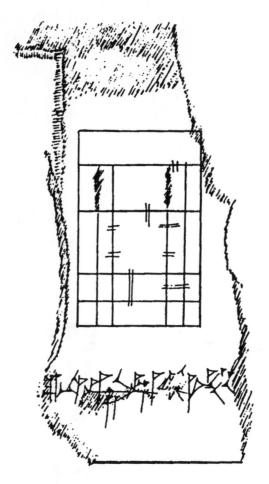

Figure VIII.6 A temple plan incised on a tablet (IM 44036, 1) in the Iraq Museum (after Schmid 1985: 289)

suggests that buildings with horns shown in Late Uruk glyptic from Susa (Fig. VIII.10) in nearby Khuzistan may already have been considered divine (Amiet 1987:99–104; Potts 1990:33–40).

As noted above it has often been remarked that there are no unequivocal, anthropomorphic representations of deities prior to the Early Dynastic II period. Therefore, the question must be asked, were Mesopotamian deities already fully anthropomorphized by the Late Uruk period when what are ostensibly temples and divine symbols, such as Inanna's reed-ring bundle (Figs. VIII.7–9), appear in Sumerian iconography? The question is a difficult one to answer. P. Amiet has suggested that, as deities were not yet depicted at this point, the temple in the Late Uruk period may have been conceived of more as the place where rites were carried out for a god or goddess by mortal priests, as shown pictorially on the Warka Vase (Fig. VIII.9), than as the 'house' of a deity who had not yet been embodied in an anthropomorph (Amiet 1975:144–5).

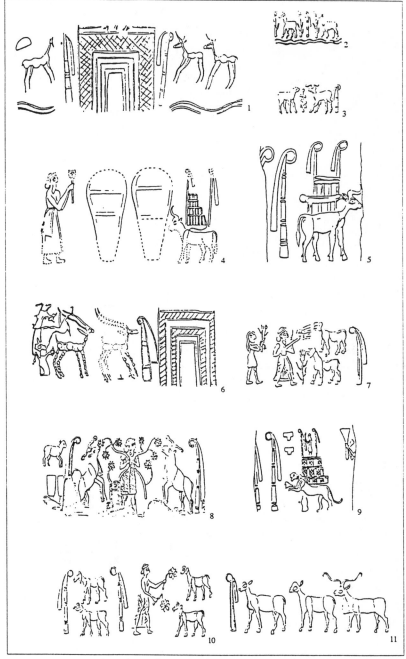

Figure VIII.7 Late Uruk and Jamdat Nasr glyptic representations incorporating the reed-ring bundle of Inanna. 1. Tell Agrab, ED II (after Amiet 1961: Pl. 42.625); 2. provenience uncertain, Haskell Museum (after Amiet 1961: Pl. 41.620); 3. provenience uncertain, J. Pierpont Morgan Library (after Amiet 1961: Pl. 41.622); 4. Uruk (after Amiet 1961: Pl. 46.652); 5. provenience uncertain, Newell Collection (after Amiet 1961: Pl. 46.653); 6. provenience uncertain, Louvre (after Amiet 1961: Pl. 42.627); 7. Uruk, Uruk III period (after Amiet 1961: Pl. 43.637); 8. probably Uruk (after Amiet 1961: Pl. 43.636); 9. provenience uncertain (after Amiet 1961: Pl. 46.654); 10. Uruk, Uruk III period (after Amiet 1961: Pl. 43.638); 11. Uruk, Uruk III period (after Amiet 1961: Pl. 41.621)

Figure VIII.8 Limestone basin from Uruk (after Amiet 1961: Pl. 42.623)

Figure VIII.9. Detail of the Warka Vase (after Lindemeyer and Martin 1993: Taf. 25)

Figure VIII.10 Drawing of a Late Uruk seal impression from Susa showing a horned building (after Amiet 1987: Fig. 1)

FROM SUMERIAN TEMPLES TO NESTORIAN CHURCHES

As a focus of worship, the early Mesopotamian temple undoubtedly differed greatly from its much more recent Christian counterpart, yet there is a remarkable coincidence between religious architectural forms of the fourth millennium BC and early churches of the late pre-Islamic era. The conservative, persistent, transcendent character of Mesopotamian civilization has long been appreciated (Yoffee 1993). In religion it has been remarked upon repeatedly (Garelli 1975:47–56). Mesopotamian-ness survived the conquests of Guti, Elamite, Kassite, Assyrian, Achaemenid, Greek, Parthian and Sasanian rulers, and did not even succumb to the Islamic conquest, for as Stephanie Dalley has recently shown, there are echoes of Gilgamesh in the *Arabian Nights* (Dalley 1991:1–17). Thus, a literary work such as the *Arabian Nights* may owe much to its pre-Islamic, local, Mesopotamian antecedents, just as it displays distinctive, obviously new elements.

One area which seems not to have been investigated from this point of view is Nestorian Christianity, the dominant Christianity of much of Mesopotamia during the long reign of the Sasanians. No doubt because of the historical and ideological watershed which Christianity seems to represent in the minds of theologians and historians, little thought seems to have been given to the degree to which Nestorian Christianity in particular does or does not display some of the distinctively 'Mesopotamian' characteristics which, in other spheres of life, seem to have persisted long after the fall of the Babylonian empire. It is well-known that scribes continued to write Akkadian and Sumerian on cuneiform tablets into the Parthian period (Sachs 1976:379–98). We know that the system of provincial administration which functioned, with some modifications, under the Ottomans, the earliest Caliphs, the Sasanians, the Parthians, and the Greeks, greatly resembled that which was in place under the Assyrians and can, in some ways, be traced back to the administrative reforms of Shulgi in the Ur III period which divided Babylonia and the Diyala region into over twenty provinces (Steinkeller 1987b:22). What of Nestorian Christianity and Mesopotamian religion?

It is not my intention to offer an interpretation of Nestorian theology in light of our knowledge of ancient Mesopotamian ritual or the ancient Mesopotamian pantheon. Rather, I wish to draw the reader's attention to some remarks made by D. Talbot Rice in 1932 which seem to have been overlooked by most scholars interested in the survival of the ancient Mesopotamian cultural imprint on the later material culture of the Tigris-Euphrates valley. Discussing the plans of the two churches excavated in mounds V and XI at Hira, hereafter referred to as Hira 1 (Fig. VIII.11) and 2 (Fig. VIII.12), and the very similar building excavated by O. Reuther at Ctesiphon, Talbot Rice remarked on the absence of an apse at one end of the church, a regular feature in Syrian and Coptic churches. Rather, he wrote (1934:58):

Close parallels and more likely prototypes are offered by the temples of Assyria and Babylonia, where we see the same rectangular sanctuaries connected with the main body of the edifice only by the narrowest of doors. Recent excavations at Kish have shown that the semicircular apse was well known to the Sasanians, and it was universal in Syria. The ancient religious edifices of Mesopotamia had avoided it, however, and there can be little doubt but that we see the continuity of this ancient idea in the churches of Hira.

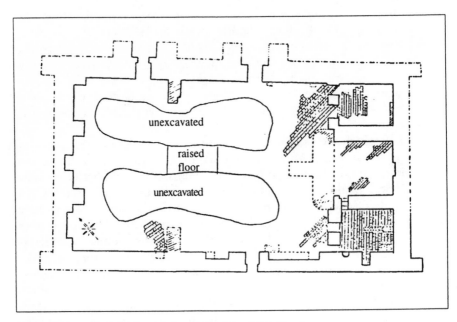

Figure VIII.11 Plan of Hira 1 (after Talbot Rice 1934: Fig. 5)

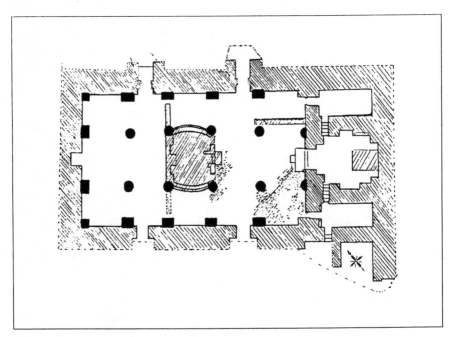

Figure VIII.12 Plan of Hira 2 (after Talbot Rice 1934: Fig. 6)

Elsewhere, he suggested (1932:266):

> The origin of these square ends to the sanctuary seems to be a feature of far earlier date, for we see such rectangular sanctuaries in Babylonian and Assyrian temples; and a comparison of the plan of such a one as the

Anu Adad temple at Assur with that of the Ctesiphon or the Hira churches is, to say the least, suggestive. It seems that we have yet another instance of the art or architecture of early Mesopotamia exercising its influence in the Christian period.

What was the basis for this statement? Plans of the Hira churches are included here (Figs. VIII.11–12), and it will be immediately obvious that they are rectangular, tripartite structures. Working from Talbot Rice's published descriptions, it is possible to describe each building as follows.

Although its precise dimensions were not published in the excavation reports, the scale in the Talbot Rice's plan of Hira 1 suggests that it measured roughly 14 × 8 m. Access was via two doorways in the eastern, and one doorway in the western wall of the building. Hira 1 is believed to have been roofed with a barrel vault, and the four buttresses which project on either side of the easterly entrances may have had a supporting function in that connection. On the other hand, whether the piers within the north wall functioned in a similar manner, or whether they were decorative, forming part of what appears to be an elaborate alternation of niches and projections, is difficult to say. Given their position opposite the walls at the opposite end of the church, it can be suggested that these buttresses are vestiges of an earlier building design (see below).

The interior of the southern end of the building was divided into three compartments, interpreted as chapels, by two massive piers. These were situated directly opposite the buttresses in the north wall mentioned above. If the piers were in fact joined to the buttresses by an imaginary line of wall, then the plan of Hira 1 would immediately appear to be fully, functionally tripartite. In the event, however, the central 'nave' appears as an open area without internal divisions.

This notion of a vestigial, underlying tripartite plan is clearer in the case of Hira 2, which varies only slightly in size from Hira 1. The building measures 14.5 × 7.5 m. Here we find two entrances on each of the long sides (again western and eastern walls), symmetrically placed opposite each other. The interior nave is divided by two rows of circular columns into two galleries and a central area. Once again, these fall in line with the walls which, as in Hira 1, divide the southern end of the church into three chambers. If the line of the columns were replaced with a solid wall, the plan would look even more tripartite than it already does.

Before discussing the resemblances between Hira 1 and 2, the Ctesiphon church, and early Mesopotamian religious architecture, there is one final Nestorian building which ought to be brought into the discussion. Discovered in 1988 and excavated more fully in 1989, the church at al-Qousour (Fig. VIII.13), near the center of Failaka (Kuwait), is the most recent addition to the small corpus of excavated Nestorian shrines (Bernard, Callot, and Salles 1991:145–81). With external dimensions of 35 × 19 m, it is also more than twice the size of the Hira churches. Like the latter two buildings, it shows a clear tripartite plan with the east end divided into three small chambers (a fourth is appended on the east side). The nave is flanked by two galleries, giving the building its tripartite appearance, but unlike the

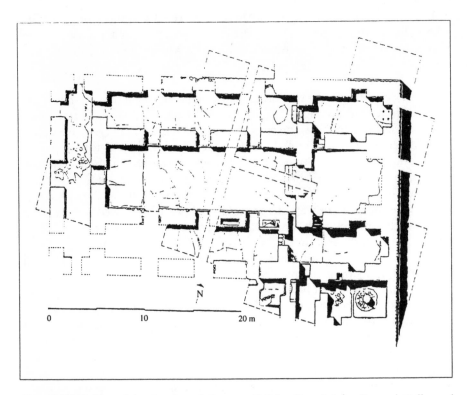

Figure VIII.13 Plan of the church at al-Qousour, Failaka, Kuwait (after Bernard, Callot and Salles 1991: Fig. 19)

Hira buildings, the galleries are divided from the nave by rectangular piers separated by openings which give access both to the nave and to the outside, for the northern and southern walls of the church are pierced by no fewer than four doorways, positioned directly opposite the passageways between the piers. Unlike the Hira churches, however, the western extremity of the church has three doorways leading into a long, narrow narthex which runs perpendicular to the central nave. From the narthex, a central doorway leads into the nave, while two side doors lead into the galleries.

If one looks for comparanda it is immediately clear that the closest resemblances are to be found in southern Mesopotamia, particularly at Uruk. The Limestone Temple (Fig. VIII.14), dating to the Late Uruk period (Uruk V) with its long, central room flanked by two rows of narrower rooms (the 'Alae'), and *Kopfbau* at the western end (Heinrich 1982:Abb. 114) is particularly reminiscent of the al-Qousour building. The two small rooms which flank the *cella* at the east end of the building would seem to represent the equivalent of the three 'chapels' or chambers in the Nestorian churches discussed above. A similar plan is seen in Kulthaus B, which formed part of the Eanna temple precinct in Uruk IVb times, and in Buildings C and D in Uruk IVa (Heinrich 1982:Abb. 119–120). On analogy with northern Mesopotamian churches these small, lateral rooms occupy the positions devoted to the *diakonikon*, or sacristy, and the *martyrion*, where

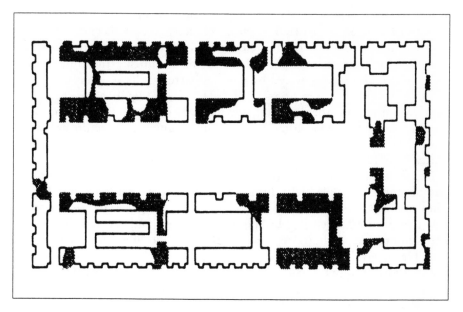

Figure VIII.14 Plan of the Limestone Temple at Uruk (after Redman 1978: Figs. 8–12)

the relics of martyrs might be housed (Ramsay and Bell 1909:315; cf. Fiey 1959:80–3; Oates 1968:107).

There can be no doubt that the four Nestorian churches under review show clear parallels to Sumerian temple architecture. The rectangular plan, the tripartite internal division and, in the case of the church at al-Qousour, the narthex which is the functional equivalent of the Mesopotamian *Kopf-bau*, are all replicated in Mesopotamian religious architecture of the Ubaid and Uruk periods. E. Heinrich has discussed in great detail the essential characteristics of tripartite *Mittelsaalhäuser* with symmetrical wings, or galleries, which he referred to as 'Alae' (Heinrich 1982:9), tracing this form back to the Ubaid period. As has often been noted, this was the typical form of early Mesopotamian temples, but Heinrich also stressed that it was found in buildings which he identified as *Kulthäuser*, i.e. religious buildings other than true temples which belonged within the temenos and which may have had profane functions such as assembly houses, treasuries, stalls, living accommodation, etc. (Heinrich 1982:xiii).

How are we to explain what, at first sight, appears to be the remarkable reappearance of an age-old Mesopotamian tradition dating to the fifth and fourth millennia BC in the late pre-Islamic era? For just as surely as early Mesopotamian religious architecture shows striking parallels with the Nestorian churches of Hira, Ctesiphon and al-Qousour, other religious monuments of the third, second and first millennia BC have floorplans which are not at all similar to the Christian monuments we have been discussing, as do buildings of the Seleucid and Parthian periods (Downey 1988). At first glance, this might seem an insurmountable problem, the result of an historical accident which was fortuitous and without meaning. But from the very beginnings of scholarship devoted to the type of church which we have before us, the vaulting of the roof areas of nave and side galleries has been recognized as showing clear links with earlier vaulted architecture in Mesopotamia. Gertrude Bell emphasized the marked 'Asiatic' character of what she called the 'barn church', 'the church with two aisles and a nave, covered by parallel barrel vaults so equal in height as not to admit of a clerestory' (Bell 1924:257), noting that the use of the barrel vault to roof the nave and side galleries harkened back to the *iwan* tradition so apparent in earlier Parthian and Sasanian architecture at Hatra, Ctesiphon and Firuzabad (Ramsay and Bell 1909: 315; Fiey 1959:80–3; Oates 1968:109).

There seems little doubt that the striking parallels between the early Mesopotamian temple plans discussed here and the Nestorian churches of Hira and al-Qousour deserve further study. More generally, they raise a point often overlooked in Mesopotamian studies and research into early Christianity but well-attested in the ethnographic literature, namely the possible survival of ancient practices from pre-Christian, Mesopotamian antiquity in Mesopotamian, principally Nestorian Christianity. Historians of Islam are well aware that there are many survivals from the religions of pre-Islamic Western Asia which are detectable in Islam. J. Henninger has argued that the ritual sacrifice of a lamb as described in a Neo-Assyrian text from the library of Assurbanipal (CT XVII:Pl. 37.Z) finds an undeniable parallel in the so-called *'Aqiqa* offering made seven days after the birth of a child (Henninger 1981b:313–6). It is quite possible that ancient Mesopotamian religious beliefs, cult practices and paraphernalia (from portable objects to entire building complexes) may be reflected in Mesopotamian Christianity and Islam in ways which scholars have largely overlooked until now, and the congruence between Sumerian temple plans and Nestorian churches would appear to embody one such case.

CONCLUSION

The study of non-Western religions has always been a focus of anthropological analysis, and anyone who has ever delved into the literature of this field will know how difficult it is to come to grips with the complex belief systems of another culture. Needless to say, the difficulties in the case of understanding Mesopotamian religion are compounded by the fragmentary nature of the evidence, the lack of living informants, and the great distance – conceptually more than geographically or temporally – which separates the modern student of Mesopotamia from the object of his study. Mesopotamian religion will undoubtedly continue to remain an important field of study for years to come. It is to be hoped that Oppenheim's pessimism will not be vindicated as that work progresses. To abandon any attempt at understanding Mesopotamian religion on its own terms would be to deny one of the principal goals of the study of human culture, for the difficulty of the subject and the intractability of the sources should not blind us to the importance of attempting to place ancient Mesopotamian belief systems in their proper context.

NOTES

1 As in Gudea Cyl B vi 23, 'He introduced [the god] with his emblems [*me*] to lord Ningirsu'. See Alster and Vanstiphout 1987:35.

2 For the relationship between An and Inanna at Uruk, long misunderstood, and for the revival of An/Anu in the Seleucid period, see Charpin 1994: 39.

3 Until the Seleucid period at Uruk when Anu came to prominence. See Chapter XIII.

4 Note, however, that this text dates to the late second millennium. See Lambert 1980–83:219.

5 Divine images varied in size greatly from small, *c*. 20–30 cm, according to materials used, to one so large it needed a whole slew of priests to carry the stand on which it was mounted during a procession around Uruk in the Seleucid period. Neo-Babylonian statues of Marduk and other gods were sometimes cast from 1–2 tons of metal. See Renger 1980–1983:309–10.

6 Lafont 1987:1–2. Numerous lyres are shown in third-millennium glyptic and examples were found in the Royal Cemetery at Ur. It is thought by some scholars that *balags* were sung to the accompaniment of a lyre. For the archaeological and iconographic evidence of lyres in ancient Mesopotamia see Collon 1980–1983:576–82. Black 1991:28 argues convincingly, however, that the identification of the *balag* as a drum 'is beyond doubt'. Cf. Barrelet 1968:238 and Bisi 1980:58 for clay figurines from Tello showing women holding drums which date to between the Early Dynastic and Isin-Larsa periods.

7 E.g. the *imittum* (?) of Ishtar, Shamash, or Ninurta mentioned in Old Babylonian texts. See Sanati-Müller 1990:149, n. 1.

8 Cf. the inscription of Entemena which says, 'Ningirsu . . . fought with Umma, and upon command of Enlil, he covered it with the great net'. See Westenholz 1970:29.

9 These identifications follow Black and Green 1992.

10 This is the etymology suggested by Jacobsen. For an alternative view of *é-an-na* as 'house of heaven', see George 1992:67, Charpin 1994:39.

IX Kinship in an Urban Society

As the brief discussion of religion should have made clear, the temple of each deity in Mesopotamia was its house, but not in the narrow sense in which we use that term today. As I.J. Gelb observed many years ago (1967:5), the deity's house was more than just a place to live in. Rather, it was:

> a full socio-economic unit, largely self-contained and autarchic, which includes residential buildings, shelters for the labor force, storage buildings and animal pens, fields, orchards, gardens and pastures, as well as the owners (or managers), labor personnel, and domestic animals . . . the full economic unit needed to support the manifold activities of the temple.

In terms of human social organization, two parallel types of 'household' can be distinguished, the public ones which served the king/crown and temples, and the private ones belonging to large landowners, many of whom were state or temple officials.

Three different social groups were represented in these households. Following Gelb, these may be distinguished as the 'free' members of the family in private households, or managers in the case of public households, the 'semi-free' men (guruš), women (géme) and children who accounted for the bulk of the labour force attached to the large households, who could not be bought and sold, and who were in regular, monthly receipt of barley, wool and oil rations (se-ba, síg-ba, i-ba) and the 'unfree' chattel slaves who could be sold freely, often had no family life, were the personal property of their owner, and generally played no productive role, functioning rather as household slaves (Gelb 1967:7). Some scholars, however, feel that in certain periods, such as that of the Third Dynasty of Ur, 'semi-free' workers such as the women (géme) employed in the grain mills of Umma, were for all intents and purposes chattel slaves owned by the state and certainly employed in a productive manner, though distinct from household slaves (Englund 1991:256 and n. 5). Beyond these global characterizations of Mesopotamian society, what kinds of information are available on actual kinship relations in the third and second millennia BC?

THE THIRD MILLENNIUM

Generally speaking, the family in third-millennium, 'Sumerian' southern Mesopotamia, was the nuclear family, consisting of parents and unmarried children. The shortage of distinguishing terms for cousins, nephews and nieces, however, often makes it difficult to differentiate filial from collateral relations. Most of the principal kin designations current in the third millennium are shown in Table IX.1.[1] In spite of some very ambiguous literary references to women having intercourse with more than one man in their lives[2] most scholars believe that monogamy was the rule in southern Mesopotamia (Ebeling 1957–1971:9). Although there may always have been

English designation	Sumerian term	Other observations
household (people + movable and immovable property)	é	
family	im-ri-a/im-ru-a	lit. 'space'; rendered in Akk. by *kimtu, nišūtu* and *salātu*, trans. as 'family, parents, kin, clan, lineage'
clan/lineage	ildú	cf. Akk. *illatu*, but meaning of Sumerian unclear
father	ad-da, ab-ba, a-a	
mother	ama	
spouse	dam	
child(ren)	dumu	
son	dumu-nitá	
daughter	dumu-munus	
brother	šeš	
elder/oldest brother	šeš-gal, PAP.PAP-gal	latter only in lex. texts
elder/eldest	pa₄/pap	
second brother	šeš-ús	
third brother	šeš-3-kam	
youngest brother	šeš-TUR	
son and heir	ibila (i₃-bí-la)	cf. Akk. *aplum*
sister	nin₉	
grandchild (?), great grandchild	dumu-KA	
paternal grandfather	a-a-a, ad-ad-da, pa-bil₃-ga	
paternal uncle	pa-bil₃-ga	
paternal uncle	šeš-ad-da	
maternal uncle	šeš-ama	
paternal aunt	nin₉-ab-ba, nin₉-ad-da	
maternal aunt	nin₉-ama	only attested onomastically
male cousin (?)	šeš	
female cousin (?)	nin₉	
father-in-law	ušbar, urum, murum, ur₇	applied to both the father's and mother's father
mother-in-law	ušbar	possibly also daughter-in-law?
son-in-law	murub₅	with ref. to wife's father
son-in-law	mí-ús-sá	also brother-in-law
future son-in-law	mí-ús-sá-tur	lit. 'small son-in-law/brother-in-law', either the future son-in-law or the youngest of a father's sons-in-law
brother-in-law	mí-ús-sá	wife's husband vis-à-vis her brother
brother-in-law	muru₅	wife's brother
sister-in-law	arib/erib	husband's sister

Table IX.1 *Sumerian kinship terminology*

exceptions (San Nicolò 1938:256), it is not until the second millennium BC that we find clear evidence for the practice of a man taking a second wife of socially inferior status (Grégoire 1981:52; Westbrook 1988:103ff.; Groneberg 1989).

Marriage was normally arranged by the groom's parents, who chose the girl to be their son's bride. It was preceded by a promise of marriage with fixed conventions, and sanctified by an oath pronounced in the name of the king (Grégoire 1991:354–5). We have, however, very little idea of exactly how the marriage was arranged, i.e. proscriptively, preferentially or freely. Thus, it is impossible to judge the degree of endogamy or exogamy in Sumerian marriage practices. Certainly, in some cases there are clear signs that political and economic considerations were taken into account by the parents arranging the marriage. Thus, a young man might renounce his own paternity in order to be 'adopted' by his father-in-law so as to place himself in a position to inherit from him. At an altogether different societal level, inter-dynastic marriages which were patently political are well attested (e.g. Pintore 1978; van Dijk 1986:159–70), though of no direct relevance to the study of the bulk of society.

Marriages were legitimized by a contract in which the phrase *dam . . . tuku*, 'to take as a spouse' appears, but we know little about the exact features of such contracts. The phrase *nì-mí-ús-sá* seems to refer to goods furnished by the groom and/or his family for the marriage celebration, while *kù-dam-tuku*, 'silver for taking the wife', may refer to brideprice, but could also refer to similarly consumed goods. The dowry, in any event, is never mentioned in Ur III sources (Grégoire 1981:54). Marital residence was patrilocal, and it was normal for the new couple to live in the same quarter of town, preferably in adjacent houses, as the groom's father. Scholars such as J.-P. Grégoire point to the difference here between multiple, nearby habitations of members of different generations linked by marriage, and true cohabitation in the form of an extended family (Grégoire 1981:54).

All filiation was strictly patrilineal, and was distinguished scrupulously from adoptive filiation. A father, however, had the right to legitimize children by a slave/concubine[3] through adoption. The mechanism of adoption[4] also served to 'free' a slave, to give a son to a wife, to effectively give someone a life annuity (fictive adoption) in order to obviate patrilineal rules of inheritance, and to pay a debt. Indeed, there was no juridical difference between biological and adopted children in terms of inheritance (Grégoire 1981:56), and the same applied to 'succession'. Thus, an adopted child could be ahead of a biological one where questions of succession arose.

A husband could renounce his marriage for the wife's failure to uphold the marriage contract, or for adultery, the penalty for the latter offence being death. However, a woman wrongfully repudiated had a right to certain indemnities according to §6 of the Laws of Ur-Nammu, in which case the husband was required to pay his wife a sum of silver as stipulated in the marriage contract. By the Ur III period this had reached the very considerable sum of one mina (500 g) of silver (Grégoire 1981:55). This is thought to have kept down the divorce rate (Neumann 1987:134).

Women were often mentioned with reference to men, for instance as *dam* (wife), *ama* (mother), *nin* (sister), or *dumu(-munus)* (daughter), and scribes often called them '*dam* PN', i.e. 'wife of X' rather than by their own given names (Glassner 1989:82–3). The superior position of the male, juridically speaking, is shown clearly in Urukagina's famous dictum, 'If a woman speaks. . .disrespectfully (?) to a man, that woman's mouth is crushed with a fired brick, and the fired brick is displayed at the city-gate' (trans. after Cooper 1986:77). On the other hand, women are by no means rare as buyers, sellers and witnesses in Old Akkadian legal documents (Steinkeller 1982:366), suggesting that their juridical position at this time was far from deplorable.

When a man predeceased his wife she did not inherit his belongings but rather protected them for the inheritors, her children, so long as they were minors. On the other hand, she (and the female offspring) was often given gifts during the life of the husband in order to ensure her survival for as long as she lived (in the case of the wife, or until marriage in the case of the daughters) (Grégoire 1981:53, 56). In general, all belongings of a deceased head of household went to the male offspring or, failing that, the females. In the absence of any offspring, property generally reverted to the deceased husband's brother, but there is also evidence for the attempted usurpation of a surviving widow's legitimate inheritance by a deceased husband's brother at Nippur in the Ur III period (Owen 1980:170–84).[5] Male offspring usually received equal portions of an inheritance, and there are no signs of primogeniture, but we know that a father could show preferential treatment to a son during life in the form of gifts which were then deducted from the inheritance upon the father's death, provided a sealed tablet existed which recorded such gifts (Grégoire 1981:53, 56).

In conclusion, the nuclear family was well entrenched in third-millennium Mesopotamia, and we have a number of examples of very formidable families, such as that of Ur-Meme at Nippur (Zettler 1984:1–14, 1987:Fig. 1), which provided three generations of the chief priesthood of the Inanna temple as well as several governors of the region. Even in the late third millennium, however, there is little sign of anything like a pattern of extended kin units of the sort which one might call lineages.

THE SECOND MILLENNIUM

It is commonplace to contrast the situation in southern Mesopotamia during the second half of the third millennium with that found during the second millennium, largely because of a presumption that a major infiltration of West Semitic-speaking Amorites from the Syrian desert region during the first several centuries of the period changed the pre-existing social structure of Mesopotamia from what it had once been. In fact, this whole subject is one of great complexity and needs careful consideration.

At the root of it is the quite simple (and certainly debatable) principle of assigning people to ethnic groups on the basis of the etymology of their name (see generally Gelb 1962). Thus, at the height of what could be called 'classical' Sumerian civilization, the Early Dynastic period, one would expect most people in southern Mesopotamia to have had Sumerian names. The presence of scribes at Abu Salabikh in Early Dynastic II times (*c.* 2500 BC) with Semitic names (Biggs 1967:55–66) thus came as something of a shock to scholars who had expected that only in the Old Akkadian period, with the creation of a 'Semitic' dynasty founded by Sargon of Akkad, did the Akkadianization of the south occur as the old Sumerian city-states were absorbed into the new empire. The Semitization of the south, however, was not nearly so comprehensive. As a study of personal names in Old Akkadian texts shows, some 80.5 per cent of the population of the south (Girsu, Umma, Me-ság and Adab) still had Sumerian names, while only 12.91 per cent had Akkadian (Semitic) ones. (The remainder could not be classified as one or the other). Conversely, in northern Babylonia (Kish, Gasur, the Diyala sites), generally considered the heartland of the Semitic-speaking Akkadians, only 5 per cent of the population whose names are attested in Old Akkadian texts had Sumerian names, while 77.66 per cent had Akkadian ones (Foster 1982:299). By the Ur III period, moreover, significant numbers of Amorites (*MAR-TU* or *MAR-DÚ*), thought by some scholars to have originated in the area of Jabal Bishri in the Syrian desert region,[6] were settled in southern Mesopotamia (Buccellati 1966). Yet even the Amorites, generally considered tribal and thought to have been led by a leader comparable to the paramount sheikh of a bedouin tribe, appear to have assimilated quickly into southern Mesopotamian society and to have lost whatever tribal organization they may have brought with them. As we have seen, moreover, speaking a Semitic language, such as Akkadian, does not necessarily imply having a 'tribal' type of social structure. Why, then, should the increase in people with Semitic names during the second millennium necessarily imply the introduction of 'tribal' social structure, as has sometimes been suggested?

In fact, when examined closely, the ethnic situation in the centuries immediately following the fall of the Third Dynasty of Ur was far from clear cut. As Kamp and Yoffee, following Michalowski, have shown, most of the references to 'Amorites' in the Isin-Larsa period concern not the area to the west of the southern Mesopotamian heartland but to the northeast, along the Elamite frontier (Kamp and Yoffee 1980:90). Indeed, the facile assumption that an 'Amorite' was always a Syrian desert-dweller originally or an assimilated one living in Mesopotamia is proven wrong by the fact that an Elamite (LÚ.ELAM.MA[ki], 'man of Elam') who is named as a witness in an Old Babylonian text from al-Hiba bore the Amorite name *Ia-mu-ut-li-im* (Zadok 1987:5). The entire question of the relationship between the Amorites of the east Tigridian region and Elam is a complex one, and, moreover, the fallacy of assuming that the etymology of a personal name automatically identifies the ethnic group to which a person belonged is clearly shown by examples such as the present one or the case of Elamites with Akkadian names (e.g. Ahi-shagish who is called *lú* ELAM[ki], 'man of Elam',) or Igmil-Sîn whose patronymic *Ku-uk-si-ga-at* identifies him as an Elamite) (Zadok 1987:7, 8).[7] Without the explicit qualification which identifies these individuals as Elamites, both would have been mistaken for an Amorite and an Akkadian, respectively, in any survey of personal names such as Foster's.

On what basis, then, have scholars presumed to differentiate family organization during the second millennium from that which obtained earlier? One way has been through examining the institution of marriage, particularly as it appears in the Laws of Hammurapi. Hammurapi's 'code' consists of some 281 rulings which 'present a set of postulated acts as having already occurred, with the circumstances considered as a protasis (if-clause) in a past tense, while the prescribed action for the respective act is presented as an apodosis (then-clause) in a present-future tense' (Yoffee 1988:101; cf. Westbrook 1988:2). As many scholars have observed, however, the laws in Hammurapi's code rarely overlap with decisions made in the vast body of legal texts which have survived from the second millennium. Indeed they are often contradicted by the decisions handed down in those documents. Moreover, as Yoffee observes, 'there is no mention of the code of Hammurabi in the thousands of legal documents that date to his reign and those of his immediate successors ... In sum, it may be inferred that Hammurabi never intended that his rules be accorded the status of practical law' (Yoffee 1988:103). One must, therefore, beware of according too much significance to the stipulations concerning marriage in Hammurapi's famous code.

Generally speaking, it has traditionally been felt that two types of marriage existed in the Old Babylonian period, one in which a brideprice was transferred, and one without brideprice (Ebeling 1938:281–6; cf. Westbrook 1988:8). Several of the paragraphs in Hammurapi's laws deal with the financial consequences of the termination of a marriage where the brideprice had been transferred, with proscriptions relating to who enjoyed rights to the brideprice and who was entitled to the dowry or other gifts given to the bride by her father on the occasion of her marriage. §159, for instance, stipulates that if a man has paid the brideprice, but then decides not to marry his intended because he has become interested in another woman, the father of the erstwhile bride keeps the brideprice. J. Renger has emphasized that there are in fact two different terms, *biblum* and *terhatum*, which appear in these laws and suggested that they are not synonyms, but refer rather to the marriage gifts exchanged by the two different families on the occasion of a marriage. In his opinion, the emphasis here is on reciprocity, for various members of the two families about to be joined in marriage receive gifts, not just the groom and the bride's father. This point is important because, as Renger observes (1973:272–3):

> It has been noted repeatedly that marriage in Old Babylonian times is not an arrangement between the groom and the bride, not even between the groom and the bride's father, but between the two families. Therefore, the exchange of gifts between the two families has a function which goes beyond the marriage of a young man and a young woman ... This exchange is a means of building or maintaining an alliance, a close relationship, between these two families.

After a lengthy consideration of all the evidence, Westbrook concludes that *terhatum* refers to brideprice ('a real price for a right over the bride, but one less than ownership'), and *biblum* to a 'a gift of various items other than money made on the occasion of "marriage" celebrations by members of the groom's family to members of the bride's family' (Westbrook 1988:59, 101; cf. Wilcke 1986:252–67).

Be that as it may, Renger suggests that alliance building of this sort was practised in urban, settled southern Mesopotamia amongst previously 'tribal' families (i.e. Amorites) as a mechanism of maintaining their identity and close ties in a new, urban context (Renger 1973:273), but it is certainly the case that gift exchange, whether reciprocal or asymmetrical, was already well attested in the third millennium (Glassner 1985:11–59), and the practice of building family alliances through marriage, which certainly goes on today, is hardly limited to families of tribal origin. On the contrary, it reflects a socio-economic strategy which can be observed, well entrenched, in Western society, amongst virtually all classes of society of any ethnic background.

Turning specifically to the question of the dowry (Westbrook 1988:89ff.), §171–9 of Hammurapi's laws specify that a woman brought a dowry with her from her father's house when she married. If the marriage failed and she was blameless, she kept it. If she died, her sons inherited it or, failing that, it reverted to her father's family (Dalley 1980:53). If we leave the legal aspects of marriage for a moment, it is interesting to see what was and was not included in an Old Babylonian dowry. Not present in several enumerations of dowries studied some years ago by S. Dalley were knives, mirrors,[8] cosmetics or sieves, and looms were present in only three out of ten texts. On the other hand, a good deal of furniture was brought, such as chairs, beds, tables and chests as well as rugs. Ceramic vessels, leather bags, grinding stones, land, silver, jewellery, clothing, reed baskets, blankets, oxen, cattle, sheep, wooden bowls, foot-stools, spoons, combs, pot-racks of wood, slave girls and bronze scrapers are also mentioned (Dalley 1980:57, 60). In the case of certain Neo-Babylonian dowries, M. Roth (1991:37) found that a definite marriage strategy seemed to have operated in the case of the Itti-Marduk-Balatu family, which was:

> wealthy and influential, and was able to command rich dowries with the women marrying into it. These dowries brought in real estate and large amounts of cash, as well as slaves and household goods . . . In contrast, although the dowries of its daughters removed silver, real estate, slaves and household goods from the family's holdings, the losses were more than offset by the considerably greater amounts their sisters-in-law brought into the family.

In northern Babylonia, as in the western frontier region along the Middle Euphrates, the situation was different according to Renger, for these were areas of truly 'tribal' organization and exogamous marriage preferences. Considering evidence from Sippar and Suhi which seems to refer to Amorite sheep/goat nomads (*Kleintiernomaden*), Renger points to the occurrence of the phrase *il hal(i) awilim*, '[the] god of someone's mother's brother [maternal uncle]', which he takes to be the protective, patron deity of a lineage, so epitomized as to make the allegiance to one's own, ancestral deity of continued importance even in an exogamous situation. The term *mar/marat ilim*, literally 'son/daughter of the god', on the other hand, is thought to identify members of a patrilineal, exogamous clan or lineage which identified itself by venerating a particular deity (Renger 1973:107). As Renger notes, it is irrelevant whether the groups which were so characterized were nomadic Amorites or already sedentary, acculturated ones living in the cities of the alluvial plain who still retained some aspects of their original lineage's structure. The important point is that identification with one's lineage-by-birth persisted in an exogamous situation.

MORES AND SOCIAL VALUES

J.-J. Glassner has shown that certain conventions existed in Mesopotamian society such as the impossibility of refusing what one has been offered (as giving offence to the host), eating and drinking a meal together as a sign of solidarity, toasting, which sometimes turned into a challenge intended to provoke a confrontation resulting in a settlement in order to bind the two parties more closely, and seeking protection with a host group on the part of a guest, in which case the guest was not without rights and might even marry a woman of the group in which he has found himself (Glassner 1990:73).

The ancient Mesopotamians were very clear about the difference between wives who were spouses, *assatum*, and women who were prostitutes or harlots, *harimtum*. For marriage, virginity was most definitely required of the woman, and we find expressions to describe a virgin before her marriage such as she 'who has not been known', 'who does not know man', 'who has not been opened' (Glassner 1989:75). It is also interesting to note that married women seem to have been veiled, 'to avoid any risk of pollution', according to Glassner. The husband covered the woman's head, an act which is revealed in a metaphor for 'night, the veiled spouse', or in the phrase, 'the veiled spouse is the goddess Gula whom nobody can look at, even from afar', referring to sunset. Indeed the same verb (*kuttumu*) is used both to express shutting a door and veiling (Glassner 1989:76). As for the *harimtum*, these harlots or prostitutes offered their services 'at the door of the tavern', 'at the crossing', or 'on the square' (Glassner 1989:74). They were specifically forbidden to wear the veil, so as to emphasize the contrast between themselves and the *marat awilim*, or 'gentlemen's daughters' (Glassner 1989:79).

Parallel to the importance placed upon virginity, it is scarcely surprising that the punishment for adultery was death, according to the Laws of Ur-Nammu (§7), the Laws of Eshnunna (§28), the Middle Assyrian laws (§13–15) or the Laws of Hammurapi §129 which calls for an adulterous woman to be tied up and thrown into the water (Owen and Westbrook 1992:202–7). The fact that the death penalty is prescribed is all the more remarkable in that it was in fact used sparingly, and indeed adultery was the only offence punishable by it in the Laws of Ur-Nammu (Ries 1976–1980:393). Interestingly, the Laws of Eshnunna (§26) prescribed the death penalty not only for adultery and several other offences but also for the deflowering of an engaged virgin by one other than the engaged man. According to the Laws of Hammurapi, death was the penalty for adultery (§129), rape (§130), adultery on the part of a woman whose husband was a prisoner-of-war (§133b) and the refusal of a wife to have intercourse with her husband (§143).

BABTUM AND NEIGHBOURHOOD

In recent years the question of neighbourhoods in ancient Mesopotamian cities has been much discussed, and indeed an entire monograph has been devoted to the subject of neighbourhoods in Old Babylonian Nippur (Stone 1987). N. Yoffee has pointed out that in the Old Babylonian period legal cases were tried in various local communities, rather than central contexts, and has pointed particularly to the *babtum* as a 'corporate group, perhaps even a lineage', numbers of which existed in individual Old Babylonian cities, each named after a prominent personage (Yoffee 1988:105–6; cf. Donbaz and Yoffee 1986:66–7). This is particularly interesting in light of the attempt by Elizabeth Stone to document the existence of neighbourhoods and house-transfers by marriage at Nippur during the Old Babylonian period (Stone 1981:24–33), or Diakonoff's study of extended family property transactions at Ur (Diakonoff 1985:47–65). Stone, however, was unsure that her 'neighbourhoods' were synonymous with a *babtum* (Stone 1987:6–7), if for no other reason, as pointed out by J.N. Postgate, than their very small size (Postgate 1990:237). In fact, reviewing *Nippur Neighborhoods*, Postgate disagreed with Stone, noting, 'The neighborhood as conceived by the author is not an administrative but a social entity, but since it cannot be defined by either spatial or kin-based limits, it is very hard to see how historians and archaeologists will be able to demonstrate its existence outside the perceptions of the modern scholar' (Postgate 1990:238).

One of the arguments put forward by Stone contends that 'urban neighborhoods were organized along kin-group lines', and further that 'sales of houses could normally not be alienated outside a social group' (Yoffee 1988:126). As Yoffee has shown, however (1988:127), at Old Babylonian Dilbat there were ways around this, for it is suggested that one individual named Iddin-Lagamal

> newly arrived in Dilbat, was able to buy land there only in conjunction with a kinsman of the sellers . . . Having made this first purchase, however, he could and did buy out the entire family and proceeded to make further purchases all over town. Further, property in Dilbat was partible and all children inherited sections of paternal (really bilateral) estates. In the Dilbat examples, rooms, not only houses, were bought and sold. In successive generations, it became a struggle to reassemble dispersed properties; principles of kinship organization seemed to break down and be replaced by occupational ties.

Thus, the situation with respect to kinship in this period was far from clear cut. Furthermore, at Nuzi several centuries later, as Yoffee observes, 'creditors were regularly adopted by debtors in order for property to be transferred' outside of kin units (Yoffee 1988:127; cf. Grosz 1988:18–42).

One conclusion drawn by Yoffee which he suggests may be projected back in time to prehistory is that the repeated rebuildings, closing up of doorways, and sub-dividing of rooms which can be observed in mudbrick architecture all over Western Asia may very well be a reflection of similar patterns of inheritance and transfer of property between kin or non-kin, indeed very much the sort of property transfer documented at Nippur by Stone (Stone 1981:24–33) and at Ur by Diakonoff (Diakonoff 1985:47–65). Otherwise it is difficult to understand why such rebuilds so consistently recur in the archaeological record. As a corollary to this discussion it is interesting to note that multi-room houses lend themselves much more easily to this sort of sub-division than large, single-room houses, and the growing differentiation of space for whatever reasons (privacy, storage, social functions, etc.) may have played a role in the much-discussed passage from circular to rectilinear architecture in the Early Neolithic of Western Asia (Yoffee 1988:128).

DESCENT AND AFFILIATION

Genealogical information in ancient Mesopotamia occurs in many different contexts, ranging from royal inscriptions where kings name their fathers, to legal transactions, such as inheritance documents naming heirs. During the later second and early first millennia a number of different ethnic groups are known to have inhabited southern Mesopotamia, including the Kassites (originally from western Iran), Chaldaeans (inhabitants of southernmost Mesopotamia) and Aramaeans (originally from the western steppe/desert zone), whose social structure and means of marking descent through family names differed from that which obtained in the third millennium. As J.A. Brinkman has noted, 'Though the individual members of each of these groups rapidly assimilated Babylonian culture and many of them bore Babylonian names, they frequently preserved a distinctive tribal or clan structure which is reflected chiefly by the way in which their ancestry was cited' (Brinkman 1968:246).

Both the Kassites and the Chaldaeans used a similar pattern of naming which followed the form 'PN$_1$, *mar* (son of) PN$_2$,' where the second name, rather than representing a biological parent, was in fact the name of the individual's 'house' (*bit*), conventionally understood as a 'clan' or 'tribe'. This is in many ways comparable to the practice of Arab groups who designate their members *Banu* (sons of) X, where X is the name of an eponymous ancestor (Henninger 1981:173ff.), or *Al* X, where *Al* denotes 'house of'. In the latter case, however, it is important to note that such a 'house', like the 'House of Saud' (Al Saud) which today rules Saudi Arabia, is a web of interconnected families and not a tribe in the anthropological sense of the term. It is difficult to know precisely how such 'houses' were constituted during the Kassite period, but we do know that while each had a head (*bel biti*, literally 'lord of the house'), that person was not always originally of the house which he headed (Brinkman 1968:255). This might suggest that an analogy between the Kassite *bit* and an Arab *Al* is more apt than an analogy with a tribe. The same may be true for the Aramaeans who, however, designated themselves in this way: 'PN₁, LÚ *(man of)* X', where X was the macro-familial/lineage name.

By the ninth century BC native Babylonians, particularly scribes and provincial administrators, increasingly styled themselves 'PN₁, *mar* (son of) PN₂' (Brinkman 1968:247). In some cases, up to three names appear after that of the person himself. Scholars have long pondered the significance of this method of naming (Ungnad 1935:319–26). M. San Nicolò suggested that the increasing number of people involved in some form of litigation, combined with a trend to repeat favoured names within a family (thus potentially causing confusion between two or more individuals with the same name,[9] prompted this elaboration of the personal name (San Nicolò 1951:2–3). W.G. Lambert has argued, however, that in cases which followed the formula 'PN₁, *mar* PN₂, *mar* PN₃,' this 'was well understood as meaning, "X son of Y, descendant of Z"', where Z is not literally a biological grandfather but a much vaguer 'ancestor' (Lambert 1957:1). Moreover, Gelb warned against a literal interpretation of names such as these, stressing the difference between a literal interpretation, in which the names were read as a series of biological ancestors representing individual generations (e.g. person-father-grandfather), and a more elastic interpretation of the names as a series of 'genealogical steps'. For Gelb (1979:26), names

> that list two or three genealogical steps may really express three, four, or more generations. As the number of genealogical steps increases, so does the likelihood that the last PN in a genealogical structure represents an ancestor who is removed from the bearer of the name by more generations than is indicated by the number of genealogical steps given in the record.

This observation is important, and if one considers naming patterns and genealogical reckoning amongst, for instance, north Arabian bedouin of the recent past, then it is interesting to see that genealogies such as 'A son of B son of C of the Zuwaiyyid Nseir of the Murath tribal section of the Rwala Aneze' refer not so much to biological ancestors as to geographically ever greater social units to which A belongs (Lancaster 1981:152). Clearly, therefore, the interpretation of descent and affiliation in late Babylonian names is a matter which requires a great deal of circumspection.

CONCLUSION

The subject of kinship in southern Mesopotamia is much more complex than this necessarily limited review has perhaps suggested. If progress is to be made in this field it is essential that scholars who approach the subject have a basic understanding of kinship theory, examining Mesopotamian social structure as an anthropologist would that of any society under study. Given the richness of the written record, Mesopotamian kinship can and should be studied from an anthropological perspective, in spite of the fact that our 'informants' have been dead for several thousand years. There are few domains in the field of pre-classical antiquity which offer such potential when integrated into a broad, cross-cultural approach.

NOTES

1 The information there is drawn from Sjöberg 1969: 201–31 and Grégoire 1981: 50–2. For more on kinship designations, see Wilcke 1986:219–41.

2 In a much-discussed passage in the so-called *Reforms of Urukagina* from the late Early Dynastic period, we read, 'Women of former times each married two men, but women of today have been made to give up that crime' (trans. after Cooper 1986:77; cf. San Nicolò 1938:256; Grégoire 1981:54). The interpretation of this passage is difficult and has been repeatedly debated. Did Early Dynastic women practise dyandry, taking two husbands, or does the text refer to a man putting his wife into 'debt servitude' or 'bondage', meaning that the woman had essentially two 'masters'? Glassner in fact proposes that this passage refers to an ancient observance of the practice of *ius primae noctis* (Glassner 1989:80), the right of a man other than the new husband to have intercourse with a newly married woman on her wedding night. Some scholars have seen a connection between this passage and Herodotus' famous statement (*Hist.* I 199) that 'each woman in the land [Babylonia] must, once in her life . . . have sexual intercourse with a stranger'. In fact, in the *Epic of Gilgamesh*, the hero was to have sexual intercourse with a woman who was to be married before her husband did on the wedding night. There we read, 'He takes the promised spouse, he first, the husband after, such is the decision of the gods in their holy assembly'. This is thought to have provoked a fight between Gilgamesh and Enkidu, who was appalled by this practice (Glassner 1989:72).

3 On concubines, see e.g. Neumann 1987:131–7; and Sauren 1990:41–3.

4 On adoption in the Old Babylonian period, see Stone and Owen 1991; Van De Mieroop 1991–1993.

5 For a good introduction to the rights of the widow in all periods, as well as a study of the widow in the first millennium BC, see Roth 1991–93.

6 For some of the suggestions on the 'homeland' of the Amorites, see Huffmon 1965:6.

7 For a Gutian, presumably of West Iranian origin, at Mari with the West Semitic name *[Y]a-si-im-*[d]IM, see Huffmon 1965:17.

8 For mirrors, see Steinkeller 1987a:347–9. Mirrors were made of copper, bronze and silver.

9 As an example of this confusion, one could take the case of the family of the Old Babylonian scribe Balmunamhe, whose family tree has been worked out by Charpin 1987:19–20.

X Mortuary Practices

INTRODUCTION

To properly understand the physical dimensions of burial in ancient Meso-potamia it is essential to have an appreciation of Mesopotamian concepts of death and the afterlife. Since the end of the last century, a series of distinguished scholars has written on this topic (e.g. Meissner 1898:59–66; Schützinger 1978:48–61; Afanasieva 1980:161–9; Steiner 1982:239–48; Cassin 1982:355–72; Bottéro 1982:373–406; Tsukimoto 1985; Groneberg 1990:244–61), and it will be our task to examine some of this literature and to see how it compares with the archaeological manifestations of rituals performed for the dead.

In Mesopotamia mortality was recognized as the condition of all humans and immortality as a condition reserved for deities. The Old Baby-lonian version of the *Epic of Gilgamesh* states quite clearly that, 'When the gods created mankind, They appointed death for mankind, Kept eternal life in their own hands' (Dalley 1989:150 (Tablet X iii 3–5); cf. Groneberg 1990:247). Having said that, we have at least two literary works, *Etana* and *Gilgamesh*, in which a search for immortality on the part of mortals under-taking heroic deeds is attempted. In fact, only Utnapishtim in *Gilgamesh* is granted immortality, though not for any deeds of his own, but rather by divine decree (Groneberg 1990:248).

Although death was the unavoidable fate of all humans, to die 'before one's time' was viewed as a curse from the gods, a sign of divine dis-pleasure. Thus, for example, we read in the lamentation over the death of Ur-Nammu that 'Enlil deceitfully changed his fate-decree', or in the case of the death of Utu-hegal, that he 'raised his hand in anger against his [Mar-duk's] city, then the river carried his corpse away' (Wilcke 1970:81–92).[1]

DEATH AND BURIAL

In the Mesopotamian world view living beings were characterized by 'gen-erative power' (Akk. *dūtu*) and 'life force/vigour'(Akk. *baštu*), buttressed by the aid of protective spirits (Wiggermann 1992). When these attributes and the protection of the beneficent spirits were removed, death was near and a healthy life (Akk. *bulṭu*) was at an end. With biological death the condition of life in this world (Akk. *napištu*) was lost. Biological death transformed an individual into a 'dead one' (Akk. *mītu*) (Steiner 1982:245) and a 'shade' or 'death spirit' (Sum. GIDIM, Akk. *eṭemmu*). This term, however, always had positive connotations in contrast to the 'death demon' (Sum. *udug*, Akk. *utukku*) which was negative. The death spirit was con-ceived of as a shadow-like being, sometimes recognizable by its friends and family as a living sign of the deceased (Groneberg 1990:251–3).

Burial facilitated the death spirit's entry into the underworld, a realm which B. Groneberg suggests, basing her ideas on the ubiquity of sub-surface, earth burials in Mesopotamia, was conceived as being in the interior of the earth (Groneberg 1990:254). The grave signified more than just an entryway into the underworld, however. It was also the place in 'this world' in which the bones of the deceased remained present and immediate and it was the house of the deceased to which the death spirit could be called back from the underworld. In Sumerian the grave was called *ki-mah*, 'exalted place', and *uru-gal*, 'great place'. In Akkadian the common Semitic root *qabru(m)* (cf. *qabr* in Arabic) was used. Only in the case of kings was the grave euphemistically called a 'house of eternity' (Akk. *šubat dārâti*) or a 'palace of rest' (Akk. *ekal tapšuhti*) (Steiner 1982:245).

The actual lead-up to burial in ancient Mesopotamia is poorly known, and considerable uncertainty surrounds the point at which the deceased was finally interred. Corpses were often wrapped in shrouds, reed mats and palm mats. The Old Babylonian dowry of Narūbtum lists 'four blankets in one. . .-chest, of which two blankets are for the grave' (Dalley 1980:72). Lexical sources (e.g. Old Babylonian Proto-Lú, l. 253) mention the profession of 'grave-digger' (Sum. *á-bi-gál* or *a-bí-a-gal*, Akk. *qabbiru, abi(n)-gallu*) and 'undertaker' or 'priest performing funerary rites' (Sum. ÙH.[d]I-NANNA or ŠITA.[d]INANNA, Akk. *uruhhu*) (Civil 1987:4–5). It seems clear that some period of mourning occurred between death and burial. In the case of kings this might last several days, and in the Neo-Assyrian period was fixed at four to five days, while at Mari more than ten days of mourning were observed on the death of one of the the queen mothers (Groneberg 1990:255, according to ARM 26: 11a). The *taklimtu* ritual consisted of 'showing' the deceased and his belongings – a bit like a wake, or lying in state (Scurlock 1991:3) – one hour after sunrise and at intervals thereafter.

The only extant descriptions of the *taklimtu* ritual concern royal burials, where we read of the 'decorated' corpse being exposed, buried and then cried over, the mourning involving music performed by singers (Sum. *gala*, Akk. *kalûm*) and musicians (Sum. *nar*, Akk. *nārum*) (Meissner 1898:59–60; al-Rawi 1992:182–4). In one case, the corpse having been laid out on a bed and its feet washed, the deceased's daughter-in-law went around the bed three times with a burning torch, kissed the deceased's feet, burnt cedar, put out the flame (of the cedar or the torch?) in wine, placed the heart of a sheep in fine flour on the 'statue/image' (Akk. *ṣalmu*) (of the deceased?), and then repeated the same ritual for the objects deposited with the deceased. In the case of a Neo-Assyrian royal funeral, the anointed body of the dead was put into a sarcophagus which was then sealed. The items which the deceased had loved, including objects of silver and gold, were then displayed for Shamash to see before being put into the grave along with gifts for the gods of the underworld (trans. in Meissner 1898:62; cf. Groneberg 1990:255, nn. 86–87). In part because of this last example, some scholars have questioned whether the *taklimtu* ritual was in fact a display of the corpse or only of grave goods since the Neo-Assyrian ritual just described shows that the deceased was sealed in his sarcophagus prior to the *taklimtu*, suggesting that the term applied only to the display of goods before they were sealed in the tomb chamber alongside the sarcophagus (Scurlock 1991:3). The burial rites often ended with a ceremony of purification (Akk. *šuruptu*), in which a selection of things which had belonged to the deceased were burnt. This served both to protect the survivors of the deceased from the death spirit, and to purify them from contact with the corpse.

As the Neo-Assyrian example cited above showed, the dead were sometimes sent on their journey into the underworld with grave goods consisting of objects which they had loved as well as gifts for the gods of the underworld. How widespread this latter custom was, and how restricted it might have been to the wealthier members of society, we do not know. Ur-Nammu, for example, took food, weapons and other warrior's equipment as gifts for the gods. In a text recounting his death, we read (Kramer 1967:114):

> The king offers the gifts of the Netherworld as sacrifices, Ur-Nammu offers the gifts of the Netherworld as sacrifices, Perfect oxen, perfect kids [and] fattened sheep. . ., A mace, a large bow, a quiver, an arrow, a fine (?)-toothed knife, A varicolored leather bottle, worn at the loins, To Nergal, Enlil of the Netherworld, The shepherd Ur-Nammu offers as sacrifices in his place.

While this is a fairly clear-cut case, others are not so easy to interpret.

P. Steinkeller has drawn attention to an important pre-Sargonic text (DP 75) which records a long series of material goods presented by Lugalanda, governor of Lagash, to his son Ur-tarsirsira, when the latter's wife, Ninenishe, was buried (Steinkeller 1990:21, n. 29). Among the objects which Steinkeller believes were actually interred with Ninenishe (Steinkeller 1980)[2] were a boxwood threshing sledge (cf. Pu-abi's sledge in the Royal Cemetery), a team of she-mules, a boxwood bed with 'thin legs', a boxwood chair, an oak foot-stool, a wooden board and small scales, a pair of boxwood combs, ten boxwood spindles, a boxwood bowl, a bucket for a ground cosmetic (?), a bronze mirror, various unidentifiable copper and bronze objects, gold and silver jewellery, six carnelian necklaces, several stone bowls, clothing, cloaks, linen, ghee and oil in pots, cosmetics and a slave girl.[3] The notion of human sacrifice in ancient Mesopotamia, as Steinkeller interprets it in this case (Steinkeller 1980; cf. 1991:188), has been extensively discussed by C.J. Gadd (Gadd 1960:51–8) and A.R.W. Green (Green 1975:46–53), most notably with reference to the Royal Cemetery at Ur, where up to eighty individuals were interred in one of the Royal Graves. In this connection it is important to recognize, as H. Schützinger has pointed out, that these individuals were themselves treated as 'grave goods', not as human beings, for nothing suggests that they were buried with any of the usual rites and accompanying objects (Schützinger 1978:50).

Another, more ambiguous text (OIP 104: App. to no. 32), which is roughly contemporary with DP 75, comes from Adab. There the goods, similar to those mentioned in DP 75, appear to have been part of the payment made in the purchase of a field. These were meant to be deposited in the grave of Làl-la, wife of Bil-làl-la after 'she dies and lives buried together with him' (i.e. her husband) (Gelb, Steinkeller and Whiting 1991:101). Texts such as these should serve as a warning against the often tacit assumption that graves and grave goods can be interpreted as a *direct* reflection of an individual's status and/or roles in life. Clearly, opportunities existed for the acquisition and deposition of goods in an individual's tomb which had never belonged to the deceased and which in no way necessarily reflected his or her being.

Moreover, it is clear that the artificial distinction between personal belongings, for example jewellery and other items such as weaponry which might have been worn by the deceased at the time of interment, and 'grave goods', as suggested by some scholars (e.g. Strommenger 1957–1971:605–8), finds no confirmation in the written record. If the Neo-Assyrian example of burying goods which 'he loved' is taken into consideration, then there can be no necessary distinction between grave goods and personal goods. Neither can we necessarily discount the possibility that, even in humble graves, a single ceramic vessel or other small object might have been there as a gift for the deities of the underworld rather than as a personal belonging.

In the category of grave furnishings we should also consider animal interments and food offerings. As noted above, Ur-Nammu took with him 'oxen, perfect kids [and] fattened sheep' when he was buried. Food offerings made in several of the graves excavated in the Royal Cemetery at Ur have already been discussed in Chapter III (Ellison, Renfrew, Brothwell and Seeley 1978:167–7), but there are other, less well-known and certainly less élite examples which can also be cited which attest to the widespread nature of food offerings in burials from the late prehistoric period onwards. At Yarim Tepe I in northern Iraq, Hassuna period burials of fifth-millennium date sometimes contained animal bones (Hole 1989:156). A burial datable to the Jamdat Nasr period (*c.* 3100–2900 BC) at Uruk (Fig. X.1) contained the distal end of the left tibia of a sheep (Boessneck, von den Driesch and Steger 1984:155; Boehmer 1984:191 and Taf. 17d), which no doubt represents a joint of meat. Joints of pork were placed in an Early Dynastic grave at Abu Salabikh (Postgate 1994:166). A Late Akkadian burial at Uch Tepe in the Hamrin contained the individual bones of cattle, sheep/goat, gazelle and pig, all of which may represent cuts of meat, as well as the skeletons of two equids (Boessneck 1990:132; cf. Gibson 1981:Pls. 45–46). Two graves at Isin dating to *c.* 2000 BC contained ceramic vessels with fish offerings (Boessneck 1977:117), while four of the Old Babylonian graves (nos. 114–116, 234) at the site contained individual parts of sheep (e.g. the distal humerus), sheep/goat (e.g. rib), pig (e.g. scapula), and cow (e.g. distal humerus) (Boessneck and Ziegler 1987). Returning again to Uruk, a double-jar burial (see below for this type) of Isin II (eleventh/tenth century BC) or later date (Fig. X.2) containing the remains of a single individual (male or female?) with a cylinder seal at the neck and a bronze beaker by the shoulder, also included remnants of an infant sheep at its feet (complete animal or a joint of meat?) as well as part of a small, unidentifiable fish (Boessneck, von den Driesch and Steger 1984:163; Boehmer

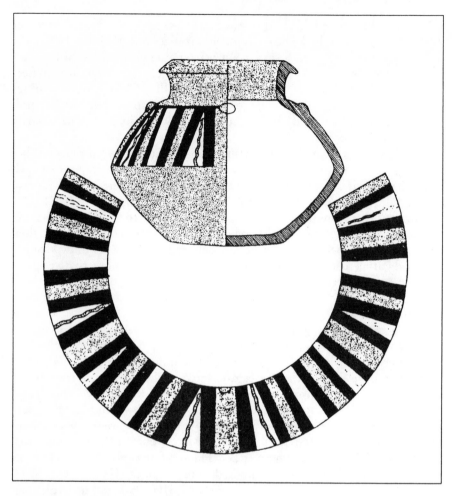

Figure X.1 Jamdat Nasr type jar from Uruk which contained the distal end of a sheep's left tibia (after Boehmer 1984: Taf. 17d)

1984:192–5 and Taf. Abb. 1). Graves 106 and 107 at Isin, which date to the early first millennium BC, contained, respectively, remains of fish (*Barbus* sp.) and sheep/goat (Boessneck and Ziegler 1987). From the Neo-Babylonian period at Uruk comes another jar burial of an adult containing the distal humerus (joint?) of a bovid, a horn core and radius of a sheep, other sheep/goat remains and part of a fish, while a double-jar burial of the same period, containing the remains of two individuals, had parts of cattle, sheep and goat as well as unidentifiable faunal material (Boessneck, von den Driesch and Steger 1984:164). At least two graves at Achaemenid Sippar contained tibia, femur and tarsal fragments of sheep and sheep/goat (Haerinck 1980:58). Food offerings were obviously part of Mesopotamian funerary rites for thousands of years, but whether these were intended for the satisfaction of the death spirit itself, or for the gods of the underworld, as in Ur-Nammu's case, is unknown.

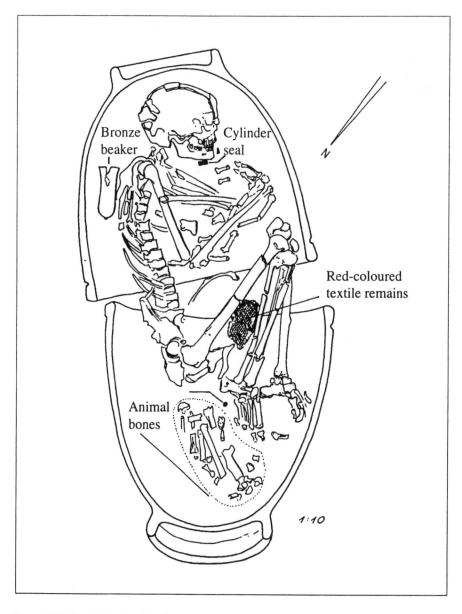

Figure X.2 Double-jar burial of Isin II or later date from Uruk which contained part of an infant sheep (after Boehmer 1984: Abb. 1)

INTO THE UNDERWORLD

From the extant descriptions of deities' journeys into the underworld it appears that the death spirit had to cross a mythical river, known as the *Hubur*, before reaching the gates of the underworld. The underworld of the gods was metaphorically likened to a city with seven walls, seven gates, and a large reception hall where the *Anunnaku* or underworld deities – Nedu the guard, Ereshkigal the princess, her husband Nergal, Namtar their vizir, Ningishzida the 'throne bearer of the world of the dead' and his wife Geshtinanna, the scribe (Tsukimoto 1985:9)[4] – lived in a palace, surrounded by a society not unlike that of mortals on earth.

On arrival in the underworld the fate of an individual was determined. Judgement, however, did not take account of 'goodness' towards one's fellows or other ethical considerations. Rather, concerns like productivity and richness were important, and the new fate was decided very much on basis of the number of one's children and the coherence of one's family. Indeed, the *Epic of Gilgamesh* expresses an almost precise, proportional relation betweeen the number of children in this world and the quality of life in the next (Groneberg 1990:260).

At all events, the Mesopotamian world view was not one of death as a paradise. Rather, existence in the underworld was unequivocally inferior to that on earth. The underworld was a dark and dusty place 'where dust is their sustenance and clay their food' (Foster 1993:420). For the protection of the living the spirits of the dead should never leave the underworld. Even the deities inhabiting it could only leave if another took their place. Thus in *Inanna's Descent into the Netherworld* we read, 'If Inanna ascends from the Underworld, she must proffer a head for a head' (cf. Afanasieva 1980:162). In fact, the only beings who moved freely between the worlds of the living and the dead were demons, powers outside the system of order who were androgenous and the enemies of humans, without families and moral conscience, beings 'who could not distinguish good from evil' according to *Inanna's Descent* (Groneberg 1990:259). The belief in an afterlife which compensated for any suffering or adversities undergone in this life was clearly not native to the Mesopotamian world view. Moreover, death was final, as descriptions of the underworld such as, 'the land of no return', or phrases like 'just as a dead [person] cannot return', or 'just as a dead [person] cannot go through the door of life', make perfectly clear (Afanasieva 1980:167–8).

AFTER DEATH

The dead were remembered and periodically called forth through offerings made after their death. A pre-Sargonic forestry text from Lagash speaks of foresters who seem to have been required to bring 'presents' as a kind of tax or presentation. One of them, Ur-Emush, brought ten bundles of *asál* wood (Euphrates poplar?) as a *mašdaria* offering (see below) 'in the festival of *d*lugal-URUx"ZÍD" . . . as a gift for the spirit of the dead *ensi* Enentarzi' (Powell 1992:105). It is not always clear whether care of the dead was obligatory, but it certainly seems to have been the duty of surviving kinsmen, although the responsibility did not usually extend beyond caring for one's grandparents (Bayliss 1973:121). Certainly some adoption documents stipulate that the adoptee must make such offerings for the adopter after his or her death (Groneberg 1990:256). Thus, for excample, a Middle Babylonian adoption contract stipulates, 'As long as Ina-UNUG.KI-ri-shat [the adopter] lives, E-ti-ir-tum [the adoptee] shall revere her; when Ina-UNUG.KI-ri-shat dies, E-ti-ir-tum, her daughter, shall pour water for her' (Bayliss 1973:120).

Pre-Sargonic Lagash offers extensive evidence of offerings for the deceased, although this should by no means be projected across the full sweep of Mesopotamian history. Let us examine the royal cult as practised for Lugalanda, second to last ruler in the First Dynasty of Lagash.[5] Offerings spanning the first five years of the reign of Urukagina, the ruler who deposed Lugalanda, are attested. In Urukagina's second year Lugalanda's widow, Baragnamtara, also died, receiving a state funeral involving over six hundred lamentation-priests and female mourners, after which her name also appeared in lists detailing offerings. From his third to his sixth year, moreover, Urukagina also took care of Lugalanda's two surviving daughters.

The offering lists give the number, kind and quality of offerings made with the names of the recipients or the persons who were meant to provide them, closing with a remark on the purpose of the offering. These texts mention alms or gifts of clothing for the deceased, including jewellery, to be made on the occasion of a major festival for Baba, food offerings for large numbers of recipients, small lists of food offerings for not more than

Figure X.3 Early Dynastic votive statuary from Khafajah (left) and Assur (right) (after Moortgat 1969: Figs. 31 and 33)

three recipients and *masdaria* offerings[6] for the deceased. Other, related texts record the numbers of animals removed from the temple herds for use in offerings to the dead.

It seems fairly clear that the clothing and jewellery offerings just mentioned were made to *statues* (Fig. X.3) of the deceased, although none of the Lagash texts name the temple or other building in which these statues stood. One text (DP 77), however, says, after listing four names, 'for the ancestors, [who] go outside'. On the other hand, the phrase 'he doesn't go out of the temple' is written after a fifth name. This would imply that some, but not all, of the statues of the deceased were paraded in processions outside of the temple just as divine statues were. The extant food offering lists for holy days also reflect the pious care addressed to the 'cult of the statues', as do the monthly accounts which record regular deliveries of barley and emmer. It is generally believed that the statues mentioned in the offering lists had all been dedicated and set up in the temple while the person they represented was still alive. It was, moreover, at this time that stipulations were made that food offerings for their statues should be continued after the death of the dedicant.

Upon the dedicant's death his or her statue became the main focus of mourning and even after the passage of a considerable amount of time the statue continued to receive offerings. Thus, eight small and one life-size (?) statue of Ur-Nanshe, founder of the First Dynasty of Lagash, stood in the temple of Nanshe, while statues of Lugalanda's wife, Baragnamtara, and of Shagshag, wife of Urukagina, stood in the temple of Baba at Lagash, just as Entemena and his wife were represented by statues in the temple of Nin-MAR-KI at Guabba. Knowledge of this practice is important for, as we have seen (cf. Chapter IX), considerable uncertainty has often surrounded the interpretation of the numerous anthropomorphic statues found in excavations. Clearly, in view of the practices just described, the bulk of those statues should probably be seen as dedicants rather than deities.

In some exceptional cases, the veneration of certain individuals in ancient Mesopotamia lasted for centuries. In the case of Dudu, an important Ningirsu-priest under Entemena, we know that his personal cult lasted into the Ur III period, several centuries after his lifetime. This is all the more remarkable as we know that even in the late pre-Sargonic period Urukagina had cancelled the monthly food offerings for Dudu. Similarly, the fact that a hymn was composed in honour of Ur-Nanshe in the Old Babylonian period shows that his memory was still alive half a millennium after his death.

During the second and first millennia BC the *kispum*, an offering of food and/or a libation dedicated to the deceased, was made bi-monthly on the occasion of the full and new moons (Tsukimoto 1985). When the Assyrian king Assurbanipal campaigned against Elam he destroyed the graves of the former kings of Susa and carried off their bones to Assyria so that no more *kispum* offerings could be made to them, saying, 'I inflicted restlessness on their ghosts. I deprived them of funerary offerings [*kispum*] and pourers of water' (Bayliss 1973:115–26). This was viewed as a terrible calamity,[7] comparable in some ways to the removal of the cult statues by an enemy, as discussed in Chapter IX. When Merodach-Baladan, the Chaldaean king, was being pursued by Sennacherib, the Assyrian, he removed not only the cult statues of the Chaldaean deities for safekeeping, but also exhumed the bones of his ancestors to take them with him lest their graves be defiled by the Assyrian enemy (Cassin 1982:365).

Funerary inscriptions carry proscriptions warning against anyone 'who rouses me from my grave', stipulating that a coffin 'may not move from its [the coffin's] place' and enjoining the living to 'bury him where he orders and he shall lie where he wants. Where he is lying you shall not disturb him'. 'To wake the sleeper' was a euphemistic way of referring to the disturbance of the dead (Livingstone 1991:1). A Middle Babylonian funerary inscription reads: 'He who invades this tomb, rather than repairing it so that it survives [or last's longer], may Anu, Enlil and Ea eliminate his descendants, may the infernal Anunnaki of the underworld destroy his progeny' (Bottéro 1982:386–7). The reason for such stern warnings is clear. If the death spirits had no one to tend them and make offerings they wandered aimlessly and had to settle for the dregs of peoples' meals. Moreover, they would vex the living, bringing disease upon them. It was the task of the *Maqlu*-priests to exorcize such spirits, and we find people dedicating goods to these displaced spirits in an effort to appease them (Meissner 1898:63). One such exorcistic text reads as follows: 'You, ghost belonging to nobody, who have nobody to bury you or speak your name, whose name nobody knows … before Shamash, Gilgamesh, the Anunnaki, [and] the ghost[s] of my family you hereby receive a present, you are honoured with a gift' (Dalley 1989:135, n. 164).

In view of these concerns, it is scarcely surprising that considerable fear surrounded the treatment or absence of proper treatment for the dead on the battlefield. As we read in the *Epic of Gilgamesh* (XII 150 ff.), 'I saw him, whose corpse you saw abandoned in the open country: His ghost does not sleep in the earth. I saw him whom you saw, whose ghost has nobody to supply it: He feeds on dregs from dishes, and bits of bread that lie abandoned in the streets' (Dalley 1989:124–5). Although not given the treatment which an individual could expect, some sort of concern for the defeated enemy seems to have governed the actions of several third-millennium rulers. Thus, we read that 'Eannatum defeated Elam … and heaped up its burial mounds', and that 'Ningirsu … fought with Umma and upon command of Enlil, he covered it with the great net, and he made its burial mounds on the plain'. During the Old Akkadian period Rimush says that when he fought Zahara and Elam, he killed 16,212 soldiers, took 4216 prisoners, and 'heaped up a *berūtum* over them' (Westenholz 1970:27). Presumably interment in a burial mound was better than no burial at all.

By the Old Babylonian period, however, we find a very different attitude expressed in the Laws of Hammurapi (§ 44). Speaking of any king who did not maintain the laws of Hammurapi, we read, 'The bodies of his soldiers should be thrown on the plain in heaps; his troops should not be granted any burial'. This last reference to the removal of the body without prior burial highlights the worst aspect of the death penalty, for the total destruction of the body, either by fire[8] or water,[9] reserved only for the most heinous crimes, prevented a proper, orderly burial and led to one's continued existence as a ghost in this world, representing a threat to family and neighbours alike.

THE PHYSICAL CONTEXT OF BURIAL

From all of the above it should by now be clear that the proper burial of an individual was of paramount importance for his or her entry into the netherworld. Without due burial, a death demon would wander the face of the earth, and if a burial should be disturbed, and proper offerings for the dead interrupted, the death demon would vex the living until such time as a priest had performed rituals to guide the demon back into the underworld. For rich or poor, king or labourer, therefore, a proper, undisturbed burial was all important. There is nothing to suggest from all that has been said, however, that the *form* of the grave had anything to do with the propriety of the burial, and indeed one is led to draw just the opposite conclusion from the archaeological evidence of mortuary practices in ancient Mesopotamia, where we have a wide variety of grave forms (Fig. X.4) attested in time and space.[10] Briefly stated, these are as follows, beginning with the various forms of earth burial.

The simplest form of burial, the inhumation of an individual in a simple pit dug into the ground, can be found in all periods. Mat burials, in which an individual was first wrapped in a reed mat and then laid in a simple pit, appear sporadically in all periods but are not well attested due to poor preservation. Shaft graves including shafts leading to large, open excavations in the earth are attested only from the Early Dynastic to the Ur III period. Shafts leading to brick grave chambers, sarcophagi, or simple pit burials are also known, mainly from the Old Akkadian period to the middle of the second millennium BC. Sherd burials, in which the body was lain on a bed of sherds or in earth and then covered with sherds, are attested in most periods.

Burial within ceramic containers was always popular and probably a kind of convenience. The term 'jar burial' refers to any burial in which the body was put into a large jar which was then sealed with a lid of wood, stone or terracotta, or with another ceramic vessel. In the early periods the jars used were normal, household vessels which do not seem to have been specially made for burial. Due to their generally small size, such early jar burials were almost exclusively those of infants. From the Ur III period onward, however, specially made grave vessels (Strommenger 1957–1971:609) appear alongside normal household ones. So-called 'sarcophagus vessels' occasionally stood upright. Children's burials often consisted of two bowls, one on top of the other, whereas proper double-jar burials, in which two jars with their mouths joining, lying horizontally, held a body, were generally used for adults. In such cases one vessel often had a smaller rim diameter than the other, the smaller mouth fitting into the larger one. Vat burials, on the other hand, involved very wide-mouthed vats set over a body either lying on the earth or on a mat.

Although wooden or reed sarcophagi are attested at Ur from the late Jamdat Nasr period onward, ceramic sarcophagi began appearing only in

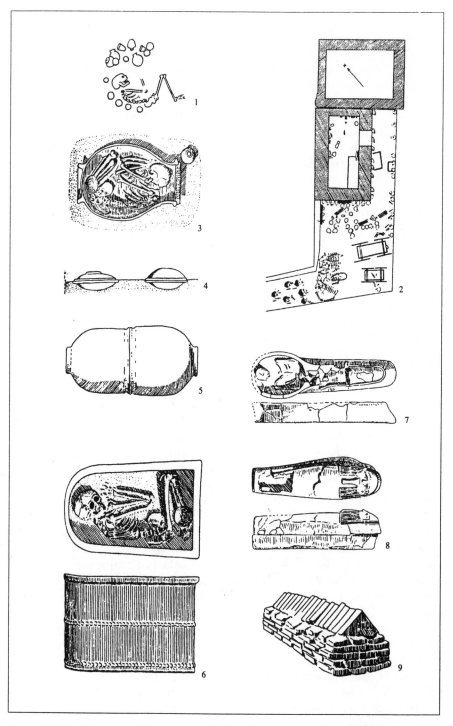

Figure X.4 Various types of burial in ancient Mesopotamia. 1. earth or pit grave; 2. shaft grave; 3. jar burial; 4. bowl burial for infants; 5. double-jar burial; 6. 'bath-tub' sarcophagus; 7. slipper coffin; 8. anthropoid sarcophagus; 9. brick cist grave (after Strommenger 1957–1971)

Early Dynastic II times, generally in a bath-tub shape with an oval outline and straight or sloping sides. These were often covered with lids of reed matting, wood or pottery. In some cases, the sarcophagus was placed over the body, rather than the body being placed in the sarcophagus. The form of the ceramic sarcophagus did not change much throughout the late third and early second millennium, but towards the end of the second millennium sarcophagi with one curved and one straight end appeared, in which the corpse was buried in a flexed position, with the knees bent. This form continued in use right into the Seleucid period, appearing sometimes in bronze as well during the Achaemenid era. Large stone sarcophagi are now known to have been used for at least some Neo-Assyrian queens, while anthropoid sarcophagi, possibly showing some Egyptian influence, appear in the Achaemenid era. So-called 'slipper coffins' were used in Seleucid and Parthian contexts alongside bath-tub coffins. These were closed coffins with an opening at one end into which the body was inserted. Clay pipes, inserted into the lid of a sarcophagus in intra-mural burials of the Neo-Babylonian period in southern Mesopotamia and the Old Babylonian era at Mari on the Euphrates are thought by B. Groneberg to represent a means of taking care of the dead (Groneberg 1990:257).

At Uruk U. Finkbeiner has been able to show very clearly that there is a sequence of burials in area U/V XVIII within a corpus of *c.* 140 burials as one moves from the Seleucid into the Parthian period. That sequence is as follows: level III – bath-tub coffins; early level II – brick cists and upturned vats; late level II and level I – slipper coffins. The change in sarcophagus form is also accompanied by a change in body position from a flexed position in the bath-tub coffins, cists and vats, to an extended position in slipper coffins. This development has been associated with an influx of Iranians, in this case Parthians, and is seen as representing a real break in burial tradition. One should, however, note that whereas it would not be possible for a body to lie in extended position in a bath-tub coffin or vat, this was possible in a slipper coffin. Nevertheless, the fact that a similar change in burial posture is also evident in sherd and simple pit graves at Uruk as well (Finkbeiner 1982:162) suggests that the change was not due solely to the use of a longer container for the body.

Finally, brick cists and chambers represent the last major type of burial attested in southern Mesopotammia. Simple brick cists date back to the Ubaid period at Tell al-'Ubaid and Eridu, where they were often covered with a roofing of brick as well. Thereafter they have a wide, if sporadic, distribution in space and time throughout Mesopotamia. Larger rectangular brick chambers, often with barrel-vaulted roofs, are known from the Early Dynastic period onwards and clearly represented a greater investment of funds and labour than a simple pit burial.

From the foregoing review of burial types in southern Mesopotamia it should be clear that the formal variation present is considerable. What is important to stress, however, is that even the humblest pit burial sufficed as a proper disposal of the dead providing the appropriate rites were performed for the corpse. Moreover, Mesopotamian burial was, from the Ubaid period onward, *primary* burial with little or no evidence for the use of ossuaries as secondary repositories of human bone. In addition, Meso-potamian burial was *individual* burial, with little evidence of collective burial[11] such as one finds at certain times in the Oman peninsula where hundreds of individuals were buried within large, presumably communal, tombs. In this regard, the Royal Graves at Ur, mentioned above, which contain the retainers of a high-ranking person do not qualify as collective burials, since their primary purpose was the interment of a single indi-vidual and the additional persons buried alongside that person must be considered 'human grave goods'.

On the other hand, there does not seem to have been any 'orthodoxy' when it came to the question of burial within a graveyard as opposed to burial beneath one's house, a common practice well attested throughout Western Asia in antiquity and perhaps one which reflected the desire to facilitate the ongoing performance of rites for one's ancestors. As Postgate has shown, intra-mural, sub-floor, house burials in the Old Babylonian period were common at Ur in the south and Sippar in the north, but absent at Nippur. He observes (1990:234):

> The fact is, of course, that we really do not know what governed the choice. One might well suppose that burying the dead within the build-ing was to enable care for the grave by means of *kispum/ki a.nag* rituals. On the other hand, separate cemeteries do also occur at different periods, particularly in old mounds. My own feeling is that the choice of whether to bury within the house or somewhere in the countryside may have been much more pragmatic than symbolic: urban families without land of their own may well have had nowhere else to use. At Nippur, or at least in the excavated sections of Nippur, this was apparently not the case, and we must presume either that the city had made communal arrangements for burials, whether within or without the walls, or that our families had their own extramural burying sites.

At Ur during the Isin-Larsa period Woolley found a markedly higher con-centration of infant burials under so-called 'house chapels' than elsewhere, and in one case discovered thirty-two infant graves beneath one chapel (Strommenger 1957–1971:591). At Uruk, on the other hand, an average of six to eight burials per house characterized the roughly two-hundred-year span covering the Neo–Babylonian/Late Babylonian era. Indeed, in one case twenty-four burials were found within a single house. In contrast, Parthian houses contained no intra-mural burials, clearly reflecting a com-pletely different attitude towards disposal of the dead than that attested in the earlier period.

Finally, it is interesting to note that there seems to have been no general rule governing the placement of a cemetery. Excavated cemeteries have been found both within settlements, as at Ur, and outside settlements, as at Arpachiyah and Tepe Gawra in northern Mesopotamia (Strommenger 1957–1971:591). But one practice which seems to have been widespread during the third millennium and attested again in the period of the Second Dynasty of the Sealand (*c.* 1025–1005 BC), the Dynasty of Bazi (*c.* 1004–985 BC) and the 'Elamite' Dynasty (*c.* 984–979 BC) was the practice of burial in the marshes or swamps of southern Mesopotamia. P.-A. Beaulieu has pointed to the reference in the late Early Dynastic 'reforms' of Urukagina to burial in the 'reed thicket of Enki', and observed that, according to the Dynastic Chronicle, the second ruler in the Second Dynasty of the Sealand, Ea-mukin-zeri, was buried in the 'swamp of Bit-Hashmar' (Beaulieu 1988:53). Moreover, both Strabo and Arrian, drawing on Aristobulus, allude to the tombs of past Mesopotamian kings in the swamps. In describing Alexander's inspection of the canals around Babylon, Strabo says that the Macedonian 'also inspected thoroughly the tombs of the kings and potentates, most of which are situated among the lakes' (*Geog.* 16 i 11), while Arrian states flatly, 'The greater number of the tombs of the Assyrian kings were built in the lakes and marshlands' (*Anab.* 7 xxii 2). In view of the absence of safely identified royal tombs in all periods of Mesopotamian history, the practice of burying kings in the swamps or marshes, close to the abode of Enki, should be considered a likely explanation.[12]

CONCLUSION

Burial is one of the few universals of human existence. Moreover, the excavation and analysis of burials is most definitely a universal of archaeological praxis. For these reasons alone it is important to have an understanding of the dimensions of ancient Mesopotamian beliefs pertaining to death and the physical treatment of the dead. Without an understanding of the specifically Mesopotamian approach to the care and tending of the death spirit, however, much of the archaeological record of burial in the region would be stripped of its intrinsic meaning. As in so many cases in Mesopotamia, the opportunity to combine written and material evidence in the analysis of burials makes the exercise both more complex and more rewarding than in areas where little accurate idea can be formed of the socio-religious dimensions of death.

NOTES

1 The new manuscript of the 'Weidner Chronicle' discovered at Sippar reads (l. 27), in F. al-Rawi's translation, 'Utuhegal the "fisherman" laid his evil hand on his city, and his corpse was carried away by the river'. See al-Rawi 1990:10.

2 I am very grateful to the author for sending me a copy of this extremely interesting paper.

3 It is not, however, absolutely certain that these objects *were* interred in the grave of Ninenishe. In any case, they read very much like a list of objects belonging to a dowry, as discussed in Chapter IX. The inclusion of a slave girl is interesting in light of the repeated presence of a single slave girl, listed without husband but sometimes with children, in an Old Babylonian text from Kish (Ki 1056) which preserves an enumeration of the family members attached to a series of households there. See Donbaz and Yoffee 1986:57ff.

4 Gilgamesh and Dumuzi also figured in the underworld. See Groneberg 1990:260.

5 All of the discussion which follows is based on Bauer 1969:107–14.

6 The precise nature of these is unknown. Sigrist 1992:190 suggests they may not have been offerings *per se* but gifts or presents.

7 In the *Epic of Gilgamesh* (XII 153ff), we read, 'Have you seen the ghost of him who has no one to care [for him]? I have seen [him], he eats scraps of food from the pots [and] bread crumbs that are thrown away in the street'. See Malul 1993:83.

8 Some examples of death by fire in the Codex Hammurapi: for a son who slept with his mother following the death of his father (§157); for a *Naditu* woman who visited a tavern or drank alcohol (§110); for robbing someone's house while it was on fire (§25). These and the examples given in the following note are taken from Groneberg 1990:249–50, nn. 42–43.

9 Some examples of death by water: for a wife who married another man while her husband was a prisoner-of-war (§133b); for a man who slept with his daughter-in-law (§143).

10 This discussion is based mainly on Strommenger 1957–1971:581–93, where full references can be found.

11 A well containing twenty-four bodies, '21 of which seem to be a mass burial', was excavated at Tepe Gawra and has been tentatively dated to the Halaf period. See Hole 1989:160.

12 The burial of Shu-Sin at Uruk, rather than Ur, is another case of royal burial in what, at first sight, seems an unlikely locale. Far from being buried at Ur, Shu-Sin was buried in the city whence his dynasty had originated, and Charpin 1992:106 even suggests that Uruk may have been the resting place for all of the kings of the Third Dynasty of Ur (with the exception of Ibbi-Sin who died in Iran in exile). Cf. Moorey 1984 on this question.

XI Functional Aspects of Writing and Sealing

INTRODUCTION

Two of the innovations for which Mesopotamia is most well known are writing and the cylinder seal. Much has been written on both topics. Sumerologists and Assyriologists have analysed tens of thousands of written sources from a philological point of view, often stressing the linguistic, lexical and grammatical over the historical, social and economic content of the texts. Art historians, in their turn, have published thousands of cylinder seals, generally concentrating on style and iconography. Here we shall be concerned rather with certain functional aspects of both writing and sealing.

EARLY WRITING

On several occasions throughout this book mention has been made of the so-called Archaic texts from Uruk, the earliest written documents in human history. The oldest of these texts date to the Late Uruk period (*c.* 3400–3100 BC) but as H.J. Nissen has repeatedly stressed, the elaborate division of labour exhibited in the Archaic list of titles and professions presumes a level of social complexity which did not simply appear overnight (Nissen, Damerow and Englund 1990:55). Far from representing the beginning of a phenomenon, these texts constitute a written résumé of a process which had reached a point of considerable advancement. That phenomenon, the elaboration of a social order, the roots of which undoubtedly lie in the Ubaid period, would never be the same after the Late Uruk period precisely because writing, as a tool of bureaucracy and social control, had now entered the social arena. This is not to say that the appearance of writing somehow differentiates prehistory from history as if the former had no connection with the latter.[1] The human biology and mental capacities of the population on either side of this notional divide were identical. Their climate, environment and basic technologies were exactly the same. The historical past was in no way superior to the prehistoric era, but writing accelerated the processes of social, economic, religious, political and even technological elaboration to an extent previously unseen. Writing suddenly put new administrative solutions to organizational problems within the grasp of the managers of private and public estates which kicked off a whole series of new experiments in human organizational management on both the micro- and macro-level. Therein lies the real difference between the 'prehistoric' and 'historic' past.

Presumably for reasons of scale, the social and economic organization of the Eanna temple complex at Uruk in the mid-fourth millennium required new techniques of social control which, one may assume, would not otherwise have emerged at that particular point in space and time. Writing and the cylinder seal were 'invented' by members of a bureaucracy whose duty it was to administer the earthly estates of Inanna, 'Queen of Heaven', from that compound of buildings excavated since the early part of this century by the German expedition to Uruk-Warka. As the Sumerian epic *Enmerkar and the Lord of Aratta* expresses it, 'The Lord of Kulab patted some clay and set down words on it as if on a tablet. Before that time there was no putting of words on tablets' (Vanstiphout 1993:13). The reference to the 'Lord of Kulab' is important, since Kullaba was an archaic district of Uruk,[2] adjacent to the Eanna precinct, which is thought by some scholars to have been prominent prior to the rise of the Eanna complex in the Late Uruk period (e.g. Nissen 1972:794–5).

As discussed in Chapter VIII, the administration of a deity's household encompassed most of the productive sectors one can think of. Herding, weaving, pottery manufacture, metalworking, woodworking, stoneworking, agriculture, gardening, forestry, fishing, beer production and baking, just to name the most obvious activities, all came within the purview of the temple administration, as did the distribution of rations in *naturalia* (e.g. barley, oil, wool, etc.) to members of the household. The Archaic texts reveal the operation of no fewer than thirteen different numerical systems falling into five major categories (sexagesimal, bi-sexagesimal, ŠE, *GAN₂*, and *EN*) for the quantitative notation of goods (objects as well as *naturalia*), personnel, rations, area measurements, weights, calendrics and volume (Nissen, Damerow and Englund 1990:64–5). In summary, the systems and their various uses may be characterized (Damerow and Englund 1987:117–66) as follows:

Archaic Numerical Notation System	*Uses*
Sexagesimal system S (1–10–60–600–3600–36,000) (numbers alternate by a factor of 10, 6, 10, etc.)	slaves, animals (sheep, goat, cattle), wool (?), fish, fishing equipment, fish products, stone objects, wooden objects, containers (e.g. of beer, milk products)
Sexagesimal system S′ (1–10–60) (numbers alternate by a factor of 10, 6)	dead animals, particular types of beer
Bi-sexagesimal system B (½–1–10–60–120–1200–7200) (numbers alternate by a factor of 2, 10, 6 etc.)	cereal/bread, fish, and milk product rations
Bi-sexagesimal system B* (1–10–60–120–1200) (numbers alternate by a factor of 10, 6, 2, etc.)	rations of uncertain type, possibly fish

GAN₂ system G   field and area measurement
(IKU–EŠE₃–BUR₃
(numbers alternate by a factor of 10?, 6, 3,
etc.)

EN system E   uncertain; weight?
(numbers alternate by a factor of ?, 4, 2, 2,
10)

U₄ system U   calendrics (day, month, year)
1 day–10 days–30 days/1 month–12
months/1 year or 10 months)
(numbers alternate by a factor of 10, 3,
12/10)

ŠE system Š   cereal, esp. barley, by volume
(small units multilied by 2, 3, 4, 5, 6 or 10,
alternating by a factor of 5, 6, 10, 3, 10)
ŠE system Š′   cereal, esp. malt (for use in beer
(units increasing by factors of 2, 5, 6)   production), by volume
ŠE system Š″   cereal, esp. types of emmer (?)
(units increasing by factors of 5, 6, 10, 3, 10,
6?)
ŠE system Š*   cereal, esp. barley groats
(small units multiplied by 2, 3 or 4,
alternating by a factor of 5, 6, 10, 3)

DUG_b system DB   milk product, probably ghee, by
(units multiplied by a factor of 10)   volume

DUG_c system Dc   types of beer, by volume
(units multiplied by a factor of 5, 2)

Literary, religious, royal and historical texts are not yet attested in the Late
Uruk or Jamdat Nasr periods, but it should be noted that the lexical tradition (Englund and Nissen 1993; cf. generally Civil 1975:123–57; Nissen
1981:99–108), so often referred to in this book, makes its first appearance
contemporaneously with the development of recording for economic purposes. Lexical texts attested in the Late Uruk (Uruk IV) and Jamdat Nasr
(Uruk III) periods cover the following categories (Englund and Nissen 1993):

Lu (titles and professions)	Food
Metal	Swine[3]
Vessels and Textiles	Cattle
City	Bird
Geographical Names	Fish
Tree	Vocabulary
Tribute	Practice
Plant	Unidentified
Officials	

THE CONTROL OF GOODS AND SERVICES

The practice of sealing official documents with a stamp of some sort is one which flourishes today in various quarters of public, religious and private administration. Generally speaking, seals serve to mark goods or documents as a validation of the authority of an institution involved in their dispatch, receipt or storage. In southern Mesopotamia, for instance at Tello (Fig. XI.1), stamp seals appear as early as the Ubaid period (Homès-Fredericq 1970; von Wickede 1990), although it is not always clear that these were employed in an economic capacity. Cylinder seals, on the other hand, appear first in the Middle[4] or Late Uruk period (Brandes 1979) where, from an early date, they were used to seal tablets, storage jars, crates and doors.

Figure XI.1 Ubaid period stamp seals from Tello (after Homès-Fredericq 1970: Pl. XLIV)

In recent years several scholars have redirected the focus of glyptic studies away from style and iconography towards function. Whereas jar sealings and seal impressions on tablets have been studied for decades, it was only in the late 1960s that the Italian scholar Enrica Fiandra began to present systematic and geographically widespread evidence for the sealing of doors in antiquity, focusing attention for the first time on the impressions of cord or rope on the reverse of a sealing, rather than on the seal impressions on the obverse. After Fiandra had applied this approach to remains found on sites extending from the Aegean (Fiandra 1975:1–25) to Iran (Fiandra 1982:1–18), the subject was taken up in particular by R. Zettler in a study of the Inanna temple at Nippur during the Ur III period, where 149 sealings were found (Zettler 1987:202).

The administrative centre of the Inanna temple, located in the northeastern part of the building (Fig. XI.2), contained a bitumen-lined, subsurface bin (locus 78), which Zettler believes was 'used for the storage of clean clay or clay which could be recycled for making tablets' (Zettler 1987:207). In addition to containing 'broken and deliberately crumpled tablets (a number recognizable as writing exercises)' as well as 'a clay figurine and four weights (one duck weight and three barrel-shaped weights)', the bin yielded thirty-four cylinder sealings (Zettler 1987:207 and n. 20). Of these three (9 per cent) showed cord impressions; fifteen (44 per cent) had what looked like clear 'hook' impressions; five (15 per cent) came from jars; one (3 per cent) had sealed a bag; one (3 per cent) came off of a box; while six (17 per cent) were miscellaneous or unidentified and three (9 per cent) no longer had their unsealed side preserved. Thus, door sealings, many of which had been placed over hooks which had presumably once secured their doors, were much more prominent in the collection

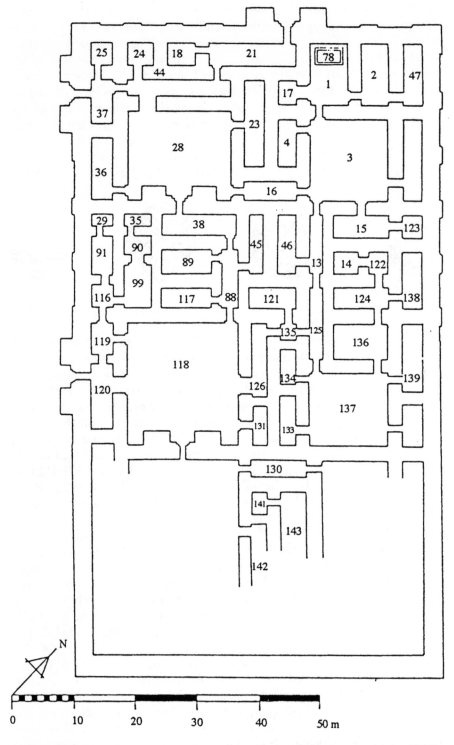

Figure XI.2 Plan of the Inanna temple at Nippur during the Ur III period (after Zettler 1987: Fig. 2)

than sealings used on bags, jars or boxes. The personal involvement of Lugal-engar-du$_{10}$, 'chief administrator of the temple', is clearly shown by the fact that four of the five jar sealings found bore the impression of his official seal, as did the seal impression from a wooden box and seven of the nine impressions with identifiable reverse sides (Zettler 1987:225).

SEALING TABLETS

Ever since the original publications of the Archaic texts of Uruk, and their counterparts from sites like Jamdat Nasr, Tell Uqair, Khafajah and Tell Asmar, it has been obvious that many of these early tablets were sealed with a cylinder seal *before* they were inscribed, a practice also observed at contemporary sites such as Susa in Iran and Habuba Kabira in Syria. This is undoubtedly a direct carry-over of the practice of sealing hollow clay balls, or *bullae*, containing numerical tokens, in the period just prior to the emergence of actual writing. What is the significance, if any, of the type of seal used on a particular document?

Some years ago H.J. Nissen formulated an influential hypothesis concerning the style and iconography of the earliest Mesopotamian cylinder seals (Nissen 1977:15–23). It had long been recognized that there were two broad categories of seals in use during the Late Uruk and Jamdat Nasr periods (Fig. XI.3). So-called 'schematic' seals were often roughly manu-

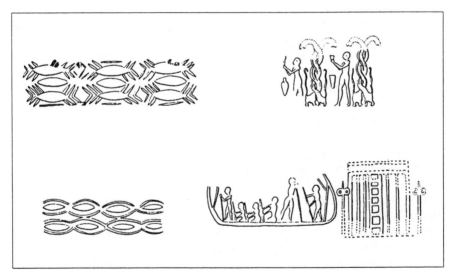

Figure XI.3 Schematic and naturalistic seals of the Late Uruk and Jamdat Nasr periods from Uruk (after Amiet 1961: Pl. 21.346, 348; Pl. 13bis. L and E)

factured using a bow-drill to hollow out the parts of bodies and objects, or a cutting wheel to slice the surface of the seal in patterns constituting either real objects such as fish or simple diagonal criss-cross friezes. 'Naturalistic' seals were characterized by much deeper cutting, using different tools. Moreover, these were decorated with highly individualistic scenes of humans, buildings, animals and objects which were much more complex than the often repetitive and simplistic scenes of the schematic group. Nissen suggested that, in the context of the Eanna temple administration, the individualistic seals were used by high-level administrators whenever a transaction required their personal sanction. The schematic seals, on the other hand, were those of less important offices or lower-level bureaucrats whose seals were recognized as reflecting the authority of a lesser level in the temple administration but not of an individually identifiable administrator.

With this distinction in mind it is interesting to turn to the seals and sealings found at a great urban centre like Uruk and compare these in broad terms with those from the much smaller, contemporary site of Jamdat Nasr. Here we are immediately faced with a dichotomy. Whereas Uruk is characterized almost exclusively by seal impressions, excavations in an administrative building complex (though not a temple) at Jamdat Nasr (Moorey 1976:95–106) yielded an abundance of seals but very few sealings. Moreover, whereas the seal impressions at Uruk were made with naturalistic seals, the original seals found at Jamdat Nasr were almost entirely of the crude, schematic sort. If we follow Nissen's hypothesis of naturalistic versus schematic seal = high-level versus low-level administrator, then clearly the sealings from Uruk reflect the presence there of many high-ranking officials, whereas the dominance of schematic seals at Jamdat Nasr would reflect the lesser status of the administration housed in the building excavated there.

To return to the question of whether the written content of the seal-impressed Archaic texts is reflected in the type of seal used on them, we must ask whether variations in iconography and tablet content co-vary in some meaningful way. As Nissen has emphasised, only some 250 out of the approximately 2000 seal impressions found at Uruk have ever been published (Nissen 1986:329). Thus, it is extremely difficult to link seal iconography with tablets, particularly as the relationship between a seal impression and the tablet from which it comes has often been ignored in publications of archaic glyptic. An Uruk III text now in the Metropolitan Museum of Art which records the distribution of barley rations bears an impression showing a male figure in a long robe/skirt leading two dogs (mastiffs?) by leashes. He and the dogs appear to be in the act of pursuing wild boar in the marshes, indicated by individual plant stalks. The human figure in this sealing is the well-attested, so-called 'priest/king' found on numerous sealings (cf. Fig. VIII.6) and relief fragments from Uruk of the same date. He appears to embody a high office but it is difficult to see any obvious link between 'his' seal, assuming this is the seal of a leading administrator of the Eanna complex, and barley rations beyond the rather simplistic notion that the authority to disburse the rations in question was sanctioned by a person with this particular seal. Perhaps the seal showed the officer in question in an attitude which was meaningful for him, but which did not necessarily depict him in a scene of 'professional' activity.

M. Brandes has observed that themes such as 'prisoner-of-war scenes', 'master of animals (lion)', 'heraldic groups', 'temple and snake', 'cattle and lion', 'herd and hut' and 'agricultural scenes' (perhaps also 'temple and procession' and 'cultic scenes') appear on jar or door sealings from Uruk but never on tablets. The scenes represented exclusively on tablets include the '"king" guiding a wagon', 'demon, snakes and animals', and most probably 'hunting scenes', particularly boar-hunting as noted above, and the sole fishing scene. Present on both jar sealings and tablets are the 'snake and bird' and 'temple and boat' scenes (Brandes 1979:30–2). Unfortunately, until such time as the individual texts are adequately published, together with their impressions, it will be difficult to take this analysis much further. As it is, only three sealed tablets (Fig. XI.4) with reasonably complete scenes were published by Brandes. Thanks to the kindness of R.K. Englund,[5] it is possible to compare the contents of these texts with the seal impressions on them. This is shown below. There are no obvious connections between iconography and text content, unless the depiction of an animal being skinned or butchered in the third example has some relation to the fact that hides are listed in the tablet from which it comes.

Tablet	Written Contents	Iconographic Theme
W 21 074,1	grain rations in bi-sexagesimal system; no ideogram representing persons involved[6]	'Demon, Snakes und Animals'
W 20 570,2	list of numbers of jars of dairy fats and strings of dried fruit; no ideograms	'Snake and Bird'
W 21 278	list of numbers of textiles, hides and unknown objects; no ideograms representing persons involved	'Temple and Butchery Scene'

One reason for supposing that the sealing habits of Late Uruk and Jamdat Nasr period officials may have reflected the nature of the transactions recorded on the tablets in question is the fact that such was certainly the case in later Mesopotamian history. For example, no seal impressions are known from the Archaic Ur texts of ED I date or the Fara texts of the ED II period (*c.* 2500 BC), and indeed from the late Early Dynastic period we have only a single sealed envelope[7] and its tablet from Lagash. Similarly, the Old Akkadian material consists of only four texts in the Yale Babylonian Collection, all impressed with the same seal, a single text from Nippur with a sealed envelope and a sealed tablet in the Oriental Institute of the University of Chicago (Steinkeller 1977:41).

On the other hand, although the sealing of tablets may have been extremely rare throughout the Early Dynastic and Old Akkadian periods, the sealing of doors and pottery vessels was well attested, for instance at Fara and Girsu. This suggests that actual security from theft or misappropriation of goods belonging to the large households (palaces or temples) was of greater concern to mid-third-millennium estate managers than the validation of written documents.

After the apparent hiatus in the practice of sealing tablets or their envelopes, the usage again became common from the Ur III period onward. An examination of sealing practice in the Ur III period by P. Steinkeller

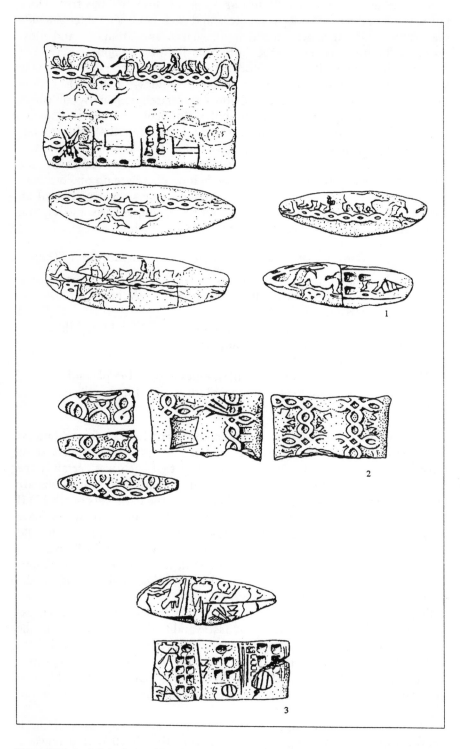

Figure XI.4 Sealed Archaic tablets from Uruk. 1. W 21 074,1; 2. W 20 570,2; 3. W 21 278

revealed that the only administrative texts which were sealed were receipts, disbursements of goods and letter-orders, whereas 'ration lists, accounts of various kinds, lists of persons, animals and commodities, inventories, the so-called "round tablets" [agricultural texts], and the "messenger texts" were not sealed' (Steinkeller 1977:42). However, it was standard practice to encase tablets (Fig. XI.5) of this period in a protective envelope, and it was in fact more common to seal the envelope than the actual tablet itself (although tablets were sealed as well). It is important to note, however, that the seal no longer functioned as a sign of the dispatching authority or institution. Rather, receipts which bear such formulaic phrases as *šu ba-ti*: 'he received [inanimate objects]', *i-dab₅*: 'he received [animate objects]' and *kišib*, 'seal [of PN]' were sealed by the *receiver* of the goods. While this may seem illogical, one should not assume that the tablet which recorded the receipt of goods was comparable to a modern invoice which has been issued by a seller of goods and signed by the receiver. Rather, the tablet which recorded the receipt of goods was written by a scribe when the delivery was made as an inventory of goods received. The tablet thus written would normally say 'PN_2 received from PN' and the envelope 'from PN the seal of PN_2', as well as bearing the seal impression of PN_2. Additionally, the receipt might be witnessed by a third party, in which case 'seal of PN_3' would appear as well.

This example could be multiplied many times by taking account of other types of sealed texts. Those which deal with labour usually exhibit the structure: N *guruš/géme* (paid) per N days/description of the work/foreman PN/seal PN_2/*gìr* [conveyor] PN3 (optional)/date/seal impression of PN_2. In some cases, when the official responsible for a transaction was absent and failed to seal the tablet, the actual sealing was often done by a brother or son, and we find the sentence 'in place of PN [the person expected to seal the document] the seal of PN_2 [was rolled]'. In at least one case we read, 'PN_2, the overseer, rolled the seal of PN_3 in place [of the seal] of PN, the foreman', which suggests that PN_2 preferred to use the seal of a third party rather than his own (Steinkeller 1977:43). One might ask, had PN_2 lost his own seal and therefore been forced to borrow the seal of PN_3?

The 'letter-order', a type of command which originated in the Old Akkadian period, was common in the Ur III period. Because these were literally letters ordering action it was normal for them to be sealed or, failing that, for their envelopes to bear a seal impression. Examples which lack the name of the sender were not thrown into the ancient equivalent of our 'dead letter' bin, however, because in most cases the sender (and not the scribe) was identifiable from his seal impression. Thus, in one case (TCS 1: 242) the letter ends *[kiš]ib [a]-hu-a*, 'seal of Ahua', and the seal used was an inscribed one the legend of which reads, 'Shul-gi, mighty man, king of Ur, king of the Four Parts [Quarters]: Ahhua, son of [PN], is his servant' (Sollberger 1966:63). The fact that less than a third of the 373 letter-orders published by Sollberger were sealed is probably due to the fact that the envelopes themselves are thought to have been sealed, but these are often missing. As in the case of the receipts discussed above, the right seal was sometimes lacking. Thus one of the letter-orders (TCS 1: 215) says,

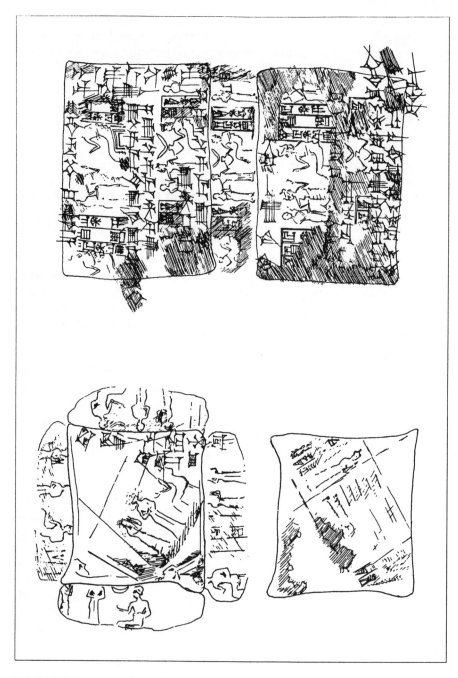

Figure XI.5 Examples of a sealed tablet (above) and envelope (below) of Ur III date from Girsu (after Grégoire 1970: Pl. LXI and LVIII)

'the seal of the chancellor [*sukkalmah*] was not available', while another (TCS 1: 305) warns, 'he must not argue on the grounds that the seal was not rolled [on this letter]' (Steinkeller 1977:44).

As for Ur III legal documents, a brief overview of seal use is presented in Table XI.1, showing clearly how different parties to a transaction might or

Document Type	Sealed by						
	Seller(s)	*Seller(s) + Guarantor*	*Guarantor*	*Seller + Person Sold*	*Person Sold*	*Buyer*	*Other/Uncertain*
sale documents	35	4	1	1	1	1	5 unclear, 5 illegible, 1 sealed using Ninurta's seal

	Borrower(s)	*Other*
loan documents	55	7 (by son of a borrower)

Circumstances

hire documents 1 sealed by owner of a slave who was hired by someone else
1 sealed by brother of individual hired
1 sealed by person not mentioned in the relevant tablet

Table XI.1 *Seal use on Ur III legal documents*

might not be involved in the actual sealing of a document or its envelope.[8] As Steinkeller has noted (1977:44–6):

> The legal texts [sale, loan, gift, hire] are sealed by the party who undertakes a specific obligation in a given transaction: in sales, the seller who abandons any claim to the sold property; in loans, the borrower who promises to return the loan (and interest) on a given date; in gifts, the donor who renounces his rights to the gift; in hiring, the owner or relative of the hired person who assures that the hireling will work in accordance with the agreement. The seals of officials rolled on six sale documents and one court record have a different function, that of authorization or attestation.

In all of these cases, the person who sealed a receipt was responsible for the goods received, the borrower who sealed a loan was bound to repay that loan and the seller who sealed a sale document was obliged not to make any further claims on the property in question. The texts which recorded these transactions would be used in court should written testimony be required to contest a claim made. For that reason, the *loss* of a seal was a serious matter since the seal could be used to engage in transactions in the name of the hapless seal-loser.

There are several such examples of seal loss known to us from the Ur III period. In one case, when the inscribed seal of a merchant of Nippur, called Ur-DUN, was lost, 'the herald blew the horn in the streets, announcing that no one might have any claim against Ur-DUN', thus effectively cancelling his seal's validity (Steinkeller 1977:49). Another Ur III text records the loss of the seal of Lu-Ninshubur 'after the 19th day of the month of the "twin sanctuaries" had passed'. As W.W. Hallo has observed, 'The precise dating implies that any document found to be sealed with the missing seal after this time would be invalid or, indeed, invalidated'. Indeed this is prescribed in texts from Nippur where the statement is found, 'Should any of their sealed tablets be lost and then found again, they are to be destroyed' (Hallo 1977:54–5). Similarly, an Old Babylonian text notes, 'Since the first day of the eleventh month the black seal of Silli-Urash has disappeared', presumably to record the day after which the seal was no longer a valid legal instrument. Finally, the Assyrian Dream Book (Tablet B) says ominously, 'If he wears a seal and one takes [it] away: either his son or his daughter will die . . . If [he wears (?)] a seal with [his] n[ame] and one takes [it] away: his son will die' (Hallo 1977:57–8).

Some Ur III scribes are known to have had up to six seals, although it is notoriously difficult to link specific seals from excavations or in museum collections with seal impressions on Ur III tablets (Waetzoldt 1989:79). Various circumstances could change the legal status of a person's seal. In some cases two seals belonging to a single person invoke the names of the two different rulers under whom they served. Thus, Ur-Lisi, *ensí* of Umma under both Shulgi and Amar-Sin, is known from seals mentioning both kings, just as his successor, Ajakalla, had seals invoking both Amar-Sin and Shu-Sin. In each case, a new seal was cut for the official in question after the death of the first ruler under whom they had served. 'Old' seals were sometimes used for quite a while after they had become obsolete, however, and this was the case with Ur-Lisi's Shulgi seal, which was employed inter-mittently alongside his later Amar-Sin seal (Steinkeller 1977:47). The more frugal Aradani, a judge at Ur who served under both Amar-Sin and Shu-Sin, had only one seal on which the sign for AMAR was replaced by SHU rather than cutting an entirely new seal (Steinkeller 1977:46).

An official who received promotion to new office normally had to have a new seal cut for himself as well. Thus, Abbakalla of Lagash, called simply *dub-sar*, 'scribe' on his first seal, is identified as 'temple administrator of Uru', an office which he inherited from his father, on his second seal. Women whose husbands received 'promotions' might also change their seals. Thus, Ninhilia, wife of Ajakalla, appears on her first seal as 'Nin-hilia, wife of Ajakalla, son of Ur-Dumu', but a later seal identifies her as 'wife of Ajakalla, *ensi* of Umma', following the promotion of her husband to the *ensi*-ship of Umma. A surprising fact is that an Ur III seal belonging to Lukalla of Umma, the 'chief comptroller of the "fiscal office" of Umma for twelve years' (Pomponio 1992:169) during the reigns of Amar-Sin and Shu-Sin, somehow made its way from southern Mesopotamia to the site of Kültepe (ancient Karum Kanesh) in Anatolia, where it was used some two hundred years later (Waetzoldt 1990:48).

THE LATER USE OF CYLINDER SEALS

The sealing of contracts was an important aspect of seal use in the Old Babylonian period. As J. Renger has emphasized, whereas modern con-tracts *create* an agreement binding both parties to fulfill certain conditions, Mesopotamian contracts attest that an agreement has been concluded and hence should be considered a 'protocol written from the viewpoint of the witnesses' (Renger 1977:75). Thus, transactions were reported in the past tense, conveying the information that a transaction had already taken place, giving, for instance, the price paid, stating that the seller had ac-knowledged receipt of payment, that certain symbolic acts had been per-formed and that the parties to the transaction had taken an oath in the presence of witnesses who were named in the document. As the idea of a signature was unknown, authenticity was guaranteed graphically by seal-ing the text recording the transaction or the envelope in which it was placed. Where disputes arose the tablet in its envelope would be presented before a judge who would call witnesses and decide the case based on their testimony. An Old Babylonian letter shows clearly how sealed tablets became important witnesses to legal transactions in ancient Mesopotamia. We read (Renger 1977:76):

> Etel-pi-Marduk, to whom you sold an unimproved lot several years ago –
> when he wanted to build a house on the lot you prevented him from
> doing so by claiming this lot from him. But he has brought to me the
> contract which states that he bought the lot from you. I have looked at
> the document. It has an envelope, your seal impression and the names of

the five witnesses are on the tablet. If he would show the tablet to the judges you would have no chance of winning the case, therefore give the lot back to Etel-pi-Marduk.

Certain peculiarities of seal use can be observed through time in southern Mesopotamia during the second and first millennia BC. In the Old Babylonian period (Leemans 1982:219–44) envelopes were generally sealed, and tablets only rarely so. Cylinder seals tended to be rolled on the left margin of the obverse and reverse of the tablet envelope or, when the tablet itself was sealed, on the left and lower and upper edges of the tablet. Such practices may have had something to do with the precise way in which the tablets were archived or filed, a practice which, in certain cases, is known to have been done on brick shelves, as at Old Babylonian Sippar (al-Jadir and al–Adami 1987:55). In a practice which harks back to the Late Uruk and Jamdat Nasr periods, the entire surface of an Old Babylonian tablet destined to serve as a receipt or loan contract was covered with seal impressions before it was inscribed. Northern Babylonian texts often have an annotation, written in very small signs, next to the seal impression identifying the seal owner, but this practice is virtually unknown in southern Babylonia. On the other hand, documents from the south often contain a clause stating that witnesses have sealed the document, a claim which can be verified on the tablets themselves since these often bear the seal impressions of several different seals, presumably belonging to several different witnesses.

Not everyone about to be involved in a legal or commercial transaction requiring a seal necessarily owned one, however. In that case there were several courses of action.[9] An inexpensive seal, for example of clay (Werr 1988:1–24), could be made. Such seals are called '*burgul* seals' after the term for 'seal-cutter' (Sum. *bur-gul*, Akk. *purkullu*) who, in such cases, generally appears as a witness alongside the scribe who wrote out the document. As Renger has observed, 'the sealcutter, who in several areas during the Old Babylonian period is listed among the witnesses, is called in cases of dispute to authenticate the seals he cut for a particular legal transaction for the writing down of which he was present' (Renger 1977:79). Such *burgul* seals were common at Nippur, but are also known from many other sites as well, particularly Tell Harmal (Fig. XI.6). The simplicity and crudeness of their designs confirms that such seals were quickly manufactured with little care, as indeed befitted their purpose. On the other hand, a person could forgo the use of a seal altogether, instead impressing the hem of his garment on the tablet (e.g. at Nippur and Sippar) which the scribe would accompany with the annotation, 'seal of PN'. Finger-nail impressions, again accompanied by an annotation identifying their owner, are found on texts from Dilbat and Ur. Old Babylonian seal inscriptions were often illegible, a fact which is perhaps understandable in view of the few extant 'practice' texts written in mirror-image writing which have survived giving the texts to be inscribed by a seal-cutter on an Old Babylonian seal (e.g. Beckman 1988:72).

Both the hem and the finger-nail impression were used during the

Figure XI.6 Impressions of cylinder seals made of clay from Tell Harmal (after Werr 1988)

Middle Babylonian period as well. On the other hand, a person who owned no seal might be represented on a document by the seal of another person, as was the case in transactions involving *naditus*, women who lived a kind of cloistered existence in the service of a deity (Postgate 1994:131). By the Neo-Babylonian period the envelope had, for whatever reason, gone out of use and the practice of making duplicate tablets, one for each party to a transaction, had arrived. In this case both tablets were sealed, and the names of the witnesses present were noted. Beginning in the Neo-Assyrian period, more specifically in the second half of the eighth century BC (Boehmer 1976:343 and Abb. 274), however, stamp seals re-emerged as the favoured medium of sealing after millennia of dominance by the cylinder seal (Fig. XI.7). By the Seleucid period the stamp itself was a cut stone set in a finger-ring, comparable in all respects to modern day signet rings. When such a ring-seal was used on a tablet, the impression was normally accompanied with an annotation reading 'ring of PN'. The resurgence in popularity of the stamp seal after nearly three thousand years is a phenomenon which cannot be easily explained, but it suggests that Nissen's views on the original appearance of the cylinder seal and its role in comparison to the late prehistoric stamp seal require modification. Nissen has argued that, within the sphere of economic management, 'cylinder seals provided a more effective control because the entire surface of an object could be sealed and thus protected from fraud and distortion, while the relatively small and restricted imprints of stamp seals could only partially secure the item' (Nissen 1977:15). Yet for over a millennium, from the late eighth century BC to the end of the Sasanian era (AD 651), the stamp seal fulfilled most of the same functions

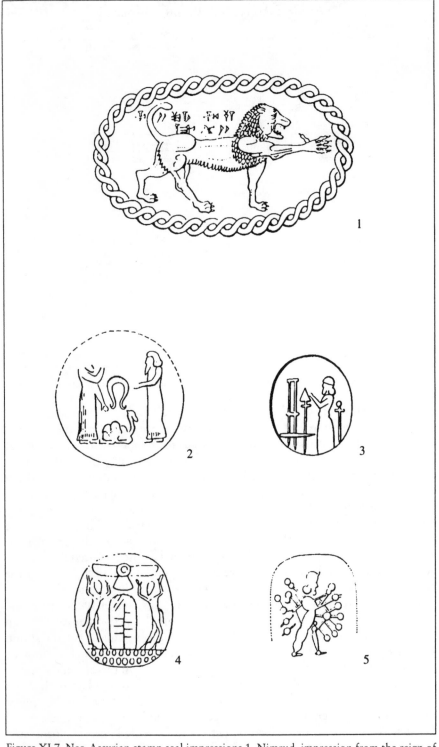

Figure XI.7 Neo-Assyrian stamp seal impressions 1. Nimrud, impression from the reign of Adad-nirari III (803-782 BC); 2. Nimrud, impression from the reign of Sargon II (721-705 BC); 3. seal impression from a tablet dated in the year of Sin-alik-pani, 615 BC; 4. seal impression from a tablet dated in the year of Bel-sharruna'id, 629 BC; 5. seal impression from a tablet dated in the year of Sin-shar-usur, 622 BC (all after Boehmer 1976: Figs. 106–107)

as early cylinder seals had. This is not to deny that it is easier to seal the entire surface of a tablet with a cylinder seal, if so desired, than with a stamp seal, but the example of Sasanian sealed clay bullae shows that bales of merchandise, leather containers, wooden boxes and parchment documents were sealed with the generally very small Sasanian stamp seals (Huff 1987:378ff). A simple, functional explanation which favours the superiority of the cylinder over the stamp does not, therefore, seem justifiable.

CONCLUSION

The seal as such, in whatever form, was always a mark of authority, validation and participation by an individual or institution. It was the primary legal instrument of the ancient Mesopotamian economic, legal and commercial system for thousands of years. In an era of human history which knew not the concept of an individual 'signature' (Renger 1977:80), the seal was the representation of identity and the means of ensuring control and security for most important transactions. In Mesopotamia the written document and the seal formed a nexus of control and authorization which was highly effective for thousands of years, and which laid the foundations for much of the later bureaucratic technology of subsequent history.

NOTES

1 For the artificiality of this divide, see e.g. Nissen 1989:179–82.
2 This was by far the most famous 'Kullab' in Mesopotamia. Note, however, that a district of Babylon called Kullab is thought to have been named after the Uruk district, while a northern Babylonian Kul'aba is thought to have existed, as well as a Neo-Babylonian town somewhere in the south, yet definitely distinct from Uruk. See most recently Beaulieu 1993:22.
3 Not dog. Cf. the discussion in Chapter III.
4 A recently discovered cylinder seal from Tell Brak in Syria appears to date to the Middle Uruk period. See Oates and Oates 1993:Fig. 31. If this is correct, then it represents the first cylinder seal ever found which predates the Late Uruk period and hence the earliest cylinder seal yet discovered in Western Asia.
5 Letter of 6.9.1994. The information under 'Written Contents' is quoted from his letter.
6 It is now known that the names of certain officials were included on some of the Archaic texts. An entire group bearing the name Kushim is presented in Nissen, Damerow and Englund 1990:66ff.
7 The practice of putting tablets into clay envelopes developed during the Early Dynastic period. Cf. the Sargon Letter (l. 53) where we read, 'In those days, writing on tablets certainly existed, but enveloping tablets did not exist'. See Vanstiphout 1993:13.
8 The information in the table is taken from Steinkeller 1977:45.
9 Unless otherwise stated, the information used in this discussion stems largely from Renger 1977:75–9.

XII East meets West

INTRODUCTION

Because of the far-flung interests of many of the kings who ruled over southern Mesopotamia, an account of its history would necessarily entail opening up the geographical purview of this study to take into account contemporary developments in areas such as Iran, Syria, Anatolia, Palestine and Egypt. In conceiving this book, however, the intention has always been to investigate Mesopotamia's infrastructure without becoming mired in the details of its political history, and for that reason an 'isolationist' approach was followed in the first eleven chapters. In the next two chapters this approach will be abandoned in order to examine certain significant items and influences which originated outside of Mesopotamia and which can only be understood in a broader geographical context.

While we have already referred to gold from Egypt and copper from Anatolia in discussing ancient Mesopotamian metallurgy, the focus in this chapter will be exclusively on certain domesticated animals, cultivars, stones and metals which originated in Mesopotamia's 'Far East'. To consider all of the items which came from somewhere east of the Tigris would require a much longer volume than the present one. Mesopotamia's closest eastern neighbours, the various polities of the Iranian plateau, were the sources of many foreign items, but the focus here will be on the Indian subcontinent and parts of Central Asia. We shall not review those items of eastern origin (e.g. soft-stone or lapis lazuli) which have already been well studied in the literature, nor shall we enter too deeply into the identification of certain place-names mentioned in cuneiform sources, such as Meluhha (the Indus Valley?), which are believed to lie far to the east of Mesopotamia and which have been discussed extensively over the years. Rather the focus here is on the goods themselves. As in our examination of the inedible resources of southern Mesopotamia, we shall proceed by considering eastern items under the rubrics 'animal, mineral, and vegetable'.

ANIMAL

Zebu bull (Bos indicus)

Many years ago E. Douglas Van Buren reviewed the then available evidence for the depiction of the humped or zebu bull in Mesopotamian art, beginning with late prehistoric, Ubaid period terracotta figurines from Uruk (Ziegler 1962:150 and Taf. 3) and including many representations in glyptic and terracotta from the Jamdat Nasr, Old Akkadian and later periods (van Buren 1939:75–6). The vast majority of the pieces which she cited, however, are not in fact representations of *Bos indicus* but are clearly either *Bos taurus*, common domesticated cattle,[1] or *Bos primigenius*, wild aurochs, the latter having been identified at such prehistoric sites as Umm Dabaghi-yah, Tell es-Sawwan, and Choga Mami (Bökönyi 1978:60, Table 2), as well as in an Old Babylonian context at Isin (Uerpmann and Uerpmann 1994:424). Indeed, it would be surprising to find zebu bull figurines in the Ubaid period when the bovine sector of the faunal assemblage from this period is overwhelmingly dominated in both southern (Desse 1983:194; cf. Huot 1989:27) and northern (Bökönyi 1978:60, Table 2) Mesopotamia by *Bos taurus*. It is not, in fact, until we reach the early second millennium that we find the first clear representations of the humped bull in southern Mesopotamia. These occur on an Isin-Larsa or Old Babylonian cylinder seal from Ur (Collon 1987:187, no. 907) (Fig. XII.1); an undated prismatic stamp seal from Latifiya (Wyatt 1983:3–6) (Fig. XII.2); and a terracotta plaque from Tell Ischali in the Diyala region which shows a man riding on the back of a zebu bull (Frankfort 1970: Fig. 124).[2] Given the paucity of faunal data from early second-millennium sites in southern Mesopotamia it is perhaps not surprising to find that no zebu are attested, but one might have expected them to turn up at a site like Isin where, however, they are absent in the Old Babylonian levels (Boessneck and Ziegler 1987:138).

Figure XII.1 Cylinder seal from Ur showing a zebu bull (after Franke-Vogt 1991: Taf. XLI.318)

The zebu is commonly associated with South and Southeast Asia, but its distribution in antiquity was far wider. As the discovery of both osteo-logical remains (Caloi, Compagnoni and Tosi 1978:87) and large numbers of baked and unbaked clay zebu figurines at Shahr-i Sokhta (Santini 1990:427–51) in Iranian Seistan attest, the zebu was clearly not restricted to the Indus Valley nor even Baluchistan. Indeed *Bos indicus* figurines far outnumbered those of any other genus or species in the period *c.* 2900–2500 BC at Shahr-i Sokhta (661 unbaked out of a total of 1045; 69 baked out of a total of 243) (Compagnoni and Tosi 1978:96, Table 2). In both the aceramic and ceramic neolithic levels at Mehrgarh in Pakistani Baluchistan (Meadow 1982:148), the percentage of the faunal assemblage represented by *Bos indicus* increased steadily from 4 per cent in the early aceramic, to 38 per cent in the late aceramic, finally reaching 65 per cent by the middle of the ceramic Neolithic around 5000 BC (Meadow 1982:56–61). As R.H. Meadow observed some years ago, 'From a paleontological point of view,

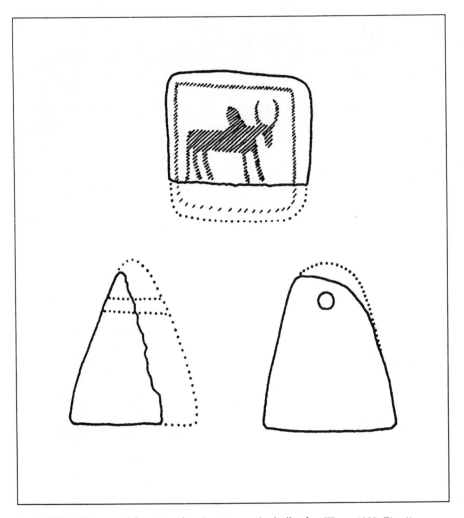

Figure XII.2 Stamp seal from Latifiya showing a zebu bull (after Wyatt 1983: Fig. 1)

the cattle remains from Mehrgarh could be very important, since there is still much debate concerning the origin of zebu cattle' (Meadow 1981:163–4). Some years later he wrote (1984:37):

> It seems quite likely, given the Mehrgarh evidence, that the zebu cattle we know today and which are represented in the iconography of pre- and proto-historic South Asia were developed in that area from a wild form already morphologically somewhat distinct from its relatives in more northerly and westerly areas.

As for the advantages of *Bos indicus*, Meadow notes:

> The evident popularity and success of cattle-keeping in the Greater Indus Valley up to the present day is probably due, at least in part, to the nature of the zebu breeds developed in the area. These humped animals are well known for their heat tolerance and for their ability to browse

marginal range vegetation. Alluvial areas, particularly along perennial rivers or around water holes, provide suitable pasturage for zebu, herds of which are also sometimes grazed in swampy areas.

Once the zebu was introduced into Mesopotamia, the same characteristics which had made it popular in eastern Iran, Baluchistan and the Indus Valley were no doubt appreciated there as well. Indeed, it was well adapted to the swamp areas of southern Mesopotamia, and may have filled a role as a draught animal, just as it does today in South Asia, where the water buffalo, on the other hand, is a supplier of milk and meat. Judging by the iconographic evidence cited above, the introduction of the zebu into southern Mesopotamia does not seem to have taken place prior to the beginning of the second millennium. From depictions of the zebu on a prismatic stamp seal from Maysar, on pottery from the island of Umm an-Nar and in the rock art of Oman, we know that the animal had been introduced into the Oman peninsula by *c.* 2400/2300 BC (Potts 1990:112, 130). It figures prominently on the early group of so-called 'Persian Gulf' stamp seals from Bahrain, datable to the last century of the third millennium (Potts 1990, I:Fig. 18), examples of which are known from Ur (Gadd 1932:Pl. I.2, Pl. III.15–17). Whether it reached Mesopotamia via late third-millennium contact with Magan, for instance during the Ur III period, through the early second-millennium trade with Dilmun (Bahrain) or indeed overland from eastern Iran is unknown. That the species represented in southern Mesopotamia during the Isin-Larsa period was ultimately of Baluchi or generally South Asian origin, whether it arrived via an intermediary in the Gulf or not, seems, however, clear, although its popularity as a draught animal in South Asia is belied by the fact that it is, for example, represented on only 3.1 per cent (N=44) of the extant corpus of stamp seals from the great Harappan site of Mohenjo-Daro (Franke-Vogt 1991:66). A famous passage in the *Curse of Agade* says, 'The monkeys, the elephants, the *áb-za-za*, and other beasts of distant lands ran into one another in the broad streets [of Akkade]' (Steinkeller 1982:252), and both A. Salonen (Salonen 1976:178) and P. Steinkeller, following the *Chicago Assyrian Dictionary*, have suggested that the animal called *áb-za-za* in Sumerian was in fact the zebu. Other scholars, however, take this to be the water buffalo as discussed below.

Water Buffalo (*Bubalus bubalis*)

The water buffalo appears for the first time in Mesopotamian iconography on cylinder seals dating to the last third of Sargon of Akkad's reign (Boehmer 1975:3), including one, known only from an impression, which belonged to a scribe of Enheduanna, Sargon's daughter. Thereafter the water buffalo is attested on the seals of various high Akkadian officials (Fig. XII.3), but it disappears suddenly from the Mesopotamian iconographic repertoire at the end of the Old Akkadian period[3] and does not reappear until the Sasanian era.

R.M. Boehmer has suggested that the original introduction of the water buffalo may have been in the form of a gift or tribute from Meluhha to

Figure XII.3 Drawing of the impression of a cylinder seal in the Louvre belonging to the scribe Ibni-sharrum, servant of the Old Akkadian king Shar-kali-sharri, *c.* 2220/2200 BC (after Amiet 1961: Pl. 111.1473)

Sargon, but he suggests that they did not survive the Guti invasion and the downfall of the Old Akkadian empire, after which whatever herds existed at the time died out (Boehmer 1975:8). Considering the *áb-za-za* in the *Curse of Agade*, Boehmer suggested that the term, rather than referring to the zebu bull, should be translated as 'water buffalo' (Boehmer 1975:11), an interpretation followed by J.S.Cooper (Cooper 1983:237), B. Lion (Lion 1992:357) and W. Heimpel (Heimpel 1993:53). However that may be, it is clear from the available faunal remains that the water buffalo was not indigenous to Mesopotamia, where no faunal remains of the species have ever been recorded.[4] Interestingly, the fragments of a horn core, a first phalanx and a rib, attributable to some sort of buffalo (*Bubalus* sp.), were discovered at the Halaf period (*c.* 5500–5000 BC) site of Shams ed-Din Tannira in northern Syria (Uerpmann 1982:33). On the basis of morphology and size, Uerpmann considers it most probable that these are the remains of wild water buffalo, and that the animal once roamed the river valleys of greater Mesopotamia. He suggests, however, that water buffalo became extinct with the expansion of human settlement throughout the region, and that it was certainly no longer extant in the area during the third millennium, when it was reintroduced, as argued by Boehmer, during Sargon's lifetime.

Like the zebu, the domesticated water buffalo originated in the east. At Mehrgarh water buffalo were rare in the aceramic (ending *c.* 5500 BC) and early ceramic Neolithic (Meadow 1982:148). Judging by the horn cores and cranial fragments recovered, the type of animal found there is the 'swamp' type of water buffalo, 'characterized by horns projecting more or less laterally and curving inward, generally remaining in the plane of the face' as opposed to the 'more commonly encountered "river" breeds which have small tightly curled horns, a trait which together with milk production was selected for over a long period of time' (Meadow 1981:165). Meadow considers the water buffalo at Mehrgarh 'crop-robbers' which 'may have been killed in nearby agricultural fields' (Meadow 1982:56–61). Water buffalo of 'swamp' type are also known from coastal Harappan sites, such as Balakot, northwest of Karachi, where a water buffalo horn core was found in an Harappan context (Meadow 1979:302). Nevertheless, Meadow suggests that the water buffalo was more at home in the Indus Valley proper than in Baluchistan (Meadow 1979:303), although the water buffalo is even rarer in Harappan glyptic than the zebu bull, appearing on only twelve stamp seals at Mohenjo-Daro (0.9 per cent of the total assemblage) (Franke-Vogt 1991:67).

Monkeys

As we saw above, the *Curse of Agade* mentions monkeys in the streets of Agade, and it has been suggested by a number of scholars that these, too, originated in the east, probably in Meluhha (Dunham 1985:240).[5] According to S. Dunham, the monkeys depicted on Old Babylonian terracottas most closely resemble the Indian Rhesus Macaque which has been, in modern times, one of the commonest monkeys kept as a pet and one which is easily carried about on the shoulder (Dunham 1985:261, n. 110). From the Old Babylonian period onwards small clay figurines of monkeys are present in southern Mesopotamia (e.g. Wrede 1990:276–7), but by the Kassite period, and certainly during the Neo-Assyrian era (Fig. XII.4), it is likely that monkeys were being brought to Mesopotamia from Egypt which had close ties to the court of the Kassite kings during the so-called Amarna period. During the Neo-Assyrian and Neo-Babylonian periods even the Old South Arabian kingdom of Saba, located in the highlands of what is

Figure XII.4 Monkeys brought to the court of Assur-nasirpal II (883–859 BC) at Nimrud as tribute (after Olmstead 1975 (orig. 1923): Fig. 59)

today northern Yemen, could have provided monkeys or baboons, either from the population of the latter species which inhabits certain parts of coastal Yemen, or from Ethiopia, which was colonized by the Sabaeans.

Indian Elephants and Ivory

By the late Early Dynastic era, as references to ivory figurines in the pre-Sargonic texts (RTC 19, DP 490) from Lagash attest, ivory objects had begun to reach southern Mesopotamia (Heimpel 1987:54). While these, in theory, could have come from either Africa or the Indus region, it is generally believed that the ivory was of Indian origin for the earliest representation of an elephant in Mesopotamia, occurring on a cylinder seal from Tell Asmar in the Diyala region of late Old Akkadian date (van Buren 1939:77; Frankfort 1955:Pl. 161.642) (Fig. XII.5), is definitely of the Indian as opposed to the African variety.

Figure XII.5 Drawing of an impression of a late Akkadian cylinder seal from Tell Asmar showing an elephant, crocodile and rhinoceros (after Franke-Vogt 1991: Taf. XLI.316)

Third-millennium representations of elephants in Mesopotamia are, however, extremely rare and aside from the Tell Asmar seal just mentioned none of the other alleged elephants can be taken as confirmed (cf. Moorey 1994:119). As we saw above, however, the *Curse of Agade* mentions elephants in the streets of Agade in the Old Akkadian period, and although this may well reflect a literary *topos* which was far removed from reality, ivory was certainly reaching the area. A text from the time of Gudea and Ur-Baba (RTC 221), which is a list of items dedicated to a temple (?), preserves the earliest attestation of ivory (Sum. *zú-am-si*) arriving in Mesopotamia in raw form, listing two pieces of ivory by length and thickness (Heimpel 1987:78). The evidence of ivory import continues to grow during the succeeding Ur III period. Most of our information comes from Ur, at this time the main gateway for goods entering the region from the south and east. UET III 1498 lists the not inconsiderable amount of 21 minas, 9.5 shekels (10.58 kg) of ivory while UET III 751 mentions an object (the word is illegible in the text) of ivory weighing 38 minas (19 kg), which was perhaps a tusk (Heimpel 1987:55). The implication here is clearly that, in contrast to the pre-Sargonic texts mentioning the import of *finished* goods in ivory, the craftsmen at Ur were in receipt of sizeable quantities of *raw* ivory which they then fashioned themselves into objects, and this is confirmed by UET III 1498 which records that a woodworker used 40 minas (20 kg) of ivory for making chairs (Heimpel 1987:55).

In the Old Babylonian period, on the other hand, economic texts from Ur mention the receipt of a wide variety of finished ivory objects, including combs, anthropomorphic and zoomorphic figurines, rings, rods and many unidentifiable items from Dilmun (Bahrain), although the ultimate source of the ivory must have been further east (Heimpel 1987:55; cf. Oppenheim 1954:6–17; Leemans 1960). UET V 678 gives us some idea of the value of ivory in noting the receipt of '1 mina of copper instead of the share of ivory' (Leemans 1960:26). Contemporary with these references is an Old Babylonian terracotta from Diqdiqah, site of a figurine and terracotta workshop near Ur (cf. Chapter VI), which shows an elephant being ridden, and although the thought of an elephant at Ur may sound far-fetched, the right thigh bone of an elephant was recovered from an Old Babylonian context at Babylon (Moorey 1994:119).[6] By the late Old Babylonian period ivory is no longer mentioned in the cuneiform sources although trade with Dilmun was still ongoing, and W. Heimpel suggests that this must have been due to an interruption of contact between Dilmun and Meluhha (Heimpel 1987:55).

From all of the foregoing D. Collon has concluded that the ivory used in Mesopotamia always came from the Indian elephant (*Elephas maximus*) and that the animals themselves were imported intermittently as well (Collon 1977:222). From the discussion of watercraft in Chapter V it may seem unlikely that elephants were ever brought by sea from the Indus region, and indeed an examination of the import of elephants in the Seleucid era, when they were used militarily, confirms that elephants always arrived in Mesopotamia by land, generally travelling from India via Bactria and the overland route through Iran (later known as the Great Khorassan Road) as when the governor of Bactria sent twenty elephants to the 'satrap' ([lú]*mu-ma-'i-ir*) of Babylonia, who dispatched them on 26 March 273 BC to Antiochus I for use against the Ptolemies at the beginning of the First Syrian War according to a late astronomical diary (van der Spek 1993:97). In fact, when the Seleucids lost Bactria around 240 BC[7] no more elephants seem to have been obtained from the region.

There is a fundamental difference, however, between the desire for exotic objects of ivory in late third- and early second-millennium Mesopotamia, and a wish to actually keep elephants in captivity. Indeed, for the Seleucids the elephant was an important instrument of war, and they used elephants in all of their major military campaigns.[8] Their initial stock of five hundred war elephants had been received by Seleucus I (305–285 BC) as a gift from the Mauryan king Chandragupta in exchange for bringing the war between them to an end. As the military centre of the Seleucid empire was at Apamaea on the Orontes, in Syria, the Seleucid elephants were always stabled there, even though they were taken overland to Babylonia in the late third century BC for use in crushing a rebellion. Elephants are ready for battle at the age of 12, reaching the peak of their physical strength between 20 and 25. In captivity they can live up to 30 years of age (as opposed to 60

in the wild). It is generally recognized that the African elephants used by
the Ptolemies in Egypt were no match for the much fiercer Indian ones, but
in 161 BC the Romans slaughtered the entire Seleucid herd in battle at
Apamea and that was the end of the Seleucid elephant corps.

Nothing suggests that whatever elephants may have reached pre-Seleucid
Mesopotamia were ever used for military purposes and there can have been
little other use for them on arrival. Thus, ivory and ivory objects would
always have been much easier to import than an elephant. It is, therefore,
all the more remarkable if some elephants were indeed brought on the long
journey from Bactria or northern India to the Mesopotamian alluvium, for
whatever reasons, prior to the coming of the Seleucids.

Mongoose (*Herpestes* sp.)

Although 'a creature with something of the appearance of the mongoose'
has been called a 'common motif' in Old Babylonian glyptic (Black and
Green 1992:132), the catalogue of Isin-Larsa and Old Babylonian cylinder
seals in the British Museum, to choose a representative sample, contains
only one seal with an animal which has been tentatively identified, among
other things, as a mongoose (Collon 1986:no. 520). Nevertheless, there
seems no doubt that the mongoose was present in southern Mesopotamia
by the end of the third millennium, for an Ur III text (AUCT 1: 296) records
the disbursement of 4.3 shekels of silver for the fashioning of a mongoose
as a royal gift (*a-ru-[a lugal]*) (Heimpel 1995). A mongoose skull of uncertain date was discovered by Woolley at Ur (Uerpmann and Uerpmann
1994:421), while the remains of the spotted mongoose (*Herpestes auropunctatus*) are also known from Old Babylonian (Boessneck and Kokabi
1981:132) and late second-millennium or Neo-Babylonian levels at Isin
(Boessneck 1977:126) as well as from Nippur (date not specified, see Uerpmann and Uerpmann 1994:420).

The big question, however, is when the mongoose, which is ultimately of
Indian origin, arrived in Mesopotamia. For even if archaeozoologists believe that its presence in Mesopotamia should be 'regarded as one of the
examples for zoogeographical connections between the Indian faunal province and Mesopotamia' (Uerpmann and Uerpmann 1994:421), it is possible
that the mongoose migrated westward without the aid of human intervention sometime around 20,000–18,000 BC when the combined effluent of the
Tigris and Euphrates flowed directly into the Straits of Hormuz (cf. Chapter I). As M. Uerpmann notes, 'Distribution along a now drowned lower
course of the Euphrates in the Gulf area would also readily explain the
occurrence of the small spotted mongoose in Iranian Khuzistan' (Uerpmann n.d.). Certainly the presence of the spotted mongoose in the IVC (*c.*
3000 BC) settlement at Tepe Yahya in southeastern Iran (Meadow 1986:36)
means that it had spread considerably west of its original homeland by the
end of the fourth millennium. Contemporary with the earliest archaeological finds of *Herpestes auropunctatus* in Mesopotamia the spotted
mongoose is found in early second-millennium levels at Qalat al-Bahrain
(Uerpmann and Uerpmann 1994:420) and at Saar (Uerpmann n.d.)[9] on
Bahrain. Although it is tempting to suggest that the mongoose may have

entered Mesopotamia from the Indus Valley, perhaps via contact with the Gulf region, it is equally possible that the mongoose has been in Mesopotamia for over 20,000 years. Later, during the earlier first millennium BC the Indian grey mongoose (*Herpestes edwardsi*) appears in the faunal assemblage from Qalat al-Bahrain, and this seems likely never to have been native to the region but to have been introduced there by human agency (H.-P. Uerpmann, pers. comm.).[10]

The fact that the mongoose was associated in Mesopotamia with the deity *Ningilin/Ninkilim* (the word for mongoose was even written with the deity's name) (Heimpel 1995)[11] suggests that it must have been relatively common. In the Sumerian literary text entitled *He is a Good Seed of a Dog* we read, 'He is a good seed of a dog, a descendant of a wolf, With the stench of a mongoose' (Sjöberg 1972:110).[12] Two Babylonian popular sayings involve the mongoose. The first of these (VAT 8807 Rev III 19–20) runs as follows: 'A mouse, out of the way of a mongoose, entered a snake's hole. He said, "A snake-charmer sent me. Greetings!"'. This clearly shows that the modern association between snake-charmers who keep a mongoose at hand should their cobra become disobedient is one of great antiquity. The second saying (Rev III 32–34) concerns a mongoose and a dog: 'A mongoose, out of the way of a dog, [entered] a drain-pipe. When the dog jumped [it got wedged] in the opening of the pipe and let the mongoose escape from the pipe' (Lambert 1960; Black and Green 1992:132).

House rats (Rattus rattus)
The high frequency of House rat remains in the Old Babylonian levels at Isin (Boessneck 1977:126; Boessneck and Kokabi 1981:147; Boessneck and Ziegler 1987:144), and their occurrence at contemporary Uruk (Boessneck, von den Driesch and Steger 1984:179–80) shows that by the early second millennium the House rat was certainly present in Mesopotamia. According to J. Niethammer (cit. Boessneck and Ziegler 1987:144), however, the House or Black rat (*Rattus rattus*) originated in the Indian sub-continent. In the Arabian Gulf today it has been described as 'an immigrant rodent, limited to the vicinity of seaports and with only limited spread into the interior' (Harrison 1981:76). As an agent in the spread of plague via the rat flea *Xenopsylla cheopis*, the House rat has had an enormous impact on human history. Given the fact that the House rat originated in the Indian faunal province, and that rats are notorious migrants on board ship (viz. their distribution around the ports of the Gulf today), it is tempting to suggest that the species originally reached Mesopotamia as a result of the seaborne trade which brought other, more highly desired goods from the east to the cities of the alluvium (cf. Armitage 1994:232).

Marine Shells
Like bone (cf. Chapter IV), shell was used extensively in ancient Western Asia for a variety of ornamental purposes. Virtually unmodified marine shells, altered only by perforation, functioned as beads in land-locked areas far from their sources, be they in the Gulf, the Mediterranean, the Black Sea or the Caspian. Worked shell, particularly mother-of-pearl, was used

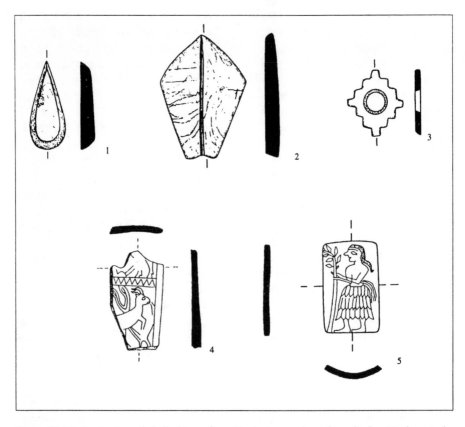

Figure XII.6 A selection of shell objects from Uruk. 1. tear-drop shaped inlay, Uruk period, 3.4 cm long, 1.3 cm max. width, 0.5–0.6 cm thick (after Lindemeyer and Martin 1993: Taf. 114.1835); 2. petal inlay from a stone and shell rosette, Jamdat Nasr/ED I, 4.6 cm long, 3.9 cm max. width, 0.5 cm thick (after Lindemeyer and Martin 1993: Taf. 118.1857); 3. stepped cross inlay, Jamdat Nasr/ED I, 2.5 × 2.3 × 0.2 cm (after Lindemeyer and Martin 1993: Taf. 119.1883D); 4. incised inlay fragment, Jamdat Nasr/ED I, 3.8 × 2.2 × 0.4 cm (after van Ess and Pedde 1992: Taf. 132.1612); 5. incised inlay, ED III, 3.4 × 2.1 × 0.3 cm (after van Ess and Pedde 1992: Taf. 131.1604)

for a variety of purposes, including the manufacture of inlays (Fig. XII.6), cylinder seals,[13] lamps and rings.[14] Of particular interest here are those objects which can be positively identified as having been made of marine shells, the habitat of which is restricted to the coast east and west of the mouth of the Indus Valley. In the past certain Mesopotamian objects, such as shell lamps from Tello and the Royal Cemetery at Ur, have been identified as being made of *Turbinella pyrum*, a gastropod which is common on the coast of India and Pakistan as far west as Pasni in Pakistani Makran, and therefore identified as imports from the Harappan civilization. All of these objects, however, turn out to be made of *Lambis truncata sebae*, a species which occurs mainly on the coast of Oman (Gensheimer 1984:67, 71). *Turbinella* was, however, used in the Early Dynastic III period for a number of massive cylinder seals, up to 4.9 cm in length and 3 cm in diameter, found in the Royal Cemetery. Gensheimer suggests that rough cylinders or semi-prepared columellae of *Turbinella* were acquired by Mesopotamian seal-cutters in order to fashion these seals (Gensheimer 1984:71). *Chicoreus ramosus* was used for a ladle found at Tello (Gensheimer 1984:71), while an unworked example from the same site of Akkadian date was inscribed 'Rimush, king [lugal] of Kish' (Tosi and Biscione 1981:47) (2278–2270 BC). As the natural habitat of *Chicoreus* includes both the area between the Rann of Kutch and the Makran coast, as well as the Muscat region in Oman, these objects did not necessarily originate in the Indus Valley. Definite imports of shell from the Harappan region into Mesopotamia are thus difficult to pin-point, but it is clear that some of the shell objects made there, particularly those of *Turbinella*, were probably made from raw materials imported from the Indus Valley. The import of finished products from the Harappan area cannot be excluded, but the Mesopotamian character of much of the shellwork found at Tello and Ur suggests local manufacture.

As for other species of Indo-Pacific mollusca not necessarily limited to the Indus Valley region but represented in Mesopotamia from the Jamdat Nasr (Tell Gubba) to the Old Babylonian periods (Tell ed-Der), many more can be named, including *Engina mendicaria*, *Oliva bulbosa*, *Strombus decorus persicus*, *Conus ebraeus*, tusk shells (*Dentalium* sp.), and *Pinctada margaritifera* (Durante 1977:Table 1; Gautier 1978; Li 1989:179; Oguchi 1992; Charpentier 1994:165–6).

MINERAL

Carnelian

Carnelian (Sum. ^{na4}gug, Akk. *samtû*) has been described as 'the evenly-coloured red variety of chalcedony, ranging in colour from orange to light brown from the unequal distribution of iron oxide impurities'. It is characterized by 'compact fibrous structure, waxy lustre, high resistance to wear, fine splintery fracture, [and] hardness 6.5 on the Mohs scale, just below quartz and flint' (Tosi 1980:448). While chalcedony occurs widely throughout the Iranian plateau, the Hindu Kush, the Elburz mountains, around the Central Asian depressions, in southeastern Arabia and in the eastern desert of Egypt, the largest sources of chalcedony and particularly carnelian are the Ratanpur metamorphic beds in southern Gujarat (near the village of Ratanpur in Kathiawad) (Asthana 1993:275). Indeed it has been claimed that, up to the present day, this area has provided 'the great majority of the chalcedony varieties used in the world' (Tosi 1980:449), for there are few areas in Eurasia where the large pebbles and veins of carnelian exist which were required for making, among other things, the longer varieties of Harappan beads.

Amongst the earliest evidence of Harappan carnelian in Mesopotamia[15] are four 14–15-cm-long barrel-cylinder beads (Fig. XII.7) from the Royal Cemetery at Ur (Tosi 1980:450) along with several of the same type from Early Dynastic contexts at Kish. Of slightly later date are seven long barrel-cylinder beads from the Old Akkadian graves at Ur (Chakrabarti 1993:266). Etched and barrel-cylinder beads of carnelian, believed to be

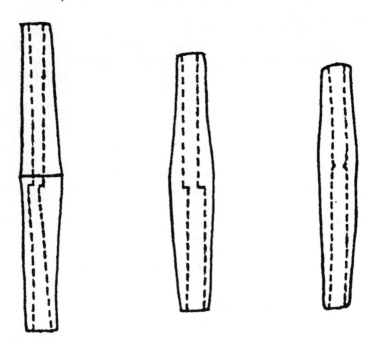

Figure XII.7 Examples of long-barrel carnelian cylinder beads from the Harappan site of Chanhu-Daro in Pakistan (after Mackay 1943: Pl. LXXXI)

Harappan, were discovered at Tello in contexts datable to the time of Gudea or the Ur III period (Inizan 1993:130 and Pl. 8.1:3). According to *Lugal-e*, a hymn to Ninurta from the time of Gudea, Ninurta received both lapis lazuli and carnelian from Meluhha (Heimpel 1993:53). This is echoed in the later, so-called 'Lipshur-litanies' which call Meluhha KUR *na4gug* (=*samtû*) (Leemans 1960:8) 'land of carnelian'. This testimony has been taken by W. Heimpel as a clear indication that the geographical term Meluhha designated the Harappan civilization or, at the very least, the area of Gujarat which supplied the bulk of the carnelian entering Mesopotamia (Heimpel 1993:54). Another indication that carnelian is meant by *na4gug* comes from an Old Babylonian text discovered at Ur (UET V 286) which mentions a *na4bir-gug* or 'kidney [shaped]' bead (?) of this stone (Leemans 1960:23). In the Harappan civilization the kidney-shape was used particularly for bone and ivory inlays, and it has been suggested that objects such as the one mentioned in UET V 286, or the actual kidney-shaped bone inlays from an Old Akkadian context at Tell Asmar in the Diyala, were Harappan imports (During Caspers 1970–1971:113).

Tin

The sources of Mesopotamia's tin, as noted already, have been sought from Southeast Asia to Cornwall. With regard to the former possibility, it has always proved difficult to establish any sort of an archaeological link between Burma, Thailand or any other part of mainland Southeast Asia and the Indian sub-continent, supposing that this was the location of Meluhha from which Gudea (Cyl B XIV 13) claims to have imported tin (cf. Chapter VII). As the Indian subcontinent has no tin itself, Meluhha's tin must have been acquired elsewhere and then trans-shipped to Mesopotamia, just as Dilmun's copper was acquired in Magan during the early second millennium BC. With a view to examining the evidence for a connection between the tin-rich regions of Southeast Asia and the Indus Valley, it is interesting to note that some years ago the claim was made that etched carnelian beads, a particularly diagnostic type fossil of the Harappan civilization, had been found at the early tin-bronze producing site of Ban Chiang in Thailand (Muhly 1981:140). This made the likelihood that Meluhhan tin was southeast Asian in origin less far-fetched than previously thought. In fact, however, scholars who have actually seen the Ban Chiang beads have confirmed that they are not Harappan at all, but date rather to the last centuries BC or first centuries AD when different types of etched carnelian beads, clearly distinct from those of the earlier Harappan period, were

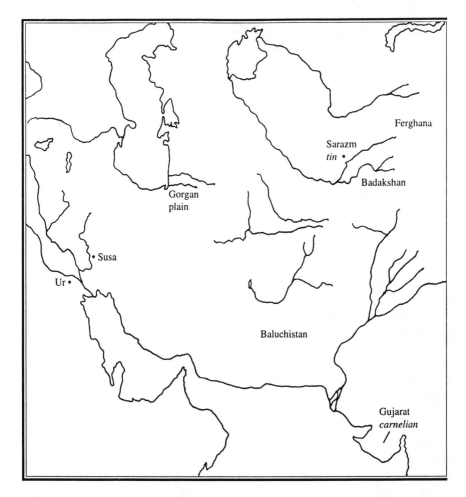

Figure XII.8 Map showing the location of Sarazm and nearby tin sources; the carnelian-rich area of Gujarat; and sites mentioned in connection with these commodities

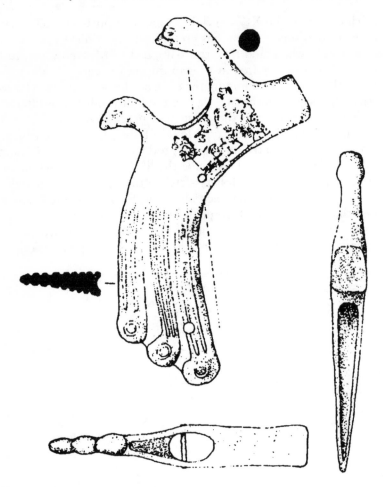

Figure XII.9 The inscribed axehead of Shulgi (2094–2047 BC) from Susa (after Tallon 1987: 178)

manufactured (Lamb 1965:90; Glover 1990:18, 38). For the time being, therefore, we should not consider southeast Asia a likely tin source based on this now discredited piece of evidence.

Although J.D. Muhly never mentioned Central Asia as a potential tin source in his 1973 *Copper and Tin*, Soviet archaeologists had pointed to tin deposits near Bukhara and in the Ferghana Valley (Fig. XII.8) of Uzbekistan in 1972 (Besenval 1988:231). In fact, both cassiterite and stannite are present throughout the mountains of Hissar, Zeravshan, Turkestan, Tien Shan and Pamir, and ancient indications of tin-mining have been observed, if not dated. At the moment, the sole reference to tin-working in this area occurs in a tenth-century AD geographical work by al-Muqaddasi (Besenval 1988:231). Recent metallurgical analyses of bronzes from Bactria (northern Afghanistan and southern Uzbekistan) attest to the manufacture during the late third and early second millennia of tin-bronzes (along with arsenical and lead alloys) so that it seems clear that the Central Asian tin sources were certainly in use by this period of time. One of the most important sites in this regard is Sarazm in the Zeravshan Valley near the border of Tajikistan and Uzbekistan, excavated by A. Isakov. Sarazm is characterized by a ceramic assemblage which includes clear imports from Baluchistan to the south, as well as types which relate to sites in the Gorgan plain of northeastern Iran, such as Tepe Hissar, Shah Tepe and Tureng Tepe of mid- to late third-millennium date (Besenval 1987: Figs. 4–8; cf. Besenval and Isakov 1989: Fig. 26). These ceramic finds demonstrate that the tin-rich region of Central Asia was certainly in contact with both the south and the west at a time when tin was beginning to enter Mesopotamia. Since lapis lazuli, which certainly originated in Afghanistan (Badakshan), is said by Gudea to have been acquired from Meluhha, it is quite probable that the tin which he received from that country originated in Central Asia as well.

Moreover, actual bronze objects of Bactrian type are known to have reached southern Mesopotamia in the late third millennium. A particularly fine axehead (Harper, Aruz and Tallon 1993:92) (Fig. XII.9) containing 7.08 per cent tin (Tallon 1987:29) and inscribed with a dedication by Shulgi (2094–2047 BC), was discovered at Susa in southwestern Iran, a city which was under the control of the Ur III state at that time, where a number of other typically Bactrian objects of stone and bronze have been discovered as well (Amiet 1986: Figs. 97–108). That tin may well have been travelling to Susa from Central Asia at the same time as the goods just mentioned is, moreover, suggested by the fact that, for a very brief interval of time during the Old Babylonian period, spanning the seventh to the ninth years of the reign of Zimri-Lim, Mari's source of tin was none other than Susa (Durand 1990:69; cf. Joannès 1991:67–76).

VEGETABLE

Cloves (Eugenia aromatica)
Having demonstrated above that the etched carnelian beads from Thailand cannot be used as evidence of late third- or early second-millennium contact between the Harappan civilization and Southeast Asia, we will now present the evidence for even more far-flung contact during the Old Babylonian period. Although it falls somewhat outside the purview of this study, a discovery made several years ago at the Old Babylonian site of Terqa (Fig. XII.10), just south of the confluence of the Khabur and the Euphrates in northern Syria, is so extraordinary that it deserves to be mentioned in the context of a discussion of eastern items found in Mesopotamia.

In the pantry of a house belonging to an individual named Puzurum, dated by tablets to *c.* 1700 BC or slightly thereafter, were found 'a handful of cloves...well preserved in a partly overturned jar of a medium size' (Buccellati 1983:19; cf. Buccellati and Kelly-Buccellati 1983:54). Prior to this discovery, the earliest attestation of cloves in the west dated to the first century AD when they are mentioned in Pliny's *Natural History* XII xxi 26–50. As J.E. Reade has pointed out in discussing this find, cloves are native to the Molucca islands off the coast of Indonesia and whether or not it was

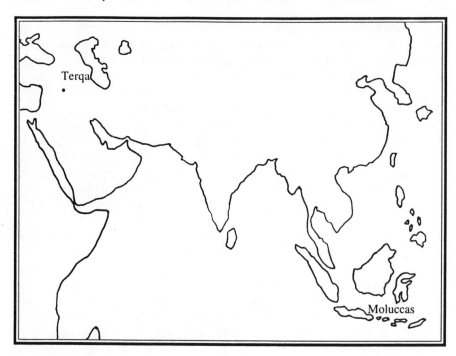

Figure XII.10 Map showing the locations of the Molucca islands, a traditional centre of clove cultivation, and Terqa, where cloves have been discovered in an Old Babylonian context *c.* 1700 BC

via India that they arrived in Mesopotamia, from which they were transshipped up the Euphrates to Syria, they are almost certainly of Moluccan origin (Reade 1986:331). Some amateur etymologists might like to suggest a link between Meluhha and Molucca, but the etymologies of Meluhha are many and varied and no consensus exists on whether the word is of Sumerian (Heimpel 1993:53) or non-Sumerian (Parpola and Parpola 1975:205–38) origin. Be that as it may, the Terqa cloves bear witness to the extraordinary range of Mesopotamia's contacts in the second millennium, even if they reached Syria via Harappan, Dilmunite, and/or Babylonian middlemen.

Cotton (*Gossypium arboreum*)

In the early seventh century BC the Assyrian monarch Sennacherib cultivated 'wool-bearing trees' (Akk. *nāš šipāti*) in his gardens at Nineveh (Luckenbill 1924:111). Ever since the discovery of the inscriptions which report this fact, this has been taken as an indication that *Gossypium arboreum*, or tree cotton (rather than the bush, *G. herbaceum*), was introduced into Assyria at that time. Later references from the time of Alexander the Great to wool-bearing trees on Tylos, the Hellenized name for Dilmun (Bahrain), echo Sennacherib's inscription and reinforce the impression that the cotton of Tylos was tree cotton as well.

The origin of Sennacherib's cotton has always been assumed to have been the Indian sub-continent. Early excavations at the sites of Harappa

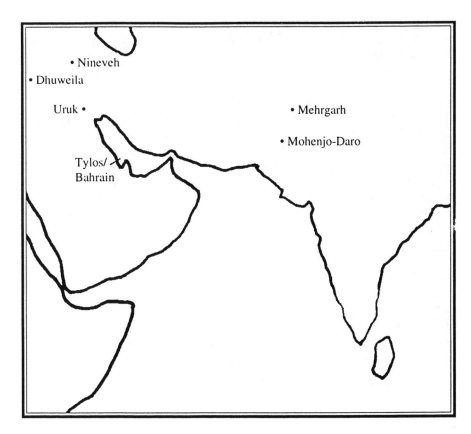

Figure XII.11 Sites of cotton cultivation mentioned in the text

and Mohenjo-Daro (Fig. XII.11) in Pakistan brought to light fragments of cotton fabric, demonstrating that it was cultivated in the Harappan civilization, but more recently seeds of *Gossypium* sp. have been discovered in a fifth-millennium context at Mehrgarh, in Pakistani Baluchistan, several millennia earlier than previously attested elsewhere in the region (Jarrige and Meadow 1980:128). While the origin of cultivated cotton in the Indo-Pakistani area is in no doubt, another recent discovery at Dhuweila, in the Jordanian desert, suggests that cotton may well have reached the West much earlier than previously thought. A range of calibrated C14 dates of 4450–3000 BC on cotton fibres embedded in plaster from Dhuweila (Betts, van der Borg, de Jong McClintock and van Strydonck 1994) confirms the presence of cotton to the west of Mesopotamia by the fourth millennium BC and, although no comparably early finds are yet known from Mesopotamia itself, this raises the question of whether Sennacherib was the first to try cultivating cotton in the region. Of course, the Dhuweila cotton may have been imported as finished textile, perhaps via Arabia, but in any case it is difficult to imagine it reaching the interior of Jordan without travelling via the Euphrates valley.

The discovery of textile fragments made of cotton in a Neo-Babylonian (or slightly later?) double-jar burial at Uruk (van Ess and Pedde 1992:257–8 and Taf. 146.1829) raises the question of whether the cotton used there was being grown in Babylonia by this time or whether it was imported from India or even Bahrain.

Cucumber (Cucumis sativus)

The cucumber is considered by botanists to be indigenous to India (Potts 1994b). Although attested in Old Babylonian lexical lists and their forerunners (Sum. *úkuš*, Akk. *qissú*) (Stol 1987:82) cucumbers, as we have seen in Chapter III, are rare in the Mesopotamian archaeobotanical record, appearing only in the Old Akkadian period at Tell Taya and at Neo-Assyrian Nimrud (Renfrew 1987:162). In the Gulf region, cucumbers in the nineteenth century formed part of the culinary assemblage of the expatriate Indian population (Potts 1994b), and it is not unlikely that their introduction into Mesopotamia was effected by migrants from the Indo-Pakistani region.

Rice (Oryza sativa)

In the past few years dates of *c.* 6000 BC have been published for rice cultivation at the site of Pengtoushan (Fig. XII.12) in northern Hunan province, China, and from this point on rice appears progressively over the next three millennia in Thailand, Vietnam and, by 2500 BC, eastern India (Bellwood, Gillespie, Thompson, Vogel, Ardika and Datan 1992:161–70).

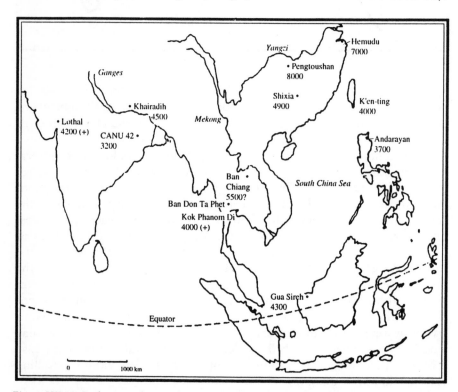

Figure XII.12 Early sites of rice cultivation in Asia (after Bellwood *et al.* 1992: Fig. 1; dates shown on the map are in years BP, not BC)

Given the fact that rice husk impressions are attested only slightly later at the Harappan site of Lothal in Gujarat, one might have expected to find rice in Mesopotamia during the course of the late third or early second millennium, but in fact the earliest written attestation does not occur until the Neo-Assyrian period when rice (Akk. *kurangu*) appears in medical texts (Potts 1991:2). Archaeologically, the earliest find in the region comes from period III (750–590 BC) at Hasanlu in Iranian Azerbaijan on Assyria's eastern flank (Potts 1991:2). The actual cultivation of rice in Mesopotamia is not attested until much later, however. Strabo says, 'Rice grows also in Bactriana and Babylonia and Susis, as also in Lower Syria' (*Geog.* XV i 18) but although some of his information is drawn from Aristobulus (fourth century BC) it is not clear whether his statement is anachronistic or reflective of his own time (first century BC). Certainly rice was being cultivated in Susiana in 318/317 BC when, as Diodorus Siculus informs us, a shortage of grain forced the Seleucid general Eumenes to feed his troops on rice, dates and sesame (XIX xiii 6).

CONCLUSION

The animals, minerals and plants of eastern origin which were used in ancient Mesopotamia arrived at different periods in the region's history, via very different mechanisms, of whose details we are, for the most part, ignorant. The strength of the ties which bound the greater Indian world and Mesopotamia was, however, much stronger than is generally assumed. Oppenheim believed that, by the end of the Old Babylonian period, Mesopotamia's links with Meluhha had been severed, perhaps as a result of the alleged 'Aryan invasion' of the sub-continent which, it was thought at the time, brought about the demise of the Harappan civilization (Oppenheim 1954:6–17). But as we have seen, some of the goods discussed here, such as rice and cotton, may well have arrived in the first millennium BC. Furthermore, this is precisely the period in which a remarkable congruence has been documented between the early Vedic system of calendrics and Mesopotamian menology (Pingree 1982:613–31). The similarities observed by D. Pingree are such that there can be little doubt of the Indian debt to Babylonian calendrics, just as aspects of Mesopotamian mathematics, astrology and astronomy seem to have reached northwest India during the Achaemenid period, judging by the survivals of formulations derived from the *Šumma ālu*-series of omens[16] in later Pali literature (Pingree 1992). The quantitatively meagre amount of material evidence of contact between the Indus Valley and Mesopotamia has often been taken as an indication that those contacts were never very significant, but as we are often told in archaeology, 'absence of evidence is not evidence of absence', and the astronomical data assembled by Pingree should serve as a warning that, for the earlier periods as well, we are perhaps underestimating the degree of contact between these two great centres of civilization.

NOTES

1 See now Wrede 1990:269 for the Ubaid period cattle figurines from the surface of Uruk. For the Late Uruk and Jamdat Nasr stone cattle figurines from Uruk, none of which show the characteristic hump of the zebu, see Becker 1993:Taf. 97–103.

2 To this could be added a representation from the Kassite period at Nippur, but as this occurs on an Harappan stamp seal, patently imported from the Indus Valley, it cannot be taken as an indication of the presence of the zebu bull in Mesopotamia.

3 Boehmer dates a terracotta representation of a water buffalo to the immediately post-Akkadian time of Gudea. An Ur III seal impression from the year Shu-Sin 2 which shows a water buffalo is thought to have been made with a re-worked Old Akkadian seal. See Franke-Vogt 1991:68 citing Collon, 'Water-buffaloes in Ancient Mesopotamia', *Ur* 2–3 (1982): 123–5 which was unavailable to me.

4 The supposed horn cores of water buffalo from the Late Uruk period (*c.* 3400–3100 BC) site of Grai Resh near Jabal Sinjar (Salonen 1976:167) have not been confirmed (H.-P. Uerpmann, pers. comm.).

5 Barrelet 1968:322 suggests that they came from Meluhha, but declines to say whether this should be firmly identified with the Indus Valley or, as was formerly believed, with a part of northeastern Africa.

6 Cf. bones identified as elephant from Middle Babylonian Nuzi and Middle Elamite Haft Tepe in nearby Khuzistan. See Moorey 1994:119.

7 The exact date is unknown and hotly disputed. See Sherwin-White and Kuhrt 1993:107–8.

8 The information on Seleucid use of the elephant is drawn from Bar-Kochva 1976:76ff.

9 Dobney and Jaques 1994:108, 116 identified this as *Herpestes edwardsi*, the Indian grey mongoose, but M. Uerpmann has shown convincingly that this identification is incorrect.

10 According to Harrison 1981:51, the modern distribution of the Indian grey mongoose does not extend beyond the east coast of Arabia where it reaches Bahrain, eastern Saudi Arabia, and Kuwait.

11 My thanks to W. Heimpel for sending me a copy of this interesting article in advance of its publication.

12 It is interesting that, from the contextual associations of the phrase 'good seed' cited by Sjöberg, this epithet is considered praiseworthy by him. In fact, in modern Persian, to call someone the 'seed of a dog' is amongst the worst insults imaginable. Since the entire tone of this composition is one of insult, viz. 'with the stench of a mongoose', it would seem to make more sense to consider 'seed of a dog' here in a pejorative sense rather than a praiseworthy one.

13 For a shell cylinder seal of Jamdat Nasr date from Tello, see Tosi and Biscione 1981:48.

14 For a wide variety of small shell objects of varying date see e.g. van Ess and Pedde 1992:226–46; Lindemeyer and Martin 1993:280–97.

15 A carnelian bead-making workshop area of Early Dynastic I date has been investigated at Larsa. See Chevallier, Inizan and Tixier 1982:

55–65. According to M.-L. Inizan, however, 'Raw material for the small beads seems to have been gathered in the immediate area of the site, and was doubtless carried by the Tigris'. See Inizan 1993:131.

16 These were concerned with interpreting the behaviour of animals and birds, e.g. at the city gates, in a temple, or near the palace. See Moren 1978, Moren and Foster 1988.

XIII West meets East

INTRODUCTION

After focusing in the previous chapter on the East, the emphasis shifts now to the West. In the present context 'West' means Greek and the purpose of this chapter is to look specifically at the encounter between the Greek world and southern Mesopotamia. That encounter cannot be treated as a series of discrete incidents, such as the great battles of the Persian Wars or Alexander the Great's conquest of the Achaemenid empire. Rather, it was a process, the roots of which lay much further back in time, and the effects of which were still being felt in the Parthian era. Evidence of that contact process took many forms, as we shall now see.

BEFORE ALEXANDER

The Greek world was certainly known to Babylonia and Assyria well before Alexander entered Babylon on 21 October 331 BC.[1] Evidence for contact dates right back to the early second millennium BC. Mesopotamian cylinder seals discovered on Crete (Møller 1983:85–104, 223–30) and documents from Mari concerning Cretan objects (Guichard 1993:53) attest to contact during the Old Babylonian period, as does a curious inscription from Kythera mentioning Naram-Sin of Eshnunna,[2] and the presence of Cypriot copper in southern Babylonia at this time (cf. Chapter VII). Mitanni Common Style cylinder seals from various parts of the region, including Cyprus (Salje 1990), Kassite cylinder seals from Thebes in Boeotia (Porada 1981:1–78) and Mesopotamian bronzes (Curtis 1994) found on Greek sites confirm that contact continued throughout the second half of the second and early part of the first millennia (cf. Guralnick 1992). The Neo-Assyrian kings extended their conquests as far west as Cyprus, and would have encountered ethnic Greeks in Phoenicia as well (Hegyi 1982:532). During one of his stays in Babylon, the Assyrian king Sargon II (721–705 BC) received gifts from the princes of Cyprus (Hegyi 1982:532). Early in the sixth century the Greek poet Alkaios of Lesbos referred to 'sacred Babylon', and the fall of Nineveh in 612 BC found an echo in a work by the poet Phocylides of Miletus who spoke of 'foolish Nineveh' (Kuhrt 1982:540). Ethnic Greeks are attested in Babylonia itself by the Neo-Babylonian period (Kuhrt 1990:184).

Thus, when Cyrus the Great (538–530 BC) and his army encountered Greek soldiers in the service of the Lydian king, Croesus, in 547 BC, it may have been the first sighting of Greek soldiers by eastern ones (Seibt 1977:23–4), but it was hardly the first time the cultures of East and West had encountered each other. By 525 BC ethnic Greeks were in the service of both the Persian king Cambyses (529–522 BC) and his Egyptian rival

Amasis, and in fact large numbers of Greek soldiers from Asia Minor, the islands and mainland Greece fought on the Achaemenid side in the Persian Wars (Seibt 1977:26, 28–9). When Cyrus the pretender visited his father Darius II (423–405 BC) in 405 BC he was accompanied on one occasion by a bodyguard of no less than three hundred Greeks commanded by Xenias of Parrhasia, but the most famous use of Greek mercenaries occurred several years later, when Cyrus, battling his brother Artaxerxes II (404–359 BC), had Xenias commanding four thousand heavily armed Greek soldiers, supplemented by Greek mercenaries who were 'unemployed' following the Peloponnesian Wars. The defeat of Cyrus at Cunaxa, somewhere upstream from Babylon on the Euphrates, gave rise to the famous retreat of the ten thousand described by Xenophon in his *Anabasis* (Ainsworth 1883:265–348). Finally, the late Babylonian astronomical diaries, so precious for the historical information they contain interspersed between records of celestial observations, refer to *KUR sa-mi-nè* (Salamis?), *KUR ku-up-ru* (Cyprus) and *KUR ia-a-mu-un-ia-am-mu* (Ionia or Greece generally) (van der Spek 1993:96).

Alexander's conquest of Babylonia and the establishment of the Seleucid empire in the East was therefore by no means the first sustained contact between Greeks and Mesopotamians in history. Centuries of intermittent contact preceded the appearance of Alexander and his army on the alluvial plain of southern Mesopotamia. A particularly graphic illustration of the penetration into Mesopotamia of Greek norms in glyptic and iconography prior to the time of Alexander is afforded by a discovery made by Sir Leonard Woolley at Ur. Beneath the floor of one of the so-called 'Achaemenid' houses was a terracotta sarcophagus which, although robbed in antiquity, still contained some two hundred clay impressions of gems of Greek, Egyptian, Babylonian, Assyrian and Persian origin as well as half a dozen impressions of Greek coins (Porada 1960:228–34). The date of this collection is provided by the impression of an Athenian coin from *c.* 450–440 BC. E. Porada interpreted the entire assemblage 'as a study collection enabling a probably non-Greek seal-cutter to produce superficially Greek style works which were obviously in great demand at the time' (Porada 1960:233). Thus, although the burial falls squarely in the middle of the reign of the Achaemenid king Artaxerxes I (464–424 BC), it clearly shows that the influence of Greek glyptic was being felt in Mesopotamia already prior to Alexander's conquest of the region.

ALEXANDER IN BABYLONIA

Much has been written on Alexander's entry into Babylon, the reaction of the local population and his manipulation of the royal traditions of the region for propagandistic purposes. In Chapter I we have already seen that, whatever else he did, Alexander immediately took steps to repair and renew the irrigation canals and drainage pattern of the lower Euphrates, a move which seems to have been motivated by practical naval concerns rather than by a sense of the welfare of the Babylonian agricultural regime. Indeed, Alexander had a fleet of warships trans-shipped from Phoenicia to

Babylonia in preparation for the invasion of Arabia (which never transpired)[3] and this certainly would have required that the Euphrates and the major canals leading south from Babylon be in good order. Arrian even says (*Anab.* 7 xix 4) that 'Alexander dug a harbour at Babylon, large enough to be a roadstead for a thousand ships of war'.

When Alexander entered Babylon, according to Quintus Curtius and Arrian, he and his men were overwhelmed by the people, who streamed forward, decorating the streets with flowers as choruses of priests sang (Curtius 5 1 17ff.),[4] all of which sounds more like opera than history. We are expected to believe that, whereas Cyrus had been tolerant, receiving similar treatment upon his arrival as well (cf. Chapter VIII), Xerxes and Darius had destroyed the temples of Babylon in the course of a failed Babylonian uprising. Hence, Alexander's reception was particularly warm as he was viewed as a liberator. Unfortunately, the 'tradition' of Xerxes' destruction of the Babylonian temples has been exposed as a late fabrication without foundation by A. Kuhrt and S. Sherwin-White (Kuhrt and Sherwin-White 1987:69–78).[5] Moreover, Kuhrt has clearly demonstrated that the *topos* of the joyful reception of the conquering hero in the account of Alexander's entry into Babylon is closely paralleled by the welcome given by the citizens of Babylon to Sargon II in 710 BC, and again to Cyrus the Great in 539 BC. Far from a spontaneous outpouring of affection, 'such a ceremonial occasion, carefully organised by both sides *after* the *fait accompli* of a major military victory and the flight or capture of the defeated king . . . represents the final outcome of complex negotiations forced on the citizens by an unenviable situation' (Kuhrt 1990:126). As P. Briant has observed (1990:55):

> Far from falling into decadence as a result of the heavy imposts of the Great King [i.e. the Achaemenid king], Babylonia experienced a period of peace and prosperity under Persian guardianship . . . All this then allows one to understand how, contrary to a thesis taken over directly from the ancient panegyrists of Alexander, the Macedonian was not received into Babylon as a liberator . . . Moving from Persian domination to Macedonian domination was clearly not regarded as progress by the Babylonian élites.

In any case, Alexander is said to have performed the offerings required of a Babylonian king when he entered the capital. He thereby became 'king of the totality' and 'king of the four world quarters' like many of his predecessors on the thrones of Mesopotamia (Schachermeyr 1973:282). In view of all that has been written about the synthesis between East and West which Alexander is alleged to have desired to forge – witness the mass marriage ceremony arranged in the winter of 325/4 BC by Alexander between ninety of his highest ranking officers and ninety daughters of aristocratic Persian families (Schachermeyr 1973:483–4) – we must consider the question of how far Alexander and his Seleucid successors altered the cultural make-up of southern Mesopotamia. Was a cultural fusion effected between Orient and Occident in this region? To answer this question we must consider a range of evidence, both historical and material, from a variety of sites in southern Mesopotamia, for the experiences of the individual cities of Mesopotamia under Alexander and his Seleucid successors were by no means entirely uniform. Given that neither Alexander nor the later Seleucids deported or otherwise fundamentally rearranged the population of southern Mesopotamia (for the case of Babylon and Seleucia-on-the-Tigris, see below), one would expect the older towns to reflect the survival of 'Mesopotamian' traditions, and the new foundations, in part peopled by Greek colonists, to be more Hellenized (Oelsner 1986:71). In fact, local circumstances differed from city to city and it is more realistic to expect something of a continuum ranging from barely Hellenized to very Greek settlements, rather than a simple dichotomy of settlement type, particularly since some of the so-called 'new' settlements were in fact already occupied sites which were 're-founded' by Seleucid rulers.

BABYLON AND SELEUCIA-ON-THE-TIGRIS

We have already discussed Alexander's entry into Babylon, and seen that it was probably just as stage-managed as the Greek accounts suggest, though not as a result of Babylonian joy at the conqueror's arrival. Thenceforth, Babylon (Fig. XIII.1) was, quite simply, an occupied capital, like Paris under the Nazis.

This did not necessarily mean that everything changed, however. The residential quarter known as Merkes was settled continuously from the Neo-Babylonian to the Parthian period, showing no really noticeable changes in the Seleucid era (Oelsner 1986:120). The theatre, perhaps begun by Antiochus I (281–261 BC) but certainly not finished until the Parthians decided to complete it in the second century AD, is the only truly Greek building yet discovered in Babylon (Schmidt 1941:844). While it has been suggested that in this region a 'Greek quarter' should be sought in the area of Babylon known locally as 'Homera', too little excavation has been conducted to confirm this. An area of burning excavated in this area was interpreted somewhat romantically by R. Koldewey as the remains of the platform built by Alexander for the funeral pyre of his friend Hephaistion, while E. Schmidt suggested that the openness of the area together with the signs of burning recalled much more the market-place or *agora* of the city which, according to various ancient sources, was destroyed by fire (Schmidt 1941:834).

Before the founding of Seleucia-on-the-Tigris (see below) Babylon was the administrative centre of the province of Babylonia (Fig. XIII.2). It was certainly garrisoned by Greek soldiers during the lifetime of Alexander and in subsequent decades, as a Greek *ostrakon* of early third-century BC date attests (Sherwin-White 1982:63). Since the payment of soldiers and mercenaries in the ancient world was one of the main reasons for the minting of coinage, the presence of a Greek garrison explains the immediate foundation upon Alexander's arrival of a royal mint (Waggoner 1979:269–80; Price 1991:64). Strabo's assessment of Babylon at this time is misleading. He writes (*Geog.* 16 i 5) that Babylon

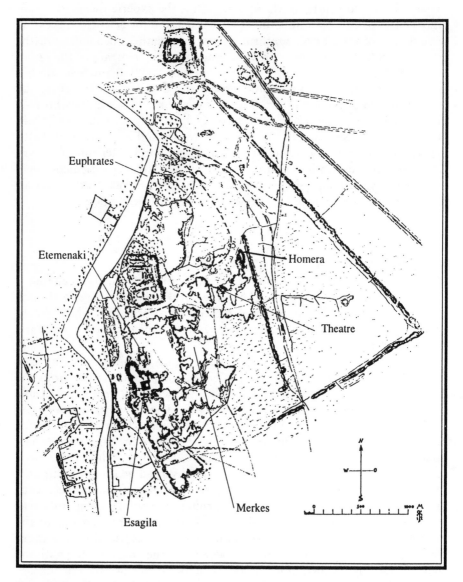

Figure XIII.1 Plan of Babylon (after Ravn 1942: Pl. III)

was neglected and thrown into ruins, partly by the Persians and partly by time and by the indifference of the Macedonians to things of this kind, and in particular after Seleucus Nicator had fortified Seleuceia on the Tigris near Babylon, at a distance of about three hundred stadia therefrom. For not only he, but also all his successors, were strongly interested in Seleuceia and transferred the royal residence to it. What is more, Seleuceia at the present time has become larger than Babylon, whereas the greater part of Babylon is so deserted that one would not hesitate to say what one of the comic poets said in reference to the Megalopolitans in Arcadia: "The Great City is a great desert".

Figure XIII.2 Map showing the locations of Borsippa, Babylon and Seleucia

What may be closer to the truth than 'neglect' on the part of the Achaeme-nids is shown by the Babylonian *Chronicle Concerning the Diadochi*, ac-cording to which Babylon was badly damaged by Antigonus in the struggle for power with Seleucus I (305–281 BC) for control of Babylonia and the 'Upper Satrapies' during the years 311 to 308 BC (Sherwin-White 1983:270). The ancient city partly in ruins, Seleucus founded the new capital at Seleucia-on-the-Tigris several years later, but probably not before 305/4 BC, according to Sherwin-White, and it was at about this time, undoubtedly as a result of the move of the seat of power to Seleucia, that the mint at Babylon ceased to function (Waggoner 1979:269).

In 274 BC, however, during the reign of Antiochus I, a portion of the population of Babylon was moved to Seleucia (see below), as both classical (Pausanias 1 16 3; Pliny, *Nat. Hist.* VI xxx; cf. Tscherikower 1927:90) and cuneiform sources (LBAT 243–244, cited in Oelsner 1986:388)[6] attest, but this was a case of reinforcement in time of war (Sherwin-White 1983:266 and n. 5) and should not be taken as a sign of 'neglect' or 'disfavour' vis-à-vis the ancient city. Nor indeed did this movement of people spell the demise of Babylon, as many lines of evidence attest. To begin with, it was at about this time that the main temple to Marduk and the Bit Akitu were renovated, and there is continuing evidence of a Babylonian and a Greek population residing in the city throughout the Hellenistic period. Cuneiform texts of many types (Table XIII.1) show that Babylonian cultural traditions were maintained and transmitted throughout the Seleucid period. The presence of stamped Rhodian and Thasian amphora handles, Attic black-glazed pottery, abundant Greek terracottas and paste copies of Greek gems help to put in context an early Parthian period inscription in Greek on a clay tablet from Babylon which (Sherwin-White 1982:55–7) lists the

> winners of various athletic competitions. The tablet reveals the operation of a gymnasium for Greeks and Macedonians who are named with Greek and Macedonian personal names and patronymics. The existence at Babylon of a Greek theatre, gymnasium and an agora, which Diodorus mentions only in the context of its destruction by fire at the hands of the Parthian satrap Himeros (*c.* 126 BC) probably does mean that the Greek community at Babylon was organized as a *polis*, though there is no direct evidence of this.

Indeed, an inscription (IG XII [5] 715) from the island of Andros, which Sherwin-White believes should be dated to the second half of the third century BC on the basis of its palaeography, honours one Dromon, whose ethnic Βαβυλωνιος, would seem to identify him as 'a Greek or Macedonian VIP' from Babylon (Sherwin-White 1982:68), yet another indication of an active Greek populace at Babylon well after the departure of part of its population to Seleucia.

The third-century BC Babylonian chronicle fragments show the crown prince (*mār šarri*), probably Antiochus, son of Seleucus I, 'signalling royal concern for non-Greek, Babylonian religion' by his presence at Babylon and his offerings in temples there sometime between *c.* 308/7 and 294/3 BC (Sherwin-White 1983:265). Similarly, the astronomical diaries contain a reference to the return of 'the satrap of Babylonia and the royal functionaries' in 274 BC to Seleucia, after which we learn, 'their parchment letters arrived at the citizens of Babylon. On the 12th day [of the XII month Adar] the citizens of Babylon went out to Seleucia' (van der Spek 1993:97). Moreover, a decree issued in 236 BC by an official of the temple to Marduk (the Esagila), and the assembly of Babylon, known in the astronomical diaries as 'the Babylonians of the Council of Esagila', endorsed a decision by Antiochus II (261–246 BC) to return a royal land grant and eight years later a chronicle refers to 'men of Babylon' (Sherwin-White 1982:69). Royal gifts from Seleucus III (225–223 BC) for the New Year's festival were received in 88 SE (224/3 BC), according to a Babylonian chronicle fragment (Sherwin-White 1983:265). Antiochus III, as the diaries report, took part in the New Year's festival at Babylon in 107 SE (205/4 BC) (van der Spek 1993:100). Finally, another astronomical diary reference from the reign of Antiochus IV (175–164 BC) for the year 169 BC alludes to what van der Spek believes was 'a festival of the Greek citizens in Babylon' (van der Spek 1993:100).

Text Category	Uruk	Babylon	Borsippa	Kutha	Kish	Nippur	Larsa	Ur	Selucia	Der
legal, economic and letters (esp. sales of slaves, property, prebends, exchange, division, disclaimers)	+500	*	*	*	*	*?	*	*	1	
historical (building inscriptions, king lists, chronicles)	*	*(Alexander-Mithridates)	*							
myths and epics (Gilgamesh, Nergal and Ereshkigal, Ishtar's Ascent)	*	(Gilg.)	(Lugal-e)							
rituals	*	*	*							
hymns and *balags* (Anu, Enlil)	*	*	*							*
incantations	*	*	*							
calendrical	*	*	*							
omens	*	*	*							
school texts	*	*	*			*				
astronomical	*	*	*							
astronomical–astrological	*	*	*							
mathematical	*	*								
medical	*	*	*							
lexical (ur_5-ra = *ḫubullu*)	*	*								

* = present in unknown quantity

Table XIII.1 Distribution of cuneiform texts in Seleucid Babylonia by site

This evidence clearly contradicts the view, espoused by Pausanias (1 16 3), that after the movement of people from Babylon to Seleucia 'only priests were left in Babylon' (cf. van der Spek 1985:546).

The cult of Esagila is last attested in the first century BC or early first century AD, and as at Uruk, the once sacred area was used for the construction of domestic Parthian houses. This then seems to mark a watershed in Babylon's existence, much more so than the movement of part of its citizenry to the new capital Seleucia.

The experience of Babylon's sister city, Borsippa (Fig. XIII.2), although much less well documented, is in many ways comparable to that of its more imposing neighbour. Although the bulk of the excavation there was done late in the last century by H. Rassam and early in the present one by Koldewey (Unger 1928:402–29), new excavations were initiated prior to the Gulf War by an Austrian expedition. Settled at least by the Old Babylonian period, Borsippa has yielded nearly as wide a variety of cuneiform texts (Table XIII.1) as Babylon and Uruk. Perhaps the most famous of these is a cylinder of Antiochus I dating to 268 BC which shows the Seleucid king restoring the Ezida, the chief temple of the city's leading god Nabu (Unger 1928:415–21), and the Esagila at Babylon. The text portrays Antiochus as a thoroughly Babylonian king, moulding the bricks for the two temples 'with my pure hands [using] fine quality oil'. Antiochus asks Nabu to regard him 'joyfully', and to ensure for him 'the overthrow of the countries of my enemies, permanent victories, just kingship, a happy reign, years of joy, children in satiety'. 'May my good fortune be in your pure mouth', Antiochus says, concluding, '[O] Nabu, first son, when you enter Ezida, the true house, may favour for Antiochus, king of lands, [and] favour for Seleucus, the king, his son, Stratonice, his consort, the queen, be in your mouth' (Sherwin-White and Kuhrt 1993:36–7).

To move from this text to Strabo's description of Borsippa is to go from the sublime to the ridiculous. After noting that 'Borsippa is a city sacred to Artemis and Apollo; and it manufactures linen in great quantities', Strabo tells us, 'It abounds in bats, much larger in size than those in other places; and these bats are caught and salted for food' (*Geog.* 16 i 7). Cuneiform texts concerning bats (Sum. *su-din*^{mušen}, *GAR/LAGAR.IB* = *arkab*^{mušen}, Akk. *šutinnu, arkabu*) (Civil 1984:5–9) attest to the use of their blood in magic (Ebeling 1957–1971:86), and they were certainly eaten in the Ur III period according to a medical prescription text (Civil 1960:57–72). 'Speckled' bats (*[su]-[di]n-dára*^{mušen}) also appear in an Ur III economic text (FLP 145) which lists quantities of various edible birds, eggs and turtles (Owen 1981:30, l. 17 and 37–38). As for the relevant zooarchaeological evidence, a large sub-species of the Naked-bellied tomb bat (*Taphozus nudiventris magnus*) has been found on a number of Mesopotamian sites, including Isin and Nippur (Boessneck and Ziegler 1987:145).

Strabo (*Geog.* 16 ii 5) makes it clear that Seleucia-on-the-Tigris which, as noted above, was founded sometime after 305/4 BC by Seleucus I, was one of the greatest cities in the Seleucid east, comparable only to Alexandria in Egypt and Antioch in Syria. As the Roman historian Ammianus Marcellinus wrote (XXIII 6) in the fourth century AD, Seleucia was the 'ambitious work' of Seleucus I Nikator (*ambitiosum opus Nicatoris Seleuci*) (cf. Tscherikower 1927:90), and it was appropriately distinguished in the cuneiform sources of the period from all other cities in southern Mesopotamia, whether old or new, by the epithet *āl šarrūti*, 'city of kingship' (Sherwin-White 1983:269). Still, it is not quite clear whether Seleucia was truly a new foundation, or whether it was founded on top of an earlier Babylonian city.[7] We have already discussed some of the sources relating to the alleged sinking fortunes of Babylon in relation to the rising fortunes of Seleucia. Pliny (*Nat. Hist.* VI xxvi 122) goes so far as to say that Babylon could not tolerate the rivalry and thereby sank into oblivion, surely an overstatement as the evidence adduced above confirms. Ancient estimates of Seleucia's population range from 600,000 soon after its founding (Pliny) to 400,000 near the end of the reign of Antiochus IV (*c.* 165 BC, Orosius) (Oelsner 1986:400, n. 539).

Excavations by an American expedition took place during the 1930s, and from the 1960s onward an Italian expedition worked at the site. The layout of the city is typically Greek with a rectilinear pattern of streets crossing at right angles to each other (Fig. XIII.3), several *agorai* and a theatre. Perhaps the greatest discovery made by the Italian expedition has been the 'Archive building' which was clearly the repository of a civic, administrative archive.

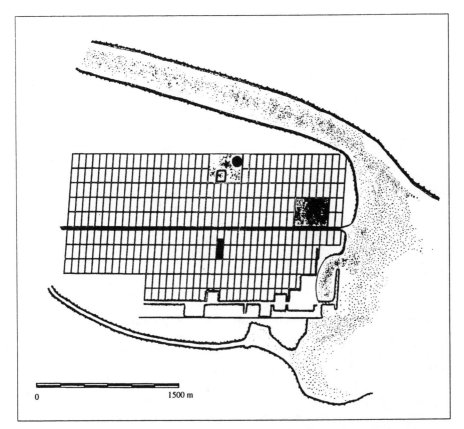

0   1500 m

Figure XIII.3 Plan of Seleucia-on-the-Tigris (after Invernizzi, Mancini and Valtz 1985: 89)

Destroyed by fire, perhaps when the Romans came through in AD 165/6 under Avidius Cassius, the building has yielded *c.* 25,000 clay bullae (including fragments) which were once attached to parchment documents (Invernizzi and Papotti 1991:33). Most of the bullae were impressed with seals bearing epigraphs relating to the salt tax (Gk. *alikē*) which, along with a general sales tax (Gk. *eponion*), a slave-sale tax (Gk. *andrapodikon*) and a canal tax (Gk. *ploiōn Euphratou*) (McEwan 1988:417), was one of the most important taxes imposed by the Seleucid government on the population (both Greek and native) of Babylonia. Considered stylistically, the majority of the seal impressions are so quintessentially Greek as to suggest that they were made by seals which were the work of trained gem-cutters from the West, possibly ethnic Greeks or Asiatics from the Greek Levant or Asia Minor. A small minority of the seal impressions are just as clearly not Hellenistic at all and are typically Babylonian, continuing the glyptic traditions of the Neo-Babylonian and Achaemenid periods (Invernizzi 1984:28–9). This preponderance of Greek over Babylonian style in the seal impressions is echoed by the fact that only one fragmentary cuneiform tablet and one bulla with a cuneiform legend were found in the Archive building, in contrast to the *c.* 25,000 largely Greek-style seal impressions on bullae.

A NEW FOUNDATION IN THE SOUTH

Seleucia was certainly not the only new foundation created by the Greeks in southern or central Mesopotamia. A number of other cities, about which we know very little, were also founded or re-founded at this time. One of Alexander's priorities in the south seems to have been the establishment of a new port-of-trade, no doubt with military responsibility for the area as well. During the Ur III and Old Babylonian periods Ur had certainly functioned as a gateway to Mesopotamia for vessels coming from the south. That same role, it would seem, had been ceded to Eridu by the time of Alexander's arrival. One of the earliest settlements in southern Mesopotamia (cf. Chapter II), Eridu was probably close to six thousand years old when Alexander entered Babylonia. F.H. Weissbach (cited in Unger 1938:464–70) suggested that Eridu was identical with the town called *Teredon* by various classical authors (e.g. Strabo, *Geog.* 16 3; Dionysios the Perieggetes 982; Ammiannus Marcellinius XXIII 6 10) and *Diridotis* or *Iridotis* by Arrian (*Indike* 41). According to Eusebius, drawing on Abydenus, Teredon was founded by Nebuchadrezzar II (604–562 BC) 'against the incursions of the Arabs' (Hodges 1876:73), an interesting allusion given the fact that Eridu is mentioned in Neo-Babylonian texts and bricks stamped with the standard inscription of Nebuchadrezzar were found on the northwest corner of the Eridu ziggurat (Oelsner 1986:320, n. 144). In view of Eridu's antiquity, however, this must be seen as a re-foundation, if indeed the testimony of Eusebius is correct.

Alexander's admiral Nearchus said that at Teredon, 'the merchants gather together frankincense from the neighbouring country and all other sweet-smelling spices which Arabia produces' (Arrian, *Anab.* 8 xli 8), and indeed Teredon became the main port of the south Mesopotamian king-dom of Characene in the first century BC and first and second centuries AD (Drouin 1890:134). In spite of these tantalizing references to the ancient city it must be admitted that, as excavations have concentrated on the earliest levels at the site, neither Seleucid texts nor ceramics or other small finds have ever been recorded from Eridu.

Not content, it seems, to go on using Teredon as the major port of the south, Alexander founded Alexandria-on-the-Tigris (Andreas 1894:1390–5) in the spring of 324 BC 'on an artificial elevation between the Tigris on the right and the Eulaeus [Karun] on the left, at the point where these two rivers unite' (Pliny, *Nat. Hist.* VI xxxi 139). There he settled some of his invalid soldiers as well as Babylonians from the 'royal city of Durine', even going so far as to order that one of the new city's quarters be called Pellaeum after his birthplace, Pella in Macedonia. The city was probably made capital of the 'satrapy of the Erythraean Sea', a term used to denote all of the Gulf/Indian Ocean/Red Sea belt, by either Seleucus II (246–226/5 BC) or III (226/5–223 BC) (LeRider 1965:38–9), but Pliny reports that it 'was destroyed by rivers', doubtless a reference to the endemic flooding in this region discussed in Chapter I, and was re-founded by Antiochus IV, prob-ably before 170 BC. Antiochus also established a royal mint at the city which, in O. Mørkholm's opinion, 'may be explained as a measure intended to revive and stimulate trade along the important sea route between India and the district at the mouth of the great Mesopotamian rivers' (Mørkholm 1970:44). Later still, Alexandria/Antiochia became the seat of power of a local dynasty, the kingdom of Characene, which existed in a more or less semi-autonomous state in the shadow of Parthia (Potts 1990, II: 8ff.).

ANCIENT SETTLEMENTS UNDER THE SELEUCIDS

How do the fates of Babylon or Seleucia compare with those of some of the other major settlements of the region? As noted above, the cities of Mesopotamia fared very differently under the new rulers. Let us examine briefly the situation at Uruk, Larsa, Nippur and Ur.

With a surface area of *c.* 300 ha Uruk (Fig. XIII.4) was by far the largest city occupied in southern Babylonia during the Seleucid period (Finkbeiner 1993:3). Moreover, we are fortunate in possessing a detailed 'topography' of the site at this time, reconstructed from the cuneiform sources (Falken-stein 1941), as well as the results of an intensive surface survey of the entire site conducted by U. Finkbeiner between 1982 and 1984 (Finkbeiner 1987:233–50).

The core of the public/religious area of Uruk was composed of the very ancient Eanna precinct, the Bit Resh shrine of Anu and his consort Antu and the Irigal of Ishtar and Nana (Oelsner 1986:77). We will now look at each of these major areas in turn. Other areas of interest for this period include U/V 18, an area of domestic houses excavated between 1969 and 1972 which produced important stratified ceramics as well as graves (cf. Chapter X) (Finkbeiner 1982:155–62), and two Seleucid era burial mounds at Frehat en-Nufegi to the north of the main site of Uruk (Pedde 1991:521–35).

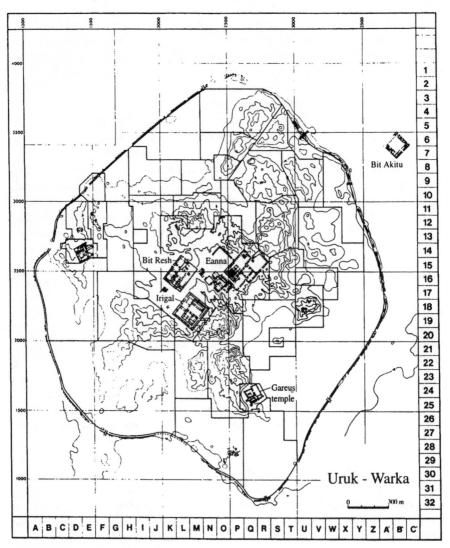

Figure XIII.4 Plan of Uruk showing the location of the main buildings of the Seleucid period (after Finkbeiner 1993: Abb. 1)

It has long been customary to believe that the Eanna sanctuary was destroyed at the beginning of the reign of Darius I (521–486 BC), as the latest, published Achaemenid text from the precinct was for many years a tablet dating to the second year of his reign (520/519 BC) (Oelsner 1986:327). A farm rental text (TCL 13: 182) from that year shows the involvement of the Eanna temple in private agriculture, for there we read, 'they will do [all] digging on the main canals at the expense of the treasury of Eanna' (van Driel 1988:129). In fact, like the destruction of the temples at Babylon, Eanna's destruction may never have happened. Moreover, whatever else occurred at Uruk in this period, 'there is certainly an un-published archive of the Uruk branch of the Egibi family which runs to almost the end of Darius I's rule' (van Driel 1987:162), as well as a small archive from Md XV 4, in the Bit Resh area, which dates to the reign of either Artaxerxes I (465–424 BC) or II (404–359 BC) (Kessler 1984:261), clearly demonstrating that the commercial life of the city was not brought to a halt by events in Eanna. The notion that Eanna was abandoned throughout the Seleucid period and that the cult centre of the city shifted west to the Bit Resh and Irigal has been countered by Oelsner, who points to brickwork of the Seleucid era on the northeast side of Eanna, and the continued use of the nearby Kassite temple to Inanna in this period as well (Oelsner 1986:79–80). Thus, although the Eanna precinct may have been less important than the Bit Resh and Irigal after Alexander, yielding neither Seleucid texts nor demonstrably Hellenistic small finds, it seems to have still been in use.

Located west of Eanna and excavated in 1912/13 (Finkbeiner 1987:233), the Bit Resh was a large building complex of unbaked brick situated on a brick terrace measuring 162 × 210 m located alongside the southwestern face of the Anu Ziggurat. According to YOS I 52, a clay cylinder inscribed with a foundation inscription, the reconstruction of the Bit Resh[8] was the work of one Anu-uballit Nikarchos, *Šaknu* (governor, city administrator) of Uruk, who completed it in April/May 68 SE i.e. 244 BC. Much has been written about this governor's name. In fact, the Bit Resh inscription calls him 'Anu-uballit, son of Anu-iksur, descendant of Ah'utu, *šaknu* of Uruk – to whom Antiochus [II], king of the lands, gave his second name, Nikarchos' (Doty 1988:96). As S. Sherwin-White and A. Kuhrt have discussed at some length, the practice of royal name-giving by Seleucid kings is one for which a number of precedents can be cited. Thus, for example, in the Bible Pharaoh rewards Joseph (Gen. 46, 45) with an Egyptian name, and in the Neo-Babylonian period, a number of high-ranking Jews at Nippur were given Babylonian names by Nebuchadrezzar II (604–562 BC). 'The purpose, primarily political, seems the same', they write, 'to reward and to assimilate people outside the ruling élite' (Sherwin-White and Kuhrt 1993:150; cf. Oelsner 1992).

This practice might be likened to the Queen's Birthday Awards or Honours List in which individuals are honoured for their good works with a knighthood or lesser order (e.g. an OBE. or MBE.). That this custom was not widespread in Babylonia, however, is shown by the fact that Anu-uballit is the only Babylonian known to have been so honoured by a Seleucid king (for Babylonians who themselves took 'extra' Greek names, see Oelsner 1992). Although this may be a reflection of spotty documentation, it must to some extent reflect the real magnitude of his effort in rebuilding the Bit Resh.

Architecturally, the Bit Resh is a typical Neo- or Late Babylonian-style temple with many courtyards and blocks of rooms within a large, rectangular perimeter wall. Later building activity associated with the cult rooms of Anu and Antu is also attested in the form of a baked brick façade, decorated with niches in Babylonian style and with glazed relief brick. According to an inscription found there this work was commissioned in 110 S.E. (202/1 BC) by another official at Uruk, Anu-uballit Kephalon, who bore the title *rab ša rēš āli ša Uruk*, which van der Spek has argued was 'chief of the clergy of Uruk' and 'the highest (administrative) authority of the temples of Uruk . . . just like the highpriest of Jerusalem' (van der Spek 1994:601, 604). The coincidence between this name and the name of the founder of the Bit Resh is more apparent than real. A glance at the list of personal names in the Seleucid texts in the Ashmolean Museum, most of which come from Uruk, shows that no fewer than twenty-seven individuals, distinguishable on the basis of their patronymics, had Anu-uballit as their first name (McEwan 1982:25–6). The latest dated document in which the Bit Resh is mentioned comes from 173 SE (139 BC), and the shrine was destroyed by fire sometime later in the Parthian era.

The prevalence at Uruk of personal names containing the theophoric element Anu- is part and parcel of the emergence of the cult of Anu (and his consort Antu) at Uruk in the Seleucid era as 'the most prominent deity at Uruk' (Kuhrt 1987:151). The scale of the Anu/Antu cult is borne out by the construction of the Anu Ziggurat in the Seleucid period. With sides measuring *c.* 110 m long, the Anu Ziggurat is the largest ziggurat in southern Mesopotamia, considerably surpassing its forerunner, the work of the Assyrian king Esarhaddon (680–669 BC), which in turn overlay the archaic terrace from the late fourth millennium BC (Oelsner 1986:83). This building history shows in fact that the area had been neglected for millennia between its first period of construction and until the Neo-Assyrian era, confirming the fact that Anu, although nominally at the head of the Sumerian pantheon (cf. Chapter VIII), had been little venerated until the Seleucid era. The veneration of Anu in this period does not, however, reflect an assimilation of Anu with Zeus under Greek influence as sometimes suggested, for personal names containing Anu as a theophoric element were already well attested in the time of Alexander. Thus, the elevation of Anu must have already taken place by the late Achaemenid period. If one is to seek an external explanation for the new interest in Anu at this time, it could be that an identification with the chief Achaemenid deity, Ahuramazda, the Iranian sky god/creator, was the cause (van der Spek 1985:541; cf. Kuhrt 1987:151).

The Irigal, excavated between 1932/3 and 1935/6 (Finkbeiner 1987:233), is an almost square building measuring 198 × 205 m to the south of the Bit Resh (Finkbeiner 1993:3). It was the shrine of Ishtar and Nana (Edzard 1979:1565–66) (not to be confused with Inanna/Ishtar). An Aramaic inscription on a glazed brick from the cult niche tells us that the Irigal was built by Anu-uballit Kephalon, probably around 200 BC (Oelsner 1986:86, 335), although earlier remains (but not pre-dating the Neo-Babylonian period) were found beneath the building and at least three or four phases of use could be discerned in the cult room itself. Most of the tablets found within the shrine date to the reign of Demetrius I (162–150 BC). After its destruction by fire, the area of the building lost its sacred associations and was covered by private houses during the subsequent Parthian period.

Finally, the Bit Akitu, the goal of an annual procession on the occasion of the New Year's celebration (Haldar 1957–1971:40–3), was a massive, square building, *c.* 140 m on a side with a huge courtyard (86.2 × 90 m) in the centre and almost two hundred rooms along three of its sides (Haldar 1957–1971:47–50). Located beyond the limits of the city wall just northeast of Uruk, the Bit Akitu was excavated in 1954/5 (Finkbeiner 1987:233), and is one of the few cult buildings in Mesopotamia for which contemporary religious texts outlining specific cult practices associated with it are extant (Falkenstein 1941).

The architectural remains, the enormous quantities of cuneiform texts of Seleucid date recovered and the sheer size of the settlement suggest that Uruk was one of the most important *Babylonian* cities in southern Babylonia during the Seleucid era. Although a palpable change is visible in local religion, best exemplified by the emergence of Anu as the chief deity of the city, this can in no way be attributed to the influence of Greek culture on the local pantheon. Both the veneration of typically Babylonian deities in temples of Babylonian style and the unbroken scribal tradition attested at the site suggest that we are not witnessing a renaissance or resuscitation of a Babylonian culture which had died out under the Achaemenids, but rather the flowering of Babylonian culture in particularly favourable circumstances (Oelsner 1986:95–6). Uruk appears in classical sources as Orchoë ('Ορχοη) (Pliny, *Nat. Hist.* VI xxvii 31), and was known to Strabo (*Geog.* 16 i 6) as the seat of a 'tribe' of Chaldaean astronomers whom he called the Orcheni. But the site is in fact rarely mentioned by Greek or Roman authors, probably because it was essentially a Babylonian city. Similarly, a satellite settlement of Uruk's known as Antioch-on-the-Ishtar Canal, founded in March 270 BC during the reign of Antiochus I (281–261 BC), is attested only in cuneiform sources, never in any of the classical texts (Sherwin-White 1983:266; McEwan 1988:415). Indeed, not a single written document in Greek is known from Seleucid Uruk, and only one from the Parthian period Gareus temple (Meier 1960:104–14). The seal-impressed bullae recovered at the site reflect the imposition of Seleucid fiscal administration, with offices such as that of *chreophylax* (finance officer, responsible for tax collection) and payment of sales tax (*eponion*) attested (Sherwin-White and Kuhrt 1993:154). However, as S. Sherwin-White has emphasized, the inscriptions of the bullae 'were in Greek because the language of the royal administration was Greek. They do not imply a Greek or Greek-speaking population' (Sherwin-White 1982:54). Little else, apart from the very exceptional Greek names of the two Anu-uballits mentioned above, belies Greek influence, and the evidence seems too deficient to accept G.J.P. McEwan's claim that Uruk became a Greek *polis* under the Seleucids (McEwan 1988:413ff.).

That there were ethnic Greeks living at Uruk and that they, both men and women, owned property and functioned as witnesses in legal documents (Funck 1984:43), attests to their complete integration into *Babylonian* society, rather than any sort of imposition of Greek norms on the ancient city. Indeed, no distinction is ever made between Greeks and Babylonians in purchase and sale documents at Uruk. Mesopotamia had always been multi-cultural, and in Babylonian legal praxis being a Greek in a legally binding transaction of whatever sort seems to have been no more noteworthy than being an Amorite, Aramaean, Arab, Elamite, Chaldaean, etc. Nowhere is this better illustrated than in a temple prebend sale text (BRM II 40) in which an individual named Sosandros, son of Diodor, son of Straton, takes part in a transaction witnessed by half a dozen people with patently Babylonian names – Ahu'utu, Hunzu, Ekurzakir, Gimil-Anu, Lushtammar-Ada, and Sin-liq-unnini – and recorded on a tablet which he then sealed. Sosandros gives his genealogy just as a Babylonian of this period would (cf. Chapter IX) but what is most remarkable is the fact that he is called *LÚ.UNUG.KI-a-a*, 'Urukean' or 'man of Uruk' (Funck 1984:44). Nothing but his obviously Greek name distinguishes Sosandros from his Babylonian brethren.

Still, it is interesting to note that some, at least, of Uruk's Babylonian inhabitants seem to have been influenced by Greek norms more than others. Thus, in contrast to Anu-uballit Nikarchos, none of whose descendants bore anything but good Babylonian names (Doty 1988:101, Fig. 2), Anu-uballit Kephalon's family was much more heterogeneous, at least to judge by the onomastic evidence. Doty has been able to identify the names of twenty-six related individuals belong to Kephalon's family in a total of fourteen texts (cf. Weisberg 1991:nos. 6, 31 and 33) and these show a striking propensity to mix Greek and Babylonian names, as shown in Table XIII.2 (after Doty 1988: Fig. 2). There we see that Kephalon himself, a Babylonian of Uruk whose ancestors all bore good Babylonian names, had three brothers with Babylonian names and one, Timokrates, with a Greek name. Kephalon's wife Antiochis, daughter of Diophantos, seems to have been Greek. Their two children bore a Greek (Diophantos) and a Babylonian (Belessunu) name, respectively. The younger Diophantos had two children, each of whom bore Greek names. Kephalon's brother Ina-qibit-Anu, christened himself with a Babylonian name, gave at least two of his three children Greek names. The name of his third child is not extant, but that individual is known to have had four children, all of whom were given Greek names. The last text belonging to this group dates to 132 BC and one can only wonder, if the family survived the Parthian conquest of Uruk, whether they began giving their offspring Parthian (Middle Iranian) names as assiduously as they had done with Greek names.

The 'end' of Seleucid Uruk is linked by Oelsner to the defeat of Antiochus VII at the hand of the Parthian king Mithridates *c.* 130/129 BC. Whether all of the temples were burned on this occasion we do not know but the signs of burning recorded in several of the shrines discussed above suggest this may have been the case. Thereafter, Uruk was much more heavily influenced by Parthian practices, as we have seen in discussing burial customs (Chapter X).

Larsa (Fig. XIII.5) is in many ways comparable to nearby Uruk, albeit on a smaller scale. The principal Seleucid period remains come from the temple of Shamash (*é-babbar*), the occupational history of which mirrored that of the Anu Ziggurat in that long gaps separated its original construction by Hammurapi (1792–1750 BC), from its renewal and renovation by Nebuchadrezzar II (604–562 BC) and Nabonidus (555–539 BC). From this point on the *é-babbar* seems to have been in continuous use till 314 BC when it is mentioned in a text from Uruk dating to the reign of Antigonus

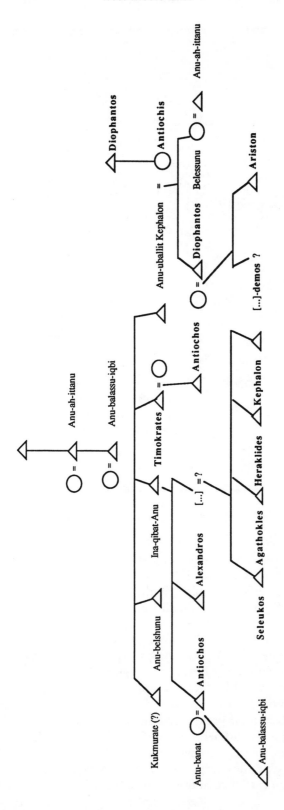

Table XIII.2 The Descendants of Aḫ'ūtu

Figure XIII.5 Plan of Larsa showing the location of the *é-babbar* (after Lecomte 1993: Fig. 1)

the One-Eyed, a Macedonian general and one of the Diadochoi (successors of Alexander) (Lecomte 1993:17).

The *é-babbar* was probably rebuilt during the reign of Antiochus III (223–187 BC), from which a cuneiform text written in Akkadian survives which names several Greeks including *Kur(?)-ri-il-lu-su* (Gk. Κυριλλος (Kyrillos)) and his brothers *Mi-in-an-dar* (Gk. Μενανδρος (Menandros)) and *A-pa-lu-ni-de* (Gk. Απολλονιδησ (Apollonidos)) (Zadok 1983:219).[9] The temple was still in use during the reign of Antiochus VII (162–129 BC) when it was destroyed by fire, perhaps in the same campaign by Mithridates which brought an end to the life of Uruk's sanctuaries around 130/129 BC. Given their proximity, it is hardly surprising that Uruk offers the closest parallels to Larsa. The Babylonian-ness of its temple, and its material culture, particularly ceramics, are all closely comparable (Lecomte 1989:83–147). With the exception of the presumably ethnic Greeks attested in the cuneiform text cited above, there is little sign of Greek influence.

Nippur, the great cult centre of Enlil whose shrine *é-kur* has been called a Mesopotamian 'Vatican' (Westenholz 1987:29), was a thoroughly Babylonian city in all respects. Little is known of its fate under Seleucid administration, however. Judging by the number of personal names from the early Seleucid period which contain Enlil as a theophoric element, Oelsner has suggested that the *é-kur* was still flourishing during the Seleucid period (Oelsner 1986:109). This is a supposition which is not supported by the cuneiform evidence, however, since the latest document from Nippur is dated after 317/316 BC (Zadok 1986:278). Still, if the case of the *é-kur* is comparable to Eanna, then the dearth of written evidence may be misleading. Pliny mentions a place called Hipparenum (*Nat. Hist.* VI cxxiii) which he says was the seat of a Chaldaean school of astronomy and which, although often identified with Sippar, is thought to be Nippur by Oelsner and others (Oelsner 1986:108, 292). Pliny's statement, if indeed it refers to Nippur, receives some slight support from the existence of an astronomical text from the site of Seleucid date.

Most of the 'late' remains from Nippur, however, date to the Parthian era. These include 'a huge fortress [which] rose around the remains of the ziqqurat' (Bergamini 1987:205) (Fig. XIII.6) of Enlil in the first century AD when Nippur was certainly an important site in Parthian Mesopotamia.

As for Ur, although it continued to be well populated during the Neo-Babylonian and Achaemenid period, the site seems to have been abandoned

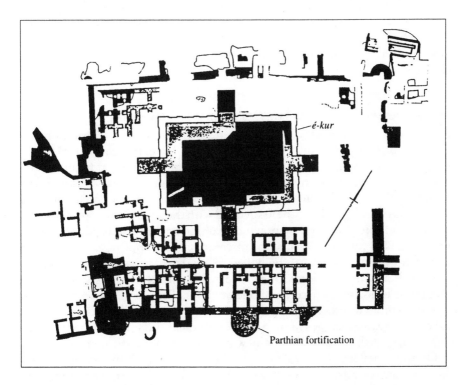

Figure XIII.6 Plan of Nippur showing the *é-kur* surrounded by the later Parthian fortification (after Bergamini 1987: Fig. L)

not long after Alexander's death (Oelsner 1986:75). The latest securely dated finds from Ur are two tablets, dating to the reigns of Alexander and Philip Arrhidaeus (323–316 BC), from a house of the Neo-Babylonian and/or Achaemenid period in the southern part of the site. Why Ur, which seemed to be flourishing during the Achaemenid period, should have been apparently abandoned by the end of the fourth century BC is unclear, but both Woolley and J. Oelsner attribute the desertion of the city to a change in the course of the Euphrates at that time (Oelsner 1986:77).

This rapid look at some of the major settlements of southern Mesopotamia under Alexander and his Seleucid successors has shown how variable was the impact of Greek rule on the Babylonian population. But throughout the period, the impression is one of continuity in the scribal tradition, religious practices and administration, and in those basic patterns of life which had obtained in Mesopotamia for centuries. Greek civil administration and taxation were no doubt present, but outside of Seleucia the impact of Greek institutions was probably insubstantial. Royal name-giving, as at Uruk, and undoubtedly inter-marriage probably played a role in welding the two cultures together at certain levels, but the character of Mesopotamian civilization remained largely unchanged until the arrival of the Parthians. One area which we have not commented on as yet is in the sphere of material culture, specifically ceramics. Much has been written over the years on the relationship between changes in the ceramic repertoire of a given area and its political, social and economic history. What impact did the Greek arrival have on local Babylonian ceramic tradition? This is a topic which has been widely discussed of late by a number of scholars, both from a Western Asiatic and from a classical Greek perspective, as we shall now see.

GREEK CERAMIC FORMS AND THE MESOPOTAMIAN TRADITION

Alexander's conquest of Western Asia resulted in the proliferation of previously unknown ceramic types (Fig. XIII.7) from the eastern Mediterranean to Bactria in Central Asia. The high degree of formal homogeneity and the repeated appearance of certain types such as two-handled amphorae and so-called 'fish-plates' strongly suggests that the spread of these 'new' types should probably be associated with the adoption of specific kinds of food and drink which were previously unknown or little-used in the area. In some cases, functional 'clusters' of ceramic types appear, as well as glass and metal vessels, which can be linked to a particular pattern of consumption, such as wine-drinking. In other cases the functional association of a given type is not so clear cut, and one of the challenges to the archaeologist is to determine whether the appearance of new ceramic forms is accompanied by observable changes in the archaeobotanical and faunal remains which might suggest the appearance of new cultivars or domesticated animals.

On the other hand, particularly in the case of Greek influence on West Asian ceramic traditions, one cannot dismiss the significance of immigrant colonists settling amongst indigenous groups or establishing new foundations. L. Hannestad, for example, believes that the spread of common (in

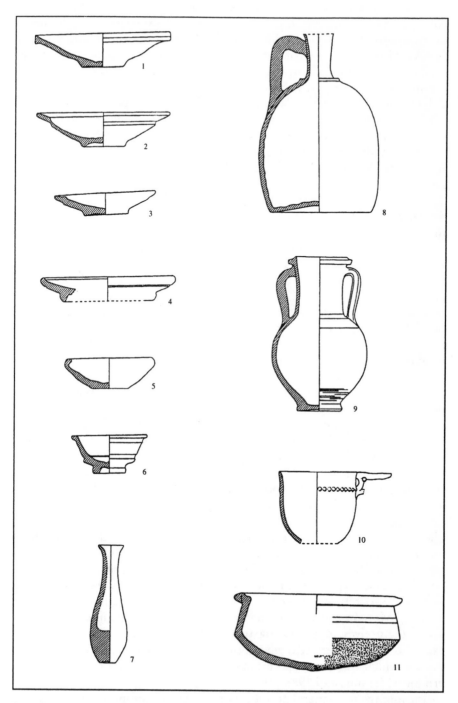

Figure XIII.7 Some typically 'Hellenistic' ceramic forms, from Seleucia. 1. glazed fish-plate; 2. glazed plate with offset rim; 3. glazed plate with thickened interior rim; 4. glazed plate with rolled rim; 5. bowl with in-curving rim; 6. glazed bowl with angular profile; 7. *unguentarium*; 8. glazed narrow-necked jug; 9. glazed two-handled amphora; 10. glazed *kantharos*; 11. glazed *lopas* (after Valtz 1991: Figs. 1–3)

this case, unglazed) as opposed to luxury (glazed) wares is a direct result of colonization. She writes, 'It is my hypothesis that a strong Greek influence on the pottery of a given site or area reflects a correspondingly strong Greek colonization, i.e. that pottery reflects Greek settlement patterns' (Hannestad 1983:84). In her opinion a 'radical change in the repertory of ceramic forms in the Near East' took place 'not with the beginning of the Achaemenian, but in the early years of the Seleucid period' (Hannestad 1983:101). This view, moreover, is shared by E. Strommenger who long ago remarked on the apparent rupture in the local, southern Mesopotamian ceramic tradition at Uruk, which was evident between the Neo-Babylonian/Achaemenid and the Hellenistic/Parthian periods (Strommenger 1967:33).

That such ruptures, where they occurred in already ancient settlements, were not normally complete is to be expected. As Hannestad observed, 'On the sites in central and southern Mesopotamia, types deeply rooted in the old local tradition continued to be produced in glazed ware side by side with the Greek shapes' (Hannestad 1983:104). While she finds that Greek influence was less apparent in common ware than in glazed ware, she points to the fact that the Greek *lopas*, a low-sided cooking pot, was copied in locally produced common ware (Hannestad 1983:104). This is, however, difficult to interpret. Does it reflect the adoption of Greek cooking practices by Babylonians, or does it signify production in local ceramics by local potters of forms for the Greek colonist market?

In general terms, southern Mesopotamia after Alexander was characterized by the continued production of local fine wares (e.g. eggshell ware, the beginnings of which go back to the Neo-Assyrian period), the introduction of completely Greek, pan-Hellenistic forms into the local glazed ceramic repertoire (e.g. the bowl with in-curving rim, the fish-plate, the bowl with angular profile and out-turned rim, the plate with thickened interior rim, the amphora, the *guttus*, the *lagynos* and the spiral bowl), the production of some of the older Mesopotamian forms (e.g. two-handled amphorae and carinated bowls) in glazed ware, the characteristic fabric of Hellenistic fine wares throughout Western Asia, the creation of some totally new glazed shapes (e.g. small bottle with pierced handles, used presumably as an *unguentarium*) unknown in the Greek world (why? produced for whom?) and the parallel use of both Greek and Mesopotamian shapes in cooking vessel types (Hannestad 1983:104–5). In sum, ceramics reflect a degree of syncretism between East and West not attested in the cuneiform sources. Moreover, it is clear that some local, Mesopotamian potters adapted themselves to producing to Greek norms when employed on the estates of Greek overlords, while others adapted their repertoire to a mass market which was more and more interested in acquiring the 'new', western forms (Hannestad 1983:119).

Turning from a general appraisal of southern Mesopotamia after Alexander to a specific examination of the new capital, Seleucia-on-the-Tigris, we can consult the valuable work of E. Valtz which details the ceramic assemblages of the site from the beginnings of Hellenistic influence to the end of the Parthian period. Once again, many Greek forms, including the fish-plate, *kantharos*, amphora, *lopas*, lamp and fusiform *unguentarium* are attested. As Valtz observes, 'The assemblages are characterized by un-mistakable details of Greek origin: the ring foot with grooved resting surface, the stemmed foot with moulded profile, the outturned and double-stepped rim, the vertical handle of various sections, the spur handle' (Valtz 1991: 54). Further, she suggests that 'city workshops were deeply and widely affected by Greek taste, also in the production of items for everyday life. A change in the ceramic stock of the city took place at the beginning of the Parthian age . . . [141–50 BC] . . . consisting mainly in a broadening of the range of previously adopted Hellenistic types' (Valtz 1991:56).

It should be pointed out that both Hannestad and Valtz approach Meso-potamian pottery in the Seleucid era from the standpoint of a classical archaeologist, familiar with classical and Hellenistic Greek forms. In con-trast, we find a very different view expressed by E.J. Keall who is engaged in publishing the Parthian period remains from Nippur, one of the most 'Mesopotamian' of all cities and a far cry from a Greek foundation like Seleucia-on-the-Tigris. Keall does not deny (Keall and Ciuk 1991:57)

that certain features present on the pottery in the Parthian period are the result of influences from the Mediterranean. But it is open to question whether these elements stem from the tradition of workshops run by Greek-speaking artisans, who had settled in what is now southern Iraq . . . or from a more general Mediterranean context, from cities such as Antioch-on-the-Orontes, where the elements of similar potting tradi-tions can be ascribed to something best covered by the loose term 'Hel-lenistic influence'. These 'foreign' elements in the Nippur corpus of pot-tery include certain surface embellishments that appear to copy Hel-lenistic decorative devices, as well as the use of a pair of handles on jugs which has led commentators to use the term 'amphora' for vessels of this kind. However, it is argued here that the actual shapes and sizes used by Parthian period potters in southern Mesopotamia, which must surely reflect what the pots were used for, represent a tradition of function that reflects a continuum of centuries of pot making in an 'indigenous mode', much more than it reflects drastic changes brought about by a taste for 'imported fashion'.

In discussing ceramic forms, Keall eschews the use of loaded, Hel-lenocentric terms like 'amphora', preferring to order pottery along different lines emphasizing volume and assumed function according to the following categories: *storehousewares*: e.g. vats, crocks, jugs, jars, cups, *kitchen-wares*: e.g. basins, pots, *tablewares*: e.g. dishes, pitchers, novelties (zoo-morphic pouring vessels) and *other specialties*: e.g. lamps, mortars, coffins. Further, Keall surveys the range of forms used in southern Mesopotamia from the Late Uruk to the Achaemenid period, emphasizing that the degree of Greek influence was much less significant than was continuity with the earlier, long-standing tradition of Mesopotamian ceramic manufacture.

In assessing this debate, the point is not the degree to which local tradi-tions persisted in southern Mesopotamia after the arrival of the Greeks, for that has been clearly indicated by the bulk of the non-ceramic data discussed earlier for all of the sites about which we have information, apart from Seleucia. The subject of acculturation and cultural syncretism, however, can never be treated in such black-and-white terms. Rather, in the face of an undeniably strong, 'Mesopotamian' character of extraordinary longevity, how are we to explain the intrusion of specific forms which come straight out of the Greek repertoire? There seems no reason to deny that ceramic forms associated with specific foodstuffs, beverages, food preparation techniques, modes of illumination (hence the appearance of lamps), etc. infiltrated southern Mesopotamia after Alexander and that these, in most cases, can be linked to specific, functional exigencies. Hannestad's belief that the adoption of Greek forms was a direct reflection of settlement by Greek colonists would hardly seem to be borne out by the available cuneiform documentation on ethnic Greeks in Seleucid Babylonia. Rather, we should consider whether Hellenistic tastes, of the palate rather than the intellect, were not more important than generally construed, and whether the conservative Mesopotamian tradition of food preparation, storage and serving was not substantially altered by the arrival of the Greeks, an alteration reflected visibly in the changes observable in the Mesopotamian ceramic repertoire of the period.

CONCLUSION

It is today widely recognized that the notion of Hellenism and Hellenization first propounded by the German historian J. Droysen in the early nineteenth century reflected the colonizing spirit of early modern Europe (Briant 1990:40). Alexander the European's 'Hellenization' of the barbarian Orient is today, in a post-colonial world, seen as a hollow claim. Far more impressive than the undisputed signs of the adoption of *elements* of Greek culture is the thoroughgoing continuity of Asiatic social, religious, economic and political forms. Nowhere is this more evident than in southern Mesopotamia where, as we have seen, most of our evidence points to the perpetuation of Babylonian civilization on all levels throughout the period of Seleucid hegemony. Fundamental changes in political administration – the transition from a period of Achaemenid domination to one of Seleucid control – obviously affected Mesopotamia, and more subtle changes, as significant as changes to the conservative dietary and food preparation domain, no doubt occurred as well. But Mesopotamia was hardly 'Hellenized' in Droysen's sense, any more than it had been Iranized by several centuries of Achaemenid rule. If anything, examples such as the dedications of Antiochus I recorded on his cylinder inscription from Borsippa, or the transactions of Sosandros, the 'man of Uruk', attest to the Orientalization of the Occidentals, rather than the Hellenization of the Orientals.

NOTES

1 'Or shortly thereafter'. For the date see Brinkman 1987:63.
2 This text has been discussed repeatedly since it was first published in 1853. For full bibliography see Potts 1990, I:225, n. 192.
3 A great deal has been written about the so-called 'last plans' of Alexander with respect to Arabia. Much of the literature is summarised in Potts 1990, II:4ff.
4 Cf. the discussion in Schachermeyr 1973:280.
5 The matter is, however, more complex. Cf. Joannès 1990: 180, n. 26, who notes that the change in titulature introduced by Xerxes, and the cessation in cuneiform documentation which one can observe both in temple (e.g. at Uruk and Sippar) and private archives (e.g. at Babylon and Borsippa) does bespeak a break in tradition and the installation of a new system. On Xerxes' titulature, see Joannès 1989:37. For an overview of the differing perspectives on Xerxes in Babylonia, see Stolper 1989.
6 The text dates the event to 18 October 274 BC.
7 Oelsner 1986:401 has proposed that Seleucia was founded on top of either Opis or Akshak, but this has been disputed by several scholars. Frayne 1991:402 has identified Opis with Tulul Mujaili' and Akshak with Tell Sinker, both of which are on the Tigris in the general vicinity of Baghdad. For more on the locations of Opis and Akshak, see Lendle 1986:214–6, 221–2, and Black et al. 1987:18ff.
8 It seems certain that, contrary to the foundation inscription, Anu-uballit Nikarchos did not build the Bit Resh from scratch. Building remains of eighth- to seventh-century BC date are located beneath the corner of the building (Finkbeiner 1993:7, Tab. 2) and both a hymn and a ritual text dating to 61 S.E., i.e. seven years prior to YOS I 52, mention the Bit Resh (Doty 1988:95, n. 1). Thus, as in so many cases of 'foundation', whether it be of cities or buildings, this was really a case of a re-foundation or rebuilding, perhaps a massive renovation, of an already extant structure.
9 The text itself is published in McEwan 1982: no. 26. Cf. Röllig 1960:376–91.

XIV Some Reflections

INTRODUCTION

The final chapter of this book is not an attempt to bring together the diverse topics discussed in the previous thirteen chapters, most of which stand on their own. Rather, it offers some reflections on the state of Mesopotamian studies with a few thoughts on how scholarship in the future might proceed. It is far from a critical appraisal of the entire field, and is offered more by way of stimulating thought amongst students and scholars little prone to reflect on these issues, than as a *status quaestionis* document.

CENTRE AND PERIPHERY IN ANCIENT MESOPOTAMIAN STUDIES

As stated in the Introduction, the topics dealt with in this book represent a selection of what, in my opinion, are essential areas which must be understood in order to have a basic grasp of what actually made Mesopotamia. It should be obvious that many traditional topics have not been dealt with, just as emphasis has been placed on topics often ignored in general works on the subject. To readers who may have found this approach too selective, I can only say that you delude yourself if you do not realize that *all* scholarship is selective. Neither Kramer's basic work *The Sumerians* nor Oppenheim's magisterial *Ancient Mesopotamia* dealt with soil and water, or rope and planks, or barley and water buffalo, in as great detail as has been done here, while their works were correspondingly richer in treating the traditional topics of Mesopotamian history, religion, literature and political ideology.

In the Introduction I spoke of the lack of general works which focused on the material basis of Mesopotamian society, from both an archaeological and a philological perspective, so here we have 'another' Mesopotamia, 'my' Mesopotamia. That there are 'many' Mesopotamias should by now be obvious to anyone familiar with the standard reference works on this area. Scholarly selectivity of subject-matter, intellectual bias and background, the national academic tradition from which one comes – all of these influence the kinds of data which are plucked from the vast corpus of available knowledge, given emphasis and sewn together to form the kind of tapestry we call social or archaeological history, be it loosely woven or tightly knit. But fundamental to any study, it must be stressed, is the *selective* approach to the data by which *all* scholarship is characterized.

It is obviously becoming more and more commonplace to speak of 'centre and periphery' in all sorts of social, economic and political studies of ancient societies, whether the data used is primarily archaeological or written. In this regard the field of Mesopotamian studies is no exception. Few Mesopotamianists would ever entertain the notion that Mesopotamia was anything but central to the ancient Western Asiatic constellation of polities in virtually all periods until the Ottoman era. Quite apart from the fact that the alleged centrality of Mesopotamia and the marginality of its neighbours is a flawed concept, which ignores the great efforts expended by a series of Mesopotamian rulers in precisely those areas considered peripheral by modern scholars (Potts 1993:200–1), what is of more interest in the present context is the notion of centre and periphery in Mesopotamian *scholarship*. One need only re-read the first chapter of Oppenheim's *Ancient Mesopotamia* to see how central certain domains of study have been in Mesopotamian scholarship, and how peripheral others. For Oppenheim, archaeology really only had a role in helping to elucidate the 'crucial millennium or more which preceded the earliest written documentation'. He never doubted for a moment (1977:10) that

> the texts on clay tablets are far more valuable, far more relevant, than the monuments that have been discovered, although the latter, especially the famous reliefs on the walls of Assyrian palaces and the countless products of glyptic art, offer welcome illustration to the wealth of factual information contained on clay tablets, stelae, and votive offerings.

Oppenheim's distinction between reliefs and glyptic art on the one hand, and the 'factual information' of written sources on the other, is as clear a rejection of archaeology's role as one could wish to find.

The traditional emphasis on Mesopotamian epic and mythic literature, in part sparked by the search for Biblical parallels (e.g. the story of the Flood), and fuelled by a desire to recover a literature of equal stature to that of Homer, long left many of the more mundane aspects of production and reproduction in Mesopotamian society ignored. Obviously, as the bibliography of this book indicates, this imbalance has been redressed in recent years, but the fact remains that whereas Gilgamesh was central to Mesopotamian studies, the analysis of most *realia* and *naturalia* was peripheral. One could say that the field has become democratized during the past few decades. The élite domains of literature, religion, law, astrology, astronomy, etc. have not been ignored, but formerly peripheral subjects, such as flora, fauna, means and modes of production, have come on strong. Furthermore, Oppenheim's belief that archaeology had little to add to the picture of life which could be gleaned from a study of the cuneiform sources has proven very wrong. The cuneiform sources themselves are silent on many aspects of production and exchange, on the sources of raw materials, and on the circulation of goods outside of the temple and palatial context (except in certain periods, like the Old Babylonian era). Flotation will recover archaeobotanical remains from sites which yield no texts and will provide the archaeologist with an indication of the cultivars, woods and weeds present. Even on sites where texts are found, it is more likely than not that they will say nothing about the flora of the site's environment, the climatic conditions, the temperatures used to fire the ceramics made there, the kind of treatment given to metal objects by the smiths of the town or the sources of the semiprecious stones used to make beads and cylinder seals. Sophisticated archaeological analyses, based on careful strategies of data recovery achieved with the use of fine-meshed sieves and scanning electron microscopes rather than hundreds of workmen, provide us with a wealth of information completely absent from the cuneiform record. Putting that information together with what is known from the written sources is a challenge which, if taken up, can only enrich our understanding of the past. Contradictions are as likely to emerge as much as confirmations, but Oppenheim was sadly unaware of the potential of sophisticated archaeological analysis, even in his own day, and of how misguided it would be to rely solely on the written record, or to use archaeological or iconographic data merely as an illustration for the texts.

THE CONSTRUCTION OF MESOPOTAMIA

Between the Bible, the Assyrian reliefs, the *National Geographic Magazine* and Cecil B. DeMille, a vivid, almost Hollywood-like picture has been built up of ancient Mesopotamia in the minds of many people. That 'construct' reflects the same selectivity and distortion as the very choice of domains of study in Mesopotamian scholarship do. Babylonian and Assyrian monuments, when first discovered, were viewed through the eyes of upper- and middle-class Europeans, schooled in the classical tradition, for whom fifth-century BC Athens, Rome and the Bible provided templates for their interpretation and evaluation. The classical tradition in Oriental scholarship is nowhere more apparent than in the work of Anton Moortgat, while Egyptological training contributed substantially to Henri Frankfort's early education. Notions of perspective, of 'arrest and movement', of naturalism and abstraction, were all part of the accumulated intellectual baggage of many of the early viewers of Mesopotamian material culture, and continue so to this day. It was, without doubt, Benno Landsberger's emphasis on the *Eigenbegrifflichkeit*, sometimes translated as 'conceptual autonomy', of the Mesopotamian world which most forcefully rejected this tendency to see Mesopotamia from anything but a Mesopotamian perspective. My belief is that the Mesopotamian perspective is not most easily arrived at by looking at the Stele of the Vultures or the *Epic of Gilgamesh*. This approach has too often led to comparisons with the art and literature of Mesopotamia's neighbours – the Bible, the Parthenon reliefs, Egyptian tomb painting, Greek epics. Comparative literature and cross-cultural studies in comparative civilizations are not unworthy fields of endeavour, but the foundation for them must be a solid understanding of each of the independent cultures being compared and this necessarily entails an appreciation of the social and economic infrastructure, not just the intellectual superstructure.

The definition of academic disciplines is, to a large extent, responsible for the image of Mesopotamia current in the literature today. Students of Assyriology will tend to know far more about Hebrew, Aramaic and general Semitic philology than they will about smelting technology, brideprice and dowry, or the salt tolerance of barley. Archaeologists, on the other hand, may be just as ignorant of many of the same domains as their Assyriological colleagues, equating material culture with concrete expressions of style and iconography, rather than the hardware of technological systems such as milling, weaving, smelting, ploughing, harvesting or shipping. Getting archaeology students to have a proper understanding of what the cuneiform sources say on any of these topics, as well as what the archaeological evidence might be, is a task which most academic archaeologists eschew, no doubt because they were often themselves brought up in the narrow strictures of an art historical approach. Anthropologically oriented archaeologists, while they may be more aware of environmental and climatic issues, not to mention the social, economic and political systems of non-Western societies, rarely have the faintest idea what the cuneiform record has to say on types of production, flora, fauna, etc. Their excuse for ignoring such information is often that they are 'prehistorians', yet the fallacy of dividing the aliterate prehistoric from the literate historic record can hardly be productive in an area which was already involved in many of the same types of production in late prehistory as were carried out in the early historic period (Yoffee 1979:11; cf. Nissen 1989:179–82).

What passes for anthropology in much of Western Asiatic archaeology is, more often than not, comparative, cross-cultural, ecological and evolutionary, involving extensive reading into the economies, social organization and political evolution of 'tribal' groups around the world. This has led to work on decision hierarchies in the Uruk period which has been informed by comparisons with the Ife of western Nigeria, the Bulamogi of Uganda and the Hawaiian and Tongan chiefdoms of the Pacific (Johnson 1973:5–9), and to speculation on marriage networks in the Ubaid period which draws much inspiration from a well-known work by the French anthropologist Claude Meillassoux (Forest 1989:219–20). By the same token, much of the early locational analysis of Mesopotamian settlement patterns adopted the central place principles which Christaller and Lösch had devised to explain the spatial patterning of market centres in central Europe.[1] If a social dimension can be added to Mesopotamian archaeology by reading such works, then they should be required reading for all members of this field. What strikes me as unfortunate, however, is the fact that in their quest for inspiration, for explanatory models and for comparative data generally, anthropological archaeologists have ignored a mass of unexploited, relevant information which derives, in effect, from the very 'native informants' they have been professing to study. Had the same zeal been applied to the reading and interpretation of the available cuneiform evidence as has been lavished on the 'tribal' literature, for want of a better term, much of relevance to the questions of greatest interest to anthropological archaeologists would have been revealed. A striking exception to the general trend just outlined is afforded by the work of Robert McC. Adams whose three masterly works (Adams 1965, 1981; Adams and Nissen 1972) on Mesopotamian settlement patterns are thoroughly laced with insights from the cuneiform record, just as they are with knowledge gleaned from reading into the more recent 'ethnohistory' of Iraq.

What accounts for this state of affairs? Why have archaeologists shied away from the rich detail of the cuneiform record? There seem to be a number of reasons. To begin with, I do not believe it is simply a case of 'you can't do it all'. Institutionally speaking, Western Asiatic archaeologists (apart from Biblical specialists) today certainly enjoy closer ties to the natural sciences than to their colleagues who study ancient languages. Particularly in the case of prehistoric projects, of which Robert and Linda Braidwood's have rightly become legendary, interdisciplinary work with natural scientists has become commonplace. Traditionally, because of the social science/humanities divide between departments of anthropology and departments of Near Eastern languages, there has tended to be little active cooperation between these two areas, although the collaboration between scholars such as Robert McC. Adams and the late A. Leo Oppenheim at the University of Chicago was a happy exception to this rule. Nevertheless, the disciplinary divide, coupled with the fact that the number of archaeologists interested in Mesopotamia, and often with an anthropological background, far outnumbers the handful of good Assyriological and Sumerological libraries in the world, has perhaps tended to exacerbate the split between the subjects. An archaeologist interested in Mesopotamia who is employed in Iowa or Arkansas may not find the CAD or the *Zeitschrift für Assyriologie* in his or her library, but is likely to find a decent selection of anthropological works there. Furthermore, he or she is probably housed departmentally, at least in the United States, with social and biological anthropologists rather than Assyriologists. The lack of a decent Assyriological library and colleagues, however, may be in some measure compensated for by the existence of colleagues in the natural sciences interested in and willing to collaborate on materials-based research. In such cases, however, it is unfortunate that insufficient use is made of the available cuneiform evidence, as the instance described in the Preface of this book revealed.

HOW TO PROCEED

There is little doubt that the notion of hypothesis-testing has exerted enormous influence on archaeologists over the past four decades, but it is equally clear that simply framed hypotheses, validated or invalidated, do not always advance the field by leaps and bounds. The past was a complex place, not one which can be reduced to a handful of simple, testable models. Studies such as those used in this book on salt gathering, leatherworking, textile manufacture, irrigation and many other topics, represent investigations of technical, economic and social domains which require wide-ranging data analysis before answers are yielded up to the inquiring scholar. As one example of scholarly method, let us emulate the 'broad spectrum revolution' in subsistence brought about by our Late Pleistocene forebears. Detailed geological and environmental awareness, studies of the technical vocabulary in Sumerian or Akkadian, cross-cultural comparisons of specific items of technology, ethnohistoric references to production, sophisticated analyses of material remains using the most advanced laboratory techniques available – these are all constituents in the 'broad spectrum' approach to *realiae, naturaliae, technologiae*. And like the multi-disciplinary teams at work in other fields, this sort of work, in

Mesopotamian studies, must necessarily involve scholars whose competence probably lies in only one of a variety of relevant fields, be it natural scientific, philological or archaeological.

The study of ancient Mesopotamia can move forward rapidly when archaeologists, Assyriologists and natural scientists cooperate. Lateral thinking and a desire to solve problems and explore domains for which no ready synthesis exists, can lead to an entirely new brand of study in which archaeology, philology and the natural sciences combine forces to elucidate problems which no one of these disciplines can, in isolation, ever solve.

But there is another dimension to multi-disciplinarity as well which most scholars tend to ignore. On any given day I may look at sherds and floor-plans, stare down the end of a microscope, pore over nineteenth-century accounts of village agriculture in lower Iraq, read an article on an Assyrian ritual for a dead king, calibrate C14 dates, or consult the CAD. All of these resources are part of the archaeologist's tool-kit. To define ourselves more narrowly as students of material culture is to place unnecessary restrictions on what we do and how we do it. Lateral thinking, lateral movement in and out of what have traditionally been considered different scholarly fields, and lateral contact with a range of specialists in other disciplines – these are the basic requirements if we are to continue making progress in our efforts to comprehend the complexity of ancient Mesopotamia.

NOTES

1 For an often overlooked critique of this approach in Mesopotamia, see Oates 1979:101–7.

Abbreviations

AAE	Arabian Archaeology and Epigraphy
AASF	Annales Academiæ Scientiarum Fennicæ, Series B
ADFU-W	Ausgrabungen der Deutschen Forschungsgemeinschaft in Uruk-Warka
AfO	Archiv für Orientforschung
AION	Annali dell'Istituto Orientale di Napoli
AKK.	Akkadian
Amherst	Pinches, T.G. The Amherst Tablets, i. London, 1908.
AMI	Archäologische Mitteilungen aus Iran
An.	Xenophon, *Anabasis*
Anab.	Arrian, *Anabasis*
AnOr	Analecta Orientalia
AOAT	Alter Orient und Altes Testament
AoF	Altorientalische Forschungen
AOS	American Oriental Series
ArOr	Archív Orientální
AS	Assyriological Studies
ASJ	Acta Sumerologica (Hiroshima)
ASOR	American Schools of Oriental Research
ATU	Archäische Texte aus Uruk
AUCT	Andrews University Cuneiform Texts
AUWE	Ausgrabungen in Uruk-Warka Endberichte
BAH	Institut Français d'Archéologie de Beyrouth, Bibliothèque Archéologique et Historique
BaM	Baghdader Mitteilungen
BAR	British Archaeological Reports
BASOR	Bulletin of the American Schools of Oriental Research
BBVO	Berliner Beiträge zum Vorderen Orient
BiMes	Bibliotheca Mesopotamica
BiOr	Bibliotheca Orientalis
BM	siglum of texts in the British Museum
BRM	Babylonian Records in the Library of J. Pierpont Morgan
BSA	Bulletin on Sumerian Agriculture
BSOAS	Bulletin of the School of Oriental and African Studies
CAD	Chicago Assyrian Dictionary
CNIP	Carsten Niebuhr Institute Publications
CRAIBL	Comptes rendus de l'Académie des inscriptions et belles-lettres
CT	Cuneiform Texts from Babylonian Tablets, etc. in the British Museum
DP	Allotte de la Fuyë, F.-M. *Documents présargoniques.* Paris, 1908–1920.

ED	Early Dynastic
FAOS	Freiburger Altorientalische Studien
FLP	Free Library of Philadelphia
FN	field name
Gen.	Genesis
Geog.	Strabo, *Geography*
GJ	The Geographical Journal
GN	geographical name
GR	Geographical Review
HdO	Handbuch der Orientalistik
Hh	lexical series ur_5-*ra* = *hubullu*
Hist.	Herodotus, *History*
Hist. Plant.	Theophrastus, *Historia Plantarum*
HSS	Harvard Semitic Studies
IG	Inscriptiones Graecae
IrAnt	Iranica Antiqua
IsMEO	Instituto per il Medio ed Estremo Oriente
ITT	Inventaire des tablettes de Tello conservées au Musée Impérial Ottoman, Paris, 1910–1921
JA	Journal Asiatique
JAOS	Journal of the American Oriental Society
JAS	Journal of Archaeological Science
JASP	Jutland Archaeological Society Publications
JCS	Journal of Cuneiform Studies
JEOL	Jaarbericht . . . van het Vooraziatisch-Egyptisch Genootschap 'Ex Oriente Lux'
JESHO	Journal of the Economic and Social History of the Orient
JNES	Journal of Near Eastern Studies
JRAS	Journal of the Royal Asiatic Society
JRCAS	Journal of the Royal Central Asian Society
JRGS	Journal of the Royal Geographical Society
KP	Der Kleine Pauly
LAK	Deimel, A. *Die Inschriften von Fara I. Liste der archaischen Keilschriftzeichen.* Leipzig: WVDOG 40, 1922.
Lau	Lau, R.J. *Old Babylonian Temple Records.* New York, 1906.
LB	siglum of texts in the Liagre Böhl collection, Leiden
LBAT	Sachs, A.J., Pinches, T.G., and Straßmaier, J.N. *Late Babylonian Astronomical and Related Texts.* Providence, 1955.
LG	(Isin-)Larsa (period) Grave (at Ur)
MB	Middle Babylonian
MCS	Manchester Cuneiform Studies
MDOG	Mitteilungen der Deutschen Orient-Gesellschaft
MDP	Mémoires de la Délégation en Perse
MEJ	Middle East Journal
MM	The Mariner's Mirror
MSL	Materialien zum sumerischen Lexikon
MVAG	Mitteilungen der Vorderasiatischen/Vorderasiatische--

	Ägyptischen Gesellschaft
MVN	Materiali per il vocabolario neosumerico
MW	Museum of the Franciscans at Werl, Westphalia
Nat. Hist.	Pliny, *Natural History*
NB	Neo-Babylonian
OB	Old Babylonian
OECT	Oxford Editions of Cuneiform Texts
OIP	Oriental Institute Publications
OLA	Orientalia Lovaniensia Analecta
OLP	Orientalia Lovaniensia Periodica
Or	Orientalia
OrAnt	Oriens Antiquus
OSP	Westenholz, A. *Old Sumerian and Old Akkadian Texts in Philadelphia*, pt. 2. Copenhagen: CNIP 3, 1987.
PG	Private Grave (Royal Cemetery of Ur)
PN	personal name
PSBA	Proceedings of the Society of Biblical Archaeology
RA	Revue d'Assyriologie
RE	A. Pauly and G. Wissowa, *Real-Encyclopädie der classischen Altertumswissenschaft*. Stuttgart, 1894–1980.
RGTC	Répertoire Géographique des Textes Cunéiformes
RlA	Reallexikon der Assyriologie
RTC	Thureau-Dangin, F. *Recueil des tablettes chaldéennes*. Paris, 1903.
SAAB	State Archives of Assyria Bulletin
SAOC	Studies in Ancient Oriental Civilization
SE	Seleucid era
SEL	Studi Epigrafici e Linguistici sul Vicino Oriente
SET	Studi Economici e Tecnologici
SET*	Jones, T.B. and Snyder, J.W. *Sumerian Economic Texts*. Minneapolis: Univ. of Minnesota, 1961.
SMS	Syro-Mesopotamian Studies
StOr	Studia Orientalia
Sum.	Sumerian
TAVO	Tübinger Atlas des Vorderen Orients
TCL	Musée du Louvre, Département des Antiquités orientales, Textes cunéiformes
TCS	Texts from Cuneiform Sources
TuT	Reisner, G. *Tempelurkunden aus Telloh*. Berlin: Königliche Museen zu Berin, 1901.
UCP	University of California Publications in Semitic Philology
UET	Ur Excavations, Texts
VAT	siglum of texts in the Vorderasiatische Abteilung of the Berlin Museum
VO	Vicino Oriente
VS	Vorderasiatische Schriftdenkmäler der Königlichen Museen zu Berlin
W	Warka (Uruk)

WdO	Welt des Orients
WMAH	Sauren, H. *Wirtschaftsurkunden aus der Zeit der III. Dynastie von Ur im Besitz des Musée d'Art et d'Histoire in Genf.* Naples: Ricerche VI, 1969.
WVDOG	Wissenschaftliche Veröffentlichungen der Deutschen Orient-Gesellschaft
WZKM	Wiener Zeitschrift für die Kunde des Morgenlandes
YNER	Yale Near Eastern Researches
YOS	Yale Oriental Series
ZA	Zeitschrift für Assyriologie
ZATU	Zeichenliste der Archaischen Texte aus Uruk
ZDMG	Zeitschrift der Deutschen Morgenländischen Gesellschaft
ZPE	Zeitschrift für Papyrologie und Epigraphik

Bibliography[1]

Adams, R. McC. *Land behind Baghdad*. Chicago and London: Univ. of Chicago, 1965.

Adams, R. McC. *Heartland of cities*. Chicago and London: Univ. of Chicago, 1981.

Adams, R.McC. and Nissen, H.J. *The Uruk countryside*. Chicago and London: Univ. of Chicago, 1972.

Afanasieva, V. Vom Gleichgewicht der Toten und der Lebenden. Die Formel **sag-AŠ sag-a-na** in der sumerischen mythologischen Dichtung. *ZA* 70 (1980):161–9.

Ainsworth, W.F. *Researches in Assyria, Babylonia, and Chaldaea*. London, 1838.

Ainsworth, W.F. A Commentary on the Anabasis of Xenophon. In: Watson, J.S., *The Anabasis, or Expedition of Cyrus*. London: George Bell & Sons, 1883:265–348.

Albright, W.F. Notes on Assyrian lexicography and etymology. *RA* 16 (1919):173–94.

Alexander, S.M. Notes on the jewelry from Ur. In: Schmandt-Besserat, D. (ed.), *The Legacy of Sumer*. Malibu: BiMes 4, (1976):99–106.

Allchin, F.R. Early cultivated plants in India and Pakistan. In: Ucko, P.J. and Dimbleby, G.W. (eds.), *The domestication and exploitation of plants and animals*. London: Duckworth, 1969:323–9.

al-Jadir, W. and al-Adami, K. Tablets from Sippar. *NABU* 1987:55.

al-Rawi, F.N.H. Tablets from the Sippar library I. The "Weidner Chronicle": A supposititious royal letter concerning a vision. *Iraq* 52 (1990):1–13.

al-Rawi, F.N.H. Two Old Akkadian letters concerning the offices of kala'um and nārum. *ZA* 82 (1992):180–5.

al-Rawi, F.N.H. and Black, J.A. The jewels of Adad. *Sumer* 39 (1983): 137–43.

Alster, B. Dilmun, Bahrain, and the alleged paradise in Sumerian myth and literature. In: Potts, D.T. (ed.), *Dilmun: New Studies in the Archaeology and Early History of Bahrain*. Berlin: BBVO 2, 1983:39–74.

Alster, B. Contributions to the Sumerian lexicon. *RA* 85 (1991):1–11.

Alster, B. and Vanstiphout, H. Lahar and Ashnan: presentation and analysis of a Sumerian disputation. *ASJ* 9 (1987):1–43.

Amiet, P. *La glyptique mésopotamienne archaïque*. Paris: Editions du CNRS, 1961.

Amiet, P. La représentation des temples sur les monuments de Mésopotamie. In: *Le temple et le culte*. Leiden: Nederlands Historisch-Archeologisch Instituut te Istambul, 1975:144–9.

Amiet, P. *L'âge des échanges inter-iraniens, 3500–1700 avant J.-C.* Paris: Notes et documents des Musées de France 11, 1986.

---

[1] Note that articles cited in *NABU* are cited by their article rather than their page number, as per the conventions of the periodical.

Amiet, P. Temple sur terrasse ou forteresse? *RA* 81 (1987):99–104.

Anderson-Gerfaud, P. L'utilisation de certains objets en céramique de Tell el'Oueili (Obeid 4): Rapport préliminaire sur les microtraces. In: Huot, J.-L. (ed.), *Larsa et Oueili, travaux de 1978–1981*. Paris: Editions Recherche sur les Civilisations, 1983:177–91.

Andrae W. *Das Gotteshaus und die Urformen des Bauens im alten Orient*. Berlin 1930.

Andreas, F. Alexandreia 13. *RE* 1 (1894):1390–5.

Anonymous. *Oman, a seafaring nation*. Muscat: Ministry of Information and Culture, 1979.

Armitage, P.L. Unwelcome companions: ancient rats reviewed. *Antiquity* 68 (1994):231–40.

Asthana, S. Harappan trade in metals and minerals: a regional approach. In: Possehl, G.L. (ed.), *Harappan Civilization* (2nd ed.). New Delhi/ Bombay/Calcutta: Oxford and IBH Publishing, 1993:271–85.

Aurenche, O. L'architecture mésopotamienne du 7ᵉ au 4ᵉ millénaires. *Paléorient* 7 (1981):43–55.

Aurenche, O. Remarques sur le peuplement de la Mésopotamie. In: Huot, J.-L. (ed.), *La Préhistoire de la Mésopotamie*. Paris: Editions du CNRS, 1987:85–9.

Bakhteyev, F.Kh. and Yanushevich, Z.V. Discoveries of cultivated plants in the early farming settlements of Yarym-Tepe I and Yarym-Tepe II in northern Iraq. *JAS* 7 (1980):167–78.

Baldwin, J.D. *Pre-historic nations: or, inquiries concerning some of the great peoples and civilizations of antiquity, and their probable relation to a still older civilization of the Ethiopians or Cushites of Arabia*. New York: Harper & Brothers, 1869.

Bar-Kochva, B. *The Seleucid army: organization and tactics in the great campaigns*. Cambridge: Cambridge Univ. Press, 1976.

Barrelet, M.-Th. Une construction 'énigmatique' à Tello. *Iraq* 27 (1965):100–18.

Barrelet, M.-Th. *Figurines et reliefs en terre cuite de la Mésopotamie antique I. Potiers, termes de métier, procédés de fabrication et production*. Paris: BAH 85, (1968).

Baudot, M.P. Vessels on archaic Near Eastern Seals. *OLP* 9–10 (1978–79):5–67.

Bauer, J. Zum Totenkult im altsumerischen Lagasch. *ZDMG Suppl*. 1/1 (1969):107–14.

Bauer, T., Landsberger, B. and von Soden, W. Lexikalisches Archiv. *ZA* 7 (1933):216–36.

Bayliss, M. The cult of dead kin in Assyria and Babylonia. *Iraq* 35 (1973):115–26.

Beale, T.W. Bevelled rim bowls and their implications for change and economic organization in the later fourth millennium BC *JNES* 37 (1978):289–313.

Beaulieu, P.-A. Swamps as burial places for Babylonian kings. *NABU* 1988:53.

Beaulieu, P.-A. Cuts of meat for king Nebuchadnezzar. *NABU* 1990:93.

Beaulieu, P.-A. An episode in the fall of Babylon to the Persians. *JNES* 52 (1993):241–61.

Beaulieu, P.-A. Notes on a local manifestation of Ninurta in the myth of Anzu. *NABU* 1993:22.

Becker, A. *Uruk Kleinfunde I. Stein.* Mainz: AUWE 6, (1993).

Beckman, G. A draft for an OB seal inscription. *NABU* 1988:72.

Bedigian, D. Is še-giš-ì sesame or flax? *BSA* 2 (1985):159–78.

Bedigian, D. and Harlan, J.R. Evidence for cultivation of sesame in the ancient world. *Economic Botany* 40 (1986):137–54.

Beke, C.T. On the geological evidence of the advance of the land at the head of the Persian Gulf. *The London and Edinburgh philosophical magazine and journal of science,* 3rd ser. 7 (1835):40–6.

Bell, G.L. *Amurath to Amurath.* London: Macmillan and Co., 1924.

Bellwood, P., Gillespie, R., Thompson, G.B., Vogel, J.S. Ardika, I.W. and Datan, I. New dates for prehistoric Asian rice. *Asian Perspectives* 31 (1992):161–70.

Benco, N.L. Manufacture and use of clay sickles from the Uruk mound, Abu Salabikh, Iraq. *Paléorient* 18 (1992):119–34.

Bergamini, G. Parthian fortifications in Mesopotamia. *Mesopotamia* 22 (1987):195–214.

Bergamini, G., Saporetti, C., Costantini, L., Costantini Biasini, L. and Masiero, C. Tell Yelkhi. In: *La Terra tra i Due Fiumi.* Turin: Il Quadrante Edizioni, 1985:41–61.

Bernard, V., Callot, O. and Salles, J.-F. L'église d'al-Qousour Failaka, état de Koweit. *AAE* 2 (1991):145–181.

Besenval, R. Découvertes récentes à Sarazm (R.S.S. du Tadjikistan): Attestation des relations au IIIe millénaire entre l'Asie centrale, l'Iran du nord-est et le Baluchistan. *CRAIBL* (April/June 1987):441–56.

Besenval, R. L'étain dans l'Asie centrale protohistorique: une source possible pour les métallurgistes moyen-orientales. In: *L'Asie Centrale et ses Rapports avec les Civilisations Orientales des Origines à l'Âge du Fer.* Paris: Mémoires de la Mission Archéologique Française en Asie Centrale 1, 1988:229–35.

Besenval, R. and Isakov, A. Sarazm et les débuts du peuplement agricole dans la région de Samarkand. *Arts Asiatiques* 44 (1989):5–20.

Betts, A., van der Borg, K., de Jong, A., McClintock, C. and van Strydonck, M. Early cotton in North Arabia. *JAS* 21 (1994):489–99.

Biggs, R.D. Semitic names in the Fara period. *Or* 36 (1967):55–66.

Bisi, A.M. Les déesses au tympanon de la Mésopotamie à Carthage. *Assyriological Miscellanies* 1 (1980):57–78.

Bjorkman, J.K. Second millennium BC prices of iron and copper. *NABU* 1989:14.

Bjorkman, J.K. The Larsa goldsmith's hoards – new interpretations. *JNES* 52 (1993):1–23.

Black, J.A. A-še-er Gi₆-ta, a balag of Inana. *ASJ* 7 (1985):11–87.

Black, J.A. A note on Zurghul. *Sumer* 46 (1989–1990):71–4.

Black, J.A. Eme-sal cult songs and prayers. *Aula Orientalis* 9 (1991):23–36.

Black, J.A., Gasche, H., Gautier, A., Killick, R.G., Nijs, R. and Stoops, G.

Habl as-Sahr 1983–1985: Nebuchadnezzar II's cross-country wall north of Sippar. *Northern Akkad Project Reports* 1 (1987):3–46.

Black, J.A. and Green, A. *Gods, Demons and Symbols of Ancient Mesopotamia: An Illustrated Dictionary*. London: British Museum Press, 1992.

Blackman, M.J., Stein, G.J. and Vandiver, P.B. The standardization hypothesis and ceramic mass production: technological, compositional, and metric indexes of craft specialization at Tell Leilan, Syria. *American Antiquity* 58 (1993):60–80.

Boehmer, R.M. Götterdarstellungen in der Bildkunst. *RlA* 3 (1957–1971):466–9.

Boehmer, R.M. Hörnerkrone. *RlA* 4 (1972–1975):431–4.

Boehmer, R.M. Orientalische Einflüsse auf verzierten Messergriffen aus dem prädynastischen Ägypten. *AMI* 7 (1974):15–40.

Boehmer, R.M. Das Auftreten des Wasserbüffels in Mesopotamien in historischer Zeit und seine sumerische Bezeichnung. *ZA* 64 (1975):1–19.

Boehmer, R.M. Glyptik von der alt- bis zur spätbabylonischen Zeit. *Propyläen Kunstgeschichte*. Berlin: Propyläen Verlag, 1976:336–63.

Boehmer, R.M. Kalkstein für das urukzeitliche Uruk. *BaM* 15 (1984):141–7.

Boehmer, R.M. Uruk: Funde im Zusammenhang mit Tierknochen. *BaM* 15 (1984):191–6.

Boehmer, R.M. Zur Funktion des Steinstifttempels in Uruk. *BaM* 21 (1990):49–65.

Boehmer, R.M. and Wrede, N. Astragalspiele in und um Uruk. *BaM* 15 (1985):399–404.

Boessneck, J. Tierknochenfunde aus Išān Baḥrīyāt (Isin). In: Hrouda, B. *Isin-Išān Baḥrīyāt I. Die Ergebnisse der Ausgrabungen 1973–1974*. Munich: Abhandlungen der Bayerischen Akademie der Wissenschaften, phil.-hist. Kl. NF 79, 1977:111–33.

Boessneck, J. Appendix B. Complete list of faunal specimens from Uch Tepe. In: Gibson, McG. (ed.), *Uch Tepe II. Technical Reports*. Copenhagen: Akademisk Forlag, 1990:131–40.

Boessneck, J. Tierknochenfunde aus Warka, Iraq (Nachtrag). In: van Ess, M. and Pedde, F. *Uruk Kleinfunde II*. Mainz: AUWE 7, 1992:267–70.

Boessneck, J. and Kokabi, M. Tierknochenfunde II. Serie. In: Hrouda, B. *Isin-Išān Baḥrīyāt II. Die Ergebnisse der Ausgrabungen 1975–1978*. Munich: Abhandlungen der Bayerischen Akademie der Wissenschaften, phil.-hist. Kl. NF 87, 1981:131–55.

Boessneck, J., von den Driesch, A. and Steger, U. Tierknochenfunde der Ausgrabungen des Deutschen Archäologischen Instituts Baghdad in Uruk-Warka, Iraq. *BaM* 15 (1984):149–89.

Boessneck, J. and Ziegler, R. Tierknochenfunde III. Serie 1983–1984 (7.–8. Kampagne). In: Hrouda, B. *Isin-Išān Baḥrīyāt III. Die Ergebnisse der Ausgrabungen 1983–1984*. Munich: Abhandlungen der Bayerischen Akademie der Wissenschaften, phil.-hist. Kl. NF 94, 1987:137–50.

Bökönyi, S. Environmental and cultural differences as reflected in the animal bone samples from five early Neolithic sites in Southwest Asia. In: Meadow, R.H. and Zeder, M.A. (eds.). *Approaches to Faunal*

Analysis in the Middle East. Cambridge: Peabody Museum Bulletin 2, 1978:57–62.

Bottéro, J. Getränke. *RlA* 3 (1957–1971):302–6.

Bottéro, J. Les inscriptions cunéiformes funéraires. In: Gnoli, G. and Vernant, J.-P. (eds.), *La mort, les morts dans les sociétés anciennes.* Cambridge and Paris: Cambridge Univ. Press and Editions de la Maison des Sciences de l'Homme, 1982:373–406.

Bottéro, J. The culinary tablets at Yale. *JAOS* 107 (1987):11–20.

Bowen, R.LeB. Arab dhows of Eastern Arabia. *The American Neptune* 9 (1949):87–132.

Brandes, M.A. *Siegelabrollungen aus den archaischen Bauschichten in Uruk-Warka.* Wiesbaden: FAOS 3, 1979.

Briant, P. The Seleucid kingdom, the Achaemenid empire and the history of the Near East in the first millennium BC. In: Bilde, P., Engberg-Pedersen, T., Hannestad, L. and Zahle, J. (eds.), *Religion and Religious Practice in the Seleucid Kingdom.* Aarhus: Studies in Hellenistic Civilization I, 1990:40–65.

Brice, W.C. *South-West Asia.* London: A Systematic Regional Geography 8, 1966.

Brice, W.C. The dessication of Anatolia. In: Brice, W.C. (ed.), *The Environmental History of the Near and Middle East since the Last Ice Age.* London/New York/San Francisco: Academic Press, 1978:141–7.

Brinkman, J.A. *A political history of post-Kassite Babylonia, 1158–722* BC Rome: AnOr 43, 1968.

Brinkman, J.A. BM 36761, the astronomical diary for 331 BC *NABU* 1987:63.

Brinkman, J.A. Meerland. *RlA* 8 (1993):6-10.

Buccellati, G. *The Amorites of the Ur III period.* Naples: Ricerche 1, 1966.

Buccellati, G. *Terqa: an introduction to the site.* Der ez–Zor, 1983.

Buccellati, G. and Kelly-Buccellati, M. Terqa: the first eight seasons. *Les Annales Archéologiques Arabes Syriennes* 33 (1983):47–67.

Buchwald, V. *Handbook of Iron Meteorites.* Berkeley: Univ. of California, 1975.

Buringh, P., Living conditions in the lower Mesopotamian plain in ancient times. *Sumer* 13 (1957):30–46.

Butz, K. Ur in altbabylonischer Zeit als Wirtschaftsfaktor. In: Lipiński, E. (ed.), *State and Temple Economy in the Ancient Near East*, 1. Leuven: OLA 5 (1979):257–409.

Butz, K. Landwirtschaft. *RlA* 6 (1983):470–86.

Butz, K. On salt again ... lexikalische Randbemerkungen. *JESHO* 27 (1984):272–316.

Butz, K. and Schröder, P. Zu Getreideerträgen in Mesopotamien und dem Mittelmeergebiet. *BaM* 16 (1985):165–209.

Cadoux, H.W. Recent changes in the course of the Lower Euphrates. *GJ* 28 (1906):266–77.

Caloi, L., Compagnoni, B., and Tosi, M. Preliminary remarks on the faunal remains from Shahr-i Sokhta. In: Meadow, R.H. and Zeder, M.A.

(eds.). *Approaches to Faunal Analysis in the Middle East*. Cambridge: Peabody Museum Bulletin 2, 1978:87–90.

Calvet, Y. Le sondage profond en Y 27 (1981). In: Huot, J.-L. (ed.), *Larsa et Oueili, travaux de 1978–1981*. Paris: Editions Recherche sur les Civilisations, 1983:15–69.

Calvet, Y. La phase 'Oueili de l'époque d'Obeid. In: Huot, J.-L. (ed.), *Larsa, travaux de 1985*. Paris: Editions Recherche sur les Civilisations, 1989:129–51.

Cassin, E. Le mort: valeur et représentation en Mésopotamie ancienne. In: Gnoli, G. and Vernant, J.-P. (eds.), *La mort, les morts dans les sociétés anciennes*. Cambridge and Paris: Cambridge Univ. Press and Editions de la Maison des Sciences de l'Homme, 1982:355–72.

Casson, L. *Ships and seamanship in the ancient world*. Princeton: University Press, 1971.

Cauvin, M.-C. Tello et l'origine de la houe au Proche Orient. *Paléorient 5* (1979):193–206.

Chadwick, R. A possible explanation for the kispum ceremony at the full moon. *Recueil de Travaux et Communications de l'Association des Études du Proche-Orient Ancien/Collected Papers of the Society for Near Eastern Studies [Montreal]* 2 (1984):45–6.

Chakrabarti, D.K. 'Long barrel-cylinder' beads and the issue of pre-Sargonic contact between the Harappan civilization and Mesopotamia. In: Possehl, G.L. (ed.), *Harappan Civilization* (2nd ed.). New Delhi/Bombay/Calcutta: Oxford and IBH Publishing, 1993:265–70.

Charles, J.A. The development of the usage of tin and tin-bronze: some problems. In: Franklin, A.D., Olin, J.S. and Wertime, T.A. (eds.), *The Search for Ancient Tin*. Washington D.C.: U.S. Govt. Printing Office, 1978:25–32.

Charles, M.P. Introductory remarks on the cereals. *BSA* 1 (1984): 17–31.

Charles, M.P. An introduction to the legumes and oil plants of Mesopotamia. *BSA* 2 (1985):39–61.

Charles, M.P. Onions, cucumbers and the date palm. *BSA* 3 (1987):1–21.

Charles, M.P. Irrigation in lowland Mesopotamia. *BSA* 4 (1988):1–39.

Charles, M.P. Traditional crop husbandry in southern Iraq, 1900–1960 AD *BSA* 5 (1990):47–64.

Charpentier, V. A specialized production at regional scale in Bronze Age Arabia: shell rings from Ra's al-Junayz area (Sultanate of Oman). In: Parpola, A. and Koskikallio, P. (eds.), *South Asian Archaeology 1993, I*. Helsinki: AASF Ser B 271, 1994:157–70.

Charpin, D. Notices prosopographiques, 2: les descendants de Bal-munamhe. *NABU* 1987:36.

Charpin, D. L'enterrement du roi d'Ur Šu-Sîn à Uruk. *NABU* 1992:106.

Charpin, D. Inanna/Eštar, divinité poliade d'Uruk à l'époque paléo–babylonienne. *NABU* 1994:39.

Chesney, Lt.-Col. F.R. *The expedition for the survey of the rivers Euphrates and Tigris, carried on by order of the British government, in the years 1835, 1836, and 1837; preceded by geographical and historical notices of the regions situated between the rivers Nile and Indus,* 2. London, 1850.

Chevallier, J., Inizan, M.-L., and Tixier, J. Une technique de perforation par percussion de perles en cornaline (Larsa, Iraq). *Paléorient* 8 (1982):55–65.

Childe, V.G. A prehistorian's interpretation of diffusion. In: *Independence, Convergence, and Borrowing.* Cambridge: Harvard Univ. Press, 1937:3–21.

Childe, V.G. War in prehistoric societies. *The Sociological Review* 32 (1941):126–38.

Childe, V.G. Archaeological ages as technological stages. *Journal of the Royal Anthropological Institute* 74 (1944a):1–19.

Childe, V.G. *Progress and archaeology.* London: Watts & Co., 1944b.

Childe, V.G. *New light on the most ancient east* (4th ed.). London: Routledge & Kegan Paul, 1952.

Civil, M. Prescriptions médicales sumériennes. *RA* 54 (1960):57–72.

Civil, M. Lexicography. *AS* 20 (1975):123–57.

Civil, M. On some terms for 'bat' in Mesopotamia. *Aula Orientalis* 2 (1984):5–9.

Civil, M. KBo 26 53 and funerary personnel. *NABU* 1987:9.

Civil, M. *The farmer's instructions: a Sumerian agricultural manual.* Barcelona: *Aula Orientalis* Supplement 5, 1994.

Cohen, M.E. *The cultic calendars of the ancient Near East.* Baltimore: CDL Press, 1993.

Cole, S.W. Marsh formation in the Borsippa region and the course of the lower Euphrates. *JNES* 53 (1994):81–109.

Collon, D. Ivory. *Iraq* 39 (1977):219–22.

Collon, D. Leier B. Archäologisch. *RlA* 6 (1980–1983):576–82.

Collon, D. *Catalogue of the Western Asiatic seals in the British Museum: cylinder seals III. Isin-Larsa and Old Babylonian periods.* London: British Museum Publications, 1986.

Collon, D. *First impressions: cylinder seals in the ancient Near East.* London: British Museum Publications, 1987.

Compagnoni, B. and Tosi, M. The camel: its distribution and state of domestication in the Middle East during the third millennium BC in light of finds from Shahr-i Sokhta. In: Meadow, R.H. and Zeder, M.A. (eds.), *Approaches to Faunal Analysis in the Middle East.* Cambridge: Peabody Museum Bulletin 2, 1978:91–103.

Conklin, H.C. *Folk classification: a topically arranged bibliography of contemporary and background references through 1971.* New Haven: Dept. of Anthropology, Yale University, 1980.

Cooper, J.S. *The curse of Agade.* Baltimore and London: Johns Hopkins Univ. Press, 1983.

Cooper, J.S. *Sumerian and Akkadian royal inscriptions I. Presargonic inscriptions.* New Haven: AOS Translation Series 1, 1986.

Courtois, L. and Velde, B. Observations techniques sur quelques poteries de Tell El 'Oueili (phases 'Obeid 0 à 'Obeid 3). In: Huot, J.-L. (ed.), *Larsa, travaux de 1985.* Paris: Editions Recherche sur les Civilisations, 1989:152–162.

Crawford, H.E.W. *Sumer and the Sumerians*. Cambridge: Cambridge Univ. Press, 1991.

Crawford, V. *Terminology of the leather industry in late Sumerian times*. New Haven: unpubl. PhD. diss., Yale Univ., 1948.

Cressey, G.B. The Shatt al-Arab basin. *MEJ* 12 (1958):448–60.

Curtis, J.E. Mesopotamian bronzes from Greek sites: the workshops of origin. *Iraq* 56 (1994):1–26.

Dalley, S. Old Babylonian dowries. *Iraq* 42 (1980):53–74.

Dalley, S. *Myths from Mesopotamia*. Oxford and New York: Oxford Univ. Press, 1989.

Dalley, S. Gilgamesh in the Arabian Nights. *JRAS 3rd ser.* 1 (1991):1–17.

Dalongeville, R. and Sanlaville, P. Confrontation des datations isotopiques avec les données géomorphologiques et archéologiques: à propos des variations relatives du niveau marin sur la rive Arabe du Golfe Persique. In: Aurenche, O., Évin, J. and Hours, F. (eds.), *Chronologies in the Near East*. Oxford: BAR IntSer 379, 1987:567–83.

Damerow, P. and Englund, R.K. Die Zahlzeichensysteme der Archaischen Texte aus Uruk. In: Green, M.W. and Nissen, H.J. *Zeichenliste der Archaischen Texte aus Uruk*. Berlin: ATU 2, 1987:117–66.

d'Anville, B. Recherches géographiques sur le Golfe Persique et sur les Bouches de l'Euphrate et du Tigre. *Mémoires de littérature, tirés des registres de l'Académie Royale des Inscriptions et Belles-Lettres* 30 (1764):132–97.

Deimel, A. Zur Erklärung sumerischer Wörter und Zeichen. *Or* 13 (1944):324–5.

Delattre, A. Les travaux hydrauliques en Babylonie. *Revue des Questions Scientifiques* 24 (1888):451–507.

Delitzsch, F. *Wo lag das Paradies?*, Leipzig: Hinrichs, 1881.

Delougaz, P. *Pottery from the Diyala region*. Chicago: OIP 63, 1952.

Delougaz, P. Architectural representations on steatite vases. *Iraq* 22 (1960):90–5.

Desse, J. Les faunes du gisement obéidien final de Tell el 'Oueili. In: Huot, J.-L. (ed.), *Larsa et Oueili, travaux de 1978–1981*. Paris: Editions Recherche sur les Civilisations, 1983:193–9.

Diakonoff, I.M. Extended families in Old Babylonian Ur. *ZA* 75 (1985):47–65.

Dobney, K.M. and Jaques, D. Preliminary report on the animal bones from Saar. *AAE* 5 (1994):106–20.

Donbaz, V. and Yoffee, N. *Old Babylonian texts from Kish*. Malibu: BiMes 17, 1986.

Doty, L.T. Nikarchos and Kephalon. In: Leichty, E., Ellis, M.deJ., and Gerardi, P. (eds.), *A Scientific Humanist: Studies in Memory of Abraham Sachs*. Philadelphia: Occasional Publications of the Samuel Noah Kramer Fund 9, 1988:95–118.

Downey, S.B. *Mesopotamian religious architecture: Alexander through the Parthians*. Princeton: Univ. Press, 1988.

Dowson, V.H.W. The date and the Arab. *Journal of the Royal Central Asian Society* 36 (1949):34–41.

Driver, G.R. and Miles, J.C. *The Babylonian laws*, I-II. Oxford: Clarendon Press, 1952–1955.

Drouin, E. Notice historique et géographique sur la Characène. *Le Muséon* 9 (1890):129–50.

Dunham, S. The monkey in the middle. *ZA* 75 (1985):234–64.

Durand, J.-M. Commerce de l'étain à Mari. *NABU* 1990:69.

Durante, S. Marine shells from Balakot, Shahr-i Sokhta and Tepe Yahya: their significance for trade and technology in ancient Indo-Iran. In: Taddei, M. (ed.), *South Asian Archaeology 1977*. Naples: Istituto Universitario Orientale Seminario di Studi Asiatici Series Minor 6, 1977:317–44.

During Caspers, E.C.L. Some motifs as evidence for maritime contact between Sumer and the Indus Valley. *Persica* 5 (1970–1971):107–18.

Ebeling, E. Baumfrevel. *RlA* 1 (1932):439.

Ebeling, E. Ehe. *RlA* 2 (1938):281–6.

Ebeling, E. Familie. *RlA* 3 (1957–1971):9–15.

Ebeling, E. Fledermaus. *RlA* 3 (1957–1971):86.

Ebeling, E. and Calmeyer, P. Gefäß. *RlA* 3 (1957–1971):182–3.

Edzard, D.O. *Die "zweite Zwischenzeit" Babyloniens*. Wiesbaden: Harrassowitz, 1957.

Edzard, D.O. Zum sumerischen Eid. *AS* 20 (1976):63–98.

Edzard, D.O. Nanai(a). *KP* 3 (1979):1565–6.

Edzard, D.O. Iturungal. *RlA* 5 (1976–1980):223.

Edzard, D.O. Meer. *RlA* 8 (1993):1–3.

Edzard, D.O. and Farber, G. *Die Orts-und Gewässernamen der Zeit der 3. Dynastie von Ur*. Wiesbaden: RGTC 2, 1974.

Edzard, D.O. and Veenhof, K. Inventare. *RlA* 5 (1976–1980):136–9.

Eidem, J. A note on the pulse crops at Tell Shemshara. *BSA* 2 (1985):141–3.

Ellison, R. Diet in Mesopotamia: the evidence of the barley ration texts (*c.* 3000–1400 BC). *Iraq* 43 (1981):35–45.

Ellison, R., Renfrew, J., Brothwell, D., and Seeley, N. Some food offerings from Ur, excavated by Sir Leonard Woolley, and previously unpublished. *JAS* 5 (1978):167–77.

Engel, T. and Kürschner, H. Holzreste und Holzkohlen (pflanzliche Makroreste) aus Uruk-Warka. In: van Ess, M. and Pedde, F. *Uruk Kleinfunde II*. Mainz: AUWE 7, 1992:271–4.

Englund, R.K. Dilmun in the archaic Uruk corpus. In: Potts, D.T. (ed.). *Dilmun: New Studies in the Archaeology and Early History of Bahrain*. Berlin: BBVO 2, 1983:35–7.

Englund, R.K. Administrative timekeeping in ancient Mesopotamia. *JESHO* 31 (1988):121–85.

Englund, R.K. *Organisation und Verwaltung der Ur III-Fischerei*. Berlin: BBVO 10, 1990.

Englund, R.K. Archaic dairy metrology. *Iraq* 53 (1991a):101–04.

Englund, R.K. Hard work – where will it get you? Labor management in Ur III Mesopotamia. *JNES* 50 (1991b):255–80.

Englund, R.K. Ur III sundries. *ASJ* 14 (1992):77–102.

Englund, R.K. and Nissen, H.J. *Die lexikalischen Listen der Archaischen Texte aus Uruk*. Berlin: ATU 3, 1993.

Evenari, M., Shanan, L. and Tadmor, N. *The Negev*. Cambridge (Mass.): Harvard Univ. Press, 1971.

Falkenstein, A. *Topographie von Uruk. I. Teil: Uruk zur Seleukidenzeit*. Leipzig: Ausgrabungen der Deutschen Forschungsgemeinschaft in Uruk-Warka 3, 1941.

Falkenstein, A. Das Sumerische. *HdO* 1/1–2 (1959):1–62.

Farber, W. Altassyrisch *addaḫšū* und *ḫazuannū*, oder von Safran, Fenchel, Zwiebeln und Salat. *ZA* 81 (1991):234–42.

Ferrara, A.J. *Nanna-Suen's journey to Nippur*. Rome: Studia Pohl Series Maior 2, 1973.

Fiandra, E. Ancora a proposito delle cretule di Festòs: Connessione tra i sistemi amministrativi centralizzati e l'uso delle cretule nell'età del bronzo. *Bollettino d'Arte* 5th ser. 60 (1975):1–25.

Fiandra, E. Porte e chiusure di sicurezza nell'antico Oriente. *Bollettino d'Arte* 6th ser. 67 (1982):1–18.

Fiey, J.M. *Mossoul chrétienne*. Beirut: Recherches publiées sous la direction de l'Institut de Lettres Orientales de Beyrouth 12, 1959.

Finet, A. Le vin à Mari. *AfO* 25 (1974–1977):122–31.

Finkbeiner, U. Seleukidische und parthische Gräber in Uruk. *BaM* 13 (1982):155–62.

Finkbeiner, U. Uruk-Warka XXXVII: Survey des Stadtgebietes von Uruk, vorläufiger Bericht über die 3. Kampagne 1984. *BaM* 16 (1985):17–58.

Finkbeiner, U. Uruk-Warka. The late periods. *Mesopotamia* 22 (1987):233–50.

Finkbeiner, U. Uruk-Warka. Fundstellen der Keramik der Seleukiden- und Partherzeit. In: Finkbeiner, U. (ed.), *Materialien zur Archäologie der Seleukiden- und Partherzeit im südlichen Babylonien und im Golfgebiet*. Wasmuth: Tübingen, 1993:3–16.

Forbiger, A. *Handbuch der alten Geographie, II*. Leipzig: Mayer and Wigand, 1844.

Forest, J.-D. Les "jetons" non urukiens et l'échange des femmes. In: Henrickson, E.F. and Thuesen, I. (eds.), *Upon this Foundation – the 'Ubaid Reconsidered*. Copenhagen: CNIP 10, 1989:199–226.

Foster, B.R. Ethnicity and onomastics in Sargonic Mesopotamia. *Or* 51 (1982):297–354.

Foster, B.R. *Before the muses: an anthology of Akkadian literature*. Bethesda: CDL, 1993.

Franke-Vogt, U. *Die Glyptik aus Mohenjo-Daro*. Mainz: Baghdader Forschungen 13, 1991.

Frankfort, H. The earliest appearance of the Sumerians. *Actes du XVIIIe Congrès International des Orientalistes*. Leiden: Brill, 1932:62–3.

Frankfort, H. *Archaeology and the Sumerian problem*. Chicago: SAOC 4, 1932.

Frankfort, H. *Stratified cylinder seals from the Diyala region*. Chicago: OIP 72, 1955.

Frankfort, H. *The birth of civilization in the Near East*. Garden City: Double Day, 1956.

Frankfort, H. *The art and architecture of the ancient Orient*. Harmondsworth: Penguin, 1970.

Frayne, D.R. Historical texts in Haifa: notes on R. Kutscher's "Brockmon tablets". *BiOr* 48 (1991):378–409.

Frifelt, K. 'Ubaid in the Gulf area. In: Henrickson, E.F. and Thuesen, I. (eds.), *Upon this Foundation – the 'Ubaid Reconsidered*. Copenhagen: CNIP 10, 1989:405–17.

Frifelt, K. *The island of Umm an-Nar I. Third millennium graves*. Aarhus: JASP 26/1, 1991.

Fujii, H. A special edition on the studies on textiles and leather objects from Al–Tar caves, Iraq. *Al-Rāfidān* 1 (1980):1–318 (in Japanese).

Funck, B. *Uruk zur Seleukidenzeit*. Berlin: Schriften zur Geschichte und Kultur des Alten Orients 16, 1984.

Gadd, C.J. Seals of ancient Indian style found at Ur. *Proceedings of the British Academy* 18 (1932):191–210.

Gadd, C.J. The spirit of living sacrifices in tombs. *Iraq* 22 (1960):51–8.

Garelli, P. The changing facets of conservative Mesopotamian thought. *Daedalus* 104/2 (1975):47–6.

Gautier, A. Notes sur quelques mollusques en provenance des fouilles de Tell ed-Der. In: de Meyer, L. (ed.), *Tell ed-Der II*. Leuven: Peeters, 1978:191–4.

Gelb, I.J. Ethnic reconstruction and onomastic evidence. *Names* 10 (1962):45–52.

Gelb, I.J. The ancient Mesopotamian ration system. *JNES* 24 (1965):230–43.

Gelb, I.J. Approaches to the study of ancient society. *JAOS* 87 (1967):1–8.

Gelb, I.J. The Arua institution. *RA* 66 (1972):1–32.

Gelb, I.J. Prisoners of war in early Mesopotamia. *JNES* 32 (1973):70–98.

Gelb, I.J. Typology of Mesopotamian seal inscriptions. In: Gibson, McG. and Biggs, R.D. (eds.), *Seals and Sealing in the Ancient Near East*. Malibu: BiMes 6, 1977:108–26.

Gelb, I.J. Household and family in early Mesopotamia. In: Lipiński, E. (ed.), *State and Temple Economy in the Ancient Near East*. Louvain: OLA 5, 1979.

Gelb, I.J. Measures of dry and liquid capacity. *JAOS* 102 (1982):585–90.

Gelb, I.J. and Kienast, B. *Die altakkadischen Königsinschriften des dritten Jahrtausends v. Chr*. Wiesbaden: FAOS 7, 1990.

Gelb, I.J., Steinkeller, P. and Whiting, R.M., Jr. *Earliest land tenure systems in the Near East: ancient Kudurrus*. Chicago: OIP 104, 1991.

Genouillac, H. de. *Fouilles de Telloh*. Paris: Geuthner, 1934.

Gensheimer, T.R. The role of shell in Mesopotamia: evidence for trade exchange with Oman and the Indus Valley. *Paléorient* 10 (1984):65–73.

Genthe, S. *Der Persische Meerbusen: Geschichte und Morphologie*. Marburg: Inaugural Dissertation, 1896.

George, A.R. *House most high: the temples of ancient Mesopotamia*. Winona Lake: Eisenbrauns, 1992.

George, A.R. An ancient mistranslation in *BRM* IV 8. *NABU* 1994:26.

Gibson, McG. *The city and area of Kish*. Coconut Grove: Field Research Reports, 1972.

Gibson, McG. (ed.), *Uch Tepe I. Tell Razuk, Tell Ahmed al-Mughir, Tell Ajamat*. Copenhagen: Akademisk Forlag, 1981.

Glaser, E. *Skizze der Geschichte und Geographie Arabiens von den ältesten Zeiten bis zum Propheten Muhammad*. Berlin: Weidmann, 1890.

Glassner, J.-J. Aspects du don, de l'échange et formes d'appropriation du sol dans la Mésopotamie du IIIe millénaire, avant la fondation de l'empire d'Ur. *JA* 273 (1985):11–59.

Glassner, J.-J. Women, hospitality and the honor of the family. In: Lesko, B.S. (ed.), *Women's Earliest Records from Ancient Egypt and Western Asia*. Atlanta: Scholars Press, 1989:71–90.

Glassner, J.-J. L'hospitalité en Mésopotamie ancienne: aspect de la question de l'étranger. *ZA* 80 (1990):60–75.

Glover, I. *Early trade between India and Southeast Asia: a link in the development of a world trading system*. Hull: Centre for Southeast Asian Studies Occasional Paper 16, 1990.

Goetze, A. Umma texts concerning reed mats. *JCS* 2 (1948):165–202.

Gomi, T. A note on g u r, a capacity unit of the Ur III period. *ZA* 83 (1993):31–41.

Gouin, P. Bovins et laitages en Mésopotamie méridionale au 3ème millénaire: Quelques commentaires sur la "frise à la laiterie" de el-'Obeid. *Iraq* 55 (1993):135–45.

Graeve, M.-C. de. *The ships of the ancient Near East*. Louvain: OLA 7, 1981.

Gragg, G. *The Keš temple hymn*. Locust Valley: TCS III, 1969.

Green, A.R.W. *The role of human sacrifice in the ancient Near East*. Missoula: ASOR Diss. Ser. 1, 1975.

Green, M.W. A Note on an archaic period geographical list from Warka. *JNES* 36 (1977):293–4.

Green, M.W. Animal husbandry at Uruk in the archaic period. *JNES* 39 (1980):1–35.

Green, M.W. and Nissen, H.J. *Zeichenliste der archaischen Texte aus Uruk*. Berlin: ATU 2, 1987.

Grégoire, J.-P. *Archives administratives sumériennes*. Paris: Geuthner, 1970.

Grégoire, J.-P. L'origine et le développement de la civilisation mésopotamienne du troisième millénaire avant notre ère. In: *Production, Pouvoir et Parenté dans le Monde Méditerranéen*. Paris: Geuthner, 1981:27–101.

Grégoire, J.-P. Le serment en Mésopotamie au IIIe millénaire avant notre ère. In: *Le Serment I. Signes et fonctions*. Paris: Editions du CNRS, 1991:345–365.

Grigg, D.B. *The agricultural systems of the world: an evolutionary approach*. Cambridge: Cambridge Geographical Studies 5, 1974.

Groneberg, B. Še'ītu and šugītu. *NABU* 1989:46.

Groneberg, B. Zu den mesopotamischen Unterweltsvorstellungen: Das Jenseits als Fortsetzung des Diesseits. *AoF* 17 (1990):244–61.

Gropp, G. Representations of deities by emblems in Middle Eastern art. In: Schotsmans, J. and Taddei, M. (eds.). *South Asian Archaeology 1983*. Naples: Istituto Universitario Orientale Dipartimento di Studi Asiatici Series Minor XXIII, 1985:453–462.

Grosz, K. *The archive of the Wullu family*. Copenhagen: CNIP 5, 1988.

Guichard, M. Flotte crétoise sur l'Euphrate? *NABU* 1993:53.

Guralnick, E. East to west: Near Eastern artifacts from Greek sites. In: Charpin, D. and Joannès, F. (eds.), *La circulation des biens, des personnes et des idées dans le Proche-Orient ancien*. Paris: Editions Recherche sur les civilisations, 1992:327–40.

Haerinck, E. Les tombes et les objets du sondage sur l'enceinte de Abu Habbah. In: de Meyer, L. (ed.), *Tell ed-Der III*. Leuven: Peeters, 1980:53–79.

Haldar, A. Fest. *RlA* 3 (1957–1971):40–3.

Haldar, A. Festhaus. *RlA* 3 (1957–1971):47–50.

Hall, H.R. and Woolley, C.L. *Ur excavations I. Al-'Ubaid*. Oxford: Univ. Press, 1927.

Hallo, W.W. Seals lost and found. In: Gibson, McG. and Biggs, R.D. (eds.), *Seals and Sealing in the Ancient Near East*. Malibu: BiMes 6, (1977):55–60.

Hallo, W.W. Texts, statues and the cult of the divine king. In: Emerton, J.A. (ed.), *Congress Volume, Jerusalem 1986*. Leiden: Vetus Testamentum Suppl. 50, 1988:54–66.

Halstead, P. Quantifying Sumerian agriculture – some seeds of doubt and hope. *BSA* 5 (1990):187–95.

Hannestad, L. *The Hellenistic pottery from Failaka, with a survey of Hellenistic pottery in the Near East*. Aarhus: JASP 16:2 [= Ikaros: The Hellenistic Settlements 2:1], 1983.

Hansman, J.F. The Mesopotamian delta in the first millennium BC *GJ* 44 (1978):49–61.

Harper, P.O., Aruz, J. and Tallon, F. (eds.), *The royal city of Susa: ancient Near Eastern treasures in the Louvre*. New York: Metropolitan Museum of Art, 1993.

Harris, S.A. and Adams, R.McC. A note on canal and marsh stratigraphy near Zubediyah. *Sumer* 13 (1957):157–62.

Harrison, D.L. *Mammals of the Arabian Gulf*. London: Allen & Unwin, 1981.

Hauptmann, A. *5000 Jahre Kupfer in Oman I. Die Entwicklung der Kupfermetallurgie vom 3. Jahrtausend bis zur Neuzeit*. Bochum: Der Anschnitt Beiheft 4, 1985.

Hauser, S. Eine arsakidenzeitliche Nekropole in Ktesiphon. *BaM* 24 (1993):325–420.

Hegyi, D. Die Griechen und der alte Orient im 9. bis 6. Jahrhundert v.Chr. In: Nissen, H.J. and Renger, J. (eds.), *Mesopotamien und seine Nachbarn*. Berlin: BBVO 1/2, 1982:531–8.

Heimpel, W. Das Untere Meer. *ZA* 77 (1987):22–91.

Heimpel, W. The natural history of the Tigris according to the Sumerian literary composition Lugal. *JNES* 46 (1987):309–17.

Heimpel, W. Ein zweiter Schritt zur Rehabilitierung der Rolle des Tigris in Sumer. *ZA* 80 (1990):204–13.

Heimpel, W. Meluḫḫa. *RlA* 8 (1993):53–5.

Heimpel, W. Mungo. *RlA* 8 (1995):423–5.

Heinrich, E. *Schilf und Lehm*. Berlin, 1934.

Heinrich, E. *Tempel und Heiligtümer im alten Mesopotamien*. Berlin: De Gruyter, 1982.

Heinrich, E. and Seidl, U. Grundriß-Zeichnungen. *RlA* 3 (1957–1971):664–8.

Helbaek, H. Notes on the evolution and history of Linum. *Kuml 1959* (1959):103–20.

Helbaek, H. Plant collecting, dry-farming, and irrigation agriculture in prehistoric Deh Luran. In: Hole, F., Flannery, K.V. and Neely, J.A., *Prehistory and Human Ecology of the Deh Luran Plain*. Ann Arbor: Memoirs of the Museum of Anthropology, Univ. of Michigan 1, 1969:383–426.

Helbaek, H. Samarran irrigation agriculture at Choga Mami in Iraq. *Iraq* 35 (1973):35–48.

Henninger, J. Einiges über Ahnenkult bei arabischen Beduinen. In: *Arabica Sacra: Aufsätze zur Religionsgeschichte Arabiens und seiner Randgebiete*. Freiburg/Göttingen: Orbis Biblicus et Orientalis 40, 1981a:170–88.

Henninger, J. Zur Herkunft eines islamischen Opfergebetes. In: *Arabica Sacra: Aufsätze zur Religionsgeschichte Arabiens und seiner Randgebiete*. Freiburg/Göttingen: Orbis Biblicus et Orientalis 40, 1981b:311–18.

Hepper, F.N. Notes on the reeds of Mesopotamia. *BSA* 6 (1992):193–4.

Heyer, R. *pû*, "Spreu" als Pferdefutter. *BaM* 12 (1981):83–6.

Heyerdahl, T. Testing wash–through watercraft in three oceans. In: Crumlin-Pedersen, O. and Vinner, M. (eds.), *Sailing into the Past: Proceedings of the International Seminar on Replicas of Ancient and Medieval Vessels, Roskilde, 1984*. Roskilde: Viking Ship Museum, 1986:24–37.

Hilprecht, H.V. Explorations in Babylonia. In: Hilprecht, H.V. (ed.), *Recent Research in Bible Lands*. Philadelphia: John D. Wattles & Co., 1896:45–93.

Hodges, E.R. *Cory's Ancient Fragments*. London, 1876.

Hole, F. Patterns of burial in the fifth millennium. In: Henrickson, E.F. and Thuesen, I. (eds.), *Upon this Foundation – the 'Ubaid Reconsidered*. Copenhagen: CNIP 10, 1989:149–80.

Homès-Fredericq, D. *Les cachets mésopotamiens protohistoriques*. Leiden: Brill, 1970.

Hornell, J. A tentative classification of Arab sea-craft. *MM* 28 (1942):11–40.

Hruška, B. Die Bodenbearbeitung und Feldbestellung im altsumerischen Lagaš. *ArOr* 52 (1984):150–57.

Hruška, B. Die Aussagen der altsumerischen Texte über die Produktionsverhältnisse in der Landwirtschaft: Versuch einer inhaltlichen Klassifizierung der Buchhaltung. unpubl. handout to accompany the lecture, 'Tempelhaushalt in Girsu', Oikos Workshop, Berlin, 19.11.1985a.

Hruška, B. Der Umbruchpflug in den archaischen und altsumerischen Texten. *ArOr* 53 (1985b):46–65.

Hruška, B. Die Bewässerungsanlagen in den altsumerischen Königsinschriften von Lagaš. *BSA* 4 (1988a):61–72.

Hruška, B. Überlegungen zum Pflug und Ackerbau in der altsumerischen Zeit. *ArOr* 56 (1988b):137–58.

Hruška, B. Das landwirtschaftliche Jahr im alten Sumer: Versuch einer zeitlichen Rekonstruktion. *BSA* 5 (1990):105–14.

Huddleston, Capt. W.B. Arab and Indian ships and seafarers of the Indian Ocean. *JRCAS* 15 (1928):341–8.

Huff, D. Technical observations on clay bullae from Takht-i Suleiman. *Mesopotamia* 22 (1987):367–90.

Huffmon, H.B. *Amorite personal names in the Mari texts.* Baltimore: Johns Hopkins University Press, 1965.

Hunger, H. Kosmologie. *RlA* 6 (1980–83):222–3.

Hunt, R.C. Hydraulic management in southern Mesopotamia in Sumerian times. *BSA* 4 (1988):189–206.

Huot, J.-L. *Les Sumériens.* Paris: Editions Errance, 1989.

Huot, J.-L. 'Ubaidian villages of lower Mesopotamia: permanence and evolution from 'Ubaid 0 to 'Ubaid 4 as seen from Tell el'Oueili. In: Henrickson, E.F. and Thuesen, I. (eds.), *Upon this Foundation – the 'Ubaid Reconsidered.* Copenhagen: CNIP 10, 1989:19–42.

Inizan, M.-L. Technologie et préhistoire récente en Mésopotamie: L'exemple du débitage par pression et de l'économie de l'obsidienne. In: Huot, J.-L. (ed.), *La Préhistoire de la Mésopotamie.* Paris: Editions du CNRS, 1987:305–15.

Inizan, M.-L. At the dawn of trade, cornelian from India to Mesopotamia in the third millennium: The Example of Tello. In: Gail, A.J. and Mevissen, G.J.R. (eds.), *South Asian Archaeology 1991.* Stuttgart: Steiner, 1993:121–34.

Inizan, M.-L. and Tixier, J. Tell el 'Oueili: le matériel lithique. In: Huot, J.-L. (ed.), *Larsa et Oueili, travaux de 1978–1981.* Paris: Editions Recherche sur les Civilisations, 1983:164–75.

Invernizzi, A. Note on the art of Seleucid Mesopotamia. In: Boucharlat, R. and Salles, J.-F. (eds.), *Arabie orientale, Mésopotamie et Iran méridional, de l'âge du fer au début de la période islamique.* Paris: Editions Recherche sur les Civilisations Mémoire 37, 1984:27–31.

Invernizzi, A. and Papotti, C.M. Sealings and fingerprints at Seleucia-on-the-Tigris. In: Schippmann, K., Herling, A. and Salles, J.-F. (eds.), *Golf-Archäologie: Mesopotamien, Iran, Kuwait, Bahrain, Vereinigte Arabische Emirate und Oman.* Buch am Erlbach: Internationale Archäologie 6, 1991:33–43.

Invernizzi, A., Mancini, M.M.N.P. and Valtz, E. Seleucia sul Tigri. In: *La Terra tra i Due Fiumi.* Turin: Il Quadrante Edizioni, 1985:87–99.

Ionides, M.G., *The régime of the rivers Euphrates and Tigris*, London, 1937.

Jacobs, L. Causes for the pale colour of second millennium BC pottery from several sites in Mesopotamia. In: Méry, S. (ed.), *Sciences de la terre et céramiques archéologiques: expérimentations, applications.* Cergy:

Documents et Travaux de l'Institut Géologique Albert-de-Lapparent, Centre Polytechnique Saint-Louis, 1992:121–36.

Jacobsen, T. The waters of Ur. *Iraq* 22 (1960):174–85.

Jacobsen, T. Religious drama in ancient Mesopotamia. In: Goedicke, H. and Roberts, J.J.M. (eds.), *Unity and diversity: essays in the history, literature, and religion of the ancient Near East*. Baltimore and London: Johns Hopkins University Press, 1975:65–97.

Jacobsen, T. *The treasures of darkness*. New Haven and London: Yale, 1976.

Jacobsen, T. *Salinity and irrigation agriculture in antiquity. Diyala basin archaeological projects: report on essential results, 1957–1958*. Malibu: BiMes 14, 1982.

Jarrige, J.-F. and Meadow, R.H. The antecedents of civilization in the Indus Valley. *Scientific American* 243 (1980):122–33.

Jasim, S.A. Structure and function in an 'Ubaid village. In: Henrickson, E.F. and Thuesen, I. (eds.), *Upon this foundation – the 'Ubaid reconsidered*. Copenhagen: CNIP 10, 1989:79-90.

Joannès, F. Méthodes de pesée néo-babyloniennes. *NABU* 1987:5.

Joannès, F. La titulature de Xerxès. *NABU* 1989a:37.

Joannès, F. La culture matérielle à Mari (IV): Les méthodes de pesée. *RA* 83 (1989b):113–52.

Joannès, F. Pouvoirs locaux et organisations du territoire en Babylonie achéménide. *Transeuphratène* 3 (1990):173–89.

Joannès, F. L'étain, de l'Elam à Mari. In: de Meyer, L. and Gasche, H. (eds.), *Mésopotamie et Elam*. Ghent: Mesopotamian History and Environment Occasional Publications 1, 1991:67–76.

Joannès, F. Metalle und Metallurgie A.I. In Mesopotamien. *RlA* 8 (1993):96–112.

Johnson, G.A. *Local exchange and early state development in Southwestern Iran*. Ann Arbor: Museum of Anthropology Anthropological Papers 51, 1973.

Johnstone, P. *The sea-craft of prehistory*. London and Henley: Routledge & Kegan Paul, 1980.

Johnstone, T.M. and Muir, J. Portuguese influences on shipbuilding in the Persian Gulf. *MM* 48 (1962):58–63.

Johnstone, T.M. and Muir, J. Some nautical terms in the Kuwaiti dialect of Arabic. *BSOAS* 27 (1964):299–332.

Kamp, K.A. and Yoffee, N. Ethnicity in ancient Western Asia during the early second millennium BC: archaeological assessments and ethnoarchaeological prospectives. *BASOR* 237 (1980):85–104.

Kay, P.A. and Johnson, D.L. Estimation of Tigris-Euphrates streamflow from regional paleoenvironmental proxy data. *Climatic Change* 3 (1981):251–63.

Keall, E.J. and Ciuk, K.E. Continuity of tradition in the pottery from Parthian Nippur. In: Schippmann, K., Herling, A. and Salles, J.-F. (eds.), *Golf–Archäologie: Mesopotamien, Iran, Kuwait, Bahrain, Vereinigte Arabische Emirate und Oman*. Buch am Erlbach: Internationale Archäologie 6, 1991:57–70.

Kenoyer, J.M. Urban process in the Indus tradition: a preliminary model from Harappa. In: Meadow, R.H. (ed.), *Harappa excavations 1986–1990: a multidisciplinary approach to third millennium urbanism.* Madison: Monographs in World Archaeology 3, 1991:29–60.

Kessler, K. Duplikate und Fragmente aus Uruk, Teil II. *BaM* 15 (1984):261–72.

Kessler, K. Rinder aus dem Meerland. *ZA* 81 (1992):92–7.

Koldewey, R. *Das wieder erstehende Babylon.* Leipzig: Hinrichs, 1913.

Kozlowski, S.K. Chipped stone industry of the Ubaid site Tell el-Saadiya in Iraq (Hamrin). In: Huot, J.-L. (ed.), *La Préhistoire de la Mésopotamie.* Paris: Editions du CNRS, 1987:277–91.

Kramer, S.N. *History begins at Sumer.* New York: Doubleday, 1959.

Kramer, S.N. *The Sumerians.* Chicago and London: Univ. of Chicago, 1963.

Kramer, S.N. The death of Ur-Nammu and his descent to the netherworld. *JCS* 21 (1967):104–22.

Krecher, J. Göttersymbole B. *RlA* 3 (1957–1971):495–8.

Krecher, J. Kauf A.I. *RlA* 5 (1980):490-541.

Kuhrt, A. Assyrian and Babylonian traditions in Classical authors: a critical synthesis. In: Nissen, H.J. and Renger, J. (eds.), *Mesopotamien und seine Nachbarn.* Berlin: BBVO 1/2, 1982:539–53.

Kuhrt, A. Survey of written sources available for the history of Babylonia under the later Achaemenids (concentrating on the period from Artaxerxes II to Darius III). In: Sancisi-Weerdenburg, H. (ed.), *Achaemenid history I. Sources, structures and syntheses.* Leiden: Nederlands Instituut voor het Nabije Oosten, 1987:147–57.

Kuhrt, A. Achaemenid Babylonia: sources and problems. In: Sancisi-Weerdenburg, H. and Kuhrt, A. (eds.), *Achaemenid history IV. centre and periphery.* Leiden: Nederlands Instituut voor het Nabije Oosten, 1990:177–94.

Kuhrt, A. Alexander and Babylon. In: Sancisi-Weerdenburg, H. and Drijvers, J.W. (eds.), *Achaemenid history V. The roots of the European tradition.* Leiden: Nederlands Instituut voor het Nabije Oosten, 1990:121–30.

Kuhrt, A. and Sherwin-White, S. Xerxes' destruction of Babylonian temples. In: Sancisi–Weerdenburg, H. and Kuhrt, A. (eds.), *Achaemenid history II. The Greek sources.* Leiden: Nederlands Instituut voor het Nabije Oosten, 1987:69–78.

Kutzbach, J.E. Monsoon climate of the early Holocene: climate experiment with the earth's orbital parameters for 9000 years ago. *Science* 214 (1981):59–61.

Lafont, B. Balag, la lyre. *NABU* 1987:3.

Lamb, A. Some observations on stone and glass beads in early Southeast Asia. *Journal of the Malaysian Branch of the Royal Asiatic Society* 38 (1965):87–124.

Lambert, W.G. Ancestors, authors, and canonicity. *JCS* 11 (1957):1–14.

Lambert, W.G. *Babylonian wisdom literature.* Oxford: Clarendon Press, 1960.

Lambert, W.G. Gott B. *RlA* 3 (1957–1971):543–6.

Lambert, W.G. Honig. *RlA* 4 (1972–1975):469.

Lambert, W.G. Kosmogonie. *RlA* 6 (1980–1983):218–222.

Lambert, W.G. Tears of Ningišzida. *NABU* 1990:127.

Lancaster, W. *The Rwala bedouin today.* Cambridge: Univ. Press, 1981.

Landsberger, B. Keilschrifttexte nach Kopien von T.G. Pinches 9. Texte zur Serie HAR.ra = ḫubullu. *AfO* 12 (1937–1939):136–40.

Landsberger, B. *The Series HAR-ra* = ḫubullu, *Tablets VIII–XII.* Rome: MSL VI, 1959.

Landsberger, B. *The date palm and its by-products according to the cuneiform sources.* Graz: AfO Beiheft 17, 1967.

Landsberger, B. *Three essays on the Sumerians* (introd. and trans. by Maria deJ. Ellis). Los Angeles: Undena, 1974.

LaPlaca, P.J. and Powell, M.A. The agricultural cycle and the calendar at pre-Sargonic Girsu. *BSA* 5 (1990):75–104.

Larsen, C.E. The Mesopotamian delta region: a reconsideration of Lees and Falcon, *JAOS* 95 (1975):43–57.

Layard, A.H. *Nineveh and its remains* (3rd ed.). London: John Murray, 1849.

Lecomte, O. Fouilles du sommet de l'E.babbar (1985). In: Huot, J.-L. (ed.), *Larsa, travaux de 1985.* Paris: Editions Recherche sur les Civilisations Mémoire 83, 1989:83–147.

Lecomte, O. Stratigraphical analysis and ceramic assemblages of the 4th-1st centuries BC E.babbar of Larsa (Southern Iraq). In: Finkbeiner, U. (ed.), *Materialien zur Archäologie der Seleukiden- und Partherzeit im südlichen Babylonien und im Golfgebiet.* Wasmuth: Tübingen, 1993:17–39.

Leemans, W.F. *Foreign trade in the Old Babylonian period.* Leiden: Studia et Documenta Ad Iura Orientis Antiqui Pertinentia 6, 1960.

Leemans, W.F. Some marginal remarks on ancient technology. *JESHO* 3 (1960):217–37.

Leemans, W.F. La fonction des sceaux, apposés à des contrats vieux-babyloniens. In: van Driel, G., Krispijn, T.J.H., Stol, M. and Veenhof, K.R. (eds.), *Zikir Šumim: Assyriological Studies Presented to F.R. Kraus on the Occasion of his Seventieth Birthday.* Leiden: Brill, 1982:219–44.

Lees, G.M. and Falcon, N.L. The geographical history of the Mesopotamian plains. *GJ* 118 (1952):24–39.

Lendle, O. Xenephon in Babylonien. *Rheinisches Museum für Philologie* 129 (1986):193–222.

Lerche, G. and Steensberg, A. Tools and tillage in Iran: observations made in 1965 in the province of Kermán. *Tools & Tillage* 4 (1983):217–48.

LeRider, G. Un atelier monétaire séleucide dans la province de la mer Érythrée? *Revue Numismatique* (1965):36–43.

LeStrange, G. Description of Mesopotamia and Baghdad, written about the year 900 AD by Ibn Serapion. *JRAS* (1895):1–76, 255–315.

LeStrange, G. Baghdad during the caliphate. *JRAS* (1899):847–93.

LeStrange, G. *Lands of the eastern caliphate.* Cambridge: Univ. Press, 1905.

Levey, M. Alum in ancient Mesopotamian technology. *Isis* 49 (1958):166–9.

Lewy, H. Nitokris-Naqi'a. *JNES* 11 (1952):264–86.

Li, H. Finds from Tell Gubba. *Al–Rāfidān* 10 (1989):167–243.

Liebowitz, H.A. Knochen. *RlA* 6 (1980–1983):41–5.

Lindemeyer, E. and Martin, L. *Uruk Kleinfunde III*. Mainz: AUWE 9, 1993.

Lion, B. La circulation des animaux exotiques au Proche-Orient antique. In: Charpin, D. and Joannès, F. (eds.) *La circulation des biens, des personnes et des idées dans le Proche-Orient ancien*. Paris: Editions Recherche sur les civilisations, 1992:357–65.

Lipke, P. Retrospective on the royal ship of Cheops. In: McGrail, S. and Kentley, E. (eds.), *Sewn plank boats: archaeological and ethnographic papers based on those presented to a conference at Greenwich in November, 1984*. Oxford: BAR IntSer. 276, 1985:19–34.

Liverani, M. The shape of Neo-Sumerian fields. *BSA* 5 (1990):147–86.

Livingstone, A. To disturb the dead: taboo to Enmešarra? *NABU* 1991:1.

Lloyd, S. *Mesopotamia*. London: Lovat Dickson, 1936.

Loftus, W.K. *Travels and researches in Chaldaea and Susiana*. London 1857.

Longrigg, S.H. *Four centuries of modern Iraq*. Oxford: Clarendon Press, 1925.

Lorimer, J.G. *Gazetteer of the Persian Gulf, Oman and central Arabia*, ii. Calcutta: Superintendent of Government Printing, 1908.

Luckenbill, D.D. *The annals of Sennacherib*. Chicago: OIP 2, 1924.

Mackay, E.J.H. *Chanhu-Daro excavations 1935–36*. New Haven: American Oriental Society, 1943.

Maddin, R., Stech Wheeler, T. and Muhly, J.D. Distinguishing artifacts made of native copper. *JAS* 7 (1980):211–25.

Maekawa, K. Cereal cultivation in the Ur III period. *BSA* 1 (1984):73–96.

Maekawa, K. Cultivation of legumes and **mun-gazi** plants in Ur III Girsu. *BSA* 2 (1985):97–118.

Maekawa, K. Cultivation methods in the Ur III period. *BSA* 5 (1990):115–45.

Malul, M. "Eating and drinking (one's) refuse". *NABU* 1993:99.

Margueron, J.-Cl. Quelques remarques concernant l'architecture monumentale à l'époque d'Obeid. In: Huot, J.-L. (ed.), *La préhistoire de la Mésopotamie*. Paris: Editions du CNRS, 1987:349–77.

Margueron, J.-Cl. Le bois dans l'architecture: premier essai pour une estimation des besoins dans le bassin Mésopotamien. *BSA* 6 (1992):79–96.

Mason, Maj. K. Notes on the canal system and ancient sites of Babylonia in the time of Xenophon. *GJ* 56 (1920):468–81.

Maxwell-Hyslop, K.R. *Western Asiatic jewellery, c. 3000–612 BC* London: Methuen, 1971.

Maxwell-Hyslop, K.R. Sources of Sumerian gold. *Iraq* 39 (1977):83–6.

Mayer, W.R. Zur Unterteilung des šekels im spätzeitlichen Babylonien. *Or* 54 (1985):203–15.

McClure, H.A. *The Arabian Peninsula and prehistoric populations*. Coconut Grove: Field Research Projects, 1971.

McClure, H.A. *Late Quaternary palaeoenvironments of the Rub' Al Khali.* unpubl. PhD. diss., Univ. College London, 1984.

McClure, H.A. Late Quaternary palaeogeography and landscape evolution of the Rub' Al Khali. In: Potts, D.T. (ed.), *Araby the blest: studies in Arabian archaeology.* Copenhagen: CNIP 7, 1988:9–13.

McEwan, G.J.P. *Texts from Hellenistic Babylonia in the Ashmolean Museum.* Oxford: OECT 9, 1982.

McEwan, G.J.P. Babylonia in the Hellenistic period. *Klio* 70 (1988):412–21.

McGrail, S. and Kentley, E. (eds.). *Sewn plank boats: archaeological and ethnographic papers based on those presented to a conference at Greenwich in November, 1984.* Oxford: BAR IntSer. 276, 1985.

Meadow, R.H. Prehistoric subsistence at Balakot: initial considerations of the faunal remains. In: Taddei, M. (ed.). *South Asian archaeology 1977.* Naples: Istituto Universitario Orientale Dipartimento di Studi Asiatici Series Minor VI, 1979:275–315.

Meadow, R.H. Early animal domestication in South Asia: a first report of the faunal remains from Mehrgarh, Pakistan. In: Härtel, H. (ed.), *South Asian archaeology 1979.* Berlin: Reimer, 1981:143–79.

Meadow, R.H. From hunting to herding in prehistoric Baluchistan. In: Pastner, S. and Flam, L. (eds.). *Anthropology in Pakistan: recent sociocultural and archaeological perspectives.* Ithaca: South Asia Occasional Papers and Theses 8, 1982:145–53.

Meadow, R.H. Pre-and protohistoric subsistence in Baluchistan and eastern Iran. *Information bulletin* 2 (1982):56–61.

Meadow, R.H. Notes on the faunal remains from Mehrgarh, with a focus on cattle *(Bos)*. In: Allchin, B. (ed.), *South Asian archaeology 1981.* Cambridge: Cambridge Univ. Press, 1984:34–40.

Meadow, R.H. The geographical and paleoenvironmental setting of Tepe Yahya. In: Beale, T.W. *Excavations at Tepe Yahya, Iran, 1967–1975.* Cambridge: American School of Prehistoric Research Bulletin 38, 1986:21–38.

Meier, C. Ein griechisches Ehrendekret vom Gareustempel in Uruk. *BaM* 1 (1960):104–14.

Meier, G. ḫuluppaqqu, ein Kultgefäß. *AfO* 10 (1935–36):365–6.

Meissner, B. Babylonische Pflanzennamen. *ZA* 6 (1891):289–98.

Meissner, B. Pallacottas. *MVAG* 4 (1896):1–13.

Meissner, B. Babylonische Leichenfeierlichkeiten. *WZKM* 12 (1898):59–66.

Meissner, B. *Babylonien und Assyrien*, I. Heidelberg: Winters, 1920.

Méry, S. Origine et production des récipients de terre cuite dans la péninsule d'Oman à l'âge du bronze. *Paléorient* 17 (1991):51–78.

Meyer, C., Todd, J.M. and Beck, C.W. From Zanzibar to Zagros: a copal pendant from Eshnunna. *JNES* 50 (1991):289–98.

Michalowski, P. Mental maps and ideology: reflections on Subartu. In: Weiss, H. (ed.), *The origins of cities in dry-farming Syria and Mesopotamia in the third millennium* BC. Guilford: Four Quarters, 1986:129–56.

Michel, C. Un problème mathématique relatif à la métallurgie. *NABU* 1989:110.

Millard, A.R. The bevelled-rim bowls: their purpose and significance. *Iraq* 50 (1988):49–57.

Miller, N.F. The interpretation of some carbonized cereal remains as remnants of dung cake fuel. *BSA* 1 (1984):45–7.

Møller, E. A re-evaluation of the Oriental cylinder seals found in Crete. In: Best, J.G.P. and de Vries, N.M.W. (eds.), *Interaction and acculturation in the Mediterranean I-II*. Amsterdam, 1983: 85–104, 223–30.

Moorey, P.R.S. The late prehistoric administrative building at Jamdat Nasr. *Iraq* 39 (1977):95–106.

Moorey, P.R.S. Metal wine sets in the ancient Near East. *IrAnt* 15 (1980):181–197.

Moorey, P.R.S. Where did they bury the kings of the IIIrd Dynasty of Ur? *Iraq* 46 (1984):1–18.

Moorey, P.R.S. *Materials and manufacture in ancient Mesopotamia: the evidence of archaeology and art.* Oxford: BAR IntSer. 237, 1985.

Moorey, P.R.S. *Ancient Mesopotamian materials and industries.* Oxford: Clarendon Press, 1994.

Moorey, P.R.S., Curtis, J.E., Hook, D.R. and Hughes, M.J. New analyses of Old Babylonian metalwork from Tell Sifr. *Iraq* 50 (1988):39–48.

Moorey, P.R.S. and Postgate, J.N. Some wood identifications from Mesopotamian sites. *BSA* 6 (1992):197–9.

Moortgat, A. Die Entstehung der sumerischen Hochkultur. *Der Alte Orient* 43 (1945):7–101.

Moortgat, A. *The art of ancient Mesopotamia.* London and New York: Phaidon, 1969.

Moren, S. *The omen series Šumma Ālu.* Philadelphia: unpubl. PhD. diss., 1978.

Moren, S. and Foster, B.R. Eagle omens from Šumma Ālu. In: Leichty, E., Ellis, M.deJ. and Gerardi, P. (eds.), *A scientific humanist: studies in memory of Abraham Sachs.* Philadelphia: Occasional Publications of the Samuel Noah Kramer Fund 9, 1988:277–83.

Morgan, J. de. Étude géographique sur la Susiane. *MDP* 1 (1900):1–32.

Mørkholm, O. The Seleucid mint at Antiochia on the Persian Gulf. *American Numsimatic Society Museum notes* 16 (1970):31–44.

Muhly, J.D. *Copper and tin: the distribution of mineral resources and the nature of the metals trade in the Bronze Age.* Hamden: Transactions of the Connecticut Academy of Arts and Sciences 43, 1973:155–535.

Muhly, J.D. *Supplement to copper and tin.* Hamden: Transactions of the Connecticut Academy of Arts and Sciences 46, 1976:77–136.

Muhly, J.D. The copper ox-hide ingots and the Bronze Age metals trade. *Iraq* 39 (1977):73–82.

Muhly, J.D. New evidence for sources of and trade in Bronze Age tin. In: Franklin, A.D., Olin, J.S. and Wertime, T.A. (eds.), *The search for ancient tin.* Washington D.C.: U.S. Govt. Printing Office, 1978:43–8.

Muhly, J.D. The Aarhus conference II. summary: the origin of agriculture and technology – West or East Asia? *Technology and culture* 22 (1981):125–48.

Muhly, J.D. Kupfer B. Archäologisch. *RlA* 6 (1983):348–64.

Muhly, J.D. Gold analysis and the sources of gold in the Aegean. *Temple University Aegean symposium* 8 (1983):1–14.

Muhly, J.D. Metalle B. *RlA* 8 (1993):119–36.

Müller, M. Gold, Silber und Blei als Wertmesser in Mesopotamien während der zweiten Hälfte des 2.Jahrtausends v.u.Z. In: Postgate, J.N. and Larsen, M.T. (eds.), *Societies and Languages of the Ancient Near East: Studies in Honour of I.M. Diakonoff.* Warminster: Aris & Phillips, 1982:270–8.

Müller-Karpe, M. Metallgefäße des dritten Jahrtausends in Mesopotamien. *Archäologisches Korrespondenzblatt* 20 (1990):161–76.

Müller-Karpe, M. Aspects of early metallurgy in Mesopotamia. In: Pernicka, E. and Wagner, G.A. (eds.). *Archaeometry '90.* Basel/Boston/Berlin: Birkhäuser, 1991:105–16.

Müller-Karpe, M. Metallgefäße I. *RlA* 8 (1993a):137–44.

Müller-Karpe, M. *Metallgefäße im Iraq I (Von den Anfängen bis zur Akkad-Zeit).* Stuttgart: Prähistorische Bronzefunde II/14, 1993b.

Mynors, H.S. An examination of Mesopotamian ceramics using petrographic and neutron activation analysis. In: Aspinall, A. and Warren, S.E. (eds.), *Proceedings of the 22nd symposium on Archaeometry.* Bradford: School of Physics and Archaeological Sciences, 1983:377–87.

Nashef, K. *Die Orts-und Gewässernamen der mittelbabylonischen und mittelassyrischen Zeit.* Wiesbaden: RGTC 5, 1982.

Nayar, N.M. Sesame. In: Simmonds, N.W. (ed.), *Evolution of crop plants.* London/New York: Longman, 1976:232.

Neef, R. Plant remains from archaeological sites in lowland Iraq: Hellenistic and Neobabylonian Larsa. In: Huot, J.-L. (ed.), *Larsa, travaux de 1985.* Paris: Editions Recherche sur les Civilisations, 1989:151–61.

Neumann, H. Bemerkungen zu Ehe, Konkubinat und Bigamie in neusumerischer Zeit. In: Durand, J.-M. (ed.), *La Femme dans le Proche-Orient Antique.* Paris: Editions Recherche sur les Civilisations, 1987:131–7.

Neumann, J. and Sigrist, R.M. Harvest dates in ancient Mesopotamia as possible indicators of climatic variations. *Climatic Change* 1 (1978):239–52.

Nissen, H.J. Grabung in den Quadraten K/L XII in Uruk-Warka. *BaM 5* (1970):101–91.

Nissen, H.J. The city wall of Uruk. In: Ucko, P.J., Tringham, R. and Dimbleby, G.W. (eds.), *Man, settlement and urbanism.* London: Duckworth, 1972:794–8.

Nissen, H.J. Geographie. *AS* 20 (1975):9–40.

Nissen, H.J. Aspects of the development of early cylinder seals. In: Gibson, McG. and Biggs, R.D. (eds.), *Seals and sealing in the ancient Near East.* Malibu: BiMes 6, 1977:15–23.

Nissen, H.J. Bemerkungen zur Listenliteratur Vorderasiens im 3. Jahrtausend. In: Cagni, L. (ed.), *La Lingua di Ebla.* Naples: Istituto Universitario Orientale, Seminario di Studi Asiatici Series Minor XIV, 1981:99–108.

Nissen, H.J. Ortsnamen in den archaischen Texten aus Uruk. *Or 54* (1985):226–33.

Nissen, H.J. The development of writing and of glyptic art. In: Finkbeiner, U. and Röllig, W. (eds.), *Ġamdat Naṣr: Period or regional style?* Wiesbaden: TAVO Beiheft B 62, 1986:316–31.

Nissen, H.J. *Mesopotamia before 5000 years.* Rome: Sussidi Didattici 1, 1988a.

Nissen, H.J. *The early history of the ancient Near East 9000–2000 BC.* Chicago and London: Univ. of Chicago, 1988b.

Nissen, H.J. Die Frühgeschichte (Mesopotamiens) als Forschungsproblem. *Saeculum* 40 (1989):179–82.

Nissen, H.J., Damerow, P. and Englund, R.K. *Frühe Schrift und Techniken der Wirtschaftsverwaltung im alten Vorderen Orient.* Berlin: Franzbecker, 1990.

Nützel, W. On the geographical position of as yet unexplored early Mesopotamian cultures: contribution to the theoretical archaeology. *JAOS* 99 (1979):288–96.

Nützel, W. Lag Ur einst am Meer? *MDOG* 112 (1980):95–102.

Oates, D. *Studies in the history of northern Iraq.* London: Oxford Uinv. Press, 1968.

Oates, J. Ur and Eridu, the prehistory. *Iraq* 22 (1960):32–50.

Oates, J. Archaeology and geography in Mesopotamia. In: Bintliff, J. (ed.), *Mycenaean geography: proceedings of the Cambridge colloquium, September 1976.* Cambridge: British Association for Mycenaean Studies, 1977:101–7.

Oates, J. The Choga Mami transitional. In: Huot, J.-L. (ed.), *La Préhistoire de la Mésopotamie.* Paris: Editions du CNRS, 1987:163–80.

Oates, J. Le Choga Mami transitional et l'Obeid 1: synthèse de la séance. In: Huot, J.-L. (ed.), *La Préhistoire de la Mésopotamie.* Paris: Editions du CNRS, 1987:199–206.

Oates, J. Babylonia and Elam in prehistory. In: de Meyer, L. and Gasche, H. (eds.), *Mésopotamie et Elam.* Ghent: Mesopotamian History and Environment Occasional Publications 1, 1991:23–6.

Oates, J. Review of Nissen, *The early history of the ancient Near East.* *JNES* 52 (1993):145–8.

Oates, D. and Oates, J. Early irrigation agriculture in Mesopotamia. In: Sieveking, G. de G., Longworth, I.H. and Wilson, K.E. (eds.), *Problems in economic and social archaeology.* London: Duckworth, 1977:109–35.

Oates, D. and Oates, J. Excavations at Tell Brak 1992–93. *Iraq* 55 (1993):155–200.

Obermeyer, J. *Die Landschaft Babylonien im Zeitalter des Talmuds und des Gaonats.* Frankfurt: Schriften der Gesellschaft zur Förderung des Judentums 30, 1929.

Ochsenschlager, E.L. Ethnographic evidence for wood, boats, bitumen and reeds in Southern Iraq. *BSA* 6 (1992):47–78.

Ochsenschlager, E.L. Sheep: ethnoarchaeology at Al-Hiba. *BSA* 7 (1993):33–42.

Oelsner, J. *Materialien zur babylonischen Gesellschaft und Kultur in hellenistischer Zeit.* Budapest: Assyriologia VII, 1986.

Oelsner, J. Griechen in Babylonien und die einheimischen Tempel in hellenistischer Zeit. In: Charpin, D. and Joannès, F. (eds.) *La circulation des biens, des personnes et des idées dans le Proche-Orient ancien*. Paris: Editions Recherche sur les Civilisations, 1992:341–7.

Oguchi, K. Shells and shell objects from area A of 'Usiyeh. *Al-Rāfidān* 13 (1992):61–86.

Oppenheim, A.L. Lexikalische Bemerkungen zu den 'kappadokischen' Briefen. *AfO* 12 (1937–39):357–8.

Oppenheim, A.L. The seafaring merchants of Ur. *JAOS* 74 (1954):6–17.

Oppenheim, A.L. *Ancient Mesopotamia* (rev. ed.). Chicago and London: Univ. of Chicago, 1977.

Owen, D.I. Widows' rights in Ur III Sumer. *ZA* 70 (1980):170–84.

Owen, D.I. Of birds, eggs and turtles. *ZA* 71 (1981):29–47.

Owen, D.I. and Westbrook, R. Tie her up and throw her in the river! An Old Babylonian inchoate marriage on the rocks. *ZA* 82 (1992):202–7.

Pallis, S.A. Early exploration in Mesopotamia. *Det Kongelige Danske Videnskabernes Selskab, Hist.-fil. Meddelelser* 33/6 (1954):3–58.

Parpola, A. and Parpola, S. On the relationship of the Sumerian toponym *Meluḫḫa* and Sanskrit *mleccha*. *StOr* 46 (1975):205–38.

Pedde, F. Frehat en-Nufeği: Zwei seleukidenzeitliche Tumuli bei Uruk. *BaM* 22 (1991):521–35.

Pellat, C. *Le milieu Baṣrien et la formation de Ğahiẓ*. Paris: Librairie d'Amérique et d'Orient, 1953.

Pemberton, W., Postgate, J.N. and Smyth, R.F. Canals and bunds, ancient and modern. *BSA* 4 (1988):207–21.

Perkins, A.L. *The comparative archeology of early Mesopotamia*. Chicago: SAOC 25, 1949.

Petschow, H. Havarie. *RlA* 4 (1972–1975):233–7.

Pettinato, G. and Waetzoldt, H. Saatgut und Furchenabstand beim Geitreideanbau. *StOr* 46 (1975):259–90.

Philby, H.St.J.B. The eastern marshes of Mesopotamia. *GJ* 125 (1959):65–9.

Pingree, D. Mesopotamian astronomy and astral omens in other civilizations. In: Nissen, H.J. and Renger, J. (eds.), *Mesopotamien und seine Nachbarn*. Berlin: BBVO 1/2, 1982:613–31.

Pingree, D. Mesopotamian omens in Sanskrit. In: Charpin, D. and Joannès, F. (eds.), *La circulation des biens, des personnes et des idées dans le Proche-Orient ancien*. Paris: Editions Recherche sur les Civilisations, 1992:375–9.

Pintore, F. *Il Matrimonio interdinastico nel Vicino Oriente durante i Secoli XV-XIII*. Rome: Oriens Antiqui Collectio 14, 1978.

Polanyi, K. *The livelihood of man*. New York/San Francisco/London: Academic Press, 1977.

Pomponio, F. Lukalla of Umma. *ZA* 82 (1992):169–79.

Pongratz-Leisten, B. Keramik der frühdynastischen Zeit aus den Grabungen in Uruk-Warka. *BaM* 19 (1988):177–319.

Porada, E. Greek coin impressions from Ur. *Iraq* 22 (1960):228–34.

Porada, E. The cylinder seals found at Thebes in Boeotia. *AfO* 28 (1981):1–78.

Porada, E., Hansen, D.P., Dunham, S. and Babcock, S.H. The chronology of Mesopotamia, ca. 7000–1600 BC. In: Ehrich, R.W. (ed.), *Chronologies in Old World archaeology* (3rd ed.). Chicago: Univ. of Chicago Press, 1992:77–121 (I), 90–124 (II).

Postgate, J.N. The problem of yields in cuneiform texts. *BSA* 1 (1984):97–102.

Postgate, J.N. Some vegetables in the Assyrian sources. *BSA* 3 (1987):93–100.

Postgate, J.N. Notes on fruit in the cuneiform sources. *BSA* 3 (1987):115–44.

Postgate, J.N. A Middle Tigris village. *BSA* 5 (1990):65–74.

Postgate, J.N. Archaeology and the texts – bridging the gap. *ZA* 80 (1990):228–40.

Postgate, J.N. Trees and timber in the Assyrian texts. *BSA* 6 (1992):177–92.

Postgate, J.N. *Early Mesopotamia: society and economy at the dawn of history*. London: Routledge, 1994.

Potts, D.T. On salt and salt gathering in ancient Mesopotamia. *JESHO* 27 (1984):225–71.

Potts, D.T. Salt of the earth: the role of a non-pastoral resource in a pastoral economy. *OrAnt* 22 (1983):205–15.

Potts, D.T. Reflections on the history and archaeology of Bahrain. *JAOS* 105 (1985):675–710.

Potts, D.T. *The Arabian Gulf in antiquity, I-II*. Oxford: Clarendon Press, 1990.

Potts, D.T. Notes on some horned buildings in Iran, Mesopotamia and Arabia. *RA* 84 (1990):33–40.

Potts, D.T. A note on rice cultivation in Mesopotamia and Susiana. *NABU* 1991:2.

Potts, D.T. The late prehistoric, protohistoric, and early historic periods in Eastern Arabia (ca. 5000–1200 BC). *Journal of World Prehistory* 7 (1993):163–212.

Potts, D.T. Rethinking some aspects of trade in the Arabian Gulf. *World Archaeology* 24 (1993):423–40.

Potts, D.T. Contributions to the agrarian history of Eastern Arabia I. Implements and cultivation techniques. *AAE* 5 (1994a):158–68.

Potts, D.T. Contributions to the agrarian history of Eastern Arabia II. The cultivars. *AAE* 5 (1994b):236–75.

Potts, D.T. Watercraft of the Lower Sea. In: Finkbeiner, U., Dittmann, R. and Hauptmann, H. (eds.), *Beiträge zur Kulturgeschichte Vorderasiens: Festschrift für Rainer Michael Boehmer*. Mainz: von Zabern, 1995:559–71.

Potts, T.F. Foreign stone vessels of the late third millennium BC from southern Mesopotamia: their origins and mechanisms of exchange. *Iraq* 51 (1989):123–64.

Powell, M.A. Sumerian cereal crops. *BSA* 1 (1984):48–72.

Powell, M.A. Late Babylonian surface mensuration. *AfO* 31 (1984):32–66.

Powell, M.A. Salt, seed and yields in Sumerian agriculture: a critique of the theory of progressive salinization. *ZA* 75 (1985):7–38.

Powell, M.A. The tree section of ur_5(=HAR)-ra=*hubullu*. *BSA* 3 (1987):145–51.

Powell, M.A. Evidence for agriculture and waterworks in Babylonian mathematical texts. *BSA* 4 (1988):161–72.

Powell, M.A. Maße und Gewichte. *RlA* 7 (1990):457–530.

Powell, M.A. Timber production in presargonic Lagaš. *BSA* 6 (1992):99–122.

Price, M.J. Circulation at Babylon in 323 BC In: Metcalf, W.E. (ed.), *Mnemata: papers in memory of Nancy M. Waggoner*. New York: American Numismatic Society, 1991:63–72.

Ramsay, W.M. and Bell, G.L. *Thousand and one churches*. London, 1909.

Rasmussen, S.T. *Den Arabiske Rejse 1761–1767*. Copenhagen: Munksgaard, 1990.

Rassam, H. Recent discoveries of ancient Babylonian cities. *Transactions of the Society of Biblical Archaeology* 8 (1885):172–97.

Ravn, O.E. *Herodotus' description of Babylon*. Busck: Copenhagen, 1942.

Rawlinson, Col. Sir H.C. Notes on the ancient geography of Mohamrah and the Vicinity. *JRGS* (1857):185–90.

Reade, J.E. Commerce or conquest: variations in the Mesopotamia–Dilmun relationship. In: Al Khalifa, H.A. and Rice, M. (eds.), *Bahrain through the ages: the archaeology*. London/New York/Sydney/Henley: Kegan Paul International, 1986:325–34.

Reade, W.J. and Potts, D.T. New evidence for late third millennium linen from Tell Abraq, Umm al-Qaiwain, UAE. *Paléorient* 19 (1993):99–106.

Redman, C.L. *The rise of civilization*. San Francisco: W.H. Freeman, 1978.

Reinmuth, O.W. Stadion. *KP* 5 (1979):336–8.

Reitemeyer, E. *Die Städtegründungen der Araber im Islām nach den arabischen Historikern und Geographen*. Munich: Akademische Buchdruckerei F. Straub, 1912.

Renfrew, J.M. Cereals cultivated in ancient Iraq. *BSA* 1 (1984):32-44.

Renfrew, J.M. Pulses recorded from ancient Iraq. *BSA* 2 (1985):67–71.

Renfrew, J.M. Finds of sesame and linseed in ancient Iraq. *BSA* 2 (1985):63–6.

Renfrew, J.M. Fruits from ancient Iraq: the palaeoethnobotanical evidence. *BSA* 3 (1987):157–161.

Renfrew, J.M. A note on vegetables from ancient Iraq: the palaeoethnobotanical finds. *BSA* 3 (1987):162.

Renger, J. Who are all those people? *Or* 42 (1973):259–73.

Renger, J. *mārat ilim*: Exogamie bei den semitischen Nomaden des 2. Jahrtausends. *AfO* 24 (1973):103–07.

Renger, J. Patterns of non-institutional trade and non-commercial exchange in ancient Mesopotamia at the beginning of the second millennium BC In: Archi, A. (ed.), *Circulation of goods in non-palatial context in the ancient Near East*. Rome: Edizioni dell'Ateneo, 1984:31–123.

Renger, J. Legal aspects of sealing in ancient Mesopotamia. In: Gibson, McG. and Biggs, R.D. (eds.), *Seals and sealing in the ancient Near East*. Malibu: BiMes 6, 1977:75–88.

Renger, J. Kultbild A. *RlA* 6 (1980–1983):307–14.

Renger, J. Zur Bewirtschaftung von Dattelpalmgärten während der altbabylonischen Zeit. In: Van Driel, G., Krispijn, Th.J.H., Stol, M. and Veenhof, K.R. (eds.), *Zikir šumim: Assyriological studies presented to*

F.R. *Kraus on the occasion of his seventieth birthday*. Leiden: Brill, 1982:290–7.

Renger, J. Rivers, water courses and irrigation ditches and other matters concerning irrigation based on Old Babylonian sources (2000–1600 BC). *BSA* 5 (1990a):31–46.

Renger, J. Report on the implications of employing draught animals. *BSA* 5 (1990b):267–79.

Ries, G. Kapitaldelikte. *RlA* 5 (1976–1980):391–9.

Roaf, M. 'Ubaid houses and temples. *Sumer* 43 (1984):80–90.

Röllig, W. Griechische Eigennamen in Texten der babylonischen Spätzeit. *Or* 29 (1960):376–91.

Röllig, W. *Das Bier im alten Mesopotamien*. Berlin, 1970.

Röllig, W. Der altmesopotamische Markt. *WdO* 8 (1976):286–95.

Röllig, W. Kisiga, Kissik. *RlA* 5 (1976–1980):620–22.

Röllig, W. Nitokris. *KP* 4 (1979):141.

Rossignol-Strick, M. African monsoons, an immediate climate response to orbital insolation. *Nature* 304 (1983):47–9.

Roth, M.T. The scholastic exercise "laws about rented oxen". *JCS* 32 (1980):127–46.

Roth, M.T. The dowries of the women of the Itti-Marduk-Balāṭu family. *JAOS* 111 (1991):19–37.

Roth, M.T. The Neo-Babylonian widow. *JCS* 43–45 (1991–93):1–26.

Roux, G. Recently discovered ancient sites in the Hammar Lake district (southern Iraq). *Sumer* 16 (1960):20–31.

Sachs, A. The latest datable cuneiform tablets. In: *Kramer anniversary volume: cuneiform studies in honor of S.N. Kramer*. Neukirchen/Vluyn: AOAT 25, 1976:379–398.

Sack, R.H. Some remarks on jewelry inventories from sixth century BC Erech. *ZA* 69 (1979):41–6.

Saggs, H.W.F. A cylinder from Tell al Lahm, *Sumer* 13 (1957): 190–5.

Salje, B. *Der "common style" der Mitanni-Glyptik und die Glyptik der Levante und Zyperns in der späten Bronzezeit*. Mainz: Baghdader Forschungen 11, 1990.

Salonen, A. *Die Hausgeräte der alten Mesopotamier II. Gefäße*. Helsinki: AASF B 144, 1966.

Salonen, A. *Agricultura Mesopotamica nach sumerisch-akkadischen Quellen*. AASF B 149, 1968.

Salonen, A. *Jagd und Jagdtiere im alten Mesopotamien*. AASF B 196, 1976.

Sanati-Müller, S. Texte aus dem Sînkāšid-Palast. Dritter Teil. Metalltexte. *BaM* 21 (1990):131–213.

Sancisi-Weerdenburg, H. The effects of cardamum. *DATA: Achaemenid history newsletter* 2 (1993):6.

Sanlaville, P. Considérations sur l'évolution de la basse Mésopotamie au cours des derniers millénaires. *Paléorient* 15 (1989):5–27.

Sanlaville, P. Changements climatiques dans la péninsule Arabique durant le pléistocène supérieur et l'holocène. *Paléorient* 18 (1992):5–26.

Sanlaville, P., Dalongeville, R., Evin, J. and Paskoff, R. Modification du tracé littoral sur la côte arabe due Golfe Persique en relation avec l'archéologie. In: *Déplacements des lignes de rivage en Méditérranée.* Paris: Editions du CNRS, 1987:211–22.

San Nicolò, M. Dyandrie. *RlA* 2 (1938):256.

San Nicolò, M. Ehebruch. *RlA* 2 (1938):299–302.

San Nicolò, M. *Babylonische Rechtsurkunden des ausgehenden 8. und des 7. Jahrhunderts v. Chr.* Munich: Abhandlungen der Bayerischen Akad. der Wiss., phil.-hist. Kl. N.S. 34, 1951.

Santini, G. A preliminary note on animal figurines from Shahr-i Sokhta. In: Taddei, M. (ed.), *South Asian archaeology 1987.* Rome: IsMEO, 1990:427–51.

Sauren, H. *Topographie der Provinz Umma nach den Urkunden der Zeit der III. Dynastie von Ur, Teil I: Kanäle und Bewässerungsanlagen.* Heidelberg: Inaug.-Diss., Ruprecht-Karl-Universität, 1966.

Sauren, H. Zu den Wirtschaftsurkunden des Musée d'art et d'histoire II. *AION* 31 (1971):165–82.

Sauren, H. á-áš, áš, aš, "concubine". *RA* 84 (1990):41–3.

Scandone-Matthiae, G. Inscriptions royales égyptiennes de l'ancien empire à Ebla. In: Nissen, H.J. and Renger, J. (eds.), *Mesopotamien und seine Nachbarn.* Berlin: BBVO 1/2, 1982:125–30.

Schachermeyr, F. *Alexander der Grosse: Das Problem seiner Persönlichkeit und seines Wirkens.* Vienna: Österr. Akad. d. Wiss., phil.-hist. Kl, Sitzungsber. 285, 1973.

Schmandt-Besserat, D. Tokens as funerary offerings. *VO* (1988):3–9.

Schmid, H. Ergebnisse einer Grabung am Kernmassiv der Zikurrat in Babylon. *BaM* 12 (1981):87–137.

Schmid, H. Der Tempelplan IM 44036,1 – Schema oder Bauplan. *Or 54* (1985):289–93.

Schmidt, E. Die Griechen in Babylon und das Weiterleben ihrer Kultur. *Archäologischer Anzeiger* (1941):786–844.

Schoff, W.H. *The Periplus of the Erythraean Sea.* New York: Longmans, Green & Co., 1912.

Schroeder, O. Assyrische Gefäßnamen. *AfO* 6 (1930–31):111–12.

Schützinger, H. Tod und ewiges Leben im Glauben des Alten Zweistromlandes. In: Klimkeit, H.-J. (ed.), *Tod und Jenseits im Glauben der Völker.* Wiesbaden: Harrassowitz, 1978:48–61.

Scrimshaw, N.S. and Young, V.R. The requirements of human nutrition. *Scientific American* 238 (1976):51–64.

Scurlock, J.A. *Taklimtu:* a display of grave goods? *NABU* 1991:3.

Seibt, G.F. *Griechische Söldner im Achaimenidenreich.* Bonn: Habelts Dissertationsdrucke, Reihe Alte Geschichte, Heft 11, 1977.

Seidl, U. Göttersymbole AI. *RlA* 3 (1957–1971):484–90.

Seidl, U. Kultbild B. *RlA* 6 (1980–1983):314–19.

Seidl, U. *Die babylonische Kudurru-Reliefs: Symbole mesopotamischer Gottheiten.* Göttingen: Orbis biblicus et orientalis 87, 1989.

Selz, G. *Die Bankettszene: Entwicklung eines "uberzeitlichen" Bildmotivs in Mesopotamien : von der fruhdynastischen bis zur Akkad-Zeit.* Wiesbaden: FAOS 11, 1983.

Severin, T. Constructing the Omani boom Sohar. In: McGrail, S. and

Kentley, E. (eds.), *Sewn plank boats: archaeological and ethnographic papers based on those presented to a conference at Greenwich in November, 1984.* Oxford: BAR IntSer. 276, 1985:279–87.

Shaffer, J.G. Indus Valley, Baluchistan and the Helmand drainage (Afghanistan). In: Ehrich, R.W. (ed.), *Chronologies in Old World archaeology* (3rd ed.). Chicago: Univ. of Chicago Press, 1992:441–64 (I), 425–46 (II).

Sherratt, A. Plough and pastoralism: aspects of the secondary products revolution. In: Hodder, I., Isaac, G., and Hammond, N. (eds.), *Pattern of the past: studies in honour of David Clarke.* Cambridge: Cambridge Univ. Press, 1981:261–305.

Sherwin-White, S. A Greek ostrakon from Babylon of the early third century BC *ZPE* 47 (1982):51–70.

Sherwin-White, S. Babylonian chronicle fragments as a source for Seleucid history. *JNES* 42 (1983):265–70.

Sherwin-White, S. and Kuhrt, A. *From Samarkhand to Sardis: a new approach to the Seleucid empire.* London: Duckworth, 1993.

Sigrist, M. Le travail des cuirs et peaux à Umma sous la dynastie d'Ur III. *JCS* 33 (1981):141–90.

Sigrist, M. Les courriers de Lagaš. In: De Meyer, L., Gasche, H. and Vallat, F. (eds.), *Fragmenta Historiae Elamicae: Mélanges offerts à M.J. Steve.* Paris: Editions Recherche sur les Civilisations, 1986:51–63.

Sigrist, M. *Drehem.* Bethesda: CDL Press, 1992.

Simonet, G. Irrigation de piémont et économie agricole à Assur. *RA* 71 (1977):157–68.

Simoons, F.J. The antiquity of dairying in Asia and Africa. *GR* 61 (1971):431–9.

Simoons, F.J. The determinants of dairying and milk use in the Old World: ecological, physiological and cultural. In: Robson, J.R.K. (ed.), *Food, ecology and culture.* London: Gordon and Breach, 1980:83–92.

Sjöberg, A.W. Götterreisen A. *RlA* 3 (1957–1971):480–3.

Sjöberg, A.W. Zu einigen Verwandtschaftsbezeichnungen im Sumerischen. In: Edzard, D.O. (ed.), *Heidelberger Studien zum Alten Orient, Adam Falkenstein zum 17. September 1966.* Wiesbaden: Harrassowitz, 1969:201–1.

Sjöberg, A.W. 'He is a Good Seed of a Dog' and 'Engardu, the Fool'. *JCS* 24 (1972):107–19.

Sjöberg, A.W. and Bergmann, E. *The collection of the Sumerian temple hymns.* Locust Valley: TCS III, 1969.

Soitzek, D. Reed-boat experiments on particular aspects of sailing on the wind. In: Crumlin-Pedersen, O. and Vinner, M. (eds.), *Sailing into the past: proceedings of the international seminar on replicas of ancient and Medieval vessels, Roskilde, 1984.* Roskilde: Viking Ship Museum, 1986:226–35.

Solecki, R. A copper mineral pendant from northern Iraq. *Antiquity* 43 (1969):311–14.

Sollberger, E. *The business and administrative correspondence under the kings of Ur.* Locust Valley: TCS 1, 1966.

Sollberger, E. and Kupper, J.-R. *Inscriptions royales sumériennes et akkadiennes*. Paris: Littératures anciennes du Proche-Orient 3, 1971.

Speiser, E.A. *Mesopotamian origins*. Philadelphia: Univ. of Pennsylvania, 1930.

Srinivasan, S. High-tin bronze bowl making in Kerala, South India, and its archaeological implications. In: Parpola, A. and Koskikallio, P. (eds.) *South Asian archaeology 1993, II*. Helsinki: AASF Ser B 271, 1994:695–706.

Starr, R.F.S. *Nuzi, i*. Cambridge: Harvard University, 1939.

Steiner, G. Das Bedeutungsfeld "TOD" in den Sprachen des Alten Orients. *Or* 51 (1982):239–48.

Steinkeller, P. Seal practice in the Ur III period. In: Gibson, McG. and Biggs, R.D. (eds.), *Seals and sealing in the ancient Near East*. Malibu: BiMes 6, 1977:41–53.

Steinkeller, P. Early Dynastic burial offerings in light of the textual evidence. unpubl. paper delivered at the American Oriental Society meeting, San Francisco, 1980.

Steinkeller, P. Two Sargonic sale documents concerning women. *Or* 51 (1982):355–68.

Steinkeller, P. The question of Marḫaši: a contribution to the historical geography of Iran in the third millennium BC *ZA* 72 (1982):237–65.

Steinkeller, P. The foresters of Umma: toward a definition of Ur III labor. In: Powell, M. (ed.), *Labor in the ancient Near East*. New Haven: AOS 68, 1987:73–115.

Steinkeller, P. On the meaning of zabar-šu. *ASJ* 9 (1987a):347–9.

Steinkeller, P. The administrative and economic organization of the Ur III state: the core and the periphery. In: Gibson, McG. and Biggs, R.D. (eds.), *The organization of power: aspects of bureaucracy in the ancient Near East*. Chicago: SAOC 46, 1987b:19–41.

Steinkeller, P. Notes on the irrigation system in third millennium southern Babylonia. *BSA* 4 (1988):73–91.

Steinkeller, P. Threshing implements in ancient Mesopotamia: cuneiform sources. *Iraq* 52 (1990):19–23.

Steinkeller, P. Comment on S. Pollock, Of priestesses, princes and poor relations: the dead in the Royal Cemetery at Ur. *Cambridge Archaeological Journal* 1 (1991):187–8.

Steve, M.-J. and Vallat, F. La dynastie des Igihalkides: nouvelles interprétations. In: de Meyer, L. and Haerinck, E. (eds.), *Archaeologia Iranica et Orientalis: Miscellanea in Honorem Louis Vanden Berghe*. Gent: Peeters, 1989:223–38.

Stiffe, A.W. Former trading centres of the Persian Gulf V. Kung. *GJ* 13 (1899):294–7.

Stol, M. Zur altmesopotamischen Bierbereitung. *BiOr* 28 (1971):167–71.

Stol, M. Kanal(isation) A. Philologisch. *RlA* 5 (1980):355–65.

Stol, M. Leder. *RlA* 6 (1983):527–43.

Stol, M. Cress and its mustard. *JEOL* 28 (1983–84):24–32.

Stol, M. Remarks on the cultivation of sesame and the extraction of its oil. *BSA* 2 (1985):119–26.

Stol, M. Beans, peas, lentils and vetches in Akkadian texts. *BSA* 2 (1985):127–39.

Stol, M. Garlic, onion, leek. *BSA* 3 (1987):57–80.

Stol, M. The Cucurbitaceae in the cuneiform texts. *BSA* 3 (1987):81–92.

Stol, M. Milk, butter, and cheese. *BSA* 7 (1993):99–113.

Stolper, M.W. The governor of Across-the-River in 486 BC *JNES* 48 (1989):283–305.

Stone, E.C. Texts, architecture and ethnographic analogy: patterns of residence in Old Babylonian Nippur. *Iraq* 43 (1981):24–33.

Stone, E.C. *Nippur neighborhoods*. Chicago: SAOC 44, 1987.

Stone, E.C. and Owen, D.I. *Adoption in Old Babylonian Nippur and the archive of Mannum-mešu-liṣṣur*. Winona Lake: Mesopotamian Civilizations 3, 1991.

Stone, E.C. and Zimansky, P. Mashkan-shapir and the anatomy of an Old Babylonian city. *Biblical Archaeologist* 55 (1992):212–18.

Strommenger, E. *Gefäße aus Uruk von der neubabylonischen Zeit zu den Sassaniden*. Berlin: Ausgrabungen der deutschen Forschungsgemeinschaft in Uruk-Warka 7, 1967.

Strommenger, E. Grab. *RlA* 3 (1957–1971):581–93.

Strommenger, E. Grabbeigabe. *RlA* 3 (1957–1971):605–8.

Strommenger, E. Grabgefäß/-behälter. *RlA* 3 (1957–1971):609.

Sürenhagen, D. *Keramikproduktion in Habuba Kabira-Süd*. Berlin: Bruno Hessling, 1978.

Szarzynska, K. Céramique d'Uruk d'après l'écriture pictographique sumérienne. *Travaux du Centre d'archéologie méditerranéenne de l'Académie Polonaise des Sciences* 6 [= Études et Travaux II] (1969):16–24.

Talbot Rice, D. Hira. *JRCAS* 19 (1932):254–68.

Talbot Rice, D. The Oxford excavations at Ḥīra. *Ars Islamica* 1 (1934):51–73.

Tallon, F. *Métallurgie susienne I. De la fondation de Suse au XVIIIe siècle avant J.-C., i-ii*. Paris: Notes et documents des musées de France 15, 1987.

Thuesen, I. et al. Analysis of Ubaid material excavated at Tell Mashnaqa: the first laboratory season – a summary. *Les Annales Archéologiques Arabes Syriennes*: in press.

Tomaschek, W. Topographische Erläuterung der Küstenfahrt Nearchs vom Indus bis zum Euphrat. *Sitzungsber. d. Kais. Akad. d. Wiss. in Wien, phil.-hist. Cl.* CXXI/8 (1890):1–88.

Tosi, M. Karneol. *RlA* 5 (1980):448–52.

Tosi, M. and Biscione, R. *Conchiglie: Il commercio e la lavorazione delle conchiglie marine nel medio oriente dal IV al II millennio a.C.* Rome: De Luca, 1981.

Tosi, M. and Cleuziou, S. Black boats of Magan: some thoughts on Bronze Age water transport in Oman and beyond from the impressed bitumen slabs of Ra's al-Junayz. In: Parpola, A. and Koskikallio, P. (eds.), *South Asian archaeology 1993, II*. Helsinki: AASF Ser B 271, 1994:745–61.

Tscherikower, V. *Die hellenistischen Städtegründungen von Alexander dem Grossen bis auf die Römerzeit*. Leipzig: Philologus Supplementband XIX.1, 1927.

Tsukimoto, A. *Untersuchungen zur Totenpflege* (kispum) *im alten Mesopotamien*. Neukirchen-Vluyn: AOAT 216, 1985.

Turchetta, B. Baluchi domains and taxonomies of herbs and spices. *Newsletter of Baluchistan Studies* 6 (1989):17–36.

Uerpmann, H.–P. Faunal remains from Shams ed-Din Tannira, a Halafian site in northern Syria. *Berytus* 30 (1982):3–52.

Uerpmann, M. Early mongooses from Bahrain. In: Buitenhuis, H. and Uerpmann, H.-P. (eds.), *Archaeozoology of the Near East II*. Leiden: Universal Book Services, in press.

Uerpmann, M. and Uerpmann, H.-P. Animal bone finds from excavation 520 at Qala'at al-Bahrain. In: Højlund, F. and Andersen, H.H. *Qala'at al-Bahrain I. The northern city wall and the Islamic fortress*. Aarhus: JASP 30/1, 1994:417–44.

Unger, E. Barsippa. *RlA* 1 (1928):402–29.

Unger, E. Dûr-Jakini. *RlA* 2 (1938):244–5.

Unger, E. Eridu. *RlA* 2 (1938):464–70.

Ungnad, A. Babylonische Familiennamen. *AnOr* 12 (1935):319–26.

Vaiman, A.A. Eisen in Sumer. *AfO Beiheft* 19 (1982):33–8.

Vallat, F. Le Kutir-Nahhunte d'Assurbanipal. *NABU* 1993:31.

Valtz, E. Pottery from Seleucia on the Tigris. In: Boucharlat, R. and Salles, J.-F. (eds.), *Arabie orientale, Mésopotamie et Iran méridional, de l'âge du fer au début de la période islamique*. Paris: Editions Recherche sur les Civilisations Mémoire 37, 1984:41–8.

Valtz, E. La campagna di Yelkhi. In: *La Terra tra i Due Fiumi*. Turin: Il Quadrante Edizioni, 1985:69–70.

Valtz, E. New observations on the Hellenistic pottery from Seleucia-on-the-Tigris. In: Schippmann, K., Herling, A. and Salles, J.-F. (eds.). *Golf-Archäologie: Mesopotamien, Iran, Kuwait, Bahrain, Vereinigte Arabische Emirate und Oman*. Buch am Erlbach: Internationale Archäologie 6, 1991:45–56.

van Buren, E.D. *The fauna of ancient Mesopotamia as represented in art*. Rome: *AnOr* 18, 1939.

van Buren, E.D. Fish-offerings in ancient Mesopotamia. *Iraq* 10 (1948):101–21.

Van De Mieroop, M. Gold offerings of Šulgi. *Or* 55 (1986):131–51.

Van De Mieroop, M. *Crafts in the early Isin period: a study of the Isin craft archive from the reigns of Išbi-Erra und Šu-ilišu*. Louvain: OLA 24, 1987.

Van De Mieroop, M. Review of Stone and Owen 1991. *JCS* 43–45 (1991–93):124–30.

Van De Mieroop, M. Reed in the Old Babylonian texts from Ur. *BSA* 6 (1992):147–53.

Van De Mieroop, M. Wood in the Old Babylonian texts from Ur. *BSA* 6 (1992):155–61.

Van De Mieroop, M. Sheep and goat herding according to the Old Babylonian texts from Ur. *BSA* 7 (1993):161–82.

van der Spek, R.J. The Babylonian temple during the Macedonian and Parthian domination. *BiOr* 42 (1985):541–62.

van der Spek, R.J. The astronomical diaries as a source for Achaemenid and Seleucid history. *BiOr* 50 (1993):91–101.

van der Spek, R.J. Review of Weisberg 1991. *BiOr* 51 (1994):600–5.

van Dijk, J. Gott. *RlA* 3 (1957–1971):532–43.

van Dijk, J. Die dynastischen Heiraten zwischen Kassiten und Elamern: eine verhängnisvolle Politik. *Or* 55 (1986):159–70.

van Driel, G. Continuity or decay in the late Achaemenid period: evidence from southern Mesopotamia. In: Sancisi-Weerdenburg, H. (ed.), *Achaemenid history I. Sources, structures and synthesis.* Leiden: Nederlands Instituut voor het Nabije Oosten, 1987:159–81.

van Driel, G. Neo-Babylonian agriculture. *BSA* 4 (1988):121–59.

van Driel, G. Neo-Babylonian agriculture III. Cultivation. *BSA* 5 (1990):210–66.

van Driel, G. Wood, reeds and rushes: a note on Neo-Babylonian practical texts. *BSA* 6 (1992):171–6.

van Driel, G. Neo-Babylonian sheep and goats. *BSA* 7 (1993):219–58.

van Ess, M. and Pedde, F. *Uruk Kleinfunde II.* Mainz: AUWE 7, 1992.

van Lerberghe, K. L'arrachement de l'emblème *šurinnum.* In: Van Driel, G., Krispijn, Th.J.H., Stol, M. and Veenhof, K.R. (eds.), *Zikir šumim: Assyriological studies presented to F.R. Kraus on the occasion of his seventieth birthday.* Leiden: Brill, 1982:245.

van Soldt, W. Irrigation in Kassite Babylonia. *BSA* 4 (1988):105–20.

Vanstiphout, H.L.J. Enmerkar and the Lord of Aratta line 503. *NABU* 1993:13.

van Zeist, W. Lists of names of wild and cultivated cereals. *BSA* 1 (1984):8–15.

van Zeist, W. Pulses and oil crop plants. *BSA* 2 (1985):33–8.

Varenius, B. The "Helga Holm" project. In: Crumlin-Pedersen, O. and Vinner, M. (eds.), *Sailing into the past: proceedings of the international seminar on replicas of ancient and Medieval vessels, Roskilde, 1984.* Roskilde: Viking Ship Museum, 1986:114–19.

Veenhof, K.R. Ad *BagdMitt* 21 (1990), 131ff. *NABU* 1991:29.

Vértesalji, P.P. al-Lahm, Tall. *RlA* 6 (1980–1983):431–3.

Vishnu-Mittre and Savithri, R. Food economy of the Harappans. In: Possehl, G.L. (ed.), *Harappan civilization: a recent perspective* (2nd rev. ed.). New Delhi/Bombay/Calcutta: Oxford & IBH, 1993:205–21.

Visicato, G. Some aspects of the administrative organization of Fara. *Or* 61 (1992):94–9.

Visicato, G. Archéologie et documents écrits: les "silos" et les textes sur l'orge de Fara. *RA* 87 (1993):83–5.

Vita-Finzi, C. *Archaeological sites in their setting.* London: Thames and Hudson, 1978.

Vogelsang, W. Gold from Dardistan: some comparative remarks on the tribute system in the extreme northwest of the Indian subcontinent. In: Briant, P. and Herrenschmidt, C. (eds.), *Le tribut dans l'empire Perse.* Paris: Travaux de l'Institut d'Etudes Iraniennes de l'Université de la Sorbonne Nouvelle 13, 1989:157–71.

von den Driesch, A. Fischknochen aus Abu Salabikh/Iraq. *Iraq* 48 (1986):31–8.

von Wickede, A. *Prähistorische Stempelglyptik in Vorderasien*. Munich: Profil, 1990.

Voute, C. A prehistoric find near Razzaza. *Sumer* 13 (1957):135–56.

Waetzoldt, H. Zwei unveröffentlichte Ur-III-Texte über die Herstellung von Tongefäßen. *WdO* 6 (1970–1971):7–41.

Waetzoldt, H. *Untersuchungen zur neusumerischen Textilindustrie*. Rome: SET 1, 1972.

Waetzoldt, H. Zu den Strandverschiebungen am Persischen Golf und den Bezeichnungen der Ḥōrs. In: Schäfer, J. and Simon, W. (eds.), *Strandverschiebungen in ihrer Bedeutung für Geowissenschaften und Archäologie*. Heidelberg: Ruperto Carola Sonderheft, 1981:159–84.

Waetzoldt, H. Zur Terminologie der Metalle in den Texten aus Ebla. In: Cagni, L. (ed.), *La Lingua di Ebla*. Naples: Istituto Universitario Orientale, Seminario di Studi Asiatici Series Minor XIV, 1981:363–78.

Waetzoldt, H. Leinen. *RlA* 6 (1983):583–94.

Waetzoldt, H. Ölpflanzen und Pflanzenöl im 3. Jahrtausend. *BSA* 2 (1985):77–96.

Waetzoldt, H. Knoblauch und Zwiebeln nach den Texten des 3. Jt. *BSA* 3 (1987):23–56.

Waetzoldt, H. Original eines Siegels und dessen Abrollung. *NABU* 1989:79.

Waetzoldt, H. Zur Weiterverwendung mesopotamischer Siegel im Karum Kaniš. *NABU* 1990a:48.

Waetzoldt, H. Zu den Bewässerungseinrichtungen in der Provinz Umma. *BSA* 5 (1990b):1–29.

Waetzoldt, H. 'Rohr' und dessen Verwendungsweisen anhand der neusumerischen Texte aus Umma. *BSA* 6 (1992):125–46.

Waetzoldt, H. and Bachmann, H.G. Zinn-und Arsenbronzen in den Texten aus Ebla und aus dem Mesopotamien des 3. Jahrtausends. *OrAnt* 23 (1984):1–18.

Waggoner, N.M. Tetradrachms from Babylon. In: Mørkholm, O. and Waggoner, N.M. (eds.), *Greek numismatics and archaeology: essays in honor of Margaret Thompson*. Wetteren: Editions NR, 1979:269–80.

Watelin, L.C. Essai de coordination des périodes archaiques de la Mésopotamie et de l'Elam. *L'Anthropologie* 41 (1931):265–72.

Weisberg, D.B. *The Late Babylonian texts of the Oriental Institute collection*. Malibu: BiMes 24, 1991.

Weissbach, F.H. Mesene. *RE* 15 (1931):1082–95.

Werr, L. al-G. Cylinder seals made of clay. *Iraq* 50 (1988):1–24.

Wertime, T.A. The search for ancient tin: the geographic and historic boundaries. In: Franklin, A.D., Olin, J.S. and Wertime, T.A. (eds.), *The search for ancient tin*. Washington D.C.: U.S. Govt. Printing Office, 1978:1–6.

Westbrook, R. *Old Babylonian marriage law*. Horn: AfO Beiheft 23, 1988.

Westenholz, A. *berūtum, damtum*, and Old Akkadian KI.GAL: burial of dead enemies in ancient Mesopotamia. *AfO* 23 (1970):27–31.

Westenholz, A. *Old Sumerian and Old Akkadian texts in Philadelphia part two: the 'Akkadian' texts, the Enlilemaba texts, and the Onion Archive.* Copenhagen: CNIP 3, 1987.

Wiggermann, F. A. M. *Mesopotamian protective spirits : the ritual texts.* Groningen: STYX & PP Publications, 1992.

Wilcke, C. Eine Schicksalsentscheidung für den toten Urnammu. In: Finet, A. (ed.), *Actes de la XVIIe Rencontre Assyriologique Internationale.* Ham-sur-Heure: Comité belge de Recherches en Mésopotamie, 1970:81–92.

Wilcke, C. Kauf A II. *RlA* 5 (1980):498–512.

Wilcke, C. Familiengründung im alten Babylonien. In: Müller, E.W. (ed.), *Geschlechtsreife und Legitimation zur Zeugung.* Freiburg and Munich: Karl Alber, 1985:213–317.

Willcox, G.H. List of trees and shrubs of economic importance in Iraq. *BSA* 3 (1987):101–6.

Willcox, G.H. Etude archéobotanique. In: Francfort, H.-P., *Fouilles de Shortughai: Recherches sur l'Asie Centrale protohistorique.* Paris: Mémoires de la Mission Archéologique Française en Asie Centrale II, 1989:175–85.

Willcox, G.H. Timber and trees: ancient exploitation in the Middle East: evidence from plant remains. *BSA* 6 (1992):1–31.

Woolley, C.L. *Ur Excavations II. The Royal Cemetery.* London and Philadelphia: The British Museum and the University Museum, 1934.

Woolley, C.L. *Ur Excavations IV. The early periods.* London and Philadelphia: The British Museum and the University Museum, 1955.

Wrede, N. Katalog der Terrakotten der archäologischen Oberflächenuntersuchung (Survey) des Stadtgebietes von Uruk. *BaM* 21 (1990):215–301.

Wright, H.T. A note on a Paleolithic site in the southern desert. *Sumer* 22 (1967):101–04.

Wright, H.T. The southern margins of Sumer. In: Adams, R.McC. *Heartland of cities.* Chicago and London: Univ. of Chicago, 1981:295–345.

Wyatt, N. A press-seal, possibly of Indus type, found in Iraq. *JRAS* 1983:3–6.

Yener, A. Kestel: an Early Bronze Age source of tin ore in the Taurus Mountains, Turkey. *Science* 244 (1989):200–203.

Yoffee, N. The decline and rise of Mesopotamian civilization: an ethnoarchaeological perspective on the evolution of social complexity. *American Antiquity* 44 (1979):5–35.

Yoffee, N. Context and authority in early Mesopotamian law. In: Cohen, R. and Toland, J.D. (eds.), *State formation and political legitimacy* [= *Political Anthropology* VI]. New Brunswick and Oxford: Transaction Books, 1988:95–113.

Yoffee, N. Aspects of Mesopotamian land sales. *American Anthropologist* 90 (1988):119–30.

Yoffee, N. The late great tradition in ancient Mesopotamia. In: Cohen, M.E., Snell, D. and Weisberg, D. (eds.), *The tablet and the Scroll: Near Eastern studies in honor of William W. Hallo.* Bethesda: CDL Press, 1993:300–8.

Zaccagnini, C. *The rural landscape of the land of Arrapḫe*. Rome: Quaderni di Geografica Storica 1, 1979.

Zadok, R. Lexical and onomastic notes. *OrAnt* 22 (1983):217–20.

Zadok, R. The origin of the name Shinar. *ZA* 74 (1984):240–4.

Zadok, R. *Geographical names according to New- and Late-Babylonian texts*. Wiesbaden: RGTC 8, 1985.

Zadok, R. Archives from Nippur in the 1st millennium BC. In: Veenhof, K.R. (ed.), *Cuneiform archives and libraries: papers read at the 30e Rencontre Assyriologique Internationale, Leiden, 4–8 July 1983*. Leiden: Nederlands Historisch-Archaeologisch Instituut te Istanbul, 1986:278–88.

Zadok, R. Peoples from the Iranian plateau in Babylonia during the second millennium BC *Iran* 25 (1987):1–26.

Zarins, J. Early pastoral nomadism and the settlement of lower Mesopotamia. *BASOR* 280 (1990):31–65.

Zarins, J. Archaeological and chronological problems within the greater Southwest Asian arid zone, 8500–1850 BC. In: Ehrich, R.W. (ed.), *Chronologies in Old World archaeology* (3rd ed.), Chicago: Univ. of Chicago, 1992:42–62.

Zarins, J. The early settlement of Southern Mesopotamia: a review of recent historical, geological, and archaeological research. *JAOS* 112 (1992):55–77.

Zettler, R.L. The genealogy of the house of Ur-Me-me: a second look. *AfO* 31 (1984):1–14.

Zettler, R.L. Sealings as artifacts of institutional administration in ancient Mesopotamia. *JCS* 39 (1987):197–240.

Ziegler, C. *Die Terrakotten von Warka*. Berlin: Ausgrabungen der Deutschen Forschungsgemeinschaft in Uruk-Warka 6, 1962.

Index

Note: wherever absolute dates are cited for
    Mesopotamian kings and dynasties these
    have been drawn from J.A. Brinkman,
    Mesopotamian chronology of the
    historical period, in Oppenheim
    1977:335–46, and Sollberger and Kupper
    1971. In general names which are
    mentioned only rarely in the text, and are
    explained there, are not annotated
    further in the Index.